SO-BCV-366

"Weaving personal experience and biblical truth, my friend Jim Daly offers hope to all those who have yearned for the belonging, the love, and the shelter that the word *home* should evoke. Whether you are a struggling parent trying to create a good environment for your family, or a grown child still longing for a home you never knew, Daly's excellent book offers a roadmap to the God who made His home among us."

—CHUCK COLSON, FOUNDER, PRISON FELLOWSHIP

"Ever felt broken? Ever longed for home? Jim Daly has a powerful, fascinating story that will encourage your heart. He is a living example of someone who has used his pain to become better, not bitter and is being used by God to change the world. Prepare to be inspired!"

—REBECCA ST. JAMES, GRAMMY AWARD–WINNING CHRISTIAN
SINGER/BEST-SELLING AUTHOR

"A true story of God's redemption."

—JASON ELAM, DENVER BRONCOS NFL FRANCHISE KICKER

"Jim Daly's book had a huge impact on me. This is a powerful story of a kid who lived in twenty-four houses by the age of eighteen yet never lost hope that life would be better, that God had a plan for his life. And what a plan! The pain of Jim's youth has been transformed into a passion for strengthening and saving others from the heartache he experienced. It is such an encouragement to see how God takes our hardships and uses them to create something beautiful if we will only let Him."

—SHAUNTI FELDHAHN, BEST-SELLING AUTHOR, *FOR WOMEN ONLY: WHAT
YOU NEED TO KNOW ABOUT THE INNER LIVES OF MEN*,
PUBLIC SPEAKER, AND NEWSPAPER COLUMNIST

"From a broken family to a champion for families, Jim Daly demonstrates how God can use the broken hearted to accomplish great things in His kingdom. Anyone with scars from their own childhood will find great encouragement in Jim's compelling story."

—RICH STEARNS, PRESIDENT, WORLD VISION US

"Jim Daly has done a beautiful job of reminding us that God is involved in the details of our lives. Through his personal journey, we see that there is purpose in our pain. Thank you, Mr. Daly, for your transparency."

—NATALIE GRANT, AWARD WINNING SINGER/SONGWRITER

"Need encouragement, help, and significance in your life? You'll find it in Jim Daly's book *Finding Home.*"

—DR. KEVIN LEMAN, AUTHOR,
MAKING CHILDREN MIND WITHOUT LOSING YOURS

"This is possibly the most inspiring story of growing up and finding God that I have heard in my short fifteen years. *Finding Home* is one of those books that bridges gaps between generations and helps us all appreciate the lengths God will go to in order to prove that in His family, there are no orphans.

"No matter what you're facing in life God is bigger. Jim Daly's story proves that. Jim Daly's story offers hope to young people who feel like they have been abandoned and wonder if God really has a plan for them."

—ZACH HUNTER, 15, AUTHOR, *BE THE CHANGE,*
FOUNDER, LOOSE CHANGE TO LOOSEN CHAINS

"For many years our family has enjoyed the ministry of Focus on the Family. I'm delighted to see Jim leading the organization. His story will shock, encourage, challenge, and inspire you."

—PAT GELSINGER, SENIOR VP INTEL CORP.,
AUTHOR, *BALANCING FAMILY FAITH & WORK*

"Jim has written from the heart and shares his experiences with honesty and sincerity. His story is one I relate to as I, too, grew up apart from a father's love and devotion. Because of God's grace, Jim encourages us to pursue better marriages, better families, better life experiences, and better lives. He never comes off sounding like he knows it all; instead he comes across as a friend offering a warm cup of coffee, a smile, and a tender heart."

—STEVE LARGENT, FORMER NFL PLAYER,
MEMBER OF UNITED STATES CONGRESS

"What a wonderful insight into a man who is devoting his life to improving the family!"

—DEAN C. BORGMAN, CHAIRMAN (RET.), SIKORSKY AIRCRAFT CORP.

"Jim's story shows us how God quiets storms in our lives and gives our lives new meaning. *Finding Home* is a must read!"

—HARRY R. JACKSON, JR., SENIOR PASTOR, HOPE CHRISTIAN CHURCH,
FOUNDER, HIGH IMPACT LEADERSHIP COALITION

"Jim's compelling story will grip you from the first page. He offers many lessons on how faith helped him overcome a very dysfunctional childhood. Thank you, Jim, for opening up your life to us."

—MAC MCQUISTON, PRESIDENT, CEO FORUM, INC.

"Jim Daly paints a very clear picture of some of the challenges kids face in broken and abusive homes today. The heart-wrenching truths you find in his story portray the beauty of healing and restoration that comes when we are recklessly abandoned to God."

—RON LUCE, PRESIDENT AND FOUNDER, TEEN MANIA MINISTRIES

"Jim Daly has revealed his life story in collections of humor, great pain, difficulty, and sometimes odd experiences that put him in the position for God to be able to do great works through him. Readers will be blessed."

—MATTHEW K. ROSE, CHAIRMAN, BNSF RAILWAY

FINDING HOME

AN IMPERFECT PATH TO *FAITH* AND *FAMILY*

JIM DALY
President of Focus on the Family

WITH BOB DEMOSS

David C Cook
transforming lives together

FINDING HOME
Published by David C Cook
4050 Lee Vance Drive
Colorado Springs, CO 80918 U.S.A.

David C Cook U.K., Kingsway Communications
Eastbourne, East Sussex BN23 6NT, England

Scripture quotations are taken from the Holy Bible, New International Version®. NIV®. Copyright 1973, 1978, 1984 by International Bible Society. Used by permission of Zondervan. All rights reserved.

"Cry Out to Jesus" by Tai Anderson, Mark Lee, Mac Powell, David Carr, and Brad Avery. Copyright © 2005 Consuming Fire Music (ASCAP) (adm. by EMI CMG Publishing). All rights reserved. Used by permission.

All names in this book are taken from the author's memory. None have been intentionally changed.

LCCN 2007930615
ISBN 978-1-4347-6894-0
eISBN 978-1-4347-6668-7

© 2007 Jim Daly
Previously published under the same title in hardcover and international trade paperback formats © 2007 Jim Daly, ISBNs 978-0-7814-4533-7 and 978-0-7814-4866-6.

Jim Daly is represented by the literary agency of WordServe Literary Group, 10152 Knoll Circle, Highlands Ranch, CO 80130 (www.wordserveliterary.com).

Cover Design: The DesignWorks Group
Cover Photo: Don Jones Photography
Interior Design: Karen Athen
Interior Photo Design: Ron Adair

Printed in the United States of America
First Worldwide Paperback Edition 2011

3 4 5 6 7 8 9 10

103116-LS

To my mom for all the lessons about life ...

And to my family, Jean, Trent, and Troy,
with whom I'm finally home.

Contents

Author's Note

Life is wonderful.

Life is hard.

I've experienced my share of both and prefer the good stuff this journey has to offer. Especially considering the train wreck that was characteristic of my childhood. As you'll soon discover, my family put the "D" into Dysfunction. My father stepped out of our cozy home when I was five. Then, at age nine, my mom died. Suddenly, I became an orphan.

I've had a few train wrecks.

I've had some major high points, too.

But in the end, I don't get to pick the events that impact my life. I have no control over such things. This I do know: How I respond to what comes my way will either make or break me. Kill me, or give me strength.

In the pages ahead I'm going to be open about my unusual path to finding faith and family. As you read, my sense is that God might just beckon you to embrace the story that is uniquely yours to tell, and to realize that, in spite of how things may appear at any given moment along the path, He has designed you to do something significant.

Message in a Bottle

There's so much about that night I don't recall. If pressed for details, I couldn't tell you about the murder weapon. Was the instrument of death a shotgun or a knife? A baseball bat or a club? I just don't know. A set of brass knuckles can do real damage, I've been told, but I never learned what went down for certain.

Although I never heard a shot, the word on the street was that a shotgun had been used. My best guess is that the killing was gang related. Perhaps a little payback in the decades-old turf war between the Crips and the Bloods for control of illegal drugs. Or, it might have been a clash between the Latino gang element, the Hells Angels, and an African American posse in our racially mixed neighborhood.

You'll have to forgive me for being sketchy.

I was only eight at the time.

There are two unmistakable images forever imprinted on my mind. First, the yellow chalk line scratched onto the pavement outlining the position where the body fell in the alley. Second, the blood stain—a brownish-red calling card left behind by the victim for the rain to deal with. My memory of those two images is clear because the murder occurred about ten feet outside of my bedroom window … a real-life nightmare worse than any dream I'd ever had. Talk about inflaming the imagination of a child—no wonder I was afraid of the dark.

We were living in Compton at the time. Yes, *the* Compton—that concrete jungle of southeast Los Angeles popularized by rappers on MTV. Compton was, and still is, a rough place, no question about it. Drive-by shootings, crime, poverty, and vice were a way of life. For years Compton had the dubious distinction of being ranked as one of the highest crime cities in all of California.

And now we called Compton *home*.

Given the grave reputation of the city, I wasn't entirely surprised to discover our apartment had served as the backdrop for a homicide. And yet, let's just say it was a bit much for me, as a child, to process. I mean, the wall separating me from that savage deed was a mere four inches thick. I wondered how often this sort of thing happened in my new neighborhood. What if a more powerful gun was used the next time? A bullet could easily penetrate the thin layer of white stucco, make mincemeat of the flimsy drywall, and plow into my chest while I was sleeping.

Suddenly, my ground-floor bedroom, at the back of a two-story apartment complex and adjacent to a dark alley, made me feel exposed.

Vulnerable.

Defenseless.

In midspring of 1970, my stepfather, Hank, and my mom, Jan Daly, had moved the family from the rolling hills of Yucca Valley, California, to the gritty streets of Compton to save a little money. I knew their goal was to eventually move to the serene ocean-side community of Long Beach, California, but that came at a price I wasn't sure we ought to pay. But hey, I was a kid. My vote didn't count. And so the wail of sirens replaced the song of birds.

Not only was Compton a dangerous place, it was *noisy*. Not a happy noisy like the sound of a merry-go-round at a carnival, where smiling tykes, munching cotton candy, lobbied dad for *just one more ride—pleeeease!* It was more of an unsettling noisy on par with the shrieks echoing from inside the haunted-house ride.

Whether white, black, or Hispanic, our neighbors had this thing about hollering and screaming and slamming doors day and night. Perhaps taking a cue from their human counterparts, the constant blare of TVs battled it out at full volume. When evening rolled around, the banging of pots and pans signaled the neighbors cooking dinner. The pandemonium was further accented by crying babies, barking dogs, kids playing stickball, or someone picking a fight in the street.

On some nights, red emergency lights splashed bursts of hot color against my windowpane. The eerie light show involved hues of police blue or fiery yellow depending on the rescue service that had arrived.

WELCOME TO THE JUNGLE

After the murder adjacent to our apartment, I wanted to spend as little time at home as possible. Getting some distance from the scene of the crime was therapeutic. You know, out of sight, out of mind. Playing outdoors with the neighbor kids quickly became a priority and, it turned out, I held the keys to unlocking new friendships: a baseball bat and ball. These tools of the trade were hard to come by in the neighborhood, making me an instant hit on the block.

After school we'd play baseball well into the evening. The apartment complex was your basic inner-city arrangement of two-story buildings facing each other with an asphalt courtyard in the middle. Naturally, we had to be careful where we hit the ball since we were surrounded by windows.

One day a grown-up wandered into our game. I had seen him before, but I didn't know his name. He wore faded blue jeans and ankle-high brown work boots. His well-tanned, muscular arms protruded from a black sleeveless T-shirt. Turned out, he was the dad of one of the kids, a construction worker by trade, evidently home early from the job site—or out of work. Didn't matter. We just liked having an adult getting involved with us.

I was at bat when, on the far side of the courtyard, the manager of the apartment complex strolled across the hot asphalt and announced his desire to get into the action too. He seemed sincere in his interest to join the game. He even had a mitt.

With two adults there'd be one for each team. Seemed to me like we were about to have our best game yet. Walking toward the makeshift pitcher's mound, the manager kept saying things like, "Here, kid, toss me the ball. I'd like to play with you guys. You know something? I'm a pretty good pitcher."

How was I to know that his real agenda was to take the ball away from us? As I'd discover later, the apartment manager didn't like kids playing ball in the quad and was determined to put an end to our sport. It didn't take but a second for the construction worker dad, who was more perceptive about such things, to figure out what was really going on. Like a volcano about to spew, he started getting worked up that the manager was trying to "rip us off" and that he'd "just have to teach him a lesson," only he used rapid-fire profanity to punctuate his growing rage.

Before I knew what was happening, this hothead erupted. He marched over to me, snatched the bat from my hands, turned, and headed toward the manager, wielding my Louisville Slugger as if it were a machete. I was horrified. I watched the bat swing through the air as the bully dad confronted the manager with a barrage of expletives.

No way! He's not gonna hit the guy, is he? I thought. I was an inner-city novice. I had spent second grade in small town USA. Yucca Valley was a quiet community where people never locked their doors. I was completely unprepared for the confrontation unfolding before my eyes. *Surely they wouldn't come to blows. What if the manager was carrying a gun? Would there be more yellow tape, more blood by the time this was over? Should I get help? Who would I ask, anyway? My mom and stepfather were both at work.*

Now what? Should I run? Hide?

Pretend I didn't see?

Paralyzed with fear, I froze at the plate.

There are some things no child should see. The sheer inhumanity of an outraged dad unleashing his anger on another human with a bat is certainly one of those things. And yet the six of us kids watched helplessly as the manager, unarmed, attempted to stave off the blow of wood against bone with just his mitt. Oblivious to the example he was setting, this father wailed away at the manager.

A moment later I heard, *Whack!* A dull thud echoed through the courtyard as the manager dropped to the ground, and doubled over, his head down between his legs. He grabbed his left wrist with the other hand. The blood dripped into a pool between his legs; his arm was badly broken with a compound fracture.

I ran. I *had* to get help.

I bolted to our apartment looking for one of my siblings, but nobody was home. I felt terrible. Responsible. Fearful. I mean, it was my idea to play baseball. Sure, I wasn't the one who belted the manager. I was just a kid. Still, I felt tremendous guilt for somehow causing his pain. I would have gladly stopped playing had I known what was going to happen.

With no one around to help and no one to talk to, I crashed on the couch and waited for my mom. I fought back a wave of tears.

When my mom finally got home, she was not happy with me. Not in the least. Boy, did she lay into me. After all, the "weapon" was *my* bat. I think she thought I had been doing something I knew was wrong, but I wasn't. How was I supposed to know we weren't supposed to play baseball between the buildings? Nevertheless, she insisted that I apologize to the manager. That evening, after the apartment manager returned from the hospital all bandaged up and with a cast on his arm, my mom ushered me to his unit and said, "I think you have something to say."

I couldn't take my eyes off of the blood soaking through his cast. To see this man in his late fifties nursing a busted arm because my bat was used to club him was almost too much for me. Between my racing heart and the fear churning in my gut, I'm not sure how I mustered the voice to offer an apology, but somehow, I did. To his credit, the manager was gracious and assured me it wasn't my fault. Looking back I'd say that God used this painful page in my life to model what grace looks like.

After that incident, my mom restricted me from going out to play for a very long time. That was the last time I played ball in Compton. In my view, none of this mayhem would have happened if Dad and Mom had just stayed together.

But they divorced three years before.

FATHER KNOWS BEST?

My biological dad, Richard Daly, had been engaged in an ongoing affair with alcohol, gambling, and horse betting, but I'd say it was primarily the alcohol that lured him away from us. Something terrible must have driven him to find constant comfort from the bottle—the liquid mistress was too seductive for him to resist.

Despite many painful memories, I can recall delightful early childhood moments with him. Take Saturday mornings, my absolute favorite day of the week. I could smell sizzling bacon, freshly scrambled eggs, and toast even before I opened my eyes. The fragrance beckoned me out from under the covers to the kitchen where Dad hovered over the skillet. A dishtowel was always draped over his right shoulder as he worked his magic. I'd stand next to him as he arranged the steaming food on the plate with the flair of a seasoned chef. I loved being close to him. I felt safe by his side.

At 6'5", he was tall, fit, trim, and solid. I loved the way Dad would reach down, scoop me up in one arm while juggling the plate full of food in the other hand, and bring me to the table where the silverware and juice awaited. My dad worked for a furniture manufacturer, and so we always had great furniture in the house. I never wanted to leave his arms, but when breakfast called, I'd ease into my seat and turn my attention to the feast before me.

Still, there was a Dr. Jekyll and Mr. Hyde aspect to my father that I'd only learn about much later in life. I'm not talking about the drunken outbursts. Although rare, they were impossible to miss. Rather, I'm referring to his clandestine side, to the fact that my dad talked occasionally with my older siblings about being a runner for Chicago's most infamous gangster, Al Capone, as a boy.

If true, that would certainly explain a lot. My dad did grow up in Chicago and worked in the furniture business. Al Capone's business card described him as dealing in used furniture. Coincidence? Maybe. Stranger things have happened. Perhaps my dad's affinity for alcohol was an attempt to repress these memories.

19

Furthermore, if Dad had some connection to the kingpin of the Chicago crime syndicate, that could explain why my siblings and I don't know the first thing about our extended family. We had a mom and dad, of course, but that was the extent of our bonsai-sized family tree. As a kid, I never could figure out why we didn't have any aunts and uncles, or cousins, or grandparents like all of my friends. I still don't know.

Everything about my parents' past was shrouded in absolute secrecy. We didn't know anything about their backgrounds until years later, when, after their deaths, we discovered both Dad and Mom had three or four social security numbers. There's even a question about whether our real last name was "Daly."

Such a bizarre collection of details led us to believe my folks might have been in a government witness protection program. At least that would explain why they moved around so much during an era when most families stayed put in the same home for decades.

I remember listening to my dad share stories about his younger days playing baseball. He told fascinating tales of the year he played with the Detroit Tigers. I can't prove that he actually played ball with that team for two reasons: He's dead, which complicates asking any follow-up questions, and there's that lingering issue about our real last name. I have tried to sort out the fact from fiction, but so far I can't reconcile the stories. He *was* good at playing baseball, that much is true.

But did he really play ball at Tiger Stadium?

Or was it his drunken imagination?

My dad coached Little League for years and taught Mike and Dave how to play but, sadly, lost interest by the time I came around. I wanted to believe my dad had made the major leagues. That would be a significant accomplishment on his part and would give me hope that I, too, might have the genetic stuff to play in the big leagues.

Or compete in the big time.

Or at least amount to more than someone who looked in the mirror every morning and doubted his future.

At the same time, it doesn't really matter whether or not Dad ever wore the Detroit Tigers jersey, batted .300, or managed to hit the winning home run. If he never threw a ball his entire life, he was still *my* dad. And I miss him. I wish he were still alive to go grab a cup of coffee, shoot the breeze, and help me find out more about my family tree.

PROMISES, PROMISES

After my parents divorced, my mother was left with the Herculean task of raising five children as a single parent. We were living in a modest rented home in Alhambra on Fifth Street where the cockroaches were bigger than breakfast, lunch, or dinner. My mom worked two or three jobs just to put food on the table, and still there were days when we had nothing to eat.

When we didn't have milk, we'd mix Kool-Aid packs with water to pour over our cereal. Dad was pretty much out of the picture, except when he'd stop by the house to pick up a few groceries. Mind you, he didn't *bring* bags of food to feed his family; he came to *take* a few things for himself when he was down on his luck.

Once, when I stumbled on him taking food out the door, my appearance seemed to catch him off guard. He masked his surprise with a broad smile and then told me how much he loved and missed me. My reaction was somewhat guarded. *Dare I believe him?* His track record as the loving, caring father wasn't so hot—at least not of late.

Sensing the distance between us, he told me he'd stop by later that day to bring me a baseball mitt for my seventh birthday.

A real, honest-to-goodness, genuine leather glove.

For me. From my dad.

This was the best news of the year. I smiled so hard, my face hurt. He tousled the hair on my head with a strong hand, turned, and then left me standing by the door, my heart hammering against my rib cage. When my best friend, Ricky, came over to hang out and play, I couldn't stop bragging. My dad was going to bring me a glove. A new leather baseball glove. Probably a Wilson special edition with a deep pocket for all of the balls I'd catch. It would be my first mitt.

Every fifteen minutes I'd run to the curb with Ricky to see if my dad was coming. We'd look down the street and study the landscape. Squinting, we saw no sign of him in the distance. Not yet. We'd go back in the house and play. Then, I'd announce, "I'm sure he's *got* to be coming now." Off we went, darting out the front screen door. Nope. No sign of him. This went on all afternoon. As the sun began to trade places with the moon, Ricky, who lived just a block away, headed home.

"Call me when he comes," Ricky offered with a friendly slug to my shoulder. Walking him to the curb, I managed a weak smile. I was only seven years old, but I wasn't entirely clueless. My dad had lied to me. At dinner, I picked at my food and asked to be excused early. My mom knew how disappointed I was. She tried to encourage me, but she couldn't replace my dad.

That night I retreated to the security of my bed. I clutched the corner of my covers and pulled them into a tight knot just under my chin. Hidden behind the soft folds of a thick blanket, I felt invincible. I was sure no under-the-bed or closet-lurking monster could get me as long as those protective covers were in place.

If only my covers could ward off the emotional blows dealt by my parents.

Alone in the darkness, I replayed the encounter with my dad in the kitchen—his smile, the roughness of his hand as he ran his fingers through my hair like a rake, the sound of his voice as he promised to return with a glove, and especially the warm feeling that came over me at the thought of his gift.

I tried in vain to silence the accusing voices in my head: *He never came. He said he was coming. He promised he would bring me my first mitt … but he never came.*

I pulled the covers around me tighter.

Would it be too foolish to hope that Dad would come in the morning? Chalk it up to childhood innocence, but part of me longed to find some plausible explanation for the no-show. *Maybe he got hung up in traffic. Could be that the store didn't have my size mitt, right? Or maybe he was having it gift wrapped?* At least those reasons were better than the alternative—that he never intended to keep his promise.

———

Dad never came.

I'd like to think that he had a perfectly good reason for failing to keep such a big promise to his seven-year-old son, but he didn't. My trust in him took a hard knock that day. I was no longer confident that he'd be there when I needed him.

Take something as simple as the issue of feeling safe and secure in the home, something that every kid ought to feel. It seems a dad ought to be the Defender of the Home. You know, the "go-to guy" when danger lurks in the neighborhood. The guy who locks up the house at night and makes sure we're safely tucked in bed. But my dad didn't even live under the same roof. Without the confidence that he'd be there for me, I lived in fear.

Especially after my clash with the Bully of Compton.

JACK THE RIPPER

I wasn't the only white kid living in Compton, but I was certainly one of the few. For some reason Jack, another white kid in our complex, decided to make me his target. Jack was three years older than me and had the tough-guy attitude down pat. The guy both looked and acted like an angry fiend, from the military crew cut and dirty T-shirt to his snarly, blistered lips. He appeared to be perpetually frothing at the mouth, and for reasons unknown, Jack derived special pleasure in bullying me.

Perhaps if we were a little closer in age, I would have found the courage to confront him. He just seemed too big, too fast, and too much older than me. I didn't have any adults in my life that could handle the problem for me. My bio-dad was living who-knows-where, and even if he'd been around, past experience had taught me that I couldn't count on him. Certainly not in a pinch. My stepfather, while capable of defending the family, wasn't making any efforts to get close to me. I didn't feel comfortable telling him about Jack the Ripper.

Instead, I told my sister Kim.

"Kommander Kim" was one tough cookie. She knew how to stand her ground and refused to take any flack. Kim didn't say a word after I told her about Jack, but I was confident she'd handle the situation in her way; in her time.

Not long after I confided in Kim, Jack was chasing me home from school. We both attended Starr King Elementary School, and since he lived around the corner from me, he'd routinely use that after-school trip home as an opportunity to show me what a tough guy he was. This time, I wanted nothing of it. I bolted as fast as my freckled legs could carry me. We came to the section of the apartment property where tall hedges lined one side of the sidewalk, forming a wall of thick foliage. With a busy street on one side and the hedge on the other, there was basically no escape for fifty yards. If I slowed down, Jack would be on top of me.

I glanced over my shoulder. Jack was right behind me, tracking me like a heat-seeking missile. A measly ten yards separated my face from his fist. With a burst of adrenaline, I managed to widen the distance between us. I sucked in gallons of air to cool my burning lungs. My shins were about to split. I tore past a slight break in the bush and saw something out of the corner of my eye. It dawned on me. My sister had come to the rescue.

Kim stepped through the hedge and popped him a good one. He never saw the punch coming. While he tried to find his legs, Kim towered over him and yelled, "Never mess with my little brother! Got that?" That was the last time I had to deal with Jack.

Kim is tough, tough as nails.

Frankly, it felt really good to have someone looking out for me. Normally, that person would have been my dad, but he wasn't in the picture. Keep in mind I'm not saying a man ought to use force to stop the taunts of a bully. Typically, a dad would talk to the bully's parents. I'll let you make your own mind up about that. However, I know I'd have taken great comfort if I could have gone to him and had the assurance that he was in my corner, that he'd go to bat for me in a heartbeat.

As an adult, I've had some space to process what went on with my father, both the good and the bad. I know that I cannot change the past by making excuses for his behavior or by whitewashing my history. He made a choice when he sent us that message in the bottle: He wouldn't be there for us, for me.

He wasn't there when I was terrorized by a bully.

He wasn't there when things got out of hand at a ball game.

And he wasn't there to teach me how to be a man, a husband, or a father who provides food, guidance, security, and love. The consequences of his choice not to get help for his struggle with alcoholism and, instead, to pursue his self-destructive ways, affected each of us Daly kids profoundly. There's something about a father wound that can really mess with you—for years, if not for a lifetime if you allow it … like the time Dad stopped by to deliver a message none of us could ever forget.

2

If I Had a Hammer

My parents divorced when I was five. One of the more compelling memories from that difficult chapter of my life was a close encounter with a monster. Although my bedroom door was shut tight that night, I had no faith that its hollow panels would offer much resistance to that *thing* lurking on the other side. Lying alone in the dark, scared out of my wits, I did what I always did under the circumstances—I yanked the blankets over my little body and then pulled them tight to the base of my neck.

In those early years I had a thing for comforters—they represented a cloak of safety against the "momphers." At age four, while I couldn't properly pronounce "monster," I sure knew one when I saw one. At the moment, there was definitely a monster outside of my door.

This particular monster flopped into the brown corduroy reclining chair in our darkened living room as if he owned the place. A jug of Gallo burgundy wine sloshed and spilled onto his shirt as he took frequent swigs—right from the bottle. Armed with an oak-handled, ball-peen hammer, he sat with his right elbow draped over the edge of the chair. With repeated *thumps*, he struck the hammer slowly against the floor, biding his time. The tool probably weighed a full pound, but whatever its weight, it could inflict real harm.

I should know. The monster had already smashed a hole in our hallway drywall. This was no dream. I saw the whole thing with my very own eyes. My brothers and sisters and I were home alone. Mom was working at a nearby bowling alley. We were just hanging out in the living room, sitting on the rust-colored shag carpet popularized during the sixties. The walls had been painted a cross between hospital green and the color of pea soup, which gave the dimly lit space a sterile, muted feel. It wasn't much to look at, but it was our new home.

We were happily watching TV in our pajamas when the monster barged through the front door, unannounced. His forceful entrance sent the door sailing backward on its hinges and into the wall with a *wham!* His eyes were puffy, reddened, and glassy, and he searched the room with a fiery intensity that instantly spiked my internal alarm. His face, unshaven with several days' growth, appeared haggard. The words he mumbled were slurred as if his tongue were too thick.

I had to remember to breathe.

Up until that encounter, I'd never witnessed such a terrifying scene. As a typical four- almost five-year-old boy, I was intrigued with the mysteries and joys of life. Preoccupied with bugs, lizards, cars, toy guns, and the stuff picked from my nose, I had a healthy innocence that every child ought to enjoy throughout their childhood. But in an instant, my world was rocked forever.

I backed away toward the green sofa, instinctively aware that my forty-pound body was no match for this giant. The towering figure spewed a host of threats as he staggered deeper into the house in search of something—or *someone*. With a roar, the monster bellowed,

"This is what I'm going to do to your mother!" *Boom!* He swung the hammer with such force it bashed a giant hole in the wall. The house seemed to shutter from the blow.

My sisters started crying.

I would have cried too, if I hadn't been so terrified of drawing attention to myself. Plus, I was pretty sure monsters didn't like crybabies. Besides, I *knew* this man, or thought I did. He was a spitting image of my dad who had the same height, weight, build, and facial features as this crazed man. But this raving-mad drunk couldn't be my father.

So, the man stalking our house, while resembling my dad, wasn't the man I knew. To walk past him now, I fully believed *this* man might grab me by my hair and start wailing on my head just like he did the wall. He plopped down in the recliner and proceeded to drink from his jug with deep gulps.

Aside from the babbling TV and the occasional sniffling from my sisters, an uneasy silence settled on us. Now what? Even at age fourteen, my oldest brother, Mike, had this way of taking charge and keeping us younger kids out of harm's way. With the monster ensconced in the chair, Mike viewed this as an opportune time to hustle us into the back bedroom where he and thirteen-year-old Dave could put together a game plan.

Because Mike was the biggest brother, he decided to stay in the room with Dee Dee, Kim, and me to protect us while Dave, who could run like lightening, would slip out of the window and dash down to the bowling alley to tell mom. She'd know how to stop the nightmare.

At least that was the plan.

ARRESTING DEVELOPMENT

For the better part of an hour, the muffled yet insistent tremor of steel against carpet pounded away at the frayed edges of my nerves. The hammer's cadence continued *thump … thump … thump …* as the monster ticked off the minutes. The steady stream of thuds was as nerve-racking as the constant drip of a faucet, only much more ominous.

Even though Mike was doing his best to keep us calm, I knew my dad was still sitting in the living room in that reclining chair. I could hear the hammer strike the carpet through the bedroom wall. I closed my eyes as tight as I could, but it didn't help. If only I could plug my ears—or become invisible and slip out unnoticed.

Where was Dave? Had he reached Mom yet? Was help on the way? What if Dad decided not to wait for her and, instead, targeted his rage against one of us? Would Mike really be able to stop him? I didn't want my dad to hurt my mom. I didn't want my dad to be who he was at that moment.

I wanted my old dad back.

Was that even possible?

Dave was in full panic mode. Hysterical at the memory of what he'd just experienced, and motivated by the thought of what else might happen if he didn't hurry, he ran until his legs burned and begged for relief. There was no time to rest. He pushed harder, faster—the urgency of his mission propelled him on.

We had no choice but to wait for Dave to make contact. You might wonder why we didn't just call her on the phone. Keep in mind this was 1966, years before the invention of cell phones and personal pagers. Back then, rotary phones with their agonizingly slow and clunky dial were the standard mode of communication. Besides, unlike today's houses with phone jacks everywhere—even in the bathroom—our only phone was located in the living room ... precisely where my dad was seated.

Dave, covered in sweat and tears, bounded across the bowling alley parking lot, burst through the doors, and started screaming for my mom. Several bowlers closest to the front doors paused to observe the curious interruption. Dave scanned the room; there was no sign of her. The sound of dozens of bowling balls thundering across the wooden lanes continued. Dave yelled and then yelled some more. People turned from their games and shot him foul looks.

Dave ran to the counter, pushed past the paying customers, and demanded that the manager find his mother—*now!* She was *supposed* to be at work. She *said* she was at work. So she *had* to be at work. One problem.

Mom wasn't there.

His panic turned to desperation. Pleading with the manager, phone calls were made and, five minutes later, my mother strolled into the bowling lobby. Dave shouted, "Where have you been?" Mom told him not to worry, to calm down, and tell her what happened. "Calm down?" Dave barked. "Dad is going to kill you! He's at the house, he's drunk, he has a hammer, and he's gonna *kill you!*"

That got her attention.

She asked about the rest of us. Where were we? What were we doing? Were we safe? Dave fought to catch his breath. His words spilled out in a rush: "Mike's there doing what he can to protect the girls and Jim.... He's locked up with them in the bedroom.... I sneaked out the window.... We've got to get to them!" With that, Dave and my mom got into a friend's car and drove the short distance to our house. Rather than pull into the driveway, they parked on the street. Dave started to jump out of the car when Mom turned partially around in the front seat, made eye contact, and told him to stay put.

"Huh?" Dave said, his forehead wrinkled into a knot. "We've got to make sure the girls are okay. Let's go, Mom!"

"Honey, be patient," she said. "Let the police handle this." As soon as she spoke those words, two patrol cars rolled down the street, lights flashing. Evidently, her friend was an off-duty police officer who had called for the squad cars. The officers pulled into the driveway, parked, then stepped out of the cars with flashlights drawn. Sitting in the backseat, Dave watched as the police approached the house in the near total darkness.

"What will they do with Dad?" Dave wondered aloud, his nose pressed against the window.

"They'll get him some help," was about all she would say. To her credit, none of us ever heard our mother badmouth our father. Even in the days after their divorce, she refused to call him a drunk or a bum or in any way demean his reputation. Moments later, the police were escorting my dad to the police car. He pleaded, "Jan, this isn't necessary. We can work this out. Come on, Jan! Call off the dogs already."

Mom didn't say a word.

These events were taking place unbeknownst to me. I was still shaking under the covers. For all I knew, my dad was still sitting in the chair, waiting. Mike, Dee Dee, and Kim, however, heard what was happening and, after my dad was arrested, left me in the room to go and find Mom. With a click, Kim closed the door behind them— which really freaked me out. I think they were just trying to shield me from what was happening.

I pulled the lime-green blanket over my head.

It felt like an eternity before someone finally entered the room. I peaked over the edge of the covers as a policeman moved to the side of the bed. He rested his hand on my chest and said, "Son, are you okay?"

I managed a nod. "Sure."

He studied my face with a trained eye. He wasn't buying my story. I sensed there was no harm in fessing up.

"Okay, so maybe I'm just a little scared."

A warm, knowing smile eased across his face. He said, "Trust me, everything will be just fine." With that, he turned and left … and then closed the door. I hated the sound of the door closing. I didn't want to be left alone. I longed to jump into the arms of my mom. I needed to know that everything would be okay.

HAPPY DAYS

Years would pass before I knew about the events that transformed my lovable dad during the first five years of my life into the lunatic bent on killing my mom in the "hammer house." To set the stage, I was born James Daniel Daly in July of 1961. I'm told my parents proudly brought me home from the West Covina Memorial Hospital to our home in Baldwin Park, California. Dad, it seems, viewed me as a special gift to them in their "old age;" he was fifty-one when I was born.

Our bungalow sat on a quiet dead-end street, largely sheltered from the unrest and commotion of life in the big city during the sixties. For the better part of four years, we had a "normal" family life. My brothers and sisters played baseball and rode bikes in the cul-de-sac. They had the time and freedom to make friends and explore the nearby woods. My mother stayed home to cook, clean, and be a mommy to her newborn child while my father held a steady job at U.S. Steel.

Best of all, both were sober.

In the years before my birth, things were downright ugly in the Daly household. Alcohol consumed my parents' every waking moment. One of my brother Dave's craziest early childhood memories was sitting in his booster seat at the kitchen table looking at a bottle of vodka in the middle of the table. Both of our parents were sitting next to him—completely passed out. They were so addicted to the bottle that they almost lost the right to raise my brothers and sisters.

I also learned there was a pattern of drunken fights predating my arrival. My oldest brother, Mike, said our parents constantly fought over stuff that he didn't understand. Even as a four-year-old, Mike saw the effects of what was going on around him and started to believe that their arguments were somehow *his* fault. Mom would say something provocative; Dad would swear and shout something nasty back. She'd throw a pan or whatever was within reach. Before long, the cops would come knocking.

Mike recalls one serious clash where Dad was beating up on Mom. When the police arrived, they put my brothers and sisters in the back of the police cruiser to take them to the Los Angeles County Children's Home. Mike was four; Dave, three; Kim, two; and Dee Dee, just one. While sitting together in the cop car, the overhead beams of red light served as a beacon alerting the neighbors of their embarrassing exile. In time, the police appeared at the front door of the house ushering my parents outside—wrapped in blankets.

Evidently, they were both too drunk to get dressed.

Dave recalls how they were removed from my parents' custody that night and taken to a children's shelter. He was directed to a bed in the back corner of a large, open dorm-style room. As he and Mike were escorted into the dorm, he wondered, *What are all these beds doing here? What am I doing here? Are we being punished for something? Where are Mom and Dad?* After a bath and something to eat, my siblings were put to bed with a head full of unanswered questions. My sisters were separated from their brothers and sent to a different wing of the same facility.

By the time Mike was in second grade, my siblings were sent to either a children's home or placed into foster care on at least four occasions. Although Mom would stop by for a number of supervised visits, they were not together as a family.

Somewhere along the way, my mom managed to snap out of her drunken stupor. During one of the visits at a foster-care facility, Mom announced, "Kids, I promise you'll never have to go through this again."

The fact that my folks struggled with alcohol was not a surprise. They first met at an Alcoholics Anonymous meeting in Chicago; they were just two broken people working to set aside their pasts and hoping to create new memories together for the future. Nothing like a fresh start and new beginnings, right? They had their first son, Mike, right off the bat. Mom was thirty-four and Dad was forty-two. Not long afterward they moved from the Windy City to New Orleans, where Dave was born, eighteen months after Mike's arrival.

Once again, they picked up and moved, this time to the Mile High City, Denver, where Kim was born. For reasons that aren't clear, they didn't linger in Denver, but headed to Los Angeles where Dee Dee and then, years later, I was born. While all of this relocating may seem normal by today's standards, at the time most people never moved beyond fifty or so miles from their hometown. They lived thirty or forty years in the same house with the same phone number and, for the most part, held the same jobs.

Why, then, did my parents move us around?

What compelled them to keep from putting down roots?

What's more, a close inspection of our birth certificates reveal a variety of different last names given by our parents. For example, my birth certificate listed my last name as "Daly" while my older brother Mike's birth certificate gave him a different last name. Adding to the mystery, my mother used three different last names between the five of us children. Clearly, there was some dark cloud hanging over them that would be important enough to keep changing addresses, names, and social security numbers. As I mentioned before, this pattern of change could have had something to do with my dad's prior involvement as a runner for Al Capone. It's possible they were in the government witness protection program. We just don't know.

What is clear is the fact that the most difficult demon to shake was their habit of reaching for another drink, which is why, when my mother promised my siblings that they'd never have to live in foster care again, she was dead serious. There would be no U-turns. No more benders. No more late-night brawls leading to arrests. Those days were over.

Someway, somehow, she dug down into the core of her being and found the inner strength to break the cycle of addiction, brokenness, and parental irresponsibility she had exhibited for so long. She wasn't particularly a "religious" person; there wasn't a "come to Jesus" moment at this stage of her life. She just *knew* things had to change—*would* change—because she didn't want to lose all that was dear to her.

I believe her change of heart is an early picture of God at work in my mom's life. Even though she didn't necessarily know where her strength to change was coming from, God was at work behind the scenes. He knew how her story would ultimately unfold—just as God knows how ours will unfold—and graciously provided her with the courage to make a stand.

Once Mom made the commitment to get sober and begin caring for her children, she laid out the options for my dad: He could join her in laying off the bottle and raise the kids as responsible parents, or, he should just clear out and let her take care of things. Again, to his credit, my dad wanted to take the high road.

He wanted to be there for Mike, Dave, Dee Dee, and Kim. Which is why, when I came on the scene, I didn't even know what "drunk" was. In what I see as a gift from God, throughout what child development experts call the ever-important "formative years," I only experienced the best that my dad had to offer. Every time I walked past my dad, he'd reach down and scruff up my hair with a playful sign of affection. I sensed that I was special to him. Sometimes he'd wrestle or toss me into bed with a tickle. And while he rarely hugged me, I felt very much loved and completely safe in his presence.

With that issue settled between them, Dad and Mom regained custody of the children, and moved to Blackwood Street in Los Angeles for a brief stint before finally settling on Cosby Street in West Covina. As it turned out, their move to Cosby Street was a divine arrangement. On the day that they moved in, the couple who lived next door introduced themselves as Bud and Esther Hope. The connection was an instant hit. They became not only best friends with my parents, but our adopted grandparents.

Grandpa and Grandma Hope. What great names.

More than that, it was a fitting name for the role the Hopes ultimately played in our lives. (That part of the story comes later.) Suffice it to say, life on Cosby Street produced the sweetest experiences for my siblings, and I have delightful memories of my early childhood there. Mom and Dad were finally settled, sober, and happy. The Hopes were great friends, and by all appearances we had a "functional" family.

However, that Kodak moment in our history would change in a flash.

Four years after moving to Cosby Street, temptation for my dad came knocking in the form of a friend from work, Joe Garcia. Joe visited several times over the Christmas break bringing his version of the holiday spirit—a fifth of whiskey. The enticement of hard liquor and the peer pressure to imbibe were too strong for my father to resist. He caved, and then caved again. In a short period of time, Dad started drinking regularly although he did a fantastic job of hiding it from me.

As a recovering alcoholic, however, Mom knew the telltale signs of his addiction and promptly reminded him of the terms of their commitment. When there didn't appear to be any serious change in his choices, she announced, "Richard, if you're going to continue this, I'm going to leave you." Of course, I didn't know anything was particularly wrong between them. My older siblings didn't comprehend the full scope of my mother's concern either.

The drinking continued.

And she left.

Mom hastily packed our bags and took us away from the only home I'd known. She timed our exodus to coincide with the time Dad would be at work. What's more, she had no intention of informing Dad of our new digs, which, as you might guess, ultimately infuriated him. When Mom told us we were moving, we were confused. Why wasn't she telling Dad? Was this some sort of new game? A grown-up version of hide-and-seek?

Mom said get packed, so we packed.

Mom said, "Don't tell your dad," so we didn't.

We moved into one of the many nondescript, single-story white stucco duplexes on Heines Street in Los Angeles, California. Two memories linger from our brief stay at that address.

First, our front yard was a battlefield of sorts: Patches of grass fought a constant encroachment by the dry earth. The dirt won most days. Occasionally, the grass would create an unholy alliance with the weeds for supremacy of the yard. We didn't live there long enough to aid the lawn in its cause. The second recollection involved the monster and the hammer. There was no way we could live within those walls after what transpired. The memories were too fresh, too painful, too savage.

The entire wretched episode might have been avoided, or at least postponed, if not for a freak encounter between my sister Dee Dee and Dad. Several weeks after we had moved away from Cosby Street, Dee Dee was riding her bike when, quite by accident, she saw Dad walking toward her in the distance. Their eyes locked for a brief second, and, with Mom's admonishment echoing in her mind not to tell Dad where we lived, she turned around and peddled for all she was worth.

She could have gotten away clean since Dad was on foot and she had wheels. They were several blocks away from our house and she had a solid start. However, when Dee Dee reached our house, she threw her bike on the front yard, darted in the front door, and announced, "Mom ... *Mom!* I saw Dad. He was coming down the street."

Dad had been searching the adjacent neighborhoods to Cosby Street looking for any sign of us. He'd been patrolling the streets for weeks. Now, spying Dee Dee's bike in our front yard, he made a mental note of our new location and then left to do two things: find a hammer to drive home his point, and get tanked up on Gallo wine to steel his nerves.

In many ways, that night was a watershed moment. Like a gravestone, it marked the death of my parents' marriage. We would never again be a family. From then on my dad became a figure that would breeze in and out of our lives—candidly, he was more *out* than *in*. I lost a lot on that sleepless night—we all did. Our identity as the Dalys would be diluted in the shuffle of temporary relationships and living arrangements that spanned more than twenty houses.

Gone, too, was the serenity and the stability of the family life we had enjoyed. Personally speaking, the most significant loss was my belief in the man I once looked up to with immeasurable admiration. Before the hammer incident, my dad could do no wrong. But with each swing of the hammer, he drove home the conviction that I would never want to grow up and be like him.

3

Mother Knows Best

I should be insane—or in jail.

At least that's what folks often say when they hear the details of my story. The fact that I've managed to avoid those outcomes has much to do with the kind of resilient woman my mother was in the face of hardship. Without Dad's regular paycheck and presence in the home, life took a turn for the worse. While Mom worked hard to make the most of what we had, little did we know how difficult things would become.

In a few short years, I'd lose my mom to cancer and become an orphan. Thankfully, the kind of home environment she worked to maintain, one that balanced discipline with an extra dose of laughter, prepared us to face the future with optimism.

My mom was tall—about 5'10"—slim, and in good shape. She had dark features—olive skin, black hair, and hazel-brown eyes. She was half American Indian and half Irish, with the Indian side the more dominate. Her tenacity probably came from the Indian side; her playful wit and humor from her Irish ancestry.

With Dad now out of the house, my mom was thrust into life as a single parent of five—long before single parenting had a network of resources and day-care services tailored to their unique needs. Without a dad to anchor the home, we were all headed into uncharted waters—the murky details of that voyage will surface in future chapters. For now, let me confess I'm afraid I didn't make things easy on Mom.

When I was born, according to my sister Kim, I was irresistibly cute. Make that "the cutest baby that's ever been born." A real happy baby, too. Always smiling. No all-night crying fits. Kim remembers the afternoon I was carried home from the hospital. Mom carefully laid me down on my parents' bed. Kim wasted no time climbing up for a closer inspection. Moments later she announced, "We've got a live dolly!" Eyes filled with wonderment, she remembers deciding right then and there that she'd be a mommy one day too.

By age six my angel wings had fallen off. I became very much the spoiled brat and could do no wrong, at least in the eyes of my mother. I was rarely punished, primarily because my older brothers and sisters would cover for me. I'm not sure why. They probably wanted to keep the peace since they knew from firsthand experience just how bent out of shape my parents could get. This pattern of covert cover-up continued long after Dad and Mom had gone their separate ways.

I remember exhibiting one of those "Picasso Moments" that children are so fond of having. I stumbled upon a tube of my sister's bright red nail polish and decided it was the perfect medium in which to express my budding creativity. Using the television screen as my canvas, I got busy.

Within seconds I had painted the red pigment all over the glassy surface with the unbridled flair of an impressionist artist. Stepping back to admire my handiwork, I heard my sisters Dee Dee and Kim enter the living room. I can't say that they shared my enthusiasm for the final product. More accurately, they flipped out.

"James Daniel Daly! What have you done?"

With a shrug, I feigned innocence.

Hand outstretched, Kim motioned for me to hand over the bottle. "That's *my* nail polish. Give it here."

I flashed a dopey grin as if to say, "Nail polish? What nail polish?" But I was busted, and I knew it.

Dee Dee chimed in. "Boy, Mom is gonna be *so* mad."

Instinctively, my sisters took it upon themselves to clean up the mess before my mom could see the damage. Dee Dee dashed out of the room; when she returned, she was armed with nail polish remover and a roll of paper towels. Together, Dee Dee and Kim scrubbed away all evidence of my infraction. Just about the time they had finished cleaning, a new thought crossed their minds:

Jim won't get punished if the evidence is erased.

They weren't being vindictive: Kim and Dee Dee just decided that I had been pampered and coddled long enough, and they were going to do something about it. Sure, life was hard, but it was time for me to grow up and face the consequences of my poor behavior. Retrieving the remains of the nail polish, they quickly rescrawled broad strokes across the TV screen.

Here's the funny part: I never did get into trouble. I'm not sure why. Maybe my mother was too tired to make an issue of it. And, technically speaking, I didn't paint what my mom saw when she came home from work. Ironically, my sisters were now out of nail polish remover, and for days we had to watch TV through the prism of red blotches. Perhaps it was mom's way of allowing all of us to share in the consequences of our actions.

While grateful that I had escaped punishment, my footloose, spoiled-brat days were numbered. Clearly, my sisters had gone over to the Dark Side and could no longer be counted on to run interference for me. And, I could sense that my mom knew something had to change. As it turned out, it took one well-placed punch to knock some sense into my young, insolent noggin.

KARATE-CHOPPING MOM

I'm pretty sure one reason Mom let me slide was because of the regrets she had. She felt incredible guilt that I no longer had a father in my life, and I believe she did what many parents are tempted to do in that situation: She overcompensated by giving me everything I wanted. Every time we'd go shopping, I'd get a toy. Being a typical six-year-old in the late sixties, I was captivated by all things G.I. Joe. I stocked up on G.I. Joe action figures, G.I. Joe clothing, G.I. Joe jeeps, G.I. Joe *everything*. I scored tons of Hot Wheels gear, too. Miles of orange Hot Wheel tracks. All of the coolest cars.

No toy was out of bounds for me.

And not just toys—chocolate shakes, too.

Now that Dad was not providing financially for us, Mom had to juggle two and three jobs at the same time. Her long hours away from home only served to further amplify the burden she felt. To compensate, she'd often bring home a chocolate shake and place it in the fridge so that it would be there in the morning for me. While a semi-melted shake might sound gross, it separated in such a great way: The rich, yummy cream sat on the top and the chocolate milk rested on the bottom.

I loved it.

If she'd forgotten to replenish my shake stash, I'd run out to the car in the morning as she backed out of the driveway to remind her. I'd grab on to the car door in my pajamas and plead, "Are you going to bring me a chocolate shake tonight? You forgot last night." Usually she would say, "Yes" or, "I'll try." Sometimes she'd actually say, "No," and I could tell it pained her to disappoint me.

But the grocery store was my ace in the hole.

I tagged along with my mom whenever she went grocery shopping because I *always* got a toy. If I didn't get one, I'd rant and rave and throw a full-body tantrum—the kind of fit that turned the heads of other moms who, with their pious looks, questioned what kind of mother would deprive Junior of such a simple request. Rather than put her foot down, she'd give in and allow me to run over to the toy section to pick something—*anything*—that would silence the whining.

My typical modus operandi was to start working on her from the backseat of the car. I planted the first thought in her mind by wondering out loud what G.I. Joe outfits might be waiting for me. We'd park, grab a shopping cart, and head through the sliding glass door. That's when I'd turn up the heat and make a bigger deal about picking out my toy. After all, there was usually an audience within earshot. I could play to the crowd with the best of the spoiled brats.

However, like most kids at that age, I had this profound fear of getting lost in the store, of not being connected to my mom. For reasons not fully understood by me at the time, my dad was no longer around. At times, an emptiness welled up in me, and I'd wander through our home totally missing him. Naturally, the last thing I wanted to do was lose my mom at the grocery store. So, on one hand I had this fear of letting Mom out of my view, even for an instant. On the other hand, I was determined to get my toy.

These conflicting feelings of fears and desire played tug-of-war in my head one Saturday afternoon when Mom and I headed to Crawford's Grocery Store in Alhambra, California, to do the weekly food shopping. As we made our way to the produce section, Mom stopped by the fresh corn display where I knew she'd take her time carefully sorting through the husks in search of the best-looking ears. I announced, "Mom, I'm going to go get my toy, okay?"

It was more of a pronouncement than a sincere request for permission. Getting a toy, after all, was my inalienable right. Without waiting for her consent, I quickly added, "Are you going to be right here when I get back?" She nodded, although I could tell she was distracted. I had clearly lost my audience to the science of selecting yellow corn. "Go ahead, Jimmy, I'll be right here," she said.

"You *promise?*"

"Yes. Now, run along. I'll be here."

Even at age six I knew exactly where the toy aisle was. That land of make-believe awaited just beyond the mountains of toilet paper, plates, and assorted paper goods a few aisles away. With my radar set on autopilot, I hustled over to find the G.I. Joe camouflage outfit I had seen on a previous trip. I didn't buy the camo gear then since I had my heart set on a different "must have" matching accessory. Due to my one-toy quota, I had to wait.

Wanting to make sure I got the garment before they ran out of stock, I sped to the shelf. Standing on my toes, I plucked it from the rack and then gawked briefly at the prize now in hand. Happy with the latest addition to my collection, I headed back to Mom. The whole trek to Toyland only took about three minutes.

That's when I saw my mom four or five aisles removed from the produce department—walking *away* from me. I blinked. There was no mistake. She was standing next to the cans of soup. I knew it was her because she was wearing her black polyester slacks (that's back when polyester was in vogue), black blouse with brown paisley swirls, and flat-heeled dress shoes. Her hair was tucked and pinned in the back.

What's this? I thought. *Mom said she'd be waiting for me ... by the corn. Where does she think she's going without me?* I panicked. The fear of abandonment and the anger I felt that she hadn't kept her promise to be where she said she'd be sent me reeling. With the energy of a charging beast on opening day of the annual run with the bulls, I tucked my head down and ran directly toward the bull's-eye on her back.

With the target almost within reach, I clenched my fist into a tight ball and raised it over my head hatchetlike. I came down on her hard. Clobbered her was more like it—right between the shoulder blades. I didn't know I was capable of such a powerful swing. I actually heard a thud as my fist hit her square in the back.

G.I. Joe would have been impressed.

The sudden and full fury of my fist completely knocked the wind out of her. With a forced exhale, she groaned and staggered a half-step forward. She instinctively groped for the nearest shelf in an attempt to recover her balance.

Still hot with anger, I stared upward at the spot on Mom's back where I'd just whopped her as if daring her to turn and face my wrath. I was prepared to unleash a barrage of indignant words. *How dare you leave me! You promised you'd be over there, not here. What kind of mom doesn't keep her promises?* But the words never left my tongue. With a slow, guarded motion, my mom turned around to make sense of what had hit her.

As she rotated full circle, the puzzlement in her eyes was only matched by the bewilderment that I felt. It was my turn to stagger backward several short steps. My heart spiked and my legs went wobbly as the earth beneath me caved in.

She wasn't my mother.

The woman whom I had just decked wore the identical top, pants, and shoes as my mom. The pale skin on her face, pulled taut as a drum, wasn't anything like the soft, warm features of my mother's face. Her eyes zeroed in on me like lasers.

"What *are* you doing?"

"I … I … I thought you were my mom."

That freaked her out.

Before she could say another word, I backed up and darted out of there. Somehow through the flood of tears soaking my face, I found my mother—exactly where she said she would be, still shucking the corn. Evidently, my sobbing caught her attention. Mom turned, lowered the husk, and said, "What's wrong, Jimmy?"

"I just hit a woman."

"You *what?*"

"I just hit a woman."

"Why in the world …"

"… because I thought it was you."

Her right eyebrow shot up indicating that I needed to offer a little clarification, especially since I had never hit my mom before. I tried to articulate my fears. *I thought she had left … because she wasn't here but there … although she was really here, but I didn't know it at the time.* I don't know whether or not my explanation made much sense. My mom's reaction, however, was crystal clear. She put down the corn, suddenly all business, and said, "Jimmy, you need to go back and apologize to her."

I balked.

Her tone revealed that there wasn't room for negotiation, I had to apologize, end of story. With her arm resting on my shoulder, she quietly escorted me to the scene of the crime. Apologizing all by myself was a frightening prospect. I started praying for a miracle … if only the lady had left the store, even on a stretcher, just as long as I didn't have to face her again. No such luck. She was still stationed midway down the aisle.

Standing next to the end cap display and just out of view of the other woman, Mom waved me forward. I froze. I felt as though my legs were bogged down in freshly poured cement. Chipping away at my reluctance, my feet managed to slowly move forward. I shuffled past the soup, feeling less like the animated G.I. Joe action figure of a few minutes earlier. As I approached, I could see her face was still tight with anger. She put a hand on her hip and waited.

I offered a sheepish, "I'm sorry that I hit you."

She looked down at me with no attempt to mask her indignation. "Why did you hit me?"

"I thought you were my mother."

I looked down at my feet just to be free of her glare. An uncomfortable moment passed. I glanced upward and added, "I'm sorry."

She shook her head, the corner of her mouth twisted up in disgust, and then turned away. I turned away too, happy to get out of there.

That experience had a profound impact on me on several levels. I never, ever hit anyone again. Choosing to use my fists to resolve conflict began and ended that day.

I also discovered that my mom's word was golden, that when I failed to control my anger, I blew it big-time, and that making things right and admitting your mistakes is all a part of life.

To her credit my mom never rubbed my face in my behavior. I didn't feel judged. She wasn't trying to shame me in front of the woman in order to preserve her own image. There'd be no "Excuse my dumb kid" lines offered on my behalf. She just wanted me to take responsibility for my actions.

The other thing I so appreciate about my mother is the way she did her best to make our house a place of fun and laughter. She knew we kids needed both guidance *and* a generous serving of lighthearted giddiness. Which most likely explains why she arranged for me to meet Larry of the Three Stooges.

NYUK! NYUK! NYUK!

At age seven, I was a member of the Three Stooges Fan Club. More of an honorary member since I never actually mailed in a postcard to join. As a quasi-member in good standing, I watched Moe, Larry, and Curly often, parroting their eye poking, face slapping, and finger snaps with my siblings. I stopped short of taking the frying pan to the coconut of my brother Dave.

There were actually six different Stooges during the span of that hit TV series. Moe Horwitz and his real-life brothers Shemp and Curly were all members of the trio during various stages of their slap-happy careers. They, along with Larry Fine, Joe Besser, and Joe DeRita rounded out the popular act. Hands down, Curly was my favorite. He seemed to catch the brunt of Moe's teasing and yet always managed to keep a smile on his face.

I haven't watched all 213 episodes, but one of my favorites was "Disorder in the Court." At one point the judge summons Curly to the stand and then attempts to place him under oath. Part of that bit still sticks in my mind:

> JUDGE: Do you swear …
> CURLY: No, but I know all the *woids!*

My mom, knowing how much I loved their antics and how I'd rehearse a few of their lines, called me one morning with a special treat in mind. She was waitressing at the Big Sky Country Club in Yucca Valley, California. My mother had this winsome way of making friends. Never shy where strangers were concerned, she befriended many of the regulars. Which is why this particular morning she asked if I'd like to meet Larry from the Three Stooges.

Clutching the phone to my ear, I couldn't believe what I was hearing. "Meet Larry? *Soitenly!*"

Mom laughed and told me to get ready; she'd pick me up around 11:00 a.m. Talk about pure excitement. This was the "poifect gift." What kid wouldn't want to have lunch with Larry? I floated to my bedroom and looked for something to wear that wasn't too dorky. This was, after all, *Larry*. The last thing I wanted to do was to come across like some kind of a knucklehead. I rummaged through my box of clothes. Satisfied with my selections, I got dressed and then waited anxiously by the front door like a puppy desperate to go for a walk.

Twenty minutes later Mom and I were walking through the expansive halls of the country club. I'd never seen such luxurious surroundings in my entire life. My feet seemed to sink into the plush green and black floral carpet. Massive white columns reached from floor to ceiling like California redwoods. We entered the dining room and strolled past tables draped in white linen tablecloths, bedecked with some pretty snazzy-looking silverware, cups, and plates.

My heart was thumping so hard I wasn't sure my chest could contain it. I wondered if Larry would look like he did on TV. You know, would he have the same Athenian-style bushel haircut with the bald spot in the middle? Would he wave his hand in my face and try to poke out my eyes while adding a "woop woop woop" sound effect?

Suddenly, I wasn't sure what to say … or what to call him. My mom always taught us to speak respectfully to adults. Saying, "Hi, Larry!" was definitely out. I wondered whether "Hi, Mr. Stooge" would be appropriate, but quickly ruled that out too. I could almost hear Larry saying, "Mr. Stooge? Don't be an imbecile."

I looked up at my mom and reached for her hand. She was wearing a black skirt and white blouse with a black pocket belt to hold her change, order pad, and other waitressy necessities. She seemed so confident. As if reading my mind, she said, "Jimmy, relax and just be yourself. This will be great!" She must have felt my sweaty palms and known I needed her reassurance.

After passing through the general dining room, we turned left at the bar and entered a semi-private eating area. Several four-top tables had been pulled together to make one longer table. A simple floral centerpiece was placed on each setting. Padded high-back chairs with bear-claw feet were situated around the table. About seven people were sitting with Larry.

Sure enough, Larry had his haircut like the Greeks of old. He wore beige pants and a white dress shirt with a T-shirt visible through his open collar. A brown leather jacket was draped over the back of his chair. Larry sat facing the window overlooking the manicured golf course. I wasn't sure if he'd ever played golf. I knew Larry played the violin professionally and was once into boxing as a lightweight fighter, but somehow the whole picture in front of me felt a little squirrelly.

I mean, to my way of thinking, the Three Stooges were ill-mannered mavericks. They threw pies in people's faces. They didn't eat pie from china and discuss how to improve their golf game. With TV shows like "Malice in the Palace" and "Pies and Guys," both with their legendary pie fight finales running through my head, it was just a little bit odd to see Larry dining in this context. Still, it was great to be standing in the presence of a real live television star.

My mom pulled a chair up for me at the end of the table right off of Larry's left elbow and motioned for me to take a seat. Taking her place on the other side, she introduced me to Larry. Larry finished chewing a bite of his sandwich, looked over at me, and said, "Hey, kid … doing all right?"

I found my voice. "Yeah, doing great."

After that rather weak introduction, I sat there staring like a dog expecting a treat. He continued to eat and talk with his other guests, tossing me an occasional smile. Several minutes passed. No face slaps. No eye pokes. The whole time I thought, *Now what? Is that it? This guy isn't even funny.*

I shifted in my seat starting to feel awkward about the visit. Larry was trying to carry on a conversation with seven adults while I wanted him to do some of his Three Stooges shtick. Ten, maybe fifteen minutes later, Mom excused us. She took me to another table in the general dining area and brought me soup and a grilled cheese sandwich. With a broad smile, she asked if it was fun to meet Larry. I told her, yeah, it was fun to meet him—because on some level it really was. None of my friends could say that they'd met a real Stooge.

What's more, my mom was doing the best she could to create a fun memory. I'm convinced that her efforts to put fun in our home went a long way in keeping us sane and on the right side of the law. She also showed us how to use humor when we were hurting or disappointed. She had this playful way of easing the pain—like taking out her teeth, messing up her hair, and placing her thick-rimmed glasses upside down on her nose. How could we keep a sad face when she did that routine?

Unfortunately, a few short years after meeting Larry, Mom fell ill with a cancer that would take her life. No amount of humor could compensate for the loss I felt, but I'm getting ahead of the story. Just before she died, I encountered one of the biggest, toughest, and angriest members of the human race.

4

Hank the Tank

entered the military when I was eight years old.

I had no say in the matter. In fact, I was enrolled against my will. Completely unprepared for this sudden turn of events, my whole universe changed overnight. One day I was a happy kid in the third grade at Bixby Elementary School, and suddenly I had to endure a regiment of push-ups and other strictly enforced maneuvers designed to break my will and transform me into a good little soldier.

Appealing the decision to enlist was not an option.

My drill sergeant was a big guy, probably 6'3" and 205 pounds of muscle. He looked a lot like Telly Savalas who played Kojak on TV, only my sergeant's ears were bigger. His head was completely shaven. He wore no glasses, chains, or rings. Unlike other military types, he didn't have any tattoos, either. He didn't need them. He had the solid build of a Ukrainian or a Viking.

But that nose—I'll never forget his overhung nose. He had this crook in his nose that reminded me of a vulture. Of course, I could never say that to his face, that is, not if I wanted to live another day.

I entered boot camp in 1969.

That's the year my mom married Hank Sheldon. There was no

church ceremony with friends to witness the event. There were no flowers, photos, or fancy embossed invitations. There wasn't a reception. Mom showed up one day at the house and announced she and Hank had gotten married in Las Vegas. None of us kids had known she was even going to Vegas.

Then again, Hank had a pilot's license and so it was entirely possible for them to fly down for the afternoon, tie the knot, and fly back all in the same day. One thing was certain. When Mom married Hank, it rocked my world in a big way. Hank, you see, was ex-navy who apparently forgot the "ex" part of the deal. The day that our new stepfather moved in with us was the day that my stint in the military started. He viewed our house as his personal barracks and my siblings and me as his little platoon.

From day one Hank made it clear he was the commander of the ship and we were to fall into compliance—or swab the deck. He immediately waged an aggressive war on dust, dirt, fingerprints, and unfolded blankets. The guy was a neat freak on steroids. With the flair of a real fanatic, he'd check under our mattresses for stuff. He'd open kitchen cupboards and drawers and require the girls to wipe out any dust lurking behind the plates, forks, and spoons. Windows and windowsills had to be spotless.

Good enough was never good enough.

Hank ran the house like a drill sergeant. Worse, he had a militaristic ... no, make that a *sadistic* discipline technique. He would make me hang up my jacket fifty times because I'd left it on the floor in my bedroom, or fold my blanket a hundred times because it was crumpled on the bed. Let me just say that this approach to enforcing the rules was a bit foreign to us.

Which is why I nicknamed him: "Hank the Tank."

Equally fed up with his control issues, my sister Kim risked a serious backlash by writing this anonymous note:

*"Our house is clean enough to be healthy
... and dirty enough to be happy."*

When Hank saw the note taped to his bedroom door, he went nuts. He demanded to know who the author was. None of us stepped forward. That only further enraged him. Hank didn't like to be crossed. Ever. Hank had come from a wealthy family. He was disinherited because he decided to join the navy against the wishes of his parents. Even then it was his way or the highway. If joining the navy meant he'd be cut out of his parents' will, so be it. He wouldn't be held hostage by such threats. Crossing this man was never a good idea.

For the better part of thirty years, Hank served in the navy. Although a real tough guy, he opted to become a chef on the side. Every port of call, he'd go ashore and learn some new aspect of cooking. Hank became a real whiz with a knife and spatula. After he left the navy, he worked as the head chef at the Glen Restaurant, an upscale eatery not far from our house. That's where he met my mom, who had taken a job there as a waitress.

Frankly, I'm not sure what she saw in the man.

To us, Hank was nothing but trouble. His love for Mom, though, was unmatched, I'll give him that much. He adored her. He doted on her. His fondness for her was unmistakable. You could see it in the way he looked at her, spoke about her, and acted around her. But Hank's love for us was missing in action. We were nothing more than excess baggage. He resented the fact that he had to share Mom with us. He'd been a bachelor his entire life and was unaccustomed to dealing with kids—the five of us were way more than he'd bargained for.

The conflict with Hank was constant and borderline legendary. He had no idea how to relate to my teenage sisters. He didn't know how to meet the needs of a nine-year-old boy. About the only person he made any connection with other than Mom was my brother Dave, primarily because Dave helped him in the kitchen. Even so, Dave had to watch his step ... or face the wrath of one knife-throwing chef.

THE IRON CHEF

When Hank walked into a kitchen, he became god of the grill. He put the "iron" in iron chef. Hank wanted things done his way or his temper would ignite like a red-hot blaze. My brother Dave, who was seventeen at the time, knew this from personal experience.

The first summer Hank was a part of our family, he got a contract to provide the food service for the Mammoth Mountain Inn in central California. That was no small deal. Mammoth Inn was a world-class ski resort, perched nine thousand feet above sea level on the eastern slopes of the Sierra Nevada Mountain Range. Nestled against the mountainside, the inn had breathtaking views from its sweeping plate-glass windows. During the summer, the ski business was exchanged for groups of hikers and assorted outdoor enthusiasts. Dave tagged along as Hank's "assistant" and was assigned to be the prep guy.

Hank also hired a local kid to be the dishwasher. According to Dave, the dishwasher was always kissing up to Hank, trying hard to make points. Dave knew better than to play that game with Hank the Tank and warned the guy to back off. No matter how many times Dave would tell the dishwasher to "stay away from Hank," the advice fell upon deaf ears.

One morning, Dave and Hank arrived in the kitchen to prepare breakfast for about 150 hikers. Try as they might, they couldn't find the omelet pans. These weren't ordinary omelet pans, mind you. These were Hank's personal pans—his pride and joy. They had served him well for years. When he couldn't locate his trusty cookware, Hank started to flip out. As any craftsman will tell you, you don't mess with a man's tools.

Having searched every inch of the place, Dave decided to check inside the giant, industrial-size dishwasher unit. Sure enough, he found the four omelet pans sandwiched inside. The kid they'd hired ruined Hank's prized pans by running them through the machine. Dave held them up and blurted, "Hank, I found them. They were in the dishwasher!"

Hank went ballistic. For the next five minutes, Dave watched as Hank launched into a salty tirade peppered with a heavy dose of spicy language: "An omelet pan is *never* to be washed … water is *never* to touch them—ever! They are conditioned with steel wool and vegetable oil … what kind of *idiot* doesn't know that?" Dave got a crash course that day in what it meant to curse like a sailor.

Midway through the meltdown, Dave watched the clueless dishwasher walk into the kitchen through the back door and then stop midstep. With a dopey grin on his face, he said, "Oh, I see you found my surprise!" Hank was beside himself. He grabbed a butcher knife and threw the blade at the culprit. With a pinging sound, the blade slammed into the wall and lodged about two feet from the startled kid. Dave shot him a look as if to say, "I told you not to mess with the Iron Chef."

That was the last time they saw the kid.

For the next eight hours, Hank made Dave take steel wool and a gallon of vegetable oil to recondition the four pans. Periodically, Dave would stop and hand a pan to Hank who, in turn, placed it on the fire. Taking an egg, Hank cracked it into the pan. After several moments of swishing it around the reworked surface, Hank would announce, "Nope. It's not ready. Wipe it out some more."

Hank's perfectionism and unbridled temper were destined to cause a major division in our home. While I was too young to do anything but follow his orders, my siblings started to mount a mutiny of sorts. My brother Mike, who, at nineteen, was serving in the navy, was the first to fire back. Mike, who freely admits he was somewhat of a hothead back then, came home on shore leave once and heard how Hank was treating us. He wasted no time in reading Hank the riot act.

Standing toe-to-toe, Mike jabbed a finger in Hank's chest and said, "I'll tell you two things. If you ever hurt my mom, or make her unhappy, or if you ever hurt one of the kids, you'll have to deal with me. Got it?" It was like watching two bucks sparring for dominance of the pack. From then on, whenever Mike was scheduled to come home, Hank disappeared until Mike left.

Don't get me wrong. Hank wasn't all bad news. In fact, there was one routine that he introduced into the family that was a good thing: He insisted that we start praying before meals. Hank wasn't a Christian, per se. He had more of a mushy religiosity somewhere in his background. I can't say that he owned a Bible. I never saw him reading from one and he most certainly never read it to us. He just had this belief that we ought to fold our hands and give thanks before a meal because "that's just what we're supposed to do."

The idea of praying resonated with me. I liked the thought that we were talking to God. Looking back, this practice of "saying grace" was another unexpected gift from God. He knew a day was approaching when I would become aware of my need to rely upon Him. These nightly dinnertime prayers, such as they were, paved the way for a much more meaningful conversation with God down the road. They were also further evidence that God was at work behind the scenes. I'm grateful that Hank took the lead in this area.

In spite of this worthy contribution, Hank was a constant source of tension. For her part, my sister Kim had had enough and refused to yield to Hank's overbearing ways. The friction was so great she ended up running away from home for several months. The tipping point was an altercation over a Frisbee, my Frisbee. We were playing catch in the backyard when I accidentally threw the Frisbee through a window on the garage. Hank barreled through the back door and barked, "Who broke the window?"

I had two choices.

I could lie—and avoid a few hundred push-ups.

Or, I could tell the truth and face the consequences.

Thanks to my mom's guidance, I had learned the importance of owning my stuff back in Crawford's Grocery Store. I opted for the truth. I started to say, "I did it," but before I could get the words out, Kommander Kim snapped. She kicked into high gear and braced for a fight.

Kim said, "I did, *Hank*. So, what are you gonna do about it?" She added a sprinkling of her own sailor lingo to underscore her point. Everything about her stance screamed, "BACK OFF." While they didn't come to blows, Hank yelled back and chased Kim around the family car in the backyard like a rottweiler. She bolted down the driveway and down the street. After successfully evading the madman, she packed what little she had and moved out.

I couldn't believe my eyes.

Just like that, Kim was gone. I was watching my world unravel right in front of me, and was powerless to prevent it from coming fully apart at the seams. My dad was gone. My brother Mike was off in the navy and rarely home. Now my sister Kim had left, leaving me stuck under the thumb of Hank the Tank. While I still had Dave,

Dee Dee, and Mom, I was completely blindsided by what was in store for us just around the corner.

FROM BAD TO REALLY BAD

I never saw the death of my mother coming.

All I knew was that she started to become tired most of the time. Exhausted was more like it. Without warning, this energetic, fun-loving, and hardworking woman—who used to bring me chocolate shakes and make us laugh—quit her job and spent her days isolated in her room. Although I couldn't help but notice the radical change in Mom's behavior, I just thought she was sick. Sick people needed to rest. Sure, she looked a little pale to me. She had lost a few pounds, too, but I just figured that went along with being ill.

How was I to know she would be dead in a few months?

Her true condition had been kept from me. My mom had been diagnosed with colon cancer and had undergone a colostomy—a surgical procedure to insert an external excretory bag. I'd only learn about that years later. At the time, however, I was preoccupied with a puzzle: Why weren't we permitted to be with her? Had we done something wrong? Did we cause her sickness? Was her illness contagious? Nothing made sense. She was my mom and we should be together, that's all there was to it.

The answers to my questions boiled down to one word:

Hank.

Mom was in lockdown because Hank had ordered it. He was so obsessed with her that he wanted her all to himself and worked overtime to keep us from seeing her. He thought we tired her out.

Sometimes she would wander out of her bedroom to sit on the sofa and talk with us in the living room. The minute Hank came home, he'd lower the boom. Right in the middle of the conversation he'd interrupt and say, "Jan, come here, you need your rest." Like a prison guard, he'd take her arm and lead her back into solitary confinement.

That really bothered me. I hated to have her taken from me. Why couldn't we be together? My mother had cared for us through both good and hard times. Why wasn't I permitted to do the same for her when she was sick? Okay, maybe a nine-year-old wasn't capable of giving her medical care, but at least I could have *talked* with her, right? I'll never understand why Hank didn't let me give my mom a hug or a kiss before she was ushered away. With a click, the door would close behind them and I'd be left on the outside longing to be by her side.

About this time, Kim returned home and couldn't believe that Hank was preventing us from seeing Mom. On several occasions Kim picked the lock on the door in order to get in and sit with her. During one of those visits, Kim asked Mom why Hank kept us locked out. Evidently, Hank claimed he was afraid one of my older siblings would steal her morphine shots for their own use. I don't think they were into drugs, so I'm not sure where Hank got that idea.

Clearly, Hank didn't know how to deal with death. He didn't attempt to explain what was going on with Mom's health. He didn't think to prepare us for the inevitable. He lacked the courage to wade into those waters. Like a storm brewing off in the horizon, this strong, rock-solid navy man knew what was coming and was beginning to crack under the pressure. His way of coping and maintaining order was to separate us. He also started hitting the bottle pretty hard toward the end of my mother's life. The thought of losing her was killing him.

As the end approached, Hank's behavior changed. He still made incredible meals. After all, cooking was his outlet. I remember he'd first take Mom, who was locked up in the bedroom, something to eat. When he returned to the kitchen, we'd sit down to dinner and, as became our habit, he'd say, "Well, let's pray."

Only now, instead of rattling off one of his formula prayers, his voice would catch. His emotions bubbled up under his fortresslike exterior and began to surface. He loved my mom, deeply. But just as soon as the feelings surfaced, he'd stuff them back down, clear his throat, and carry on.

Since I had been kept in the dark and didn't know Mom was dying, I just figured Hank was really, really sad that she was sick. Looking back now, I'm pretty sure the reality of her impending passing overwhelmed him. Especially the thought that he'd have to take care of kids whom he didn't love and with whom he had no real connection. He must have thought, *Dying and leaving me with five kids wasn't part of the deal, Jan.*

Dave remembers a particular Sunday when Hank charged into his bedroom and, with a shake, woke him up and said, "Dave, come on, we're gonna go to church." Mind you, our church affiliation at this time was nonexistent. Since Hank didn't know which church to attend, the two of them drove around looking for the biggest church they could find. Perhaps he thought that the bigger the church and the higher the steeple, the closer they were to God. Of course, that's not how it works.

They ended up at an Episcopal church with large stained-glass windows and heavy wooden pews that appeared to have been hewn by the Pilgrims. Massive brass organ pipes covered the walls behind the pulpit. The thick red carpet, which covered the narthex floor by the front doors, rolled down the main aisle and then up three short steps to the altar. The sanctuary wasn't particularly full. They entered and sat toward the rear.

As the choir sang, Hank's emotional dam breached; tears of grief flowed freely. Dave had never witnessed Hank showing any real, unbridled emotion whatsoever and was at a loss for what to do. He wasn't about to put an arm around the man. They didn't have that kind of relationship. Dave wasn't even sure if he should look in Hank's direction for fear of getting hammered by a hymnal. Tough guys didn't like people staring when they cried. Dave played it safe and just focused on the dimly lit surroundings.

Hank buried his face in his hands and continued to fall apart. As the service ended, Dave decided he had better get some help. Walking to the front, he set his sights on finding the priest with the biggest, fanciest robe. Dave approached the older gentleman and said, "Please, you've got to come talk to my stepfather." When the priest asked what was wrong, Dave said, "I'm pretty sure my mom is dying and I don't think he knows how to handle it." He gladly obliged. While Dave sat out of earshot, the priest spent thirty minutes talking to Hank.

On the drive home, Hank stared straight ahead and didn't say a word. He could have shared the insights and comfort spoken by the priest. I'm sure Dave would have appreciated that. At the least, he could have used those private moments to probe Dave's feelings. This was, after all, Dave's mother who was dying. Oblivious to the needs of the seventeen-year-old young man riding next to him, Hank remained quiet.

Evidently, his pride as a self-made man got the better of him in the days ahead, too. He acted as if the whole close encounter with God on that Sunday morning never happened. While Hank was a closed book, my mom took a different approach with me. She never mentioned that she was about to die, and yet she creatively planted in me a remarkable picture about life, death, and new beginnings that I'll carry with me the rest of my life.

FLOWERS FROM HEAVEN

For my ninth birthday, Mom surprised me with the ultimate gift. No, not another G.I. Joe toy. I was pretty much through with that stage. She got me a bicycle. Not just any regular old kid's bike. This was a blue Stingray with racing tires and an extra-large sissy bar—a tall, U-shaped chrome bar rising six feet into the air from the back of my sparkling metallic-blue banana seat.

I went everywhere on that thing. I was the King of the Road.

One particular afternoon, I arrived home from school and noticed my mother's bedroom door was both unlocked and ajar. I knew Hank would be hacked, but since nobody was around, I figured it might be safe to venture in. When she heard me hesitating by the door, she called out.

"Jimmy?"

"Yes, Mom?"

"I'm glad that's you. Come here, Son."

Happy to finally be in her presence, I covered the ground between us quickly and stood next to the edge of her bed. I really wanted to climb up and hug her, but she seemed surprisingly frail. There was so much I wanted to say. I mean, this visit was one of the precious few times that I got to see her in several months.

As my eyes adjusted to the soft, indirect lighting, I noticed her reddish brown, shoulder-length hair had been cropped short. She was much thinner now, of that I was pretty sure. She appeared somewhat smaller, as if her peach nightgown was a few sizes too large. She rested on her left side, a pillow propped against the headboard for support. It was difficult to believe that this was the same lady, with that great sense of humor, who dressed up as an infant by wearing a giant diaper to a party just for laughs.

With a weak yet beautiful smile, Mom explained her request.

She asked me to go to the nearby department store, which had a nursery, and buy a packet of chrysanthemum seeds. She wanted me to plant them outside of her bedroom window in the flowerbed.

Chrysanthemums?

Never one to miss a teachable moment, she told me to get a pen and paper. I zoomed out of the room, grabbed the items from a kitchen drawer, and then hustled back as fast as I could. I had to return before Hank came along and locked me out. After all, I was about to be sent on an important mission and didn't want Hank to sandbag it.

Mom slowly spelled out "chrysanthemum" and made sure I had written it down correctly. She pressed some money into my hand and, with a love tap, sent me on my way. I, of course, was happy for the chance to do anything for her. This was a big deal. She had singled me out from the rest of the kids. The fact that she trusted me with such a big assignment was like a gust of wind at my back. I rocketed toward the store.

Of course, I had never planted anything in my life. I didn't know seeds from weeds. But, if Mom thought I was up to the challenge, then I just had to get this right. The last thing I wanted to do was to fail her. Upon my return, I read and then reread the instructions on the back of the seed packet. I wanted to be precise with my gardening. If the directions called for three seeds per hole, planted every four inches apart, then that's what I'd do.

With ruler in hand, and garden hose ready, I planted a dozen chrysanthemum clusters in the flowerbed just outside of her window. It was a perfectly straight row, too. I measured those coordinates twice before pushing my forefinger down to the appropriate depth. I think even Hank, the perfectionist, would have approved of the job I was doing.

In an odd way, I felt connected to my mom as I worked. This

was our project. We were a team. She had the idea and I got to make it happen. I kept thinking, *Boy, she's gonna really love 'em ... and won't she be surprised when they bloom just like the picture on the packet.*

With a steady hand, I counted out the precise number of seeds, dropped them lovingly into each hole, and, with a gentle pat so as not to crush the life out of them, painstakingly refilled the holes. I served the thirsty seeds their first splash of water. That was the only time I remembered to water them. Gardening was not a priority for a nine-year-old, especially one with a blue Stingray and roads to conquer.

Thankfully, I planted in mid-February, when California was entering the rainy season. Mom's chrysanthemums would get the moisture they needed. After cleaning up, I went inside to tell Mom that the job was done. She was asleep, breathing slow and steady in the darkness. I retreated from her room, careful not to wake her. As it turned out, that would be the last time I was permitted to be with my mom at home until the very end.

THANK YOU, MOM

Several weeks later, Mom was transferred to the hospital. As far as I was concerned, she was still just really sick. Mike, Dave, Dee Dee, and Kim knew better. Mom's health was failing fast. She had very little time left. Maybe days. Perhaps a week. Hank knew this, too, and went off on a bender. His drinking spree took him out of the picture for days. The man fell completely apart. Without any adult to turn to for direction, my siblings went into group mode.

After a family meeting, they were convinced that I should see Mom at least one more time. One problem. Back then, children under sixteen weren't allowed to see patients. My siblings staged a covert operation to smuggle me into the hospital on Saturday morning. It went off without a hitch.

We stood in a semi-circle around her bed. A thin, light-brown blanket lay loosely over her body. She sat in a semi-upright position with the bedrails in place. A translucent tube ran from the back of her left hand to an IV drip. But what struck me most about our brief visit wasn't the array of monitors with their constant beeps, or the hospital with its disinfectant smell.

My most striking memory is how my mom was so uplifting and positive. In spite of the pain she must have felt as the cancer worked overtime to shut down her vital organs, she joked with us. She laughed with us. She teased us. And her smile made each of us feel like everything would be "okay." Mom was giving us a gift—our last memory of her is one of laughter, of joy, and of love.

As we were leaving, Mom pulled Mike aside and said, "Look, I just want you to take the kids somewhere. I want you to go and have a good time, you know, get away from here. Maybe go up to the desert or the mountains and see friends."

Mike hesitated. "Shouldn't I be here with you?"

She persisted. "Will you just do it—for me?"

He agreed. This was what she wanted and he wasn't about to argue. With the exception of Dave, who decided to stay at our house, we left the hospital and headed east of Los Angeles. I'm not sure how we knew about this family out in the boondocks, but Mike was sure that we could hang out with them. Midway through our afternoon visit, Mike announced that he wanted to call Mom and see how she was doing. But, I learned later, he didn't want to call from the house because in his heart he had this sense that she had died.

Instead, he drove to the nearest pay phone and placed the call. He asked to speak with Jan Daly—or was it Jan Sheldon? The nurse asked him to hold. The minutes dragged on. Mike was starting to become anxious. The tight quarters of the phone booth didn't help matters. At 6'5", he was, after all, a big guy. He shifted in the cramped space and continued to wait. Was his premonition right?

The nurse came back on the line and announced, "You'll have to call the doctor."

Mike said, "Wait a minute, I don't need to talk to the doctor. I'm her *son*. I'd like to talk to my mom."

"I'm sorry," she said, maintaining a practiced professional demeanor. "You'll need to speak with the doctor."

"Fine. Then put him on."

"He's not here."

Mike was ready to reach through the phone and grab her by the collar. "So why don't *you* tell me what's going on? I was just with her this morning."

"I can't tell you. The doctor has to tell you."

A wave of fear washed over him. *Tell me what?* Mike cleared his throat and said, "Look, get the doctor … get any doctor on the phone. I just want to talk to my mother." That's when reality hit him full force. He swallowed hard, and when he found his voice, said, "She's dead, isn't she? She died; that's why I can't talk to her, right?"

The nurse wouldn't budge. "You have to talk to the doctor."

Mike slammed the phone down. In his anger, he busted the telephone booth. Stumbling out, he fell down into the sand, crying. With fists clenched and repeated pounds to the earth, he wailed, "*This isn't right…. This isn't right…. There's no reason for Mom to die. This can't be happening. Not now.*"

Mike stood, kicked the sand, and got back in his car. He knew he had to compose himself during the short drive back to the home we were visiting. One by one, he called Dee Dee, then Kim, and then me into the kitchen to break the bad news. I remember Dee Dee coming out, first, crying. I thought, *This isn't good.* When Kim appeared, she was crying too. I thought, *Nope, not good at all.*

When my turn came, Mike said, "I don't know how to tell you this, Jimmy, but I think Mommy has died." Even though I wasn't sure what it meant to "die," I knew it had to be really bad. I mean, Dee Dee and Kim were bawling away in the other room. Suddenly, I realized that I'd never see her again. I fought back the tears. I could feel the edges of my ears start to burn and an emptiness settling into the place where my heart once was.

I reached for Mike's arm and squeezed—hard. Mike tells me I squeezed with such force I left deep nail marks. It's as if by holding on to Mike's forearm, I was somehow refusing to let go of my mother … if I could only hold on, maybe she'd still be with us. I think by clamping down I was recognizing the ache I felt inside. Dad was gone. Hank was off somewhere disconnected from our pain.

Now, Mom was gone.

One by one, the adults in my life had vanished.

And yet, over the next few chaotic days, Grandma and Grandpa Hope would deliver some of the greatest news I could ever receive.

5

Home Alone

I stood beside my mother's graveside sporting my best corduroy pants, white shirt, and blue clip-on tie—the kind nine-year-olds wear on important occasions. I might have looked sharp, but inside my jumbled emotions had my stomach in knots. When my fourth-grade classmates at Bixby Elementary had heard the news, they sent me a batch of fifty cards, including several from the teachers. They said how sorry they were to hear about my mom. Some promised they'd pray for me.

The graveside service was about to begin. Though I was in a crowd of well-wishers, I longed for space. If another well-meaning stranger pinched my cheek and asked, "Are you okay, Jimmy?" (according to the word on the street, I still hadn't cried), I'd probably have gone nuts. Couldn't a kid be allowed to process his feelings in his own way? And what's with the pinched cheek?

United in their sadness at Mom's passing, hundreds of people I'd never met, and didn't know, had followed us from the funeral home to the cemetery. While these people had been Mom's friends, I felt overwhelmed by the crowd and definitely on the outside of the group. Everyone was older than me. I don't recall seeing one kid standing with us among the sea of gravestones.

I concluded this was not a place for children.

Maybe the death of my mother was just a bad dream, a nightmare from which I'd soon awaken. I looked upward. Had it really been just five days since Mom died at Long Beach Memorial Hospital? I searched the sky for answers that didn't come.

A thick blanket of cottony-looking clouds hovered overhead, cloaking the afternoon sky behind a shroud of gray. Unlike thin, wispy cirrus clouds on a sunny day, this array hung low across the horizon, obscuring the sun. I watched as unseen currents of air shuffled and reshuffled the gray-bottomed clouds, as well as the pages of the minister's Bible.

The pastor started to speak, pulling me back to earth. He offered words of assurance and read from the Bible. Much of what was said didn't register with me. My mind was elsewhere and nowhere at the same time. It's as if I had pulled an invisible blanket over me—as I had done many times before in bed with my covers—to shield me from the fear of the unknown. This time I needed to keep the ghostly feelings of abandonment from haunting me. I felt terribly alone. I desperately wanted to be held by my mother.

Why did she have to leave me?

Where was she now?

People said she was in heaven, but where was that?

My mind drifted like a kite without a string. I floated back to a memory from the funeral service earlier that afternoon. The chapel had been filled to overflowing, with maybe five hundred in attendance. People were lined up around the outer wall and spilled out of the back door. Since we didn't have any extended family, these people were all her friends.

After all, Mom was quite the extrovert. She'd walk up to a complete stranger if she wanted to meet them and say, "Tell me about yourself."

Position meant nothing to her. In her view, you were a person no different from herself. If she wanted to talk to you, she did. That's how she met and befriended all three of the Three Stooges at the Pomona Fairgrounds. No wonder the chapel service had been packed.

I recall how a tall, somber man in a black suit had directed each of us to the casket, one at a time, to place a rose and say our final good-byes. Mike went first. Then Dave, Dee Dee, and Kim. I went last. I don't know why they always made me go last. I was always out of the loop; the last to learn about how sick Mom really was … the last to know she had died … and now, the last to say good-bye.

When my turn came, I walked toward the open casket feeling the eyes of everyone in the chapel boring a hole into my back. I kept telling myself, *I've gotta be grown up. Don't cry. Just don't cry.* The pressure of being studied by a room full of strangers was enough to terrify me. And the thought of kissing my mom good-bye, which Kim had suggested, was not sitting well with me. I didn't think Kim would go forward with it, but she did. She leaned into the coffin and actually kissed Mom before placing a rose in there.

As I made my way down the aisle, I debated whether or not I could, in fact, bring myself to kiss Mom. Moments later, I found myself peering over the casket, numbed by the whole surreal experience. Being a few months shy of my tenth birthday, I was tall enough to be chest high with the top of the elevated coffin. My mom lay slightly below my eye level. She appeared pale and gray and definitely not "her." I tipped up on the balls of my feet to lean in closer.

I whispered, "Mom? It's me …"

Boy, did I struggle to fight back the tears when I realized she'd never answer, couldn't answer. She was really gone. Slowly, tentatively, I reached forward and touched her hands. That was a real shock. Her fingers felt fake, like cold wax. They didn't feel anything like the hands that used to scratch my back. Mom would sometimes cup my face in the palms of her hands and look me in the eye to tell me she loved me; those hands were soft and warm—nothing like these stony limbs, which were more suited for a mannequin.

For a long moment I froze, trying to process the sight of my mom lying lifeless in the casket. The casket was an ornate bronze, water-tight model we kids had picked out since Hank was too distraught to coach us into making a wise decision. Nobody told us it was just a coffin. We spent far more than we could afford. At least Hank had the foresight to purchase two plots at Roosevelt Memorial Park, one for each of them.

Looking at her porcelainlike face, I couldn't bring myself to kiss her. Instead, I told her that I loved her and placed my rose with the others. I turned and, refusing to cry, faced the packed room. I didn't want them to think I was just an emotional kid. I had so many unanswered questions running through my head. *What was death? Where was Mom now? Could she see me? Hear me? Was this really the end?*

Would I see her again?

That day changed me; at nine years old I became an adult out of necessity. I didn't know if my biological father was dead or alive, or where he was living. He had been a no-show at the funeral, just like Hank. Both of the men in my life were AWOL. We later found out that my dad didn't learn about Mom's death for several months after the funeral. And, for his part, Hank was back on the bottle, an old habit that resurfaced with all the pressure caving in.

We were on our own. Walking away from the casket, I started to feel stress about issues children shouldn't worry about. My mom's passing affected my survival. *Where would we live? What would we eat? What school would we go to? Who would pay the bills and take care of us? Hank? Was Hank capable of taking care of us? Would I even want him to?*

It's funny how your mind works in moments like that. While wrestling with adult-sized questions, there were also practical, little-kid things that tugged at my heart. I was sad that Mom wouldn't make me breakfast anymore. There'd be no more chicken and dumplings with scalloped potatoes and spinach on Sundays, a tradition and one of my favorite meals. My tenth birthday party was just four months away and mom wouldn't be throwing me a party.

I collapsed into the seat next to my siblings in time to overhear my sisters fuming. They were steamed about the way Mom was "presented." They didn't like her hair, her makeup, and they absolutely detested her outfit—the lime-green chiffon dress looked "ridiculous." Personally, I was too lost in my own fog of emotions to have formed an opinion one way or the other. I remember thinking: *Does it really matter?*

STAIRWAY TO HEAVEN

With a host of thoughts weighing on my heart, I looked over at the minister. His voice sounded strained as he fought to be heard without a microphone. The brisk March wind didn't help matters. Pointing skyward with Bible in hand, he declared, "Friends, Jan is in a better place. For the Scriptures tell us, 'To be absent from the body is to be present with the Lord....'"

While I liked the sound of that, I wasn't exactly sure how it worked. I mean, I was pretty sure her body was in the box suspended over the giant hole in the ground several feet from us. How, then, could she be in heaven at the same time? At the time we weren't religious. Heaven, hell, and the afterlife were vague concepts. In matters of faith, we were, at best, CEOs—Christmas and Easter Only churchgoers.

Of course, like true CEOs, we never went to the same church twice. We might attend a Baptist church on Christmas and a Catholic parish for Easter. The next year we'd go to a Presbyterian church for Christmas and a Methodist for Easter. The churches with the kneeling pads were my favorite. I thought the pads were footrests. I often felt like lying down on them, but Mom would have frowned on that.

You can imagine, then, how my ears perked up when Grandma and Grandpa Hope stopped by with some unusual news earlier that week. Their visit came a couple of days after Mom had died. We were at home talking about the funeral arrangements. Actually, I wasn't doing any of the talking. Those were issues for my siblings to work out. The Hopes were kind to visit, and I was comforted to see them again.

You may recall the Hopes were our neighbors on Cosby Street— back during the happy days of my childhood. Dad and Mom became their best friends, and we kids quickly "adopted" the Hopes as grandparents. They, in turn, loved us as if we were their grandkids. When the Hopes learned Mom was dying, they had paid her a visit in the hospital.

Sitting on the sofa, Grandpa Hope conveyed the story. Over the weekend their daughter, Penny—we affectionately called her "Aunt Penny"—had asked, "Is Jan saved?" Unsure about Mom's faith in God, Grandpa said, "I don't know. Let's go find out." Off they went. Aunt Penny, and Grandma and Grandpa Hope took up positions around Mom's hospital bed. I could picture the room as he narrated the story.

According to Grandpa, he had taken her hand and said, "Jan, you know how much we love you. Because of that love, we want to make sure you're going to go to heaven. Do you believe that Jesus died for your sins? Have you invited him into your heart to be your savior?"

As he spoke, Grandpa's questions for my mom had taken me by surprise. While I had never given such matters much thought, I always assumed Mom would get into heaven because she was a "good person." She did her best to teach us right from wrong. She even taught us the Golden Rule—to treat others the way we wanted to be treated. That had to count for something, right? Plus, she made it clear that lying and cheating were out of bounds. Now, by the sound of it, those things weren't good enough to get her into heaven.

Mom must have felt something was missing in her life. Come to think of it, she'd been struggling with spiritual issues for some time. About six months before her death, Mom placed me in a weekly "release time" program at a local church. Every Wednesday afternoon, I was dismissed early from public school and "released" to go study the Bible at a nearby church for an hour. She wanted to make sure her "little guy" would get some kind of spiritual training and religious instruction.

And, she admitted to Grandpa that she couldn't say for *sure* whether or not she had a place in heaven. With the question of her spiritual destiny unresolved, Grandpa had asked, "Would you like to settle that issue right now?"

A smile eased across her face; "I'd love to!"

They joined hands around her bed as Mom prayed and gave her heart to God. Fourteen hours later, Mom stepped out of her frail, cancer-ridden body and into the arms of the One who awaited her in eternity. Grandma and Grandpa Hope had the honor of sharing that life-changing moment with her—and couldn't wait to tell us.

While I didn't understand the full implication of Grandpa's story, at least not until later in life, his confidence that Mom was in heaven comforted me. It sure sounded like good news. I liked the idea that she felt no more pain. I had this sense that God would take good care of her. I still didn't understand how her body was *here* and she was *there*. Maybe I'd grasp it one day, I thought. With the memory of Grandpa's visit and the story he shared fresh in my mind, I looked skyward again.

Was Mom in heaven right now looking down on me?

Did she know how much I missed her?

Lost in those reflections, I half heard the minister asking us to bow our heads for a final petition before he dismissed us. As he began to pray, I confess I hesitated to close my eyes. Frankly, I couldn't stop staring at the swirling clouds. They began to drift away with remarkable speed. Like a curtain pulled back from a window, the gray veil above was giving way to the deep blue skies beyond. I was captivated.

By the time the minister said, "Amen," a remarkable thing had happened. Most of the clouds had dissipated. Sprays of warm sunlight hurried to trade places with the shadows, like some sort of time-lapse film shot in the plains of Montana. We were now immersed in the golden glow of a late-afternoon sun. A handful of large cotton ball-shaped clouds lingered. Considering that the other clouds had jetted off to parts unknown, these lone stragglers stood out.

As the minister prayed, the wind continued to blow, causing the remaining clouds to morph gracefully into the definite likeness of a staircase, leading from cemetery to heaven. By the end of the prayer, the wind had finished its sculpture. Everyone was looking up now.

The image was unmistakable. The five of us Daly kids who, as nominal churchgoers, didn't look for symbolism in the skies, witnessed the sight. The Hopes saw it too. People to our left and right were elbowing each other, discreetly pointing toward the stairway to heaven.

Was it some sort of a sign?
Perhaps a message from Mom?

LEAVING ON A JET PLANE

Mike, Dave, Dee Dee, Kim, and I piled back into the longest car in the world, at least that's what it seemed to me. Some sort of black stretch Cadillac DeVille, or maybe a Lincoln Continental, with charcoal-tinted windows. As the lead car in the slow-moving processional, we snaked our way through a maze of granite tombstones. Here and there I saw monuments with bouquets of flowers resting in their shadows. Several elaborate headstones towered over adjacent plots, as if boasting, "My gravestone is bigger than your gravestone."

While the staircase in the sky had scattered, I turned my head and, with a squint out of the rear window, briefly focused on where the flight of stairs had first appeared. In my mind's eye, I pictured those heaven-bound stepping-stones and wrestled with what they might have meant—if they meant anything at all. Minutes later, the limo pulled past the entrance gate, aided by a policeman who halted the oncoming traffic. The manicured, parklike cemetery faded from view as we merged into the congestion of Los Angeles traffic.

It felt strange to leave Mom behind.

I rode in relative silence. It would be a short trip to the McCormick Gardena Chapel where our car was parked, and I didn't feel like talking. Someone suggested we grab dinner on the way home, but I wasn't hungry. More than anything, I was drained. I was plagued by far too many fears and misgivings that, like a swarm of

81

gnats, wouldn't go away. I couldn't help but wonder: *What horrible thing would happen next?*

After picking up our car at the chapel, Mike drove us home. The sun was beginning its nightly descent; its warm orange rays glinted across the windshield. I felt chilled. I couldn't shake the uneasy feeling that something horrible was around the corner. Minutes later, Mike pulled into the driveway. I was glad to be finally home and far away from the cheek-pinchers. Heading for the house, I was anxious just to spend time in my room, away from any commotion.

I stepped through the front door and gasped. I felt as though I'd been sucker-punched. I stopped dead in my tracks, gawking at the sight before me. Nothing made sense. I was exhausted, but I wasn't dreaming.

I blurted out, "Guys, where's all of our stuff?"

While everything had looked normal on the outside of the house when we arrived, the living room was completely vacant. The television was gone. The lime-green sofa was gone. The pictures, the books, the vacuum—everything had vanished. Mike, Dave, Dee Dee, and Kim pushed past me and quickly fanned out to the other rooms. The reports were shouted like a series of blasts from a rapid-fire gun.

Empty. Empty. Empty. Empty in here, too.

The beds, the chairs, the dishes, the towels, the refrigerator, and every lick of furniture—the house was completely empty. Well, almost empty. Our clothes and a handful of personal possessions had been tossed from the dressers and dumped on the floor in jumbled heaps. This was not a good sign. A week ago, Hank would have punished us with a hundred push-ups for piling our things on the floor.

Did someone forget to pay the rent?

Were we being evicted?

Had we been robbed?

We gathered in the now barren living room to consider our options. That's when Hank appeared from his bedroom carrying two suitcases. Mike was livid. Kicking into battle mode, Mike said, "Just where do you think you're going? What happened to the furniture and our things?" Hank waved him off. Usually quick to respond with a verbal jab, Hank didn't say a word. There was no fight left in him. Brushing past Mike, he headed out the front door and to the curb.

His shoulders slumped as if pulled down by the weight of the earth's gravity. No spark remained in his eyes. He had mentally checked out months ago. Hank the Tank was a broken man. We meant nothing to him when Mom was alive—and apparently less now that she had died. We followed him in the near darkness to the sidewalk, with the sun already below the horizon. When Hank finally spoke, the once confident bulldog shook his head and said, "I can't deal with this. I'm moving back to San Francisco."

He didn't say, "I'm sorry about your mom," or, "I hate to leave you guys this way," or, "Here are the arrangements I made for you guys after I'm gone." Nothing.

Mike was itching to get in his face, but probably knew a confrontation would accomplish nothing. Almost on cue, a taxi pulled to the curb. The driver helped Hank toss his bags in the trunk. They climbed in and headed for the airport. Like a phantom, Hank had appeared and then evaporated before our eyes. I never saw or talked to him again.

Back inside, we stood around the empty living room talking about how Hank just left. The fact that he was an emotional wreck was clear. I can't say we were that surprised he chose to abandon us on the evening of Mom's funeral. And, at least one mystery had been solved. It dawned on us why Hank didn't attend the funeral—he was too busy packing up our house. He must have had a crew with a truck ready to haul everything away the moment we went to the service that morning. He had sold everything.

In some ways, we felt relieved not to be under his thumb. But didn't he have some obligation to us? What were we supposed to do now? We had no adults, no money, and no furniture, except for the Formica-top kitchen table—with no chairs. Someone decided to check the phone mounted on the kitchen wall. It worked. At least that was something. While the Hopes were too old to handle all of us, Kim said, "Is Aunt Penny someone who can help us?"

Mike took the lead. He placed the call, explained our situation, nodded a few times, and finally said, "That's okay, Aunt Penny, we understand, we'll figure something out...." My stomach started to sink. More bad news. Mike slowly returned the phone to its cradle. "Aunt Penny's husband, Bill, is dying of stomach cancer," he said. "She'd love to help, but under the circumstances it's not a good idea." He leaned against the doorjamb, head tilted back.

Now what?

I looked over at Mike. Something was eating at him. With a sigh, he said, "Look, guys, I hate to break this to you, especially with all that's going on. But I head back to Vietnam tomorrow. My furlough is only through midnight tonight. I've got to be back at the base this evening." Mike was assigned to the USS *Kansas City*, a giant ship assigned to refuel and rearm the battle groups. I had once visited, and now wished it would take me away too.

I sank to the floor. Who would take care of us, of me?

Mike started stuffing his things into his duffel bag. I knew he wasn't abandoning us. What choice did he have? Duty called. Still, the thought that he'd soon be leaving seemed to press the air out of my lungs. I pulled off my clip-on tie, tossed it on my pile of clothes, and headed for the door. I needed to get away from the chaos, if only for a minute.

Honestly, everyone was too busy trying to figure out what we were going to do to notice I was about to go outside. I didn't want anyone to show concern. I wandered off on my own most of the time anyway to ride my bike or play with friends. Nothing unusual about that. As I headed out the door, I heard Dave announce to the group, "Hey, I know a family that might take us in, at least for a while." He started to place the call as I closed the door behind me.

A WALK TO REMEMBER

To say that I had been unprepared for the events of that day would be a gross understatement. It's as if the instant I got up that morning, I'd been swept away by a whirlwind of chaos. Seeing my dead mother's body. Watching my siblings cry. Standing by the grave. The parade of well-wishers. All of the talk about heaven. Seeing the stairs in the sky. Coming home to an empty house. Discovering that Hank had sold everything—and left us with nothing. Mike preparing to leave. Getting the news that Aunt Penny's husband was dying. How was I to make sense of it all?

Standing under the darkening sky, I hit rock bottom. I couldn't handle another thing. I was officially an orphan without a place to live or food to eat. And yet, at my absolute lowest, I remembered the flowers. What were they called?

Chrysanthemums.

I had completely forgotten about the chrysanthemums. The thought of them gave me a much-needed spark of hope. After all, Mom had asked me to plant them. It was our project, something just the two of us shared. I never told anyone about them, partly because it was personal and partly because I never gave them a second thought. But did they grow?

I had to find out.

I ran around the house to the flowerbed where, a few weeks before, I had so carefully planted them. As I approached, I didn't see anything at first. It was dark. For a second I wondered if I had the right spot. Getting down on one knee for a closer look, I was shocked that they were actually growing. I'd never planted anything in my life, and here they were; the first tiny sprouts pushing their way through the ground. While only an inch or two high, they were as wonderful to me as if they had been in full bloom. I kept thinking, *It worked. I must have planted them right!*

What a great confidence builder.

That's when a new idea struck me. When Mom had asked me to plant the flowers, she wasn't thinking of herself. They weren't for her enjoyment. She did it for my benefit. She must have known they'd become a living metaphor about life and new beginnings. It was almost as if she were saying, "Jimmy, I'm counting on you to carry on after I'm gone. Spring will come. The skies will brighten. You'll be just fine."

Whether or not that was what she had in mind, that's the impression the flowers had on me. On some deeper level, I also had a distinct spiritual impression that God was at work too. That even though Mom was gone, God was going to take care of me.

Resting on both knees, not caring that my corduroy pants were getting dirty, I tucked a few handfuls of earth around each of the plants. As I worked, I had a one-way chat with my mom. In my own childish way, I wanted to thank her for the flowers, for asking me to plant them, and for being such a great mom.

As I stood to leave, I debated digging up the flowers and taking them with us, but I didn't want them to die. I decided leaving them behind made more sense. I dusted my hands together, brushed the dirt from between my fingers, and headed for the door.

Rounding the corner of the house, I could see Dave, ear pressed against the phone, pacing the floor through the kitchen window. For the first time all day, I sensed that one way or the other, something would work out. We were due for a break. I walked in the door as Dave got off the phone all excited. He'd found us a place to stay. We were going to move in with the Reil family.

Life was about to get really weird.

6

No Place Like Home

There's an old saying: *Home is where the heart is*. As sentimental catchphrases go, there's definitely a Norman Rockwell ring to it. I'd say it falls into the category of those timeless expressions best embroidered on a quilt draped over the back of a well-worn leather armchair next to a roaring fireplace.

Home is where the heart is.

Sure sounds nice, inviting, even cozy. I don't know who first penned the line. Maybe a writer for *The Saturday Evening Post*, or perhaps someone at Hallmark. But what if your heart has been drawn, quartered, and bruised beyond recognition? Where's home then? Our hearts were first broken when Dad and Mom separated. They were further splintered when Mom remarried, and finally shattered when she died. And even after all of that, Hank sold all of our possessions and left us penniless orphans.

Home is where the heart is.

On the night of Mom's funeral, home became anywhere we could find a place to lay our heads. Although Dave's phone call had yielded a place for us to stay, his friends lived more than a hundred miles east of Los Angeles. Dave decided that was too far to travel at such a late hour. Frankly, I was relieved. I wanted to hold on to what was left of my world as long as possible.

After Mike left for his ship, Dave, Dee Dee, Kim, and I made the best of our circumstances and settled in for the night. We huddled together on the carpeted floor in the living room. We had no pillows or blankets to pull over us, but at least we were together in our home. If I tried hard enough, I felt certain I could still smell Mom's perfume lingering in the hall.

I'm pretty sure Norman Rockwell would have never painted us sprawled out on the floor in the vacant room, with nothing but clothes in rumpled piles, doubling as cushions and blankets. Why capture the dark shadows of a nightmare when the world is filled with warmer, happier hues?

Besides, practically speaking, who wants to live like that? I didn't. Like Dorothy in *The Wizard of Oz*, I wanted to click my heels together three times and be instantly transported to the home I longed for … a place where laughter and good times were shared … where Mom and Dad teased each other with the snap of a kitchen towel after dinner … a place we once called home.

While the prospect of living with a family I didn't know wasn't my first choice, I took comfort in the fact that at least my siblings and I hadn't been split up like baggage at the airport, separated and sent to different final destinations. Unbelievably, that was a solution proposed by Hank a few days after Mom had died. In some of the most colorful tones I'd ever heard, Dave made it clear such a breakup would *never* happen.

With all of the talk about going to live with Dave's friends, the Reils, I couldn't help but wonder why we didn't go and live with Dad. Sure, he had problems, but maybe he had changed. He was still *my* dad, and I liked that option much better than stepping into the unknown. Of course, we hadn't seen him in years and had no idea where he was living, so that option wasn't really on the table.

Lying on the floor, eyelids at half-mast, my gaze was drawn to Mom's bedroom door. Part of me wanted to believe she'd walk out at any moment and call my name—that everything would be okay. What was she doing now that, according to Grandpa Hope, she was in heaven? Did people sleep in heaven? Could she see me missing her? Did she know how much I wanted to talk with her like before, to hear her voice again? Thankfully, Mr. Sandman rescued me from dwelling on what I no longer had.

FORK IN THE ROAD

California's Interstate 10, locally known as the San Bernardino Freeway, is a twelve-lane, east/west concrete artery connecting Arizona to the Pacific Ocean. With Dave behind the wheel, Dee Dee riding shotgun, and Kim and I in the back, we drove eastward for what seemed like an eternity. Everything I had known—our house, my school, my friends, and Dad—was now a hundred miles away. Each passing mile separated me from the world I once knew and loved.

Would I ever get to go back? Would I ever see my dad again?

Was that even possible?

With my head against the window, I watched the trees and scrub brush whiz by in a blur of sameness. The rhythmic hum of tires over pavement put me in a trancelike state. I listened to the scratchy sounds emanating from the AM car radio: The Beatles wanted to hold someone's hand, the Monkeys were believers, and Carol King was feeling the earth move under her feet—whatever that meant.

Although sad to leave everything behind, I nevertheless felt safe and secure because my brother and sisters were with me. Even though Mom was gone and Mike was somewhere on the Pacific Ocean, I believed I could go anywhere and face anything as long as the rest of us stuck together. What's more, I was happy that Mike had promised to visit us one day when back at port. Maybe this change wouldn't be so difficult after all; at least that's what I told myself.

Every now and then I'd lean forward and rest my chin on the seat back for a better view. I was fascinated by the sporadic ping of bugs against glass, the windshield serving as their final resting place. I thought about how Mom would have joked, "Those bugs should have known better than to play tag with the windshield!"

With temperatures in the mideighties and without the luxury of air-conditioning in that car, we had to roll down the windows. I could feel the freeway bake with enough radiant energy to fry chicken, and maybe my face while it was at it. The sweltering air seemed reluctant to touch down where earth met sky, producing a hazy diffusion in the distance.

As if answering the unasked question endlessly circling my mind, Dave announced, "We're almost there." I fell back against my seat and resumed my watch for Route 62, also known as Twentynine Palms Highway. Although Dave was fully capable of the task, he had asked me to keep an eye out for our exit, probably to give me something to do. A sign announcing the city of Palm Springs came into view. Our exit was twelve miles away.

At the mention of Palm Springs, my sisters were quick to point out a laundry list of the famous celebrities who had a second home there ... Clark Gable, Cary Grant, Steve McQueen, Donna Reed, Bob Hope, Liberace, and Frank Sinatra. They were names I didn't recognize, but the fact that they had a *second* home while we were homeless must have meant they were doing okay.

When someone mentioned that Elvis and Lucille Ball had houses there too, I understood we were talking about *really* famous people. People on TV. People like Larry from the Three Stooges. I'd later learn that Al Capone once used Suite 14 at the Two Bunch Palms resort to evade the police and rival thugs.

We passed the playground of the rich and famous and continued east toward Morongo Valley, a dry, dusty, barren stretch of land on the western edge of the Mojave Desert. Unlike Palm Springs, which had made the cover of *LIFE* magazine, Morongo Valley didn't have a shot at making the national news. After all, no movie stars lived there, at least none that Dee Dee and Kim knew about. In fact, with a population of less than 1,800, almost *nobody* lived there.

At least there was a family kind enough to take us in.

Dave exited onto Route 62 and followed the two-lane road north along the foothills of Mount San Gorgonio, a majestic 10,834-foot mass, the tallest mountain in Southern California. Living in the Long Beach basin, I'd forgotten how enormous it was. I craned my neck for a better view.

According to Dave, the rugged rock formations leading to the peak were the stomping grounds of bighorn sheep. I had hoped to catch a glimpse of those creatures, but the road parted company with the mountain and veered toward the high desert. The occasional patches of greenery on the foothills traded places with sagebrush, desert flora, and cacti that dotted the scorched earth.

Making a right turn onto T-Circle Drive, Dave gave us the skinny on the Reil family. They were, after all, our new house parents and we should know something about them. Vernon and Betty—Mr. and Mrs. Reil to us—were originally from Iowa and knew a thing or two about farming. They had four boys: David, nineteen; Paul, eighteen; Gary, fifteen; and Marky, age eight. Perhaps living with them might not be so bad.

Dave explained that Mr. Reil used to work as a butcher at the Hormel Foods Corporation meatpacker plant in Osceola, Iowa. He and the other meat cutters would butcher a hog, and then place various cuts of pork onto iron gaffing hooks. Like a mini-monorail, the hooks hauled the meat overhead on a track system to the next station to turn it into Spam, Black Label Ham, or one of their other signature products. Evidently, one of the hooks broke, dropping a hefty side of pork on Mr. Reil, and three discs in his neck were ruptured.

With Mr. Reil disabled and unable to continue working at the meat plant, the Reils moved west and somehow stumbled onto a five-acre lot at the end of T-Circle Drive. There, Mr. Reil and his boys built chicken coops, rabbit cages, and goat pens. The Reils raised their own fruits and vegetables and lived off the land. That sounded pretty neat. I pictured their family as modern-day pioneers; Mr. Reil probably had a lot in common with Davy Crockett or maybe Paul Bunyan. You know, a burly, salt-of-the-earth, lumberjack type.

Almost on cue, Dave shattered my impression when he added that Mr. Reil had had three heart attacks, was a chain-smoker, and took nitroglycerine. I wasn't sure how much I was supposed to read between the lines. Did that mean Mr. Reil might die any day? What if he had a stroke while we were there? I was quick to push the questions out of my mind, having dealt with enough thoughts about death to last a lifetime.

Dave slowed the car and his narration as the pavement abruptly yielded to a bumpy dirt road. A row of rusted mailboxes perched on crooked wooden posts marked the transition from civilization to the wild frontier. After navigating several miles of car-eating craters, we reached a deep, wide channel cut into the earth—what country folk call a "wash" since your car or truck or whatever would sometimes have to wade through water to reach the bank of the other side.

We drove down into the wash, which happened to be dry, and, maybe thirty yards later, ascended the dirt road on the other side. I inched forward in my seat as we crested the incline. My heart hammered away as the Reils' private plateau came into view. Nothing Dave might have said could have prepared me for the scene unfolding before us. This wasn't Palm Springs. Not even close. By all appearances, we had entered a dimension closer to the *Twilight Zone*.

ALL IN THE FAMILY

Dave leaned on the accelerator as we ascended the embankment from the wash. Free-range chickens squawked and leaped, startled by our sudden appearance. Feathers flapping, they made a mad dash for the safety of the henhouse on our left. Brownish-gray planks of wood, bleached by the unmerciful sun, appeared to have been haphazardly tacked together to construct the enclosure.

Adjacent to the chicken coop, a large wood stump with an ax stuck in the flat top caught my attention. Red-brown streaks stained the top and sides of the stump clearly suggesting blood. What else could it be? In true city-slicker fashion, I thought: *Do they really chop off chicken heads? I could never do that.*

The pea-gravel crunching beneath our tires announced our approach. Dave followed the circular driveway toward the house on the opposite end. A vegetable garden sprouted in the center of the private turnaround drive. Hunched over, Mr. Reil was fussing at the ground with a hoe. Slim as a scarecrow, he was no more than 5'6" and maybe 145 pounds. With a turn, he straightened up and offered a smile and a wave. With no visible teeth, his lips seemed to pucker inward as if curling over his gums. I'd later learn he did own, but rarely wore, his dentures.

Scanning the yard beyond him, I saw the skeletons of several vehicles in various stages of disrepair, hoods raised, resting either on cinder blocks, or crouched on the ground with a platoon of weeds holding the tires captive. I would soon learn that the picked-over carcasses of the cars, trucks, or tractors deemed unsalvageable ended up in the ravine where the Reils dumped their trash.

The ravine was no more than fifteen feet from the back of the house and just beyond the clothesline. Running north to south, the gorge, while not particularly deep, had to be the width of two football fields. Without trash service, the Reils apparently decided to conduct their own landfill operation by tossing in their daily garbage, as well as busted chairs, auto parts, paint cans, animal carcasses, and whatnot. I'm fairly sure they didn't have government approval for that.

On the far end of the circular drive, Dave rolled to a stop in front of the one-story house, a square, cinder-block structure with a flat roof. Their home wasn't what I had pictured at all. The house had been painted pink, the color of Pepto-Bismol, or perhaps a little more like Barbie Doll pink. Given the choice of house color, I wouldn't have been surprised to see a clutch of plastic flamingos staked in the flowerbeds.

An enclosed patio jutted off the rear of the house, which, I'd soon learn, was where six of us—the four Reil brothers and Dave and I— would sleep on beds lined up in a row like an army barrack. Did I mention that the cramped, makeshift room was well within sniffing distance of the decomposing trash in the ravine?

Their house was a patchwork of poorly constructed additions as Mr. Reil annexed the outdoors to make more living space. Let me just say he appeared long on ideas but short on talent when it came to being a carpenter. I doubt a building inspector ever set foot in the house, because there's no way the ragtag workmanship would have been approved.

A short, stocky woman appeared by the screen door. She wore a loose-fitting muumuu dress and unlaced sneakers. Her hair was pulled back into a matted ponytail. "That's Mrs. Reil," Dave said, turning off the car and stepping out. I followed, though somewhat reluctantly. Like a master of ceremonies, Dave launched into a series of introductions. When my turn came, I shook Mrs. Reil's hand, which felt weathered like leather.

At least she didn't pinch my cheek.

A stale, ripe smell emanated from within the house, like a locker room overdue for a good hosing down. And, as I'd come to find out, with just one bathroom, no bathtub, one shower, one sink, and a toilet to serve twelve people, personal hygiene became a contest of wills.

Was staying with my dad really out of the question?

Carrying armloads of clothes from the car, we started to settle in our new shared home. We brought no possessions with us because Hank had sold everything—including my blue Stingray bike. In some respects, the fact that we had no furniture was probably a good thing considering how tiny the house was. The Reils had been crowded with six people; with us, that number swelled to ten.

To say that our time living with the Reil family was "strange" would be kind. More accurately, if *Ripley's Believe It or Not!* were to list the most bizarre places to live, the Reil home would probably be close to the top. While thankful for a roof over my head, it didn't take me long to wonder: *So ... where did Dave meet these people?*

Don't get me wrong. The first couple of weeks were relatively "normal" as we adapted to each other, to our new surroundings, and to my new school. I was sent to the only school in Morongo Valley, Morongo Valley Elementary School. Since it was March and the school year was well on its way, I entered the fourth-grade class and did what I could to fit into the existing cliques.

On the homefront, learning the Reils' daily routine was actually rather simple since it rarely changed. Every morning was like a scene from Bill Murray's *Groundhog Day*. While we kids jockeyed for a few precious minutes of privacy in the bathroom, Mrs. Reil made breakfast. She would toast up a loaf of bread and mix a vat of instant hot chocolate, occasionally adding a hint of goats milk. She'd sprinkle cinnamon and sugar on the toast, and stack the slices on a plate. Everyone dipped the toast into his or her hot chocolate.

The breakfast menu never changed.

We always had cinnamon toast and hot chocolate.

For variety, some days we had hot chocolate … and cinnamon toast. With all of the chickens running around, I wondered why we didn't have eggs at least once in a while. I can't recall ever drinking a glass of milk. No wonder I broke so many bones when I reached high school. We also never prayed before eating. Hank the Tank would have been miffed. I had grown accustomed to giving thanks for our food and missed that practice.

After dinner came a ritual that I observed, but never participated in. Their idea of a good time was to gather around the kitchen table to talk and smoke, smoke and talk, night after night, all the while rolling endless batches of cigarettes. Even Gary and Paul smoked and rolled cigarettes with their parents. While Marky didn't smoke, he helped with the manufacturing process. The table, with a Formica top and tubular metal legs, became their workbench.

With a "thunk," Mrs. Reil would place a large tin of tobacco on the table, fetch a cache of rolling papers and filters, and then pull up a chair. Using a cigarette roller machine they all took turns loading the paper, the filter, and then the tobacco. For its part, the machine whirled with a "chi chi" sound and, moments later, spat out a perfectly rolled cigarette. I was never tempted to try one of those things … it just seemed not too smart to smoke it.

While they worked, the AM radio blared away in the corner. Either they couldn't afford a television, or didn't have reception out in the boondocks, because the radio provided our only entertainment. After dark, the stations in the area signed off until sunup, and when the signal faded, we called it a night. After all, it was pitch black outside with no streetlights and no neighbors for at least a mile.

I think we might have been able to handle living with the Reils if hot chocolate and toast for breakfast, and rolling cigarettes listening to AM radio at night, had been the extent of their weirdness. Far from it. During the course of the one year we were in their foster care, for example, David Reil, who was nineteen, decided to marry his forty-two-year-old cousin. Even at ten years of age, I knew that was kind of strange.

And that wasn't the half of it. For the Reils, life was a never-ending, convoluted sitcom.

RUN, CHICKEN, RUN

Every culture on earth has a rite of passage. In various African tribes, when a boy turns thirteen, the men assemble and hand him his first hunting spear. In Jewish tradition, a thirteen-year-old boy is given a bar mitzvah, a ceremony recognizing him as an adult member of the community. Catholics experience this rite of passage through the process of confirmation.

Some see significant events in life as a rite of passage: a toddler's first haircut, a young woman who starts wearing makeup, or a young man who has his first shave. A first girlfriend or boyfriend, a first cigarette, or enduring college hazing are milestones signifying a transition in life. I discovered the Reil family's version of a rite of passage one Saturday morning several weeks into our stay.

After a hearty breakfast of hot chocolate and cinnamon toast, Mr. Reil rounded up Marky, Gary, and me, and we headed for the chicken coop. I figured we were just going to collect some more of the eggs that we never ate at breakfast. Reaching the henhouse, Mr. Reil lit up a cigarette and surveyed the coop with a practiced eye. He took a long, unhurried drag, pointed to a plump bird, exhaled a cloud of smoke, and told Gary to bring the unfortunate specimen to the wood stump.

I knew full well that the meat we ate came from the chickens, rabbits, and goats raised by the Reils. I just wasn't around for the killing, which was fine by me. With the exception of swatting flies or stomping spiders, I'd never killed anything in my life.

Before I knew what was happening, Mr. Reil, in full butcher mode, had a chicken pinned down on the chopping block, neck exposed. In one smooth, effortless swing, he knocked its head off. The headless chicken flopped to the ground and took off running. Watching it flail about was as unnerving as anything you might read in a sci-fi novel. For a good five minutes, the chicken staggered around and bumped into things, blood squirting out of its artery like a fountain. I backed away as it did a few headless flips. That was a new experience for me.

About the time the bird ran out of nervous energy, I heard Mr. Reil call my name. Marky, with a smirk I'll not forget, readily produced another chicken. Like he was initiating some sort of rite of passage, Mr. Reil held out the handle of the ax for me to take. Speaking through puckered gums, he said, "Jimmy, it's your turn to cut off the head." The look in his eye implied this was a command not a suggestion.

Right. As if I wanted to do that.

I hesitated.

Mr. Reil puffed away with his left hand while extending the ax to me in his right. Everything about his stance seemed to say, "Son, I have all the time in the world. You can either take this ax and get 'er done, or fret for a few hours. But we'll not leave this place until you take the head off of that bird. Suit yourself."

I stole a look at Gary and Marky who were having a total kick over my anxiety. They knew that their dad was the law in these parts. This was his land. His house. Mr. Reil was both the judge and the supreme court of the valley. I didn't have any option but to comply. There wasn't a higher authority to appeal to, and not wanting to end up like the headless hen, I stepped forward and took the ax.

I raised the blade and held my breath. It was one thing to eat chicken and quite another to do the deed. Time seemed to move in slow motion. While I felt sorry for the hen, I didn't want to miss and embarrass myself in front of them. I winced and let the ax fall. With my eyes partially closed, I felt the ax connect with a "Whomp!"

I'm not sure how I managed to hit the neck. But I did. With its head successfully lopped off, the chicken took off running, leaving a trail of blood everywhere—on the stump, the ax … even on my pant leg. I didn't spend a lot of time going back to the chicken coop after I cut that chicken's head off. I'm sure the Reils had a good laugh at my discomfort during supper. My only defense was to tune them out and withdraw into the safety of my own little world. I picked at my plate and went to bed hungry.

The mood between our families began to change not long after that incident. A clear line in the sand was being drawn, with their kids on one side, and us on the other. Things got so strained that Kim ran off not long afterward and married a guy, probably to put some distance between herself and the Reils' wild and wacky world.

That left Dave, Dee Dee, and me to take the brunt of the antics of this household. Well, mostly Dee Dee and me since Dave was gone most of the time at work.

Two brief examples come to mind. Marky, whom I originally had hopes of befriending, turned out to be a closet kleptomaniac. He liked stealing my stuff, what little I had to my name. He'd take things from the bundle that I kept under my cot and then stash the items in his dresser drawer. When confronted, Marky would deny it.

When I'd go to Mrs. Reil to explain what was going on, Marky would say, "I didn't steal from him—he's a lying pig." She just shook her head and took his side. Mrs. Reil would say, "Not *our* Marky. You must be wrong, Jimmy. Your problem is that you lose things and want to blame someone for it. No, it's not Marky." Years later, long after we were gone and Marky had turned eighteen, I heard that he was sent to the state penitentiary for fraud and forgery. I wonder how his life might have turned out differently had he been taught to own his "stuff," like my mom taught me.

I could deal with Marky pilfering my stuff and lying to my face to cover his tracks. What was a bit more difficult was discovering that Gary was a homosexual who looked at me in ways I didn't understand at the time. Keep in mind I had just turned ten—a birthday the Reils didn't even celebrate. I never had "The Talk" about sex with either of my parents. To me, girls still had cooties.

Imagine my surprise when Gary, who was five years older than me, started to take an interest in me. I'd come in from playing in the canyon looking for lizards and such, eat dinner, and then hear Gary say, "Hey, you're kinda cute." He approached me about his desires, but nothing happened. Frankly, it struck me as odd. Apparently, a little resistance was enough to keep him at bay.

I was in a no-win situation. After the way the Reils turned a deaf ear to my concerns about Marky's stealing, I knew they'd brush me off if I told them about Gary. I could hear Mrs. Reil say, "Not *our* Gary. This must be your problem. Maybe *you're* the one who is attracted to men, Jimmy."

I'd pull the covers tight and hope my brother Dave would hurry home from work. Dave had been working two jobs at the time just to give us a little spending money. Thoughts of finding and moving in with my dad resurfaced. Anything had to be better than unwanted sexual advances. No kid should have to face that.

Thankfully, God heard the cry of my heart, and nothing physical ever happened between us. When it was clear that I had no intention of becoming Gary's special friend, he didn't hassle me as often. Nevertheless, the tensions between the Reil family and us continued to increase. It was a matter of time before something bad was bound to happen.

YOU'RE KILLING ME

Although the entire Reil family was melodramatic, no one could top Gary. He bled drama. If Gary stubbed his toe, the whole family would panic and say, "We've got to rush Gary to the hospital—they may have to amputate his leg." Gary would lock himself in the bathroom and threaten to kill himself with a bottle of aspirin over the slightest infraction.

Such vaudeville theatrics seemed more pronounced and more frequent as summer ended and the fall rolled around. The crowded conditions of the house, the fights over who got to use the one bathroom, the body odor and stale smell of smoke hanging in the air—no wonder everyone was nuts.

By then, Mr. Reil joined the act with his own histrionics. Somehow he got the idea in his head that someone was trying to kill him. I learned about his paranoia during a meeting with the social worker assigned to supervise our case.

We'd been at the Reils' for six months when she dropped by for the first visit and professional evaluation. While I don't remember her name, I do recall she was about thirty years old and had a winsome smile. Dave and I sat across from her at the kitchen table. Apparently, she'd already met with the Reils and now it was our turn. Hooking her hair behind her left ear, she smiled again, and said, "Look, I think we have a problem."

I'm thinking, *Yeah, tell me about it.... This place is crazy.*

She lowered her voice a notch and added, "Mr. Reil said that you tried to kill him."

I shot my brother a look. "Dave?!"

Before Dave could respond, she said, "No, Jimmy, Mr. Reil claims *you* tried to kill him."

"Me?"

She nodded, slowly.

It was Dave's turn to be surprised. "Jimmy?!"

"But ... I'm ten years old!"

Was everybody losing their mind? I was sure Dave knew that I wasn't capable of killing anything—except for flies, spiders, and now chickens. I was a harmless wallflower. Would this lady believe me? Or, would she take sides with the Reils and just send me off to jail? I wasn't even sure whether social workers could send people to jail. About all I could say in my defense was ... "How?"

She leaned forward, raised an eyebrow, and said, "Mr. Reil claims you tried to push him off of a cliff."

"You're serious?" I mean, this was one of those ten-year-old observations: *We were living in the desert.* There were no cliffs for miles. Sure, there was the ravine out back, but that was more of a gentle slope. At best I might have been able to roll Mr. Reil down there to join all of the stuff they'd been dumping for years. But it was definitely not a cliff. I just wasn't sure if my view would hold up in court.

The lady cleared her throat. "Yes, that's what he said. Which is also why Mr. Reil has been sleeping in the rabbit hutch for several days."

So that's what he's been doing out there, I thought. My heart started bumping around in my chest like, well, like a chicken with its head missing. She must have perceived my growing panic. With a smile, she winked. In the following minutes, she explained that she thought Mr. Reil was going senile.

She said, "There really are just two options. First, we can keep you guys together and you can hunker down here until we find another solution. If so, I'll do what I can to make sure Mr. Reil understands you don't mean him any harm. Or, we can separate you and place you into the appropriate foster-care homes for your respective ages."

I didn't like the sound of either of those options. In my view, there was a third idea: find Dad and live with him. Hands down, that was my first choice. But we still didn't know where to find Dad, and Dave and Dee Dee were unconvinced that move was wise. Not wanting to break up the family, we agreed to stay for another six months. While that decision made the most sense at the time, a fresh round of trouble was just around the corner.

The Reils invited another family to move in.

$$\frac{7}{}$$

The Prowlers

Being falsely accused of attempted murder at age ten is not the kind of thing a boy easily shakes off. The memory of sitting with the social worker as she broke the news that Mr. Reil thought I was trying to kill him had a significant impact on me. Her visit lingered in my mind long after she snapped her thin, padded briefcase and drove off to the next foster-care case.

She was nice enough to believe me, which I was thankful for. Still, the encounter felt as if I had received a summons to report to the principal's office for some wrongdoing that I had no part in, like spraying graffiti on the bathroom wall. My guilt or innocence wasn't the issue. The fact that I was *accused* marked me as someone to watch.

Where there's smoke there's fire, right?

Try though I did, I couldn't fathom what fiendish act I could have committed that would have given Mr. Reil a reason to think I wanted to kill him. I didn't harass him. I didn't joke about tearing him apart, limb from limb. I didn't even have those feelings so it wasn't as if he could read something between the lines. I was about as threatening as a houseplant. The social worker apparently said something to Mr.

Reil before she left that calmed him. He stopped sleeping in the rabbit hutch, but still, I felt watched, as if on probation.

From that day forward, my best defense was to stay far away from the Reils whenever possible—no small task given how cramped the house was. Like sardines, we marinated in each other's space. After school, I kept out of sight by playing in the ravine. However, once the sun went down, my options were limited. I found the best idea was to retreat to my bed before the others called it a night. That worked for a while—at least until the prowlers showed up.

One evening, long after the sun had called it quits for the day, I was lying on my cot out on the enclosed patio staring at a network of cobwebs where the ceiling met the house. Although Mrs. Reil was constantly doing laundry, she rarely attended to things like the spider webs overhead or the dust bunnies on the concrete floor. I'm not faulting her; she simply didn't have time to be Suzie Housekeeper.

That's understandable considering how much effort went into washing clothes for ten people, especially with one of those prehistoric washing machines. Mrs. Reil had the kind of antiquated device that sported two top-mounted, hand-cranked rollers that, when turned, squeezed the excess water out. Sort of a manual spin cycle. Then, she'd hang the clothes out to line-dry. The process took forever.

That night, the cobwebs failed to provide enough action to hold my attention. I couldn't find a moth or unlucky fly struggling to break free before a spider came for his dinner. Bored, I decided to go to sleep. I wanted to read a comic book, but I didn't have one. We were never given any spending money, and even if I had a dime, there were no stores within walking distance.

I rolled off the cot, careful not to bang my knees on the adjacent bed less than a foot away. I crossed the room and turned off the lamp. Slipping back under the covers, I looked out the window. It didn't take long for my eyes to adjust to the darkness and for the stars to come into view. That was one of the great things about living in the desert—the sky is so clear. The stars seem to gleam like a freshly washed chrome bumper in the sun.

Against the backdrop of the night sky, the Big Dipper and its galactic companions generated enough light to cast a soft bluish glow against the windowpane. September had brought with it slightly cooler evening temperatures; the clean, cool air carried with it the scent of desert flora that drifted through my partially opened window.

I could hear the Reils swapping stories in the adjacent room, but tuned them out in favor of my own thoughts. School was back in session. While the kids in my fifth-grade class were nice enough, I didn't feel particularly connected to them. I was still very much the new kid in town without a shared history. I missed my friends back in Long Beach.

Lost in my reflection about what the new school year might hold, I heard, or thought I heard, approaching footsteps. The enclosed patio walls were thin and, most likely, not insulated—something similar to plywood, painted pale green on the inside, tacked to two-by-four wooden posts. Sound traveled easily through the flimsy exterior surface. The barking of a dog or the closing of a car door a mile away sounded as if it were nearby.

The fact that someone might be walking out there in the dark was unusual. The Reils rarely had visitors, and never at this hour. I listened more carefully. Nothing. Maybe I had been mistaken. Or, maybe it hadn't been human footsteps. Perhaps a goat had weaseled out of its pen and was heading to the garbage dump for a late-night snack. No. There it was again, the distinct sound of soles against gravel, moving toward the house.

I sat upright, but didn't approach the window. My pulse quickened, more out of curiosity than fear. That is, until I perceived another set of footsteps. Two visitors? Or, were there three?

Definitely more than one. The number was hard to distinguish over the accelerated thumping in my chest. Were they friendly visitors? Guests? The Reils hadn't mentioned they were expecting company. I'm pretty sure they would have said something.

How would anybody find this place? The house wasn't visible from the main dirt access road until you drove down through the wash and up the other side. That was odd. I didn't hear a car pull up. I ruled out the possibility that it might be one or more of the Reils in the yard. When I had left the kitchen, everyone was accounted for. They'd taken up their usual seats around the table and were busy rolling cigarettes. If someone had stepped out, I would have heard the screen door smack the doorjamb.

These footsteps were slow and tentative. They were not the bold, confident steps of someone who lived there and knew the place like the back of their hand. Whoever they were, and whatever their business, I decided they had no good reason to be out there.

When the face appeared in the window, I stopped breathing.

WATCH AND PREY

The trespasser wore a black ski mask pulled taut across his face—the kind used by bank robbers. Only this wasn't a bank, and we had no money. With the exception of two slits for the eyes, and one for the mouth, his features were concealed. I quickly ruled out the idea that this was a surprise visit from an old friend. I was equally sure he wasn't a representative from the Morongo Valley Welcome Wagon finally coming around to greet us kids.

The spike pinning my heart against my rib cage assured me this wasn't a dream. I was very much awake wishing it *were* a nightmare. That's the thing about bad dreams. In even the most terrible nightmares, you always survived. In real life, the outcome was always up for grabs.

A large masked face blocked the spot in the window where I had been watching the Big Dipper. With less than five feet between us, I dared not move. Could he see me? My room was dark and the blanket covered my legs, but I was sitting upright on the bed. Maybe he was allowing his eyes to adjust to the interior darkness, or perhaps my face had been briefly illuminated by the moon's glow and he was deciding what to do next.

But he just waited. And stared.

I fully expected him to slip a gloved hand through the gap at the bottom of the window and nudge it open farther. If so, then what? For a second, I debated reaching forward to slam the window shut. However, if he *didn't* know I was there, such brashness would be a dead giveaway that the room was occupied. And, come to think of it, I wasn't even sure that the window lock worked.

Afraid that any sound might betray my position, I remained as mute as a stone sculpture. Even the slightest movement on the bed would provoke the rickety, steel-spring mesh beneath the mattress to squeak. I felt as if I were sitting on live dynamite. Although frozen in place, my mind sped through the options. Should I scream? Run for help? Stand my ground?

More footsteps approached. The intruder turned his head in the direction of his partner. I used the momentary distraction to breathe. His head rotated back and then he looked at me. I was convinced he *knew* I was there. Alone. I didn't know whether or not he was armed and dangerous, or just intent on terrorizing us for fun. I didn't care to find out. An exchange of muffled voices broke his stare and, seconds later, drew him from his post by my window.

But for how long?

My stunned silence gave way to a gasp. There was no time to waste. With a sharp tug, I ripped the blanket off of my legs, popped up from the bed like a jack-in-the-box, and cracked my right knee against the metal frame of Dave's cot. I winced, but managed to stay standing, then backed away from the window where the black figure once stood. Stubbing my toe on some unseen object left on the floor by the baseboard, I found the doorknob and, with a yank, pulled the door open.

I burst into the kitchen, yelling, "They're out there! They're out there! Two or three men!" The conversation stopped as everyone looked up at the crazy kid in the doorway. For a moment, nobody spoke. Mr. Reil blew a steady stream of smoke through his nose. His eyebrows knotted into a brown wrinkle. With a squint, he looked at me as if I had grown two heads. Bewildered at what might have come over me, he said, "Slow down, sonny. What men?"

Didn't he hear what I just said? I pointed back toward the patio door. "Some guy … with a black mask … in my window … staring right at me!" Mr. Reil reached up with his left hand and stroked his chin. Head tilted to the side, he stared at me as if I were speaking Russian. When nobody moved to check out my story, I said, "There were more, too."

"More what?" Marky asked, toying with me. "More of your little dreams?"

I felt my face flush. I knew what he was doing. He was comparing this to the time when I had accused him of stealing my stuff. Siding with Marky, Mrs. Reil insisted I had imagined the whole thing. She didn't believe me then, why should she—or anyone— believe me now? My credibility was zero with this bunch.

"More bad guys. And I wasn't dreaming, Marky."

I stood there like Paul Revere sounding the alarm, while the sleepy townspeople paid no attention to the warning. What reason would I have to lie about something like this? On the off chance I was right, wouldn't it make sense to find out if, indeed, we were in some sort of imminent danger? How could they be so dismissive? I knew my brother Dave would have backed me up, but he was working third shift at the Circle K.

Gary who, at times, was a great conversationalist, was also the original Mr. Theatrics. Breaking the silence, Gary said, "Jimmy, are you sure you aren't hallucinating? Or maybe exaggerating just to get some attention?"

"You can see for yourself," I started to say, when Marky cut me off.

"Why don't you just go back to bed, Jimmy." Marky's contempt was as thick as the gray cloud of cigarette smoke hanging in the air. I can't say I ever met another eight-year-old with so much raw hostility. Reasoning with him was pointless. Invariably, he'd just call me a liar, or worse.

I wasn't sure if I was more hurt or angry that not one person believed me. I *knew* what I saw—the masked face was not my imagination. And, no, this wasn't some game to get noticed. I didn't want attention—certainly not from them. In fact, I was doing my best to avoid them. If they didn't care about the prowlers, fine.

As I turned to leave, my sister Dee Dee left the naysayers behind and followed me out of the kitchen. As we took a seat in another room, she slipped her arm around my shoulder. Pulling me close, she said, "It's okay, Jimmy. I believe you. If you want, you can sleep in my room tonight. Don't listen to them."

That was easier said than done. I could overhear Marky and Gary mimicking me in the other room, embellishing my words as if I were certifiably nuts…. *"They're out there! Run for your lives! Yeah, watch out for the men in masks. They've come to take us away!"*

Sitting with my sister helped insulate me from their ridicule. A variety of verbal jabs came to mind, but I didn't say a thing. My mother didn't raise me that way. She was fond of saying, "Treat others the way you want to be treated, Jimmy," and for that reason, I held my tongue.

To say that I withdrew into my own world after that experience wouldn't be accurate. To be withdrawn implies I wasn't connected to reality. I was connected. I just didn't like what I was connected to. Like Alice in Wonderland, I wanted to be free of that strange house, these strange people, and especially these strange happenings.

SHOWDOWN AT SUNDOWN

The rest of the evening and throughout the next day, I was the resident joke. I was the crazy kid who had cried wolf … that is, until the howling started. The prowlers who supposedly didn't exist began circling the house once again, this time yelping like hungry coyotes. For a short moment, the Reils suspended their cigarette rolling and fell deathly silent. The noise in the yard couldn't be dismissed as my imagination run wild, and they knew it.

Not that anyone offered an apology.

When several masked faces darted past the kitchen window, it was Gary's and Marky's turn to become melodramatic. "What are we gonna do?" "We're all gonna die!" "Somebody call 911!" Mr. Reil pulled the curtain closed and told his sons to knock it off, adding, "I can't think above your racket, daggumit."

After much animated debate, they decided that they couldn't ignore the problem. Something had to be done. The Reils weren't about to be intimidated by these hoodlums. A show of force was necessary. This was their land, and they'd defend it like Davy Crockett's last stand at the Alamo. David Reil volunteered to play the part of Davy Crockett.

I wasn't so sure that was a good idea. I mean, what did he plan to do once he was outside? What if these guy were armed? We had no idea why they'd come, what they wanted, or how many bad guys were circling the house. What was David going to do against two, three, or more men?

Besides, I didn't think the Reils understood the severity of getting involved with thugs. I knew from my Compton days that sometimes these things ended up really bad—as in yellow chalk outlining the position of a dead body. Personally, I would have called and waited for the police—not that anybody was asking for my opinion.

By the sound of the screeching, the trespassers were in the backyard running in several directions. Flashlight in hand, David Reil, Righter of Wrongs, stepped out the door. Within two minutes, the whooping stopped. As far as we could tell, nobody had heard David shouting at the bad guys to get off of the property. There hadn't been the sounds of a struggle—you know, grunting, groaning, things smashing, and the like.

With a click, Mr. Reil snapped off the radio for a more careful listen. Aside from the barking of a dog, we heard nothing unusual. No footsteps. No movement outside. And no David. Just an uneasy stillness. Had David somehow scared them off just by his presence? Had he chased them to the edge of the property? If so, where was he? Why hadn't he returned? What was taking him so long?

The silence was deafening.

Several more tense minutes passed, and still no David. Not a peep from the prowlers, either. Agitated, Gary got up from the table and paced the floor. "We can't just sit here. What if David's dead? Huh? What if they kidnapped him—did you think of that? I just *knew* he shouldn't have gone after them."

Although not as dramatic, Mrs. Reil agreed. "Maybe you should do somethin', Vernon." She tucked a cigarette between her lips, struck a match, and lit up.

From left to right: Jim, DeeDee,
Mike, Dave, and Kim in front of
the Cosby house

Grandma and
Grandpa Hope

My mom, Jan Daly

My siblings and I -
top: Kim; bottom from left to
right: Mike, Jim, DeeDee,
and Dave

May 2007 - left to right: Jim, DeeDee, Mike, Kim, and Dave

Mike in Navy

Jim Daly - 2nd grade

The meeting at the Reils - from left to right: Mike, Dad, Jim, DeeDee, and Dave

Standing by the front door, Mr. Reil scratched the back of his head. "Like what?"

"Like ... maybe go find David?" she said.

"Aw, he's a big boy, he's fine."

"He's a kid."

"He's nineteen, Betty," Mr. Reil said. "He can handle himself, otherwise he wouldn't be out there."

She tapped the end of her cigarette into the ashtray with a yellowed finger. "I'm just saying, he might need a hand, that's all."

"Yeah, Dad," Gary said, plopping back down in a chair. "Why don't you go get yourself killed too."

With a wave of her hand, dismissing his concern as overblown, Mrs. Reil said, "Gary, come on now ... nobody's gonna get killed."

Gary rolled his eyes. "But, Mom, how do you know they're not escapees from death row or something, huh?"

Mr. Reil had had enough. Without a word, he reached for the front door and started to leave. Crossing the threshold and walking out a few yards, he stopped in his tracks.

"Whatcha see, Vernon?" Mrs. Reil said, leaning forward.

"I found David."

Gary and Marky jetted to the door before Mrs. Reil could free herself from her chair. Mr. Reil held up a hand, palm forward, like a policeman directing traffic, stopping them at the door. "Back inside, Marky. Gary, stand there and hold the door."

"Not fair," Marky said.

"Go! Now! Let Mom through."

I kept my distance. I couldn't really hear what was going on outside, between Marky's protests and Gary, as Gary held the screen door open with an arm, whining, "He's dead, right? I *knew* he was dead.... I told you, but you didn't listen to me!"

Mr. and Mrs. Reil struggled to support David's weight as they carried their son through the door; Mr. Reil's arms cradled his neck and back while Mrs. Reil lugged his limp legs. They laid him on the sofa in the living room. That's when I saw the side of David's head was covered in matted blood. Moving faster than I'd ever seen her move before, Mrs. Reil grabbed two washcloths, filled one with ice, and dipped the other in water. As she tended to the wound, Mr. Reil straightened and said, "He ain't dead, just unconscious."

"Not dead? He's not dead?" Gary gasped in relief.

"No. Just a nasty cut. Got walloped with a plank of wood, or maybe a pipe. Probably needs stitches," Mr. Reil said, taking a seat. Although he sounded surprisingly composed, I could tell by his knotted forehead that he was shaken up.

Lying prone on the couch, David groaned. Mrs. Reil held the ice, wrapped in the washcloth, to David's head. "Shh. Don't move. Just lay there, Son."

"So, why aren't we taking him to the hospital?" Marky asked.

Mr. Reil said, "No car."

"What! Where's the car?" Gary said, panicked. "He needs a doctor or he's gonna die."

"Betcha Bill's got it, right?" Marky said.

Mr. Reil nodded. About a week before the prowlers arrived, the Reils took in Bill Appletree, a full-blooded Native American Indian, along with his wife, their infant, and pint-size dog. The already crowded house, now with thirteen people, was an unbearably cramped circus. I never found out where Mr. Reil met Bill, or why he invited his family to stay with us.

Bill was on the heavy side. His shoulder-length black hair was as straight and as fine as silk. He wore a leather bandanna around his head and sported several turquoise-colored rings. His eyes were as intense as a storm and seemed to hide a dark secret. Privately, my brother Dave and I nicknamed him "Wild Bill."

Bill's wife was blonde, fair skinned, heavyset, and almost never spoke—at least not in front of us. Her time was consumed by doting on their infant. Almost from the minute they arrived, Bill spent virtually all of his time rebuilding the engine of his red Pontiac GTO. While he didn't give us a reason to be afraid of him, his friends spooked us—at least, we assumed they were his friends. Throughout the day, the biker-guys, as Dee Dee and I called them, would show up to talk to Wild Bill.

These were characters from the rough end of the spectrum. Festooned in chains and black leather jackets with skulls and crossbones plastered on the back, they'd rumble into the yard as if they owned the place. One biker, with a bushy handlebar mustache, got his kicks hitting on my sister Dee Dee.

"Gee, that was dumb, Dad." Marky was speaking. "Why'd you give Bill *our* car?"

Mr. Reil sat hunched forward, resting his forearms on his legs. He appeared drained and in need of his heart pills. When he didn't immediately answer, Marky said, "Oh, wait … let me guess, he needed parts for his piece-o'-junk car. Is that it?"

"Leave him be, Marky," Mrs. Reil said.

"You know, none of this crazy stuff happened until Bill got here," Gary said, pointing toward Bill's bedroom. "I bet he ripped off one of those biker friends of his."

"They're Hells Angels," Marky replied.

"Hell's Bells, hippies on wheels, call 'em what you want." Gary started pacing again. "Nope. We never had prowlers until you took in those people."

"Hush your mouth, Gary," Mrs. Reil said.

"Well, it's true."

Mr. Reil lifted his head. "You heard her. Shut your trap."

The kitchen screen door opened and closed with a *thwack*. Wild Bill tossed the keys on the kitchen counter, plucked a cigarette from the stack on the table, and tucked it over his right ear. With wide strides, he paraded through the living room and headed straight for his sleeping wife and child in the back bedroom.

Marky blurted, "Hey, where've you been?"

"Out. What's it to you?" Wild Bill stopped long enough to answer, apparently unaware of David's condition.

"Only that David is dying." Gary pointed toward the couch.

"He's not dying," Mrs. Reil said. "But he needs a doctor. Vernon, give me a hand already."

Bill surveyed the situation and glided to David's side. "Here, let me." His thick arms lifted David from the couch effortlessly. Heading toward the kitchen, Bill said over his shoulder, "Who did this?"

Marky and Gary spoke almost in unison: "The prowlers." Over breakfast that morning, Bill had listened without speaking as the boys made a big joke about the masked man in my window. At the time, I couldn't tell whether Bill believed them or me. He just maintained a faraway look, as if deep in thought.

Now, at the mention of the prowlers, Bill said, "Don't worry about them. I'll handle it."

WILD BILL TAKES AIM

David Reil didn't die. Not even close, contrary to Gary's prediction. The doctor determined David had suffered a concussion, but assured the Reils that the surface wounds and the internal damage would heal nicely with time. We were all relieved. The excitement of the night gave way to the routine of the new day. With one exception. Wild Bill announced at breakfast that he had some news.

Having gotten up with the sunrise, Bill spotted footprints left behind by the attackers and tracked them back in the direction of the chicken coop. Bill was prepared to take countermeasures. He intended to stand watch that evening—with his .30-06 rifle. I got the impression that he was a shoot-first-ask-questions-later kind of guy. My brother Dave wasn't scheduled to work and offered to make the rounds with his tiny six-inch knife. That didn't seem particularly wise, but Dave wanted to help.

As Dave later relayed the story, he and Bill took up positions in the yard. According to Bill's plan, he'd sit in the chicken coop as the first line of defense. With a point, he directed Dave to stay in the brush near the house in case the prowlers sneaked across the ravine and approached from the rear.

Occasionally, they'd leave their posts and, under the moonlight, make the rounds. After a quick tour of the immediate property on foot, Bill heading to the left and Dave to the right, they'd return to their spots and wait. And wait some more.

Several hours passed without any sign of trouble. Still crouching behind the thicket, my brother started to rethink the wisdom of engaging some trespasser with his puny blade. Besides, was he really prepared to stab someone? To kill them maybe? The more he thought about it, the more he became convinced that confronting the prowlers was nuts.

Abandoning his post, Dave hiked over to the chicken coop, softly calling Bill's name as he approached. The last thing Dave wanted was to be mistaken for a bad guy and get shot. He found Bill holding his rifle like a sniper, scanning the yard from the wash to the house and back. He was all business, dead set on killing someone to avenge what was done to David Reil. He'd probably planned to toss the body—or bodies—into the ravine behind the house. For several minutes, neither man spoke as Wild Bill, with his hand on the trigger, scanned, searching for the enemy.

Evidently, about the moment my brother Dave was going to tell Bill to call the whole thing off, I came bounding out the front door looking for Dave. At the sudden sound, Bill wheeled his gun around to shoot me. Acting on impulse, Dave part-grabbed and part-knocked the gun up into the air before Bill could get off a shot. No question, if Dave hadn't been there, I would have been wounded, if not killed.

Back safely inside the house, my brother told me how close I'd come to taking a bullet. I couldn't believe what I was hearing. I mean, I was thankful that Dave had rescued me. And yet, I'd recently been accused of attempted murder ... and now *I* had almost been murdered.

Closing my eyes that night, I felt utterly alone. At no point did I ever feel integrated into the Reils' family. At best, we were two families—make that three, counting Wild Bill—living in one house rather than one big happy family. Everyone had to fend for themselves. There was no love or kindness or tenderness displayed toward us. Not to mention I was never fully trusted by Mr. Reil.

I'll be the first to admit it was gracious of the Reils to take us in. I'm sure they originally wanted to help us out of a jam. But that noble motive was quickly tainted by the money they received through the social security survivor benefits from my mom. We never saw a penny; they never bought us anything to wear. We didn't receive presents at Christmas, and, for the most part, we were made to feel very much on the outside.

I wondered how living with my dad could be any worse.

In some ways, living with the Reils on the western edge of the Mojave Desert was a fitting metaphor for my life. The Mojave Desert is the location of Death Valley—a place where those who lose their way have no hope. That's exactly how I felt in my soul. At 282 feet below sea level, the Mojave Desert is the lowest point in North America. I was at the lowest point in my life. I felt utterly alone, abandoned, anxious.

Powerful feelings of loneliness had a way of overwhelming me at the most inconvenient times, like while I was sitting in my fourth- and fifth-grade class at Morongo Valley Elementary School. On several occasions as I listened to my teacher, Mr. Todd, a wave of sadness would broadside me. Tears would burn at the edges of my eyes. I'd literally get up in the middle of the lesson and walk outside, sit on the sandy hill at the edge of the school property, and just cry.

You know, I always sensed that God met me there. While I didn't have a Christian experience until I was fifteen, I'd sit on the hill and say, "God, where are you? Where's my dad? Why did Mom have to die? Will I always have to live with the Reils? Why does my life have to be like this?" The answers didn't have to come—just pouring out my heart to God seemed to keep the burden from crushing me.

At times the school nurse, Mrs. Bandy, would join me. She'd take a seat next to me and slip her arm around my shoulders. She usually wouldn't say anything more than, "It'll be okay, Jimmy. Hang in there, kiddo." *But Mrs. Bandy, you don't know the Reils!* I thought. Gary hit on me. David married his cousin. Marky stole my things and called me a liar. Mr. Reil thought I was trying to kill him. And the prowlers haunted us at night.

How would everything be okay?

One particular afternoon after these events had taken place, Mrs. Bandy sat down and handed me a Kleenex and some amazing news. She said, "I have a message from your brother."

"Dave?"

"No, from Mike. He's coming to visit you tomorrow."

8

Dad: Take 2

Sleep was out of the question … *Mike was coming!*

I hadn't seen my brother in a hundred years. Okay, so it was more like four months, but the time apart might as well have been a century. I wouldn't be more excited if the Lone Ranger himself rode into town on the back of his white horse to rescue me.

The only news that might top this would be to learn my dad was with him. Mike and my dad had their share of conflicts, but were alike in a number of ways. Same height. Same facial features. Similar mannerisms. Athletic. A visit with Mike would be like having my dad drop by … almost.

With Mike in town, I knew I'd have an escape from my crazy, mixed-up life—at least for a few wonderful hours. Like sunshine after a long, cold Alaskan winter, I could feel a part of myself thawing, that part of me I'd locked safely away in a deep freeze to preserve. The funny, playful, expressive side of me didn't seem to fit into the Reils' *unusual* world.

When Mike sailed into town, he was tanned and brawny, his hair clipped as short as a bristle brush. He was full of tales from the high seas. He spoke of a jungle called Vietnam on the other side of the world, of war protesters in tie-dyed shirts, beads, and bell-bottoms, and of a man on his ship who introduced him to something called Christianity. While Mike didn't go into details, I got the impression that whatever Christianity was, Mike still had his doubts.

Being with him, I felt safe. Mike was an entire navy battle group of hope pulling into port. To me, the Reils lacked a vision or even the desire to rise above infighting and pettiness. By contrast, Mike inspired confidence. He represented strength, bravery, and a man on a mission. I'd sail anywhere, face any storm, with Mike as my captain at the helm.

Although just twenty years old, Mike was perceptive. His military training conditioned him to be particularly discerning. Even though his visit was brief, he quickly detected the friction in the house. The tension at the Reils was as thick as a handmade milkshake. What he saw concerned him. He could tell the Reils were sending us a message. Their actions made it clear we were not a part of their family, that our welcome was wearing off, and perhaps we ought to be leaving.

Finding us a different home, while important, wasn't Mike's top priority. Rather, he wanted to know how I was dealing with the living arrangements, with school, with my feelings about Mom. We'd go for walks, hang out, and just talk. Guy talk. Throughout the day, Mike pursued my heart. He'd ask, "Jimmy, how are you doing?" and, "Are you sure you're okay?" This probing didn't feel like the inquiry of a school official, or the impersonal cross-examination by a social worker. We spoke brother to brother. You know how that made me feel?

Loved.

Mike didn't have to bring me gifts, new clothes, or a treat. This big navy man—who'd faced far more serious battles than our ongoing skirmishes at the Reils'—cared about my well-being, and that was enough. Sure, he was visibly upset that Marky was a thief, that Mr. Reil was going senile, and that we lived in such primitive conditions. Who, in their right mind, wouldn't be? But most importantly, he *cared* about *me*. His unconditional love put fresh wind in my sails.

What's more, Mike had a news flash of his own. He pulled Dave, Dee Dee, and I together to tell us that he'd been in contact with Dad—more accurately, that Dad had been searching for us. Unbelievable! I was floored. I couldn't get over the fact that my dad had been looking for us. Not with a hammer, bent on revenge, but out of a desire to find us—to find me. The wave of euphoria I felt just about knocked me over.

We ambushed Mike with rapid-fire questions: Where was Dad living? How was he doing? Did he know Mom had died? Was there any chance he'd come and visit us? What about us going to see him? At one point Mike and Dave ended up in a heated exchange over the most obvious question: Could we go and live with Dad? Anything had to be better than our current circumstances, or so Dave believed. But Mike didn't think the idea of handing us off to Dad was wise.

Not yet. Maybe never.

But what about a visit? Mike wasn't sure Dad could handle three of us descending on him all at once. Evidently, he was emotionally fragile and not doing particularly well after learning about Mom's death. By the time we'd finished discussing the pros and cons of a family reunion, Mike agreed that a few days spent with Dad would probably be a good thing, especially for me. In the end, everyone agreed I should be the one to go. But how? Dave graciously offered to pay for my bus fare. Since Mike was heading back to sea, Dave would also make the arrangements.

To me, that was Christmas in October.

Dinner rolled around much too quickly for my tastes. Sitting elbow-to-elbow with Mike, I ate slowly as if that would delay the inevitable. I knew that when we finished, Mike would return to his ship. I must have chewed each bite ten times. I almost choked at the thought of his leaving. Mike was a bridge to memories of better times, when Mom was alive, and we were a family living in our own home. Soon his chair would be empty, and I felt the sadness gnawing away at the edges of my heart.

I had to laugh, though, at the look on Mike's face when he learned what we were eating for dinner. At 6'5" and 300 pounds of muscle, Mike could pack away the food. He'd been lifting weights and needed his protein. Licking his fingers, he said, "This is the *best* beef I've ever had. They sure don't cook like this on the ship."

Marky smirked. "Beef? Where'd you get that idea? That ain't beef."

"Really?" Mike said, skewering another piece. "Could have fooled me. What is it?"

Gary said, "Remember that burro that knocked you off its back?"

Mike nodded, his mouth full of "beef." The last time Mike had come to visit, he thought it would be great fun to catch a ride on a donkey the Reils had in the yard. The donkey, however, didn't take too kindly to Mike's girth on its back. Mike was as startled as the rest of us when the donkey took off running, dumping him in the bushes. Picking the briers from his skin, he had no shortage of choice words for that "hideous creature."

Mike chewed a little slower, then swallowed. "Yeah, what happened to that thing anyway?"

Marky said, "That's what you're eating!"

The look on Mike's face was priceless.

HOMEWARD BOUND

When I lived at the Reils', there was this thought I'd carry around with me, much like a kid who refuses to give up his tattered Linus blanket. I always thought I'd find my dad, that he'd be glad to see me, that we'd live together, and maybe, just maybe, we'd feel like a family once again. Now that Dad had made contact with Mike, and plans were set in motion for me to go see him, I was several steps closer to realizing my dream.

Mike must have read my mind. Before he left, he made a point of warning me that Dad "still had his issues." I know he was trying to protect me from getting my hopes up only to have them dashed against the hard reality of his addictions. He might have thought that I was too young to remember Dad's history of bad choices with gambling and alcohol and his difficulty keeping promises—as if I'd forgotten about the mitt Dad promised to bring me.

Time has a way of reconstructing history, either for better or worse. Mike probably assumed I was glossing over the past with rose-colored glasses. I wasn't. I just liked to focus on my dad's positive qualities. I preferred to dwell on those things about him that I admired. Still, I knew he had problems and a few eccentric ideas, not in a Mr. Reil sleeping-in-the-rabbit-hutch sort of way. He was more of a *frustrated perfectionist.*

When I was four, for example, back when we were living on Cosby Street, I recall that my dad got really, really mad with the city trash collector. Back then, most everybody had those forty-four-gallon aluminum trash cans with the corrugated ridges on the sides. I'm not sure what ticked him off. Maybe the garbagemen didn't put the lids back on after emptying the cans, in which case the lids would blow down the street or get flattened by a passing car. Perhaps the guys dented the sides of the can against the back of the trash truck, or left pieces of litter on the sidewalk. Whatever the infraction, they made Dad so mad he refused to pay for garbage pickup.

Instead of the regular Tuesday-Friday waste pickup, he wanted to prove he didn't need them and their lousy service. His plan? He closed and locked the front of our garage door. For a solid year, we packed the garage—from floor to ceiling, wall to wall, and front to back—with garbage. How was I to know that sort of thing was abnormal? My dad said to put the trash in the garage, so we did.

Keep in mind that the weather in Southern California never really cools down. Year-round the temperatures tend to hover in the seventies. With the sun roasting the air like a solar microwave, our garage became like a giant version of an Easy Bake Oven. Between the decaying trash and the worms who, I'm sure, were enjoying themselves entirely too much, our garage became the world's largest compost box.

One night after discovering he couldn't shove any more trash through the back door, Dad announced, "I'm going to get a trailer." He didn't mind hauling the filth to the dump; he was too pleased with himself that he didn't need "that stinking trashman." Looking back, I'd have to say there are better ways to make your point.

Like I said, I tended to be forgiving of such flaws while embracing his strengths. For example, I have fond memories of the way he'd make breakfast on Sunday to let my mom get some rest. After lunch, he'd take us for a Sunday-afternoon drive to places like the Joshua Tree National Monument where we'd climb rocks, scuff our knees, and enjoy each other's company.

Dad was particularly sensitive to Mom's need for rest. We owned a 1957 Chevy station wagon, and he placed a mattress in the back so Mom could sleep during those long drives. We'd get home and Dad would fire up the grill. He was, in my mind, the most fantastic barbeque chef in the world. Which is why, among other reasons, I was just about jumping out of my skin to see him for the weekend.

I ducked out of school early that glorious Friday, just after lunch, to catch the bus. Dave sat with me on the bench at the bus stop until the red, white, and blue Greyhound rumbled into view. The behemoth, a forty-foot MCI-M7, stopped at the curb with a blast of its air brakes and a belch of diesel. Its tires were almost as tall as me. The shiny chrome door swung outward, and the driver, wearing sunglasses, a blue shirt, and holding a cup of coffee, emerged. He took a final sip, tossed the empty container in a garbage can, and called out the destination.

I hugged Dave, and boarded clutching my ticket and my knapsack, taking a window seat toward the back. I sat up so high I could see the other end of the world. I could even see the driver's bald spot on the top of his head as he inspected the tires beneath me. As it turned out, I was the only passenger departing from that station. With just one ticket to collect and no luggage to stow, the driver had us rolling down the road within a few short minutes. I leaned against the window for a final wave good-bye. I felt like a grown-up, taking a trip by myself—at only age ten.

Aside from the yellow Blue Bird buses used by my public school, I'd never been on a *real* bus, one with carpet and cloth seats that reclined. Acquainting myself with my surroundings, I counted forty-three seats and nine other passengers. There were three other kids on the bus; I was the only one without an adult. I had hoped there'd be a bathroom. Dave said some buses had them. No such luck. I'd have to hold it.

The trip to San Gabriel would take several hours, but I didn't care. I was finally going to see my dad. When we passed by the Palm Springs exit twenty minutes later, I knew I wasn't dreaming. I was really on the road. I yearned for the chance to be "normal" for a few days and to sleep without fear of the prowlers. I still struggled with memories of the face in the window.

But, most of all, I couldn't wait to eat regular food.

Because the Reils were on welfare (although they did receive Mr.

Reil's disability payment and our foster-care check), and in light of the fact that there were so many mouths to feed, they'd shop in volume at an army surplus store. Once every couple of weeks, they'd come home with five-pound blocks of cheese, bins of butter, cases of noodles, sacks filled with instant hot chocolate mix, and peanut butter by the gallon. These staples would supplement what was grown and killed on their property.

Nothing against donkey meat, but a genuine hamburger and a milkshake sounded really nice.

I hadn't had a shake or ice cream in eight months—back when my mom was still alive. What I wouldn't give to have something other than hot chocolate and cinnamon toast for breakfast. Maybe eggs the way Dad used to serve them, sunny-side up, with a side of bacon, and toast with peanut butter and jelly on it. I could picture Dad serving my plate, the steam rising like a smoke signal telling me that breakfast was ready.

With visions of milkshakes and eggs on my mind, I rocked in my seat as if that would help the bus roll down the road faster. When that failed to make a noticeable difference, I slid to the aisle seat where I could see the bus driver in his mirror. Maybe he'd notice how anxious I was to get to San Gabriel and step on the pedal.

REACH OUT AND TOUCH SOMEONE

I got to my new seat just in time to watch a bit of drama unfold up ahead. A man wearing a weathered tan hat with a floppy brim—the kind worn by fishermen—and a wrinkled windbreaker started talking to one of the other kids on the bus. The boy wasn't much older than I was. He sat across the aisle from the hatted stranger.

I assumed the man was a stranger because the boy's father glared at him. Raising a hand as if to say, "No problem, I'll move," the hatted stranger rose and made his way toward the rear, gripping the top of the seat backs as he walked.

He stopped midway down the aisle as if momentarily disoriented, or perhaps to scan the faces, then continued. With a half smile, he took the seat directly across the aisle from me. He slumped back into his seat, removed his hat, and dabbed his forehead with a handkerchief. He rolled his head in my direction, placed his hat on his lap, and started to make small talk.

"So, what's your name, kid?"

"Jimmy."

"Nice name. Jimmy. I got a friend named Jimmy. Yeah, that's a real nice name. Sure is."

I turned to look out the window on my side of the bus when he nudged my arm.

"Is this your first bus ride, Jimmy?"

"Yes."

"Where'd you say you were going?"

"I didn't. I'm going to see my dad."

"That should be fun. And your mom, too?"

"No … she's dead."

His eyebrows narrowed. He reached over and squeezed my arm. "Gee, Jimmy. That's a tough break. Sure is." He fell silent for a moment, then added, "Um, you know what? My mother's dead too."

"Really?"

"Yeah … I know how you must feel, Jimmy." He started gently tapping my forearm. I offered a smile, unsure what to say. He looked over his shoulder and then back at me.

"So … does that mean you're traveling alone?"

I nodded.

A wide smile eased across his face. "Really? Me, too. Isn't that something? We guys should stick together, right?"

Another nod. Another silence.

I really wasn't trying to be rude. I just didn't feel like talking. I had too many thoughts in my head about seeing Dad. You know, would he be as glad to see me as I was to see him? Would he hug me? Would he look the same? Where did he live? Work? Would there be time to play catch? Should I hug him if he didn't hug me? Would he make his famous Saturday-morning breakfast?

"Care for a LifeSaver, Jimmy?" the hat man said, interrupting my thoughts. He popped a candy in his mouth and then peeled back the multicolor wrapper. He extended the treat toward me. "Go ahead, have one."

"That's great, thanks."

I plucked one from the pack. He said, "You know something, Jimmy?"

I handed back the LifeSavers. "What?"

"Well, I was kind of wondering if you'd do me a little favor."

"What's that?"

"Do you mind if I … if I held your hand?"

"Huh?"

"You know, Jimmy, like friends do. I'd like that."

He seemed nice enough. He sounded as if he were alone in the world, like my dad. What did I know? At least I couldn't see the harm in his request. Keep in mind I didn't have anyone coaching me about the prospects of meeting a pedophile on the bus. I had no idea what that was, just as I didn't understand why Gary would tell me I was cute.

"I guess that's okay," I said.

The man's eyes widened as he reached over and took my hand in his. I figured he was glad for the company. The bus driver, however, figured something different. He was watching this action unfold in his mirror. Evidently, the driver had his suspicions about this guy.

Without warning, I felt the bus start to brake and veer to the right. That was odd. We weren't getting off at an exit. Maybe we had a flat tire? Did buses with those huge tires get flats?

The driver pulled the bus onto the shoulder of the highway, opened the door, and then worked his way toward us. His sunglasses were off. So were his gloves. The hat man dropped my hand as if I were suddenly infected with a contagious disease. The driver pointed to the man, all businesslike.

"I don't know what you're into, pal, but you need to get off of my bus. Now."

"Hey—hold on. We were just having a little friendly conversation, right, Jimmy?"

"Leave the kid out of this," the driver said, folding his arms. "Get your things and get moving before I throw you off."

"But what about my ticket? I paid to go—"

The driver cut him off. "Sorry, pal, this is the end of the road for you."

We left the hat man with his luggage by the side of the road and then drove off. *What did he do?* I thought. I'd learn later in life about the significance of what had happened. The Greyhound driver, however, knew full well what was going on, and put the brakes to it. Thanks to him, I dodged another bullet.

HOME RUNS, HOT DOGS, AND PLEDGES OF ALLEGIANCE

The bus driver encouraged me to take a seat closer to the front, which was fine with me; this way I could see the bugs colliding with the windshield. Before I knew it, we were pulling into the Greyhound terminal. Dad planned to meet me at the loading dock. I figured picking him out of the crowd would be easy since he was so tall. I was almost shaking with anticipation.

A moment later, we parked at the curb. The brakes exhaled with a gush of air, as if they'd been holding their breath for the last two hours, and the door opened with a *whoosh*. The driver descended down the stairs with me riding his heels. I saw Dad waiting by the boarding gate; when he saw me, his smile almost didn't fit on his face.

We hugged forever—and yet it wasn't long enough.

Since Dad didn't own a car, we boarded a local transit bus for the trip to his place. I can't recall the details of what we spoke about during the brief commute, but it didn't matter. I was with my dad and for those unforgettable moments that was all I needed. I sat straight and proud and as close to him as the seats allowed. Nobody could pull us apart.

Dad lived in a modest, one-bedroom flat in San Gabriel. Probably the most unexpected thing I remember about his apartment was the plastic furniture. The white chairs with stick arms and legs and matching table sort of resembled an outdoor patio set—definitely a far cry from the table and chairs we owned as a family when Dad worked at a furniture factory.

While he hadn't draped a Welcome Home sign above the apartment door, he shocked me when he handed me a brand-new baseball and asked if I wanted to get a Dodger Dog. What? Was he serious? Go see the Los Angeles Dodgers vs. the Cincinnati Reds ... in a doubleheader? Best of all, if we got there in time, we might get my ball autographed. I floated. I was going to my first major league baseball game—with Dad. Mike and Dave would be so jealous.

Dad told me to toss my stuff in the bedroom and wash up. We'd have to hurry to catch the bus to Dodger Stadium. Minutes later, we ran to the bus stop, but the taillights of our bus could be seen moving away just as we arrived. Dad tried to assure me another bus would come along soon enough, but I was brokenhearted. I kept saying, "We're *never* going to get there in time."

My dad, seeing the disappointment, flagged down a cab. I knew that was a big sacrifice on his part; Dad disliked paying taxi fare the same way he disliked paying for our trash service back on Cosby Street. The trip from San Gabriel to Los Angeles was upward of thirty miles. Thanks to some fancy Friday-night driving, we arrived a half an hour before the game with enough time to meet some of the players.

I smiled so wide my face could barely contain it. My baseball had been signed by Johnny Bench, Steve Garvey, Joe Morgan, Pete Rose, and Davey Lopes. Best of all, I was with my dad. For hours I cheered until my voice was hoarse, downed Dodger Dogs and Orange Crush soda, and, for the first time in years, felt like a kid again.

Here's the funny thing about that ball. Weeks later, a bunch of guys from school wanted to play baseball at lunch. One problem. We didn't have a ball. Remembering my autographed treasure, which, amazingly, Marky didn't steal, I brought the autographed ball to school. Needless to say, by the end of recess my shiny white ball was black; the merciless asphalt pavement had taken off all the signatures, too. That ball would probably be worth a few hundred dollars today.

After the Dodgers game, we caught the last bus to San Gabriel. With a full heart and the rhythm of the wheels humming against the pavement, I fell asleep on my dad's lap. Saturday morning, the smell of bacon and eggs enticed me out from under the covers. I went to the kitchen and found my dad working his magic at the stove as if he were auditioning for Emeril's cooking show. A towel hung from his shoulder as he put the finishing touches on our plates.

I rubbed the sleep from my eyes and took a seat. I was afraid to blink for fear that when my eyes reopened, he'd be gone and I'd be back at the Reils'. Within a moment, he joined me and served us the best sunny-side up eggs this side of heaven. He hadn't lost his touch.

As we ate, we talked about the Dodger game. Dad was such a big fan with no shortage of opinions on what our manager might have done differently—maybe start a lefty against their righty. Stuff like that. He asked me how I was doing at school and at the Reils'. But, as I answered, I secretly hoped Dad would get around to asking me the big question, the one I'd been longing to answer:

Jimmy, do you want to live with me?

I'd privately rehearsed the answer in my head for months.

I wouldn't be any trouble....

I'd be happy to sleep on the floor....

I'd eat anything—well, preferably not donkey....

I could even do a few chores. Just ask me the question, Dad. Please ask me to stay.

Dad fell silent for a minute, as if deep in thought. When he finished eating, he wiped the edge of his mouth with his napkin. When he cleared his throat to speak, my heart jumped.

"Jimmy, would you like seconds?"

9

Great Expectations

My eyes were pinched shut. I inhaled a deep, searching breath. Nothing. I filled my lungs again. Still nothing. I was lying on my cot at the Reils' trying to detect a trace of my father's scent lingering on my clothing from his hug good-bye. His unique blend of Old Spice covering the tracks of lime-scented Gillette Foamy had taken up residence on my shirt and stayed there for hours.

I breathed in, but the fragrance had vanished. Even the details of his face seemed to fade from remembrance far too quickly; almost with the speed of a sweet dream I wanted to remember but couldn't recall when I blinked awake. I wanted to remember and so I kept my eyes pinned tight; I refused to let go of my memories of the time spent with Dad.

I had returned to the depressing land of headless chickens, donkey meat, Wild Bill, prowlers, and vats of hot chocolate, but I didn't immediately acknowledge that reality. I lay motionless in my cocoon, a reluctant butterfly dreaming of the day I'd break free of that place.

My dad never got around to asking me to live with him during that otherwise great weekend. I'm not sure why, but he didn't bring the idea up on his own and I wasn't entirely comfortable inviting myself into his world. I certainly didn't want to say anything that might cause him to regret inviting me or jeopardize the prospects of future visits. Most of all, I didn't want him to disappear from my life again.

Sure, I was disappointed. I had a dad-shaped hole in my heart like every other boy on the planet. I yearned for him to play sports with me and take me hunting and fishing. I wanted to learn how to pound crooked nails into scraps of wood, build a rocket ship to the moon, and design the best go-cart on this side of the planet.

I wanted to know my dad would be there to show me the ropes as I got older. I needed him to show me how to shave once the peach fuzz on my chin demanded a real razor, and tell me how to ask a girl for a date without my voice cracking. I needed him to prepare me for the Round Table of manhood, where I might one day fight with the bravest of knights to win the hand of a beautiful maiden.

Most of all, I needed someone who believed in me.

True, I had a male figure in my life—Mr. Reil. But he wasn't the mentoring type, and I had difficulty picturing King Arthur inviting him into the fellowship of the knights. While Mr. Reil had plenty of opportunities to be a mentor, he never took the initiative. Even with all of the cars scattered around his property in need of repair, he never took the time to introduce me to a socket wrench. He didn't show me how to change the oil, or a flat, or even an air filter.

Yes, I did get a lesson in chicken chopping, but knowing my way around a car would have been of more long-term value than knowing how to decapitate a bird—unless, of course, I was contemplating a career in heavy metal music.

If the roles had been reversed and I were the dad, I know I would have asked my son to come and live with me in a heartbeat. And why not? We were family. Though I needed a mentor, and wanted my dad, I wasn't entirely surprised that he hadn't reached across the table and, with a squeeze to the back of my neck, said, "Jimmy, how soon can you move in with your old man?" Like I said, I was disappointed, but not crushed. I might have been young, but I was well on my way to developing a personal philosophy of life, for lack of a better phrase. The first principle life taught me went like this: *Keep your expectations low. That way you don't get hurt.*

The seeds of that viewpoint had been sown back when my dad didn't bring me the baseball mitt he promised. The roots were watered when I met Larry of the Three Stooges, who didn't turn out to be the funny, crazy person I expected, like the guy on television. When Hank the Tank rolled into our family with a mission to love my mom without targeting any of his love toward us, the seedlings of low expectations put down deep roots.

When nobody in my life prepared me for the death of my mother, when the Reils sided with Marky and suggested I was the troublemaker, when Mr. Reil accused me of attempting to kill him, and—the hardest hurt of all—when my own dad didn't want me to live with him, my emerging outlook on life helped me survive the impact. Keeping my expectations low was like strapping a bullet-proof vest around my spirit.

Although I had no control over my circumstances, I could control my response. I had low expectations, but I never crossed over to pessimism. I believed that something better was waiting around the corner; my life and my circumstances *would* improve if I plowed ahead and stayed focused on doing my best with what I had. I also couldn't shake the sense that God was somehow there with me, just as Grandpa Hope had said God was with my mom when she died. I didn't know how it all worked, but God must have known the hunger of my heart and given me the strength to move forward.

ONCE UPON A DREAM

A remarkable turn of events occurred about four months after I returned to Morongo Valley from seeing my dad, and not a moment too soon. The tension at the Reils' was incredibly thick. Not a good thick, like the middle of an Oreo Double Stuff cookie. More like a destructive thick, like a hot lava flow inflaming everything it touched. Mr. Reil continued to lose touch with reality as dementia started to set in, which, I later learned, is why he viewed me as Public Enemy Number One. Naturally, Mrs. Reil felt the need to protect her family's well-being and was quick to favor her kids over us.

I stopped talking around them since anything I said seemed to fuel the paranoia. I drank my watery hot chocolate and ate my chewy cinnamon toast in silence. I went to school where at least nobody thought I was plotting to push them off of a cliff. In fact, my athletic ability even gained me respect on the playground. Then I'd return to the Reils' where I took cover by being as invisible as I could. I'd play outside, out of sight until dinner, ate without daring to ask Mr. Reil to pass the salt, and went to bed early, where I watched spiders and moths and wondered if the prowlers might return.

When school let out for the summer, I spent the day exploring the outdoors, looking for soda bottles to return for a little spending money, and generally kept clear of the Reils. Never once did they suggest that I invite anyone from my fifth-grade class over to play. And rather than create more friction, I didn't ask. As I hiked, stick in hand, I held on to the hope that something good was around the corner.

There just had to be.

One particularly hot mid-August Friday night, I had already switched off the light and fallen asleep when I heard Dave come home late from work. He sat on the edge of his adjacent cot, and the springs bearing his weight protested. A raspy series of squeaks simultaneously announced his arrival and pulled me out of my sleep. Dave poked my side.

"Pssst! Jimmy. You awake?"

"Hmm?"

"Guess what?" Dave said, just above a whisper.

I rolled over on my side, blinked my eyes open with a yawn. "Um, is Mr. Reil sleeping with the rabbits again?"

"No, silly...."

"Hold on, what time is it?"

"Midnight. But, listen, Jimmy, Dad's coming!"

I scratched my head while his statement made its way through my ear canal, and across a network of semi-alert electrodes to the corner of my brain trying to process this information. The fog in my head lifted a notch.

"Dad? As in our dad?"

"Isn't that great?"

I was understandably suspicious of anything that resembled good news, especially when offered in the dead of night. After all, good news was about as rare as scrambled eggs at breakfast—we just didn't get it.

"You're serious?" I said, a little too loudly. Marky stirred, but kept on snoring.

"Serious as a heart attack," Dave said in hushed tones. Not wanting to share the glorious news with Marky or Gary—at least not yet—I matched Dave's volume.

"How do you know?"

"He called. He's really coming, Jimmy."

"When?"

"Tomorrow. Probably around lunch."

With the fog now lifted, I tried to envision Dad eating lunch at the kitchen table with the Reils.

"I can't believe it. Dad's really coming … here?"

"Would I joke about something like that?"

For a moment, I was conflicted. I wanted to believe Dave. But would this turn out to be another one of my dad's broken promises? A twinge of doubt surfaced in my heart, tethering the wings of hope back to reality. I laid down and stared at the gray ceiling; my feet wiggled left to right under the covers as I tried to process the conflicting emotions.

"But how? Dad doesn't even have a car."

Dave didn't answer at first. I turned and saw, even in the darkness, a glint of white as his smile widened. My eyes narrowed in expectation. I got the impression Dave was withholding something.

"Mike's bringing him." The words hung in the air.

"*Mike?* For *real?*"

"Ha! Can you believe it?!"

If I hadn't already been sitting down, I think I would have fallen over. Instead, I fell back against my pillow and floated somewhere over the moon. *Dad and Mike were coming. Here. Tomorrow.* Having dropped this bombshell, Dave gave me a quiet high five before leaving to take a shower.

Sleep was impossible. I lay awake with a few million thoughts. *Why was Dad coming? Just a friendly visit? Had Mike told Dad how difficult life was for us? Was Dad coming to rescue me from the Reils? This time, would he ask that question: Do you want to live with me? If he did, I'd answer him with the biggest bear hug in the world.*

The next morning I dressed quickly and then skipped breakfast, which, to Mr. Reil, was probably a sign that I was planning some sort of mutiny. Rather than try and explain anything, I headed to the front of the property to hang out by the chicken coop. Dad was coming and I'd be waiting. The chickens, however, deserved to know that I came in peace. I explained that I wasn't there to wield the ax, just to pass the time.

They appeared to appreciate that.

I kicked rocks, searched for lizards, and waited. The empty dirt road on the other side of the wash beckoned, and for a minute I contemplated hiking down those dusty miles to wait by the mailboxes. That way I could spot the first signs of Mike's yellow and white '57 Chevy on the horizon. But Dave said they wouldn't arrive until lunch, so I decided to stay put. At least hanging by the henhouse provided some level of interest: I could watch the chickens peck away at the ground in their endless search for the perfect bug-meal—it was sort of like watching a special on the Discovery Channel today.

When the chicken-watching grew old, I scratched the backs of the rabbits right behind their floppy ears, which I knew they loved. If, on the off chance my dad asked me to live with him, I knew I'd miss the animals. Maybe I felt a certain affinity for their plight considering we were both trapped in a cage of sorts, longing to be free. Spending a little extra time that morning seemed an appropriate way to say good-bye—just in case.

SAY THE WORD

There's a world of difference between having a roof over your head at night and being at home. Staying at a hotel, while providing shelter, just isn't home. The pillows are harder. The towels feel as if they've been dipped in industrial laundry soap that washed away their original softness. The pictures on the wall, with their pastel splatters, seem mechanically designed by a computer program to maximize the color coordination with the drapes.

Life at the Reils' never felt like home to me. Sure, I was thankful for a roof over my head, a place to bathe, and food to eat. But I never felt settled. I certainly didn't feel loved. I didn't even have the freedom to wander into the kitchen and help myself to a snack. I couldn't ask to have the patio room where we slept painted something other than warehouse gray. I couldn't hang a portrait of my mother on the wall, even if I'd had one. I was increasingly aware that the management viewed my siblings and me as undesirable guests and was counting the minutes until checkout time.

The feelings were mutual. I wanted to get out of the Reils' almost from the moment we drove up to their flamingo-pink house. Maybe when Dad arrived, he'd pick up on the negative undercurrent flowing through the place and decide to break me out. Dave and Dee Dee, knowing I held such hopes, kept telling me that my dad wasn't a stable guy. Living with him might not be such a good alternative.

Whenever they'd make that point, I'd think, *How could Dad be any less stable than Mr. Reil?* I didn't feel like I was trying to pick between two bad choices. Living with Dad was a good option. In my heart I knew it was the *best* option—if only he'd say those magical words I longed to hear.

Just before noon, I heard tires crunching gravel in the distance. Because of the dust that plumed overhead, I couldn't see the vehicle until it almost reached the wash, but I could tell the car was close by. When Mike's '57 Chevy appeared, I jumped up and down, waving my arms as if directing a jet across the tarmac.

As promised, my dad came.

He really came.

The euphoria of being found, of being with Dad again, was

almost too much for me to handle. My heart pounded so hard I was sure Dad could hear it. Even with all of "that stuff" that my siblings said he had struggled with, I couldn't have been happier to see him. Grinning ear to ear, Mike hit the horn as they rode down and then up the other side of the wash as if it were opening day at Disneyland and they were riding the Matterhorn.

While I was still waving my arms like a rooster, Mike tapped the horn and pulled the car toward the house. I chased after them like a tailwind, a clutch of chickens following in my wake. Within seconds, Dee Dee and Dave bounded out the front door of the house and surrounded the car as if royalty had arrived. Mike cut the engine and Dad emerged.

Dad wore a bright orange shirt, chocolate brown slacks, and a light tan jacket. His hair seemed a tad grayer, but his smile was as wide and as grand as the canyon. He was still in good shape. As I hugged my dad, I inhaled deeply as if that would help me memorize his scent. If only I could somehow bottle it. With the exception of Kim, who had married and moved away, we were a family once again.

It felt good. I felt whole.

At Dad's suggestion, we piled into the car and drove to town to have lunch together. I wouldn't be surprised if Mike had a hand in promoting that idea, considering the donkey meat he was served during his last visit. Come to think of it, we were so swept away by the reunion, we didn't think to introduce Dad to the Reils until after we returned.

We hadn't been together since well before my mom had died, and the three hours of laughing, swapping stories, and catching up flew by far too quickly. The main question running through my mind was, *Is Dad gonna ask me to stay with him?* As the afternoon drifted toward evening, and nobody had raised that "big question,"

I started to feel a sense of urgency. I was determined to bring it up even if nobody else did. I wasn't going to let the chance pass me by.

Not this time.

The sun started its slow descent, and we gathered by Mike's car for a photo. As Mrs. Reil prepared to snap the picture, I could feel my father's hand resting on my right shoulder. The warmth of his body at my back as he stood behind me was more comforting than a thousand blankets. And yet, even with my dad standing so close, my heart felt as if it were sinking right along with the setting sun. *Why didn't anybody talk about the one question that mattered? Had they privately decided among themselves that I'd be better off staying at the Reils' than with my dad? Didn't my vote count?*

After Mrs. Reil took the picture, she handed the camera back to Dee Dee and left us alone to say our good-byes. My dad fished a Pall Mall cigarette from his jacket. I watched his hands as they maneuvered through the familiar routine of lighting up. He struck the match and, behind the safety of a cupped hand, lit the end. Tossing the matchstick to the ground, and grinding it in the dirt with his shoe, he exhaled.

"So, Jimmy, I hear you don't like living at the Reils', is that right?" he said.

I glanced at Dave and Dee Dee. They obviously *had* talked about what I was feeling. I just hadn't noticed. I felt the edges of my ears start to tingle as if sunburned. The problem was I didn't know where my dad was headed with his question. If I said, "Dad, it's nuts," would he launch into a pep talk about being thankful for a roof over my head? Or, would he pop the question I had hoped he'd ask? I decided to be truthful.

"Dad, it's pretty crazy, that's for sure."

He took another slow drag. "The Reils seem nice enough to me...."

"That's because you don't have to *live* with them," I countered, looking at Dave and Dee Dee for backup. Dave started to say something, but Dad raised a hand and cut him off.

"Jimmy, if half of what I heard today is true, I can see why you'd feel that way," he said, referring to our lunchtime conversation when we'd brought Dad up to speed on the prowlers, the dismal breakfast menu, the stealing, the taunts by Marky, everything. "I'll tell you what. I've been thinking, and I've decided you and Dee Dee can come back and live with me if you'd like. How's that sound?"

"Wow! Really, Dad?" I hugged him until my arms hurt.

"Whoa, champ. A man's gotta breathe," he said, patting me on the back. I straightened, took a step back, and pointed toward the house.

"Should I go get my stuff?"

"Slow down a second, Jimmy," he said with a grin. "I'll get it worked out. We'll take care of it in the next week or two."

Those were the longest two weeks of my life, just waiting for the big day when Dad would return to take us away. After Dad left, I asked Dave why he wasn't moving too. He said he didn't feel right about walking away from the two jobs he was working—at least not yet. Plus, being older, he had developed a network of friends.

As I counted off the days, I thought that by leaving the Reils' bizarre world behind, my life would become "normal." I had some idea of what a normal family ought to be thanks to my mom. Even though she was dead, I carried with me those wonderful early childhood memories of what a family was and what a home ought to be like.

Now it was just Dad in charge.

How bad could that be?

Take Me Out of the Ball Game

Dee Dee and I moved into Dad's apartment and, in many ways, living with him was a blessing. Having the man I loved back in my life would have been enough, but there were other immediate benefits. I didn't have to share one bedroom with five guys or compete with ten people over a single bathroom. I drank whole milk and ate eggs and bacon. I'd spend hours at the pool after school, diving for coins or swimming laps.

However, I was no longer five years old as I had been the last time we'd lived under the same roof. I was eleven going on twelve and much more cognizant of what was going on around me. During those first few weeks of being reunited with Dad, I got the distinct impression that he wanted to do right by us, which is why he rescued us from the Reils'. At the same time, I could tell Dad was a troubled, haunted man.

The root cause of his distress was never talked about. His generation didn't openly share their feelings, at least not with the kids. I guess he preferred to engage his personal battles somewhere deep in his spirit. There were several times when he'd lose the fight and then turn to alcohol to cope. In those moments, I had to remind myself to continue to keep my expectations low so I wouldn't get hurt.

Every Friday night Dad would watch boxing on television. Dad loved his boxing. Sometimes with a dishtowel over his shoulder, he'd watch from the kitchen while preparing a snack. Whether sitting in the room or making popcorn by the stove, he maintained a running commentary with the fight. *Hit him—come on, don't be a wimp. Knock his lights out! Hey, that's a low blow, Ref!* Stuff like that.

He'd yell at the tube, clench his hands into fists, and punch the air in front of him as if it were *his* heavyweight title on the line. Sometimes I sat by his side for hours, content to watch him shadow-boxing.

Saturday nights we ate hot dogs, pork and beans, and "black cows," that great combination of vanilla ice cream and root beer soda. Sundays, we never went to church, but Dad would make barbecue religiously, as if competing in the county cook-off.

While those treats with Dad were a highlight, his behavior wasn't always healthy, especially when the drinking got out of hand. His episodes really troubled me. I didn't like the person he became when he was drunk, and I hated the distance his behavior created between us. I still loved him, I just didn't *like* him at times—like the Saturday he decided to come to my Little League game.

I loved baseball. Still do. Back then, when I slipped my hand into my leather glove, I knew I was becoming a part of something larger than myself. I was a member of a team. We called ourselves the Mets and, with a win/loss record above .500, we were quite good. Whether or not there was a scheduled practice, I'd walk five blocks to the ball field where, for hours, I'd snag fly balls and practice hitting with the team or whoever showed up on a given day.

Whenever we had our games, I was about the only kid who didn't have his dad around to cheer for him. Of course, that didn't keep me from talking up my dad to the guys—you know, bragging about how he had coached Little League most of his life and could pound a ball over the center-field fence as effortlessly as Babe Ruth.

One particular evening our game was scheduled to be played on the nicest of three adjacent fields, the one with the manicured grass infield and overhead lighting. Those towering lights bathed the field in artificial shafts of sunlight, which made me feel nervous, as if we were actually in the big leagues being watched by millions on TV. Since I was the shortstop, and sometimes covered first or third base, I always felt the energy of the crowd cheering me on.

About the third inning, I was sitting in the dugout with my team, when I heard, then saw, my dad in the crowded stands with the other parents. He was intoxicated. I had been so proud of him and couldn't wait for the day he'd come to see me play—until that moment. He wasn't just drunk; he was loud and obnoxious.

At home, when my dad would shout at the TV during fights, I thought it was funny. Here, his behavior was embarrassing. Dad stood and criticized the calls the umpire was making. *Come on, Ump, are you blind or stupid? That ball was a strike. How about getting a new pair of glasses?* His words were slurred, and his inebriated protests were definitely over the top.

More than a few times, he began to launch into a ridiculous diatribe when the action on the field picked up. Thankfully, the crowd response drowned him out. I wanted the noise to continue so that his lone drunken voice couldn't be heard.

When "that crazy man" in the stands pointed toward us, people around me started asking, "Whose dad is that?" I pulled my cap down and plowed my cleats into the earth beneath the bench. If I dug fast enough, maybe I could carve a hole large enough to crawl into. I refused to acknowledge *that man* was my father. When I stepped into the batter's box, he blew my cover. He called out my name, adding, "Thaaat's my bouy!"

I was humiliated.

After the game, I avoided walking home with him. I hid my team information so he wouldn't know when I was scheduled to play again. I wish I could say that was the last time he drank excessively. It wasn't. He became severely drunk five or six other times during the year we lived together. While he never threatened me with physical harm as he had threatened my mom, my siblings were growing concerned about the wisdom of me continuing to live with him.

As I said at the outset, the first principle life had taught me thus far was to keep my expectations low so I wouldn't get hurt. Watching Dad's public misbehavior, however, demonstrated that my philosophy wasn't foolproof. I *was* hurt by my father's actions. Further, I'd soon be crushed again, this time by yet another man I'd come to admire.

SCHOOL OF HARD KNOCKS

Living with Dad required a change in schools. From the moment I started to attend San Gabriel Elementary School as a sixth grader, I was in panic mode. Everything about the school was new to me. I had to transition from a friendly country school in Morongo Valley, to a rough, big-city school in East Los Angeles. I was a new kid who didn't know anybody or anything about the system.

I didn't have just one teacher who covered all of the subjects. Instead, I had homeroom and a confusing array of teachers who taught different periods that required me to change classrooms several times during the day—all before the bell rang. I dreaded being assigned a locker with a built-in combination. What if I forgot the code? What if I couldn't get my books out fast enough to find the right room before the bell sounded?

Talk about pressure.

Thankfully, my homeroom teacher, Mr. Freid, was kind and, in many ways, a mentor to me. Mr. Freid was a reserve deputy sheriff for the city and taught karate as a fifth-degree black belt instructor. Everything about him—his manner of speaking, his stance, and the way he patrolled around the halls—exuded power. He was what every boy thought a man should be. I know I did.

When Mr. Freid suggested that I take his karate class, I felt like somebody cared. For six months I studied the Japanese art of karate under Mr. Freid. I was fascinated by the pressure-sensitive points on the body of an opponent where a well-placed kick or blow would neutralize him.

The highlight of our class was when Mr. Freid announced a special guest, Chuck Norris. We already thought a gung-ho guy like Mr. Freid with his police badge and black belt was invincible. But to discover he was also friends with famous people like Chuck Norris—*the* Chuck Norris who fought Bruce Lee in the then-popular movie *Way of the Dragon*—was incredible. Watching them spar on the mat was enough to convince me that my homeroom teacher was a rock.

Mr. Norris was invited, in part, to speak with us about the dangers of drugs and alcohol. The part of Mr. Norris's story that especially resonated with me had to do with his background. He was the son of an alcoholic. So was I. He talked about how his dad missed so much of his childhood. I knew the feeling. His mother was half Irish and half Indian—just like my mom. And yet, while his childhood sounded about as daunting as my own, he'd managed to rise above the challenges he'd faced to become a world-class competitor.

I was captivated as Mr. Norris described his pathway to

achieving multiple black belts, including those in Tang Soo Do, tae kwon do, and Shito-Ryu karate. Frankly, he inspired me to want to take my skills to the next level. I would have continued in karate except I was the only kid in the class who wore street clothes. I couldn't afford a Gi.

Mr. Freid said, "Sorry, no Gi, no Karate."

Chuck Norris's visit made me realize I wanted nothing to do with drugs, and that I could accomplish whatever I set my mind on doing. The fact that Mr. Norris didn't have a dad to show him the ropes didn't prevent him from climbing high and reaching the top in his field. As Mr. Norris bowed toward us, hands pressed together, I knew he was a man worthy of respect. The kind of guy I'd like to be. Definitely the warrior type King Arthur would break bread with.

After Chuck Norris left, Mr. Freid asked us to create a poster with some sort of antidrug headline. I decided to draw an overview shot of a Formula 1 racing car, which I was getting pretty good at. Across the top, I made up and inked the slogan, *Keep Speed on the Right Track*. I don't know how I knew what "speed" was. I just did. I probably heard about the drug from my older brothers and sisters.

I remember working on that poster at home until every inch was perfect. I was proud of the final product and knew in my heart that if Chuck Norris could see it, he'd agree it was ad agency quality. *Who knows,* I thought, *maybe he'd even want to use it in his antidrug talks.* When I turned in the poster, I didn't expect Mr. Freid to ask me to stay after class. When he did, I figured he was going to tell me how wonderful my poster was—or that he planned to show it to his famous karate buddy.

"Son, have a seat." It wasn't a suggestion. He parked his frame against the edge of the desk and I complied. His arms bulged when he folded them together.

"Jimmy, do you know what plagiarism is?"

I offered a blank stare. "No. Should I?"

He plucked my poster off the top of the desk and tilted it forward like a lawyer making his case before the judge. This was Exhibit A.

"Plagiarism is when you pass someone's idea off as your own. You *did* know that your slogan was supposed to be an original idea, right?"

I nodded, unsure what the problem was.

"So, where did you get yours from?"

I didn't know what to say. I mean, my teacher, a man whom I respected and admired, who just so happened to be a policeman, was telling me that I had stolen something—plagiarized the idea or whatever. But I didn't steal it.

"Mr. Freid, I made it up, honestly."

"You're in sixth grade, Jimmy," he said, letting the poster fall back against the desk. "How do you know anything about a hard drug like speed?"

When I told Mr. Freid that I didn't know how I knew about speed, that I must have heard about it from my older siblings, he didn't buy it. And, he maintained that I must have stolen the slogan for my poster. Mr. Freid doubted my honesty and his lack of faith crushed me. It wasn't my creativity that was in question; it was my integrity. When Marky Reil called me a liar, I could handle that because I didn't respect him. But when Mr. Freid didn't believe I was telling the truth, it completely undid me.

I'd like to tell you there was a happy, fairy-tale ending, that Mr. Freid later believed me and awarded me a prize for my outstanding poster—an autographed Gi from Chuck Norris or something. But that's not the way it happened. In fact, just when I thought things couldn't get any worse, they did.

11

Journey's End

Nothing about the wallet was particularly remarkable. That is, nothing except for the circumstances under which it was found. The wallet was brown, a threefold case purchased more for function than style. According to the faded gold foil stamping along its edge, the billfold was made from "100% Genuine Imitation Leather."

The wallet rested, flaps open, on the kitchen table with its inner chambers methodically emptied of their contents. Adjacent to the billfold was a driver's license, social security card, a couple of credit cards, and a number of wallet-sized photos arranged faceup. If the items had been tossed haphazardly, it would have suggested a robbery. Instead, these personal effects were arranged systematically in two orderly rows.

The wallet was discovered just after lunch on a Friday. A single, tarnished brass key, evidently no longer necessary to perform its duty, rested to the left of the identification. While no note was left nearby explaining the enigma, the staging suggested that a statement had nevertheless been intended by the owner. Dee Dee was the first to stumble upon our dad's wallet. Now seventeen and soon to be eighteen, she was in the process of moving to her own apartment. Having inherited her work ethic from my mom, Dee Dee had graduated from high school a year early and taken a job at an insurance company. That Friday afternoon she'd returned to collect a few remaining possessions, but got more than she bargained for.

Trying to make sense out of what the array of Dad's things might mean, Dee Dee reached out and, with a careful eye, studied the items one by one. When no plausible explanation came to mind, she snatched the phone and dialed Kim.

"Hey, Sis," Kim said. "What's up?"

"I just stopped by the apartment and ... well ... do you know where Dad is?"

"On a Friday? He'd be at work, right?"

"That's what I thought ..." Dee Dee's voice trailed off.

"You sound worried. What is it?"

"Just that ... this is *so* bizarre." Dee Dee hooked her hair behind her left ear. "Maybe it's nothing, but I found his wallet and the apartment key on the kitchen table. What do you think that means?"

"Could he have forgotten to take them to work?"

"I don't think so, Kim." Dee Dee lifted the driver's license and studied the photo. "I mean, it's totally empty, and all of his ID was just laid out in rows on the table."

Kim absorbed that piece of the puzzle. "Maybe he was drying them out, you know, if he'd spilled a beer on them or something," Kim said, then paused as if weighing the likelihood of that scenario. She added, "Did you see him? Are you sure he's not there?"

"No. Hold on."

Dee Dee held the receiver to her chest and called his name. When Dad didn't answer, she put the phone down and did a hurried sweep of the place. She retrieved the phone.

"He's not here."

"What about Jimmy?"

"No, he's at school. Now what?"

"Call Dave, call Mike. See if they know what's up."

"Sure … I just don't have a good feeling about this, Kim."

"What do you mean?"

"Well … did Dad just leave us?"

A silence fell between them. Kim said, "If he did, he'd have taken his wallet, right?"

"My point exactly. So …"

"Is there anything missing?"

Dee Dee glanced around. "Doesn't look like it. Look, I'll call the guys and get back to you, okay?"

Dee Dee returned the phone to the cradle with a soft click. She stared at the table, momentarily paralyzed by what this turn of events might mean. When she was younger, long before I was born, Dad would disappear unannounced, sometimes for weeks at a time. The fact that he might be up to his old tricks concerned her, especially now that she'd moved out. She knew if Dad had hopped a train or a bus to Reno or Las Vegas to gamble, he'd be back.

One problem. I'd be alone in the apartment until he returned, perhaps days later. But that disappearing act reflected his past behavior, not Dad's somewhat more responsible actions of late. And Dad would have taken his wallet and key with him had he gone on a trip. Leaving those things behind made no sense … *unless* … she leaned on the chair back to steady herself. What if Dad had no intention of returning because he'd be *unable* to return?

Could that be it?

Had someone or something from his past caught up with him? Had he become so distressed that he concluded life wasn't worth living? Whatever my dad's reason for disappearing, Dee Dee had to immediately address the fact that I was uncared for.

She had reached for the phone to call Dave when the apartment door opened.

DEAD MAN WALKING

At the sound of the door swinging on its hinges, Dee Dee jumped from the chair, almost tipping it over in the process. Dad stood at the threshold, apparently as startled to see Dee Dee as she was to see him. A blanket, hastily gathered together and tucked under his left arm, made him appear as if he had returned from a picnic. His pants were stained with dirt at the knees as if he'd slid into home plate. His shirt was disheveled, partially untucked at the belt. He seemed momentarily disoriented as if he had returned from an alternate reality.

He took several steps into the room before speaking.

"I see you found my things."

Dee Dee's face flushed. She felt an odd mixture of guilt and relief; she was relieved to see Dad, but felt a twinge of guilt over prying through his personal stuff. She found her legs and hurried to his right side for a hug. His stance stiffened the moment she wrapped her arms around him, as if he were hiding something.

"I was so worried, Dad."

"Really? About what?"

For a split second, Dee Dee wondered if she had misread the significance of discovering his wallet and key. Had she overreacted and let her imagination get the better of her? Might there be a perfectly harmless explanation? She decided to press him.

"Well, for one thing, Dad, why was all of your ID just laid out on the table like that? Doesn't that seem odd?"

"If it's all the same to you, I'd rather not talk about it." He dropped the blanket on the floor and headed to the kitchen. She followed him and leaned against the counter while he retrieved a beer from the refrigerator.

"Come on, Dad. You don't look so good. Where've you been?"

He twisted off the top and took a swig from the bottle. "The park."

"The park? With a blanket? What for? Aren't you supposed to be at work?" Her words came out sounding more accusing than she felt.

Blank stare. He was somewhere on the dark side of the moon and she didn't know how to reach him. She softened her voice and tried again.

"Look, Dad, I understand this might not be easy for you ... but if you at least tell me what's going on ... maybe there's a way I can help."

Another swallow of beer. He looked up from his bottle and searched her eyes as if questioning her capacity to hear what he had to say. Dee Dee was always very levelheaded and more mature for her age than her peers. He must have known that creating an elaborate fabrication wouldn't work with her. That, or he'd lost the will to fight.

"The truth?"

"That would be nice," she said with a nod.

Dad slouched into a chair at the kitchen table. Dee Dee pulled up a seat across from him. Picking at the edge of the label on his beer, he started to peel away the foil. He pursed his mouth and blew out a long, restless breath.

"I ... look, there's no easy way to say this."

His eyes seemed to go out of focus. A moment later, he bit his bottom lip and started to study the contour of the beer bottle, as if peering into the amber glass would help him gather his thoughts. Dee Dee waited. She didn't understand the mind of an alcoholic, even after so many years of having two parents who struggled to remain sober. At the same time, she knew enough not to stifle him with too many interruptions.

"Look, I went to the park because … I didn't want to live anymore." His eyes met hers, then he quickly looked away, embarrassed by the confession. Dad shifted in his chair. His shoulders drooped forward. He was a defeated man. Dee Dee felt the air start to burn in her lungs.

"I took the blanket to cover up after … you know, after I cut my wrists. I didn't want to make a scene." He drained the bottle and then slumped against the chair back. "Obviously, I couldn't go through with it."

The room felt unusually warm. Dee Dee began to feel light-headed, as if her world had just spun out of its orbit. Her throat, now dry as the desert, wouldn't allow her to form a response. She swallowed, hard. Even though he was just across the table, she had the urge to run to his side and comfort him. She wanted to hug him with an embrace that would forever wipe away the sadness he wore on his face. She heard herself say two words.

"Why, Dad?"

"I guess … well, living with you and Jimmy reminded me of what I had." He paused. "I lost everything after Mom took you guys away."

"You're blaming Mom?" Dee Dee said.

He waved her off. "No. Your mom did what she had to do. I know that." He closed his eyes for a moment. When he reopened them, tears formed at the edges. "I had it all and blew it. How does a man live with that?"

Dee Dee had some appreciation for the depth of his regret. Right before Mom died, Dee Dee and Kim risked the wrath of Hank the Tank by breaking into Mom's bedroom to talk. They laid down next to Mom and during those few intimate moments, Mom said, "Girls, all I ever wanted to do was to be a good mom, a good wife, make breakfast, help you with your schoolwork, take care of your clothes, and keep the house clean." That's exactly what Dad had wanted too, but the only time they had ever been happy was when we lived on Cosby Street.

But Dad's drinking had burned the last bridge home. He lost the only thing that was important to him—his family. As much as Dee Dee wanted Dad to be strong and to assure her everything would be okay, he didn't have the strength or the will left in him to fight. Dad needed to get help. Having his kids back home should have been a good thing, but Dee Dee was convinced Dad couldn't handle the pressure—or the memories of the better times.

"We'll get through this, Dad," she said, with a pat to the back of his hand. How they'd get through it, she wasn't sure. The last thing she wanted to do was to leave me alone with Dad, now that he was drinking more heavily and had come close to attempting suicide. Slipping out of his chair, Dad stood then returned to the refrigerator for another beer.

"I guess you're gonna tell the others, right?"

READY, FIRE, AIM

My siblings were quick to lobby me with their laundry list of concerns. I understood their misgivings. Living with Dad wasn't wise, they said. What if I came home from school one day and found that my father had committed suicide in the apartment? I was only twelve. He was unstable, unpredictable, unreliable, and definitely making unhealthy choices. He didn't seem interested in getting help for his drinking. They were convinced that things *had* to change before something dreadful happened.

In spite of their concerns, I didn't want to leave my dad. I understood my siblings were looking after my best interests, but I loved Dad. And I'd already been through so much. The death of my mother. Hank leaving us. The Reils. The excitement of being reunited with Dad. And now they had this notion that I should check out of his world because he had issues. The thought of yet another change was too much for me to handle.

Adding insult to injury, they wanted *me* to break the bad news to Dad—and the sooner the better. That broke my heart. Why did I have to do the dirty work? I felt sure my dad would get the impression that I didn't love him because I was leaving him. Nothing could be further from the truth. I did love him. He wasn't perfect. Far from it. But he was *my* dad.

Yet, once again, what choice did I have?

The inevitable family meeting was called. I dreaded that day as if it were a date with the hangman. Dad, Mike, Dave, Dee Dee, Kim, and I sat in a circle at my brother Dave's house in Yucca Valley. When Dee Dee and I moved in with Dad, Dave had stayed behind at the Reils' to work. Dave, who was twenty at the time, got married to a minor and had a baby. They rented a modest house on Cherokee Street, which now hosted our family summit.

The drapes were drawn to protect us from the uncharitable afternoon desert sun. The air felt stuffy. The swamp cooler strained to provide some relief. Although the room was sparsely furnished with little more than a couch, a TV, and the extra chairs rounded up for the group, I felt as though the walls were closing inward. The thought of dismissing my father from my life was overwhelming.

More than anything, the finality of announcing the decision was weighing on me. Like a drowning man hanging onto a plank for dear life, I didn't want to let go of my dad. I had the sinking feeling Dad would hear the news and sail out of my life forever. But, since I was only twelve, I was following the leadership of my older siblings. I was also troubled because I wasn't sure anybody had the presence of mind to lay out a strategy or think through the issues of my long-term care beforehand. I was about to cut my ties to Dad without a backup plan.

After a little chitchat, we got down to the matter at hand. I'm sure Dad must have had an idea why the meeting had been called. At least he didn't appear startled when the conversation was directed to the topic of his drinking, his behavior, and its impact on me since I was living under the same roof. While I don't remember the exact flow of the conversation, I'll never forget when Mike, sitting across the room from me, said, "So, Jimmy, what's your decision?"

D-Day had arrived and I was about to drop the bomb. I turned, looked at my dad, and hesitated. I knew once I spoke the words I'd practiced in my head, there would be no going back. I didn't know a broken heart could beat so hard. Somehow I found the words. "Dad, I don't … I don't think it's a good idea to, well, to live with you anymore." The words seemed to hang in the air.

Dad scratched the side of his head and asked me something that I didn't anticipate. "Why?"

I was caught off guard. I'd practiced reciting my one-sentence statement, but I wasn't prepared for a follow-up question. I couldn't think of a good answer. I actually *did* want to live with him. I'd only said that I didn't because that's what was expected of me.

Finally, a bold thought hit my mind. I blurted out: "Because of all the stuff you did to Mom." There was definitely real hard truth behind those words. To his credit, Dad didn't attempt to shift the blame or dodge what had happened in the past. With a nod, he said,

"I can accept that. I wasn't a good husband or father."

The meeting ended abruptly and Dad stood to leave. I was so emotionally wrung out that I actually forgot to hug him good-bye. Noticing the oversight, Mike came to me and said, "You should hug Dad. It might be the last time you hug him." Still numb from the whole surreal experience, I complied. I crossed the room and gave him a hug more out of duty than passion. I felt neutral. Certainly not the way I felt during our embrace when I took a bus to see him, or the time I hugged him with uninhibited joy when he arrived at the Reils'.

Even with all of my practice, I never got used to saying good-bye.

Although I managed to survive that confrontation, there was no concrete decision as to where I'd live. Afterward, since I wasn't returning to San Gabriel with my dad, Dave pulled me aside and told me I had two options. I could throw myself on the mercy of the foster-care system—although, speaking from his personal experience back when Dad and Mom were too drunk to care for him, he didn't think that was such a great idea. "Or," Dave said, with a squeeze to my shoulder, "why don't you move in with me?"

Dave was gracious to make the offer and I accepted his hospitality. He was always good about trying to keep us together. Although a disaster, the experience at the Reils' was Dave's way of keeping us a family. Now, once again, he was taking the lead and holding things together. I never did return to my dad's place.

Dave retrieved my stuff from my dad's, and I started my life sharing the cramped quarters with Dave and his wife, who interestingly was named Dee, and their infant, Kelly. What made this arrangement somewhat ... *unusual* ... was the age difference between myself, at twelve years old, and Dee, who was sixteen. My new foster mom was just four years older than me. Considering how unorthodox my life had been to date, I guess just about nothing fazed me.

THE END GAME

While I was getting settled at Dave's place, my father, rather than live alone, agreed to move in with Mike. Having finished his service in the navy, Mike was attending the University of Nevada in Reno, and playing on the football team. For his part, Dad used his social security checks to drink and play the slots. On hindsight, considering that Dad was a gambler and Reno was a gambling town, that wasn't the best idea in the long run. But it was his choice.

One evening, Mike came home to his apartment and found Dad seriously drunk. Dad could get mean when under the influence of alcohol, as we learned in the hammer house. It didn't help matters that Mike and Dad had their share of confrontations over the years. Had we considered the wisdom of pairing the two of them together, a different arrangement might have been advisable. While they didn't come to fists, the heated skirmish placed Dad on a course of action from which there'd be no return.

This particular night, Mike confronted my dad about his unacceptable behavior. Between making his grades at school, working two jobs, and tackling the grueling football schedule, Mike was under a great deal of pressure. Pulling the extra weight of a drunk was more than he could handle. Mike said, "Dad, I can't keep this up. I can't keep living this way with you drunk all of the time. I refuse to support your habit."

That was like throwing fuel on the fire. Enraged at the thought that he was some kind of a burden to Mike, Dad took a $100 bill from his wallet and threw it at Mike, saying, "Here then, take this blankety-blank money" (only he had filled in the blanks). Exercising an amazing amount of restraint, Mike said, "Look, Dad, I don't want your money. I just want you to be sober. If you can't sober up, I'll find you another place." Rather than return to Alcoholics

Anonymous, Dad said, "Then, I guess I don't need to be here."

Mike found a nearby one-room studio and paid for three months rent up front. Dad stayed all of three weeks and didn't return. Every time Mike would stop by to check on him, the landlady said she hadn't seen our dad in a long while. She finally decided to box up Dad's few possessions and re-rent the room. When Mike checked in one last time, he learned that Dad did finally stop by. He collected his things and the unused portion of the rent money, and then disappeared. We had no idea where he went.

Several months later, I was lying on the couch at Dave's house watching the *I Love Lucy* show. I wasn't a big fan, it just happened to be on after dinner. I was doing well in my studies and in sports. Living with Dave and Dee seemed to be working out. Sure, we had our struggles, but unlike with the Reils, the feeling in the home was calm. Dee was very kind toward me and took the new living situation in stride. It was November and we hadn't heard from Dad in months, but that wasn't a surprise.

The phone rang.

Dave, who was closest to the kitchen, picked up after several rings and listened. Although I continued to watch TV, I sensed that something about Dave's demeanor had changed—almost as if an invisible fog settled over him. Since the phone cord was long enough to stretch to the dining room table, Dave took a seat as he continued to listen. He said little and, within a few minutes, hung up.

"Jimmy," he called.

"Yeah?"

"Dad's dead."

Still lounging on the couch, I looked over my shoulder and said, "Oh, that's too bad." I really didn't feel anything. No waves of sadness. No tears. I was numb. I realize that may sound coldhearted. Maybe I had prepared myself for the worst for quite some time.

Dave clicked off the TV and said, "Jimmy ... you okay?"

"Sure." In truth, it would take three full years for my tears to force their way out of the vault where I had safely tucked away my feelings.

"That was Mike."

"Really? Was he with Dad?"

"No. Mike said he was playing football when his coach asked him if he knew where Dad was." Dave pulled up a seat. "Mike said that was strange since he never talked about Dad with the coach before." Dave, clearly more shaken by the news than I was, went on to recite the conversation between Mike and his coach.

Mike had said, "He's dead, isn't he?"

The coach was startled by Mike's quick assessment. "Why do you say that?"

Mike said, "Because he was a drunk and a bum."

The coach told Mike they'd received a call from the coroner and that Mike needed to go downtown to identify the body. Mike went to the police station and said, "I'm Mike Daly. My dad was found someplace. I'd like to know where."

He was told, "You really don't want to know."

Mike replied, "I'll make that decision."

They explained that a twelve-year-old boy discovered Dad's body in an abandoned Laundromat warehouse building across the street from the police station. Dad evidently died of hypothermia. Unlike Mom, who had her children and her loved ones around her as death approached, Dad died alone.

After identifying our dad's body, Mike went to see where Dad had been living. The building had no electricity, no heat, and was strewn with litter. Dad had made the corner of an office his "home" with little more than a dirty, beat-up old mattress and a few personal effects in a paper bag.

His wallet was never found.

I would later learn that Dad had been placed in a paupers casket, which was essentially a cardboard box. Dave, Mike, and a woman official from the funeral home, whose name I never learned, conducted the service. My sister Dee Dee was almost eight months pregnant and wasn't permitted to make the trip. Kim was at a Palm Springs hospital with her husband who had a hernia operation and couldn't break free.

I don't think anybody thought about me going.

In the end, my father was buried by two sons who really didn't like him that much and a stranger. There had been no talk of faith, no minister offering assurances of him being in a better place, and certainly not the crowd of well-wishers who wanted to honor his life as hundreds had done for my mother. The contrast couldn't have been greater.

I couldn't help but wonder why his life had to end that way. He knew that my mom gave her heart to God just before passing into eternity. What prevented him from doing the same? Pride? Ego? Fear? One thing was certain: Having watched the way my mom and my dad had lived and died, I knew which example I wanted to follow.

There was, however, one bright spot. After the burial service, such as it was, Mike and Dave learned that Dad had been volunteering at the Good Shepherd Lutheran Church not far from the warehouse where he'd been found. The church folks loved him and appreciated the way he'd show up day after day to help out with their programs.

Was it possible that Dad had a change of heart?

12

Holy Huddle

Not long after my father died, I turned thirteen and my body became a stranger to me. With puberty, the rules of the universe seemed to change overnight. I started to sprout hair where none had been before. I was introduced to a razor, underarm deodorant, and mouthwash. I became self-conscious around the girls at school who, up until then, suffered from that contagious disease called "cooties." For reasons I couldn't explain, I found myself suddenly fascinated by God's fairest creation and actually enjoying their company.

Unfortunately, at the most inconvenient times, like talking to those newly discovered cute girls or answering a question in class, my voice developed a mind of its own. I'd start to speak when, without notice, my vocal cords would betray me with honking sounds like those played by first-year clarinet students. I could hide my sweaty palms and racing heartbeat, but that caterwauling always brought snickers.

I was regularly making the honor roll at school, but my transformation from boyhood to manhood required some coaching. Now that Dad was dead, I suppose I was looking for someone—a man— to be a role model, or at least a friend. About that time, my brother Dave's wife, Dee, was paid a visit by her older brother, Ronnie

Hughes. I immediately thought I found someone with whom I could connect.

In some respects, Ronnie reminded me of my dad. Both men were athletic. Both loved baseball. Ronnie had played baseball for the University of California at Irvine the year they won the NCAA (National Collegiate Athletic Association) championship. He was such a good athlete that he went on to play for an Angels farm team. So, when Ronnie invited me to play catch just before sundown one evening, I was thrilled.

Of course, at the time I agreed, I'd never witnessed the fury of a ninety-five-mile-per-hour fastball. Ronnie was a pitcher with a rocket launcher for an arm. Not only did the ball sail into my mitt as fast as a shooting star, he threw what he called a "rising fastball." This ball moved like nothing I'd ever seen. It took all of the focus I had to keep up with him.

When his mom called out that dinner was about ready, we agreed he'd throw one more pitch. Ronnie fired a missile that tailed up suddenly, clipping the edge of my glove. Bouncing off my mitt, the leather fireball hit me square in the cheekbone, totally shattering the left side of my face.

I thought I was dying. Like slamming a car door on your fingers, waves of pain surged from my head through my body, practically sending me into shock. Trying to cope with this sensory overload, my enflamed network of nerves started shutting down as if a thick curtain of numbness had been pulled across my face. I was in a fog. Blood began to pour out of my mouth and nose.

I was rushed to the hospital where I spent two weeks undergoing, and healing from, extensive reconstructive surgery. I later learned that I had a broken nose, broken cheek, broken eye socket, busted jaw, and fractured skull. Ronnie's pitch was so hard, you could see the imprint of the baseball stitches welded into my cheek for days. On the upside, I was excused from school for several weeks—that part was a nice change of pace.

Interestingly, I can't remember blaming God for this accident or for any of the hard breaks along my journey. My prevailing attitude was that "things just happen."

My doctor informed me that, had the baseball made contact an inch and a half to the right, it would have killed me. Thirteen-year-olds typically think they're invincible and don't spend a lot of time dwelling on death or dying, but his assessment was a wake-up call. One minute I was playing baseball, the next minute I could have been dead. I had to wonder, was God trying to tell me something?

Although I was young, I had an acute sense that this life wasn't the end of the story. Death was all too real to me, having lost both parents. Now my own close encounter prompted me to do some heavy-duty thinking. I felt pretty sure another chapter would be written once I stepped across the threshold of life and into eternity. Grandpa Hope seemed convinced that giving your heart to God was important—a step I hadn't made and didn't know how to make. Lying there wrapped in bandages like a mummy, I had more questions than answers.

Thoughts of death and the afterlife aside, I was so banged up that two officers from the San Bernardino sheriff's office came to my hospital room to investigate the cause of my injuries. They said, "Jim, we don't think you've been straight with us. Given the extent of your injuries, we think you've been involved in a gang fight. We believe this was no accident. Were you, in fact, hit by a baseball bat? Are you lying to us to cover it up? Nobody gets this hurt just playing catch. What gang did this?" When I explained that Ronnie was a pitcher who played college baseball and spent time in the Angels organization, it seemed to placate them. They closed their notebooks and left.

The force of the ball actually cut the ganglion, a group of nerve cells, leaving the left side of my face numb. To this day, my teeth, my cheek, and my lips on the left side have no feeling aside from a minor tingle. As skilled as my doctor was, he wasn't certain whether my damaged nerves would heal properly. Back then, there were no precision microsurgery techniques that increase the odds of a successful outcome. Thankfully, I did get some movement back in my upper lip after the surgery.

It's worth jumping ahead of the story for a moment. Several years later, I had turned sixteen and was sitting in algebra class daydreaming about dating Cheryl Wheeler. Cheryl and I had known each other since the second grade when we attended Yucca Valley Elementary School together. Although I had changed schools several times, when I moved back to Yucca Valley to live with Dave, we were reacquainted. Now I couldn't take my eyes off of her. Cheryl was terminally cute. She had flowing brunette hair that smelled of roses when she walked by and a smile so warm it could melt snow. She and about three other girls were *the* "catch" of the class.

I was really out of my league, reaching for the top.

I'd always wanted to ask Cheryl out for a date. We were friends, but I hoped there could be more between us. The fact that we were assigned seats side by side in the front row of class had to be a signal that we were destined to be together, right? I remember thinking, *This is it. I'm going to ask Cheryl out Friday night for a date.* Since my desk was on the far left row adjacent to the wall, my left side, the numb side, wasn't actually seen by anybody unless I turned my head.

I mustered all of the courage I could summon, took a quick breath to settle my nerves, then turned to look at the angelic being sitting three feet from me. I said, "Hey, Cheryl, do you want to go out Friday night?" She took one look at me ... and started chuckling—not a mean, black-hearted laugh. It was more of a musical chuckle. I flushed and felt like Bozo the Clown.

I thought, *What's going on? Did I say something funny?* I can't say that I could see anything humorous about my question. Seeing my dream girl grin and point toward my face made me think of an explanation. I turned away and touched my upper lip on the left side of my mouth.... My hunch was confirmed: I had something moist streaming down my lip from my nose, only I hadn't felt it because my face was numb. If the floor would have opened up at that moment and swallowed me, I would have been eternally grateful. I was so embarrassed. I slumped back into my seat.

She allowed me a minute to collect myself. I walked up to the teacher's desk where Mrs. Pruett kept a box of Kleenex for students in need. When I returned to my seat, Cheryl simply turned toward me with that great smile and said, "I'm sorry, Jim. I'm busy Friday night." In my view, that was close enough to the familiar brush-off, "I gotta wash my hair tonight."

Now my face *and* my heart were broken.

Not long after recovering from my accident, my brother Dave and his wife, Dee, started to have marital difficulties. Considering how young they were, I wasn't surprised. I don't know all the reasons, but they simply did not have enough life experience under their belts to sustain them when things got tough. After four years together, they divorced. Dee moved out, and Dave and I became bachelor roommates. I washed my own clothes, paid bills, worked a job at the Dairy Queen cleaning fry vats and windows, went to school ... and wondered if there were good guys in the world who modeled what being a man was all about.

Most of the men in my life didn't have their acts together: drugs, alcohol, addictions, poor judgment—I'd seen it all. True, Mr. Freid, my sixth-grade homeroom teacher back at my old school—the one with the black belt and Chuck Norris as a friend—was a rare exception. But even Mr. Freid had basically accused me of lying and refused to take me at my word. I still held that as a disappointment.

God must have known the longing of my heart because a surprise was waiting for me in 1976 when I returned for my second year of high school football. Everyone was talking about the new coach, Paul Moro. A graduate of Long Beach State, Paul played linebacker and was selected to the collegiate All-American First Team along with notables like star quarterback Pat Haden. Pat led his University of Southern California team to three Rose Bowl contests and went on to play for the NFL's Los Angeles Rams.

Paul was a little undersized to pursue a professional football career and, instead, wanted to invest his life coaching high school football—and mentoring young men. We were the first team he coached. Strolling onto the field, I got the impression "Coach Mo" was a real tough, no-nonsense kind of guy. Fit, blond, and tan, with sunglasses and white sunscreen on his lips to block the sun, he commanded our attention—and got it.

Coach Mo and I immediately clicked. He became my first true mentor and got involved in the details of my life. As we got to know each other that first semester, Coach Mo and his wife, Joyce, reached out to me, inviting me to their house for dinner from time to time. They were so … *normal*. I'd forgotten what normal was, considering that the last time I'd experienced an intact family situation was when I was four. It felt good. Very good. Almost scary good. Brokenness I understood. "Normal" was just not in my vocabulary.

On the field, Coach Mo pushed me toward excellence. He'd say, "Jim, you need to be the leader. I want you to set the example. Be the first to finish the wind sprints and show the others how to hustle." I liked that. I appreciated the fact that Coach saw me as a natural leader. Talk about a real confidence builder. He knew how to bring the best out of me.

Not only was he a rock-solid man, I learned that Coach Mo was a man with deep moral convictions. Faith in God was a big part of his life. I'd never really met anyone like him before and wanted to understand how a burly linebacker could believe in something—in Someone—whom he couldn't see. When I said as much, Coach invited me to go with him and several others from our team to a football camp sponsored by the Fellowship of Christian Athletes.

I was curious to find out what faith and football had to do with each other. About fifty guys from several area schools loaded up in a parade of vans and headed to Point Loma College, an oceanfront college in San Diego. The days were structured around sharpening our football skills. For eight intense hours we worked on technique, conducted drills, scrimmaged, and listened to coaching instructors who gave us group and personal training.

At night, although exhausted and nursing our sore muscles, we were told to gather in a room to participate in something our leaders called "devotions." Most of us felt like collapsing in bed. I know I did. But we filed in anyway, grunting and groaning like trolls tromping home from a brutal day at the coal mines. We flopped down on the floor like beached whales as the meeting was called to order.

Somebody with a guitar and an overhead projector did his best to get fifty ruff-n-tumble guys to sing along. At first, few took the bait. We were a tough crowd, beefy linebackers and all. I mean, the level of testosterone in that room must have exceeded the recommended limits allowable by law. More than anything, we macho teens didn't want to appear too eager to sing along. Singing was something girls did. Rather than risk public ridicule from our peers, most half-sung, half-mumbled through the tunes.

But the room seemed to fade around me when the guest speaker, whose name I don't recall, started his talk. I hung onto every word as he described the emptiness he felt in his life: how in spite of his accomplishments, and regardless of what he had tried, nothing seemed adequate to fill the void in his soul. I felt as if he were speaking to me because I knew that feeling all too well.

I figured a large part of that emptiness had to do with my transient home life. I had no stability. My life had been nothing more than a fragmented series of events, or so it seemed. And yet, as this speaker talked about God's pursuit and His unconditional love, he began to untangle a mystery for me. I started to connect some of the dots and see glimpses of God's love at work throughout my life. For instance, it was no accident that God had brought people of faith like Coach Mo into my life.

Sitting on the floor, listening and yet reflecting, I remembered Grandpa Hope had described Mom feeling that there was something missing in her life too. And how, when given the chance, she invited God into her heart. She was with God, according to Grandpa. That memory reminded me of the clouds forming a stairway to heaven in the sky at Mom's graveside service, and, for the first time, I made a connection. Was God saying Mom had taken a step of faith that I, too, would one day take? Maybe.

I also thought about how I felt God's presence when I cried out to Him sitting on the sand hill in fourth grade and how God had spared me from being shot by Wild Bill or being killed by a fastball. Considering my path in light of what the speaker was saying, I got the distinct impression that God was pursuing me. He had never given up on me. All of those years I had been on a spiritual quest, but I hadn't recognized it for what it was.

The speaker finished his comments by reading a verse that says, "The thief comes only to steal and kill and destroy; I have come that they may have life, and have it to the full." That sounded good. Life to the full. No more emptiness. No more restlessness. No more wondering what would happen to me if I were to die. I knew right then that I wanted God to be a part of my life.

When he asked if anyone wanted to come to the front of the room to invite Jesus Christ into their life and have Him forgive their sin, I went forward. I could feel the eyes of the guys on me, but I didn't care. More than anything, I wanted peace within. Of course, the only prayer I knew was the one Hank the Tank taught us to pray at mealtimes: "Bless us, O Lord, for these thy gifts that we are about to receive from the hand of Christ our Lord, Amen." I was pretty sure this was different. Thankfully, one of the leaders put his arm around my shoulder and coached me through the biggest decision of my life.

In the days following my profession of faith, I sensed a change in my heart but I never experienced an epiphany. I didn't hear angelic music playing in my head, but still, I was different. Coach Mo noticed the change and was excited for me. Even though I had no clue what to do next, transformation was under way.

And that was good enough for me.

DON'T LET IT HURT

Here's a perfect example of how I had begun to change on a spiritual level. By the time my senior year rolled around, I was heavily invested in football, which had become really important to me. I worked hard to be the starting quarterback. I spent long hours on the practice field perfecting my performance, and I pushed myself to be at the top of my game.

Thanks to efforts from my coach, I received letters of intent from the University of Nevada, Las Vegas; Texas Christian University; and a couple of other big-time college campuses. As far as I was concerned, the sky was royal blue. Nothing but clear sailing for me. Maybe I'd take a scholarship to one of the colleges courting me and then go on to play pro ball. Why not?

About that time, my brother Mike, who'd played defensive tackle for the University of Nevada at Reno, came to watch me play. Frankly, he didn't like what he saw. I mean, I played strong. He was impressed, but he was concerned about my arrogant behavior. After the game, Mike said, "Jim, you know what? You're getting a big head about playing football. You're not the same guy you used to be." His words hit me like a bucket of ice water in the face. I felt blitzed.

Normally, I would have ignored a comment like that. I might have dismissed it as jealousy or whatever. Instead, I reflected on Mike's concern in light of my commitment to the Lord. Rather than disregard Mike's insight, I decided to pray. I said, "Lord, what does this mean? Has football become an obsession? Should I give it up?" I wrestled with Mike's assessment because I didn't want to have this ego thing going on. At the same time, I really loved the game and belonging to the team.

That's when I heard God speak. Not an audible voice, mind you. Rather, I had a sense, or maybe an impression, that continuing in the direction I was heading wouldn't be healthy. I began to entertain the unthinkable—maybe I should give up the game? And yet, since I was such a young believer, I wasn't sure God would ask me to do something so radical.

Did He really want me to give up football?

Two events cemented His answer for me. The first sign came when I separated my right shoulder on a fluke play. I had been hit by a defensive lineman when we were out of bounds—a hit that should never have happened. That injury took me out of play for a month, giving me plenty of time to gain some much-needed perspective. I came off the injured list just in time for our first league game. The feeling around town seemed to be, "Daly's back and we're gonna win."

Before the game I knelt down and prayed. I said, "Lord, if you don't want me to play big-time college football, break a bone today … but please don't let it hurt." You see, one of my early lessons as a young believer was that you've got to be careful what you pray—careful *and* specific. Big, general prayer requests leave too much room for interpretation. Instinctively, I must have known that I needed to be specific when I prayed about the matter of pain.

Rather than praying that God would break a bone but not let it hurt, I could have asked for something that didn't involve breaking a body part, like having it rain at halftime. I'm not typically a glutton for punishment. But so much was on the line—my entire career in football—that I guess I wanted there to be no wiggle room to explain away whether or not God did, in fact, answer my prayer.

In the third quarter of the game, one of our running backs was ejected for throwing a punch—the only time in my four years of playing high school football that a member of our team had been thrown out during a game. That was odd. The coach decided to bring in Parrish Robbins, a sophomore, to play fullback. We quickly huddled and I called the play—a straight, drop-back pass. I could tell by Parrish's eyes, wide as saucers, that he didn't know what to do. I told him to step to my right and hit anybody inside out.

The roar in the stadium reached a fevered pitch as we lined up for the second-down play. I took the snap, dropped back, and saw my receiver going deep. I waited for him to hit his mark downfield. Out of the corner of my eye, I noticed that the outside linebacker was charging toward me like a bull. Whether it was fear or a bad case of the jitters, Parrish didn't even touch him. He let out a "Whoah!" and then actually jumped out of the linebacker's way.

The guy creamed me.

I went down as he hit me underneath the shoulder, driving through the armpit. My first thought was that my separated shoulder injury was toast. As I pulled myself up from the turf, my right shoulder appeared to be fine, but something was wrong with my left arm. While it didn't hurt, I did feel a dull pressure. I reached under my shoulder pad and felt that my collarbone was broken. I could actually feel the points of the bone pushing up under the skin.

We huddled up again and I said, "Guys, I think God is answering my prayer."

That got a look from the team. They said, "What do you mean? Are we going to score a touchdown?"

I said, "No, I broke my collarbone."

More puzzled looks. Someone finally asked the obvious, "What kind of prayer is that?"

"I'll tell you later," I said, glancing toward the sideline. Evidently, the coach didn't notice how severely I'd been hit. Rather than make a scene, I sprinted off the field and told the team trainer that I thought I broke my collarbone. He sat me out for the third-down play. When we didn't get enough yardage for the first down, the head coach yelled over to me, "Daly! You gotta get in there and kick the ball," since I was also the team punter.

As I went to put on my helmet, I found that I couldn't raise my left arm hardly at all. It had been a few minutes so my left arm was kind of getting locked. Taking my position for the kick, I thought,

Boy, this better be a good snap. Fortunately, the snapper hit me right in the chest. I was able to catch the ball with one hand and make the kick. Even before the play downfield was finished, I walked off the field unable to continue.

I had my answer. I had broken a bone and it didn't hurt. That day was the last time I put on a uniform. Through that experience, I felt God as a father. It was as though He had whispered, "You know what, Jim, I appreciate that you stopped to ask Me which direction to go. I've answered your prayer." Isn't that amazing? That experience was a dramatic start to a lifelong pursuit of discovering God's agenda and putting it ahead of my own. Thankfully, it's the only time that broken bones were part of the discovery process—at least so far.

13

Finally Home

It would be difficult to top the craziness that characterized the first fifteen years of my home life. By the time I started my senior year in high school, I'd experienced just about every imaginable variation of home life as a child. I lived in a two-parent household, which, five years later, became a single-parent home led by Mom. With Hank the Tank, I experienced a stepfather running the home. I had a taste of foster care at the Reils'. I lived with my dad as the single parent, then shared a roof with my brother Dave and his wife. I also lived briefly with my unmarried sister, Dee Dee. Interestingly, I once counted and discovered that I'd lived in almost two dozen different houses or apartments along the way.

While moving around might not sound that unusual today, back then society was much more stable. Families stayed put. For better or worse, you had the same neighbors for years, even decades. On the positive side, families developed a network of friendships. You had a sense of belonging, of roots, of security.

While I had no idea what that feeling of continuity felt like, something inside of me longed for a place to call home. However, when I turned seventeen, I was out on my own. No parents. No contact with my siblings. Just me. My brother Dave and I had lived together as bachelors, but parted ways not long after he remarried. Let's just say that his new wife didn't warm to the idea of having "the kid brother around." I think she resented the fact that Dave insisted on taking me under his wing. When the tension reached a boiling point, I knew I needed to move on.

Thankfully, Joe and Ramona Campbell, the grandparents of my high school girlfriend, offered me a humble trailer, which was parked forty feet behind their home, under an oak tree. I was thrilled to have my "own" place to live.

The trailer was no more than 6' x 12' and was built by Joe years before. It was made out of wood with masonite exterior siding and an asphalt shingle roof. The inside featured dark pine paneling and shag orange carpet with a musty smell. I had one small window with a little drape over it. I had a space heater for cold nights, a bed, a small dresser, and that was about it. No phone. No refrigerator. No shower or running water. I went to the main house for those amenities.

But it was home.

Being around the Campbells was surprisingly comforting. I remember coming home late from football practice and sitting on the sofa with Ramona eating raisin toast. Together we'd snack and watch *The Tonight Show* starring Johnny Carson. You might say God was providing me with another glimpse of what "normal" family life felt like. When the program was over, she'd ask me about my day. We'd talk for a while, then I'd say "good night," brush my teeth, and go out to my trailer under the tree. Lying there in the dark, I'd think, *So, that's what a family is like.*

By the time I graduated from high school, I'd lived in twenty-three houses ... and one trailer. When I got the news that I'd earned a small scholarship for college, I thought things might start to turn around for me. And yet, I still kept my expectations low so I wouldn't be disappointed. The future felt like it could be promising. It had to be.

COLLEGE BOUND

In the fall of 1979, I moved into a dorm on the campus of Cal State San Bernardino to start a new chapter in life. I was accepted to other universities, but I chose this school because it was close to the Campbells'. Their expression of kindness to me the previous year was one of the most gracious acts I'd ever experienced.

Although I hoped that this change would bring good things, I got off to a rough start. The freshman year of college is tough for students under normal circumstances. I didn't have parents to talk with about my class selection. I didn't have a home to go to for the weekend. Without the security that a family and a home provide, I couldn't shake the feelings of loneliness even though I was surrounded by thousands of students.

Making matters worse, I rather innocently alienated my professor of philosophy that first semester who, in turn, made my life in class miserable. It all started when my incoming freshman counselor said that, with my grade-point average, I should consider taking an upper-level class, a 300-level philosophy course even though I was just a freshman. With a class size of twenty, the setting was intimate and encouraged student-teacher interaction. I was told I'd have a great time.

From the first day, it was clear that my professor was enamored with the Greek philosophers Aristotle, Plato, and Socrates. He waxed eloquently about the wisdom of their teachings, the brilliance of the Socratic method, and recommended their writings as the key for achieving self-knowledge. I honestly wasn't attempting to start a brawl when I slipped up my hand and asked, "What about the words of Jesus?"

With that simple question, the professor became unhinged. I mean, he totally unraveled right before our eyes. Red in the face, he barked, "There's no evidence that Jesus ever lived. Most *intelligent* people know the Bible is nothing more than a myth … a compilation of stories that human beings want to believe about a perfect man to make themselves feel better."

For the next several minutes he railed against Jesus and the Bible with vein-popping anger. When I pushed back and asked a follow-up question, he unleashed his wrath on me. I ended up having to drop the course after about five classes because he appeared to enjoy ripping into me. Interestingly, that heated exchange put me on a journey of spiritual discovery that semester. I started reading about Aristotle and Plato, since they were held in such high esteem.

Probably my biggest surprise was learning that the earliest surviving copy of the writings of Aristotle was dated around 1,400 years after he lived. For Plato, the earliest surviving copy of his material was dated around 1,200 years after he lived. My professor had no problem referencing what these philosophers taught as fact—even though the only copies of their works were dated more than a thousand years after the original documents.

By contrast, regarding my professor's assertion that there was no evidence that Jesus existed, I found that there are over 24,000 manuscripts of various parts of the New Testament written by eyewitnesses who lived during the time of Jesus. Many wrote down their personal accounts within seventy years of His death. And, the oldest document of the New Testament we have today is a fragment of the gospel of

John written just twenty-nine years from the original.

I felt as if I'd caught my philosophy teacher being intellectually dishonest. He was unwilling to admit that Jesus lived, despite all of the eyewitness accounts. In my view, Jesus passed the test of historicity, and that knowledge grabbed me intellectually. While I had given my heart to God at age fifteen at the Fellowship of Christian Athletes football camp, I now realized that Jesus actually was who He said He was, and that His claims were backed up by the rules for measuring writings of antiquity.

That insight cemented my earlier step of faith and opened my heart to a deeper relationship with God. And, at the same time, I had a new thought. With all of the books I had been reading on the ancient philosophers, why wasn't I reading the most important book of all, namely, the Bible? Convicted, I sometimes played hooky from my classes to read the Bible for hours at a time.

While my spiritual life was slowly maturing, my sophomore year was the pits. I felt lost. I remember going to the counseling center to talk with a counselor. In addition to the questions common to freshmen, such as, "What am I doing?" "Who am I?" "Where am I going?" "What's life all about?" I needed to deal with my mom's death, my dad's death, and my crazy, mixed-up family life. More than anything, I needed a good cry. A hug.

And a place to call home.

Being homeless in college was no small deal. After I broke up with my girlfriend, I didn't feel comfortable visiting the Campbells' and staying in the trailer. I didn't think that would be fair to my ex-girlfriend and her family. So, during my sophomore year while living on campus, I had to apply for special permission to stay through the Christmas holiday in my dorm room. I was politely informed that the college shut down the dormitories and I would need to leave. When I explained that I didn't have anywhere to go, they made an exception. I was permitted to stay—with the understanding that there'd be no heat.

While friends were enjoying Christmas dinner and exchanging gifts with family and loved ones, I sat on the edge of my bed snacking on food from the vending machines. The campus was a ghost town. Walking the deserted streets at night was eerie and only reinforced my feelings of incredible isolation and loneliness—especially against the backdrop of the Christmas season. About all I could do was pour out my heart to God.

Here I was, the kid from Compton … the little guy at the Reils' … trailer boy. I thought that my life was quickly shaping up to be meaningless. Part of me desperately longed to travel—maybe study abroad and experience other cultures, but I figured that would never happen. I wasn't a fatalist. On the contrary, I was, and am, a very optimistic person. But that Christmas, I hit rock bottom. I felt trapped, stuck in a rut with no help of getting out. Even after reading in the school catalog about a study program in Japan for seniors, I shook my head in unbelief.

How could I ever afford to do that?

I won't suggest that I heard an audible voice, but something stirred in my heart. It felt as though God were saying, "Jim, trust Me." Of course, the fact that I had no money appeared to be an insurmountable obstacle. Then again, I had a lot to learn about God's endless resources and His ability to provide a way when, humanly speaking, I couldn't see a solution.

During my junior year, I visited with Ramona, whom I hadn't seen for a while. Just like the old times, we sat on the sofa, ate raisin toast, and watched Johnny Carson. Between the commercial breaks, I mentioned the idea of studying in Japan as a senior. Without hesitation, she offered to loan me the $5,000 necessary. I was floored. I really did not ask for or expect her help. But she and Joe were kind toward me. God, working through these dear friends, had answered my prayer. I only wished I could have called my mother with the great news.

JAPAN WAS AH-SO GOOD

In 1982, I traveled to Tokyo to attend Waseda University, the Harvard of Japan. I was enrolled in their School of International Liberal Studies, also known as the Kokusaibu division and was assigned to live with a Japanese family who spoke very little English. The city of Tokyo is overwhelming in every way, even to the most seasoned traveler. With more than twelve million people, the city never sleeps. While I have many memories from that incredible experience, two are worth highlighting.

About three weeks into school, I remember sitting in my elementary Japanese language class. Our professor, Mr. Kobaiyashi, was a third-generation teacher who, like his grandfather and father before him, was writing his own English/Japanese dictionary. You might say he was a stickler for the correct usage of words. This particular day, he decided to use a new drill on us. Professor Kobaiyashi asked the class to construct a simple sentence in Japanese and express it aloud.

With three weeks of language training under our belts, none of us were very sharp. My classmates formed elementary sentences like, "See the dog run," or, "See the cat run," or, "See Spot run." Standing in the front of the class, Mr. Kobaiyashi would listen, correct their pronunciation or inflection, and then move on to the next student.

This particular day I had a severe headache. I thought it would be original if I translated the English sentence "Today, Teacher, I have a terrible headache" into Japanese. When my turn came, I proudly said, *"Kiyo wa sensei, otama gai itai desu!"* Mr. Kobaiyashi immediately started laughing. Turning his face from the class, he composed himself, and then turned back to begin drilling the other students. *What did I say that was so funny?* I thought.

I wanted to ask him after class, but in the Japanese educational system you just don't have a relationship with the teacher as you might in the United States. The teacher-student relationship is much more formal. The minute I got home that night, I told my Japanese home mother what I had said in class. She started cracking up too—her eyes were even tearing up. Again, I was at a loss. What was so humorous about having a headache? Noticing my puzzled look, she got the cat and flipped it over. She pointed between its legs and smiled. Evidently, in perfect Japanese, I had said, "Today, Teacher, my testicles hurt."

Understanding the nuances of the language, while important, wasn't the main lesson I learned while studying in Japan. Experiencing another culture and seeing things that were so different from my limited vantage point as an American, especially in the area of faith, was fascinating. Shintoism teaches that you have to pay money for a good name so when you die you get closer to the Creator. It saddened me that poor people would pool their money to buy a name for their deceased loved ones. It also seemed suspicious that you had to pay the priest to get the name.

Learning about Shintoism, Buddhism, and Hinduism, all of which are a big part of the Asian cultures, actually helped me to go deeper in my understanding of why I believe what I believe. Rather than feel tempted to explore one of these Eastern religions, I found myself hungry to study the Bible. I would start reading the Bible and look up at the clock only to realize hours had passed.

I set myself up on a reading schedule and literally read, read, read the Bible every available moment I could. I was like a human sponge absorbing all of the insight I could get. I took breaks to attend class or go to a meal, and then returned to my room to read some more. I longed to know this God who had His fingerprints all over my life—even through the most difficult times.

LENNY & PENNY

When I returned from Japan, I wrapped up a few remaining classes necessary to graduate. After graduation in 1984, I needed a place to stay after taking my first real job. I felt God impressing on my heart to call my mother's best friend, "Aunt Penny," the daughter of Grandma and Grandpa Hope. You may recall on the day of my mother's funeral, when Hank took a taxi leaving us orphaned and deserted, Dave called Penny to see if we could live with her. Penny's husband, Bill, was dying of cancer and, as much as she wanted to take us in, she really wasn't in a position to do so. Dave's second choice was to go to the Reils'. The rest is history.

This time, when I called Penny to reconnect after thirteen years, she was thrilled to have me live a couple of months with her and her new husband, Lenny Mitchell. I've always thought God seems to have a thing with names ... Lenny and Penny. Cute. Getting to know Lenny was a blast. I learned that he was a well-known saxophonist during the Big Band era, played with the Tommy Dorsey band, and was a part of creating more than a hundred albums.

Lenny had an exciting career in film and television, too. He was in the original *A Star Is Born* picture with Judy Garland, as the saxophonist. He played the trumpeter in Cecil B. DeMille's epic *The*

Ten Commandments. There's a key scene in that film that shows a hand blowing a horn, and Lenny told me a funny story about what it took to get that shot right for the film. It's one of those huge crowd scenes with thousands of people.

Lenny kept ripping out of his costume because it was too tight for him. Keep in mind that Lenny was a bodybuilder. Mr. DeMille would shout, "Okay, Mitchell, get your costume repaired. Take a ten-minute break." Lenny put his watch on to make sure he got back in time. The costume crew stitched him up while thousands of people were waiting for the shot.

Ten minutes later, Mr. DeMille called, "Action." One problem. Lenny forgot to take off his watch. When he put his horn to his lips to sound the trumpet, the director called, "Cut! Mitchell, take your wristwatch off!"

A number of years later, Lenny got a job as the saxophonist for the sixties hit music variety TV show *Shindig!* In spite of his professional successes, Lenny felt something was missing in his life. At the end of one of the *Shindig!* shows, he literally threw his arms up while the camera was panning the stage and said out loud, "God, there has to be more to life than this!" While his comment wasn't heard by the television audience, God was listening. Not long afterward, Lenny's hearing became impaired. He dropped out of performing music, gave his heart to the Lord, and became a music instrument repairman in East Los Angeles.

When Lenny committed his heart to God, he pursued studying the Bible with the same passion that made him a great musician. When I moved in with Lenny and Penny, Lenny was instrumental in cementing my faith in the Lord. He and I sat for three or four hours a day just to study the Bible together and pray. I've never seen someone with such deep convictions. Through Lenny, the Lord was getting a hold of my heart in a deeper way.

Living with Lenny was like enrolling in a crash course in biblical studies, an experience that helped me grow as a Christian young man. Lenny took it upon himself to talk to me about what it meant to be a man, and the importance of living as a person of integrity, honesty, honor, and faithfulness. I never saw these traits in my father. I had much to learn and, thankfully, Lenny was a patient mentor. He knew life was about learning and sometimes it takes time to get it. When it came to the topic of dating, Lenny challenged me to wait on God for the woman I'd one day marry. I wasn't sure how that worked, but I was about to find out.

THE CHAPEL OF LOVE

I was sitting at a Wednesday-night church service at Lake Arrowhead Christian Fellowship when the pastor stopped his preaching and walked right up to me in the middle of the service. He said, "I have a word from the Lord for you." Me? I looked over my shoulder to make sure he wasn't talking to someone else. "I believe God has your mate picked out for you," he said. "She's going to have a heart for the things of God. She'll be your crown."

I didn't know the pastor well. We weren't friends. I'm not sure if he even knew my name. We'd never talked about my dating life—or lack thereof, since I had stopped dating for some time. In the back of my mind I thought, *I can't come back to this church. It's obviously not a Bible-believing church. I don't think God still sends messages this way these days. Maybe this guy is one of those false prophets the Bible warns about.*

When he finished, the pastor moved on to two or three other

people with a message for them. I thought he was simply stating the obvious. I figured he targeted me since I was twenty-four and didn't have a wedding ring on. I was obviously the eligible bachelor type. I was uncomfortable with the experience and left that evening with no plans of ever returning to the church.

Just three days later on Saturday, I was the best man at the wedding of Dan, a friend I studied with in Japan, and his bride, Tina. Dan told me, "Tina's got a friend I think you'll like. You're both Christians. We think you guys will really hit it off." Evidently, their friend Jean was at the same place I was—neither of us dated. Instead, we were waiting on God. Dan and Tina made a point of introducing us before the night was through.

Shortly after the brief introduction, Jean needed to leave. With no thought of what the pastor had said a few nights earlier, I remember saying to a friend, "I think that's the woman I'm going to marry." Still, I didn't pursue dating her. In fact, it took Dan and Tina nine months to get us to agree to go out with them on a double date, an Amy Grant concert at Pacific Amphitheater in Costa Mesa. That night, as we later learned by comparing notes, we both knew that we were going to marry one another. Isn't that amazing? On August 24, 1986, about a month after I turned twenty-five, Jean and I were married.

While we got off to a wonderful start, married life wasn't always rosy. Marriage is hard work. Both of us had things in our past that threatened to derail us from staying together. One evening we were getting ready for bed and I stepped into the bathroom to brush my teeth. When I came out, Jean was sobbing.

I sat on the edge of the bed next to her and said, "What's up?" "I just don't think you should stay married to me," she replied. I knew she was wrestling with depression, as well as a lack of confidence that she'd be a good mother once we started having children.

Of course, I had the same kinds of questions of my own: whether or not I'd be a good dad since I didn't have a solid example to model.

I slipped my arm around her and said, "Jean, it seems to me that there are only two options for us, because divorce is not an option. We can do marriage one of two ways: happily or unhappily. With all of the stuff that's gone on in my life, I'd much rather do this happily."

That bedrock of commitment sparked a desire in us to get Christian counseling, which ultimately helped untangle the difficulties in our background that kept us from winning at our marriage. That was eighteen years ago. As a result of seeking a marriage counselor, our relationship today is stronger than ever. As of this writing, we've been married twenty years and I can say with certainty that God has blessed us in ways we never dreamed.

THE BOYS

One of the things I love about my wife is her incredible nurturing heart. I first noticed Jean's innate mothering flair in the way she related to animals. We had five indoor cats and four outdoor cats at one point because Jean would find strays or unwanted kitties who needed love. One cat in particular was partially paralyzed. We called her Little Kitty and loved her as if she were no different from the rest.

When we started discussing having kids, Jean wasn't sure that she was capable of being a good mother. I wanted to have kids, but didn't know if the timing was right. Again, I felt the Lord saying to me, "Jim, don't pressure Jean." About age thirty-eight, Jean had a change of heart. With the window of childbearing closing, and having completed her college course work in biology, she felt it was time. When she came to me and said she was ready to start, I was excited at the chance to be a dad.

Jean had a really long labor with our firstborn son, Trent—upward of twenty hours. When the nurses brought Trent into the birthing center, Jean was understandably exhausted. She needed to sleep. The nurses, however, were trying to make sure that Trent stayed with us that first day as much as possible—part of the bonding process.

I was so captivated by Trent that I literally held him in a rocking chair throughout the night. I never tired of gazing into his precious face or smelling his fresh newborn scent. I prayed over him, thanking the Lord for such a blessing. I asked God for the strength and wisdom to do a better job raising him than my dad did for us. I also prayed that the Lord would take away my fears—my apprehension because I didn't know how to be a dad.

Our second son, Troy, arrived on the scene almost two years later to the day. Both boys were August babies, but if Trent took his time in labor, Troy decided to get a running start. At first, Jean thought she was just having back pain. Like some women, she tended to go into denial when in labor. But at two o'clock in the morning, her water broke.

We lost no time jumping into the car. We strapped Trent in the car seat and I called my sister Dee Dee on the way and asked her to meet us at the hospital. I ran several red lights, fearful that Troy would be born in the front seat.

In the hospital parking lot, Dee Dee and I made a hurried hand-off with Trent, our two-year-old. That done, I raced into the lobby and to the evening nurse's window. Banging on the glass, I called out, "My wife's going to have a baby right now." A woman approached and told me to calm down. She was really taking her time and I was annoyed.

Thankfully, a nurse wheeled Jean in as I dealt with the mountain of paperwork. Moments later, somebody came running out of the birthing room and said, "Mister, if you want to see your baby being born, you'd better get in there." I walked into the room as Troy was being born. They cut the umbilical cord and then the catch nurse took Troy's vital signs at a workstation.

Behind me, I overheard some murmuring from the nurses who had gathered around our baby boy. When I went over to look at Troy, I was told his color was not quite right. When the doctor finished with Jean, he turned and looked at Troy. Within a minute, they whisked him out. Evidently, Troy had ingested a lot of fluid and his lungs were full.

He was taken into the neonatal intensive care unit where he was put on an IV drip. A series of X-rays were taken. For the first forty-eight hours, that poor little guy was poked and pricked and tested to identify why his vital signs were so low. We didn't see him for twenty-four hours, which caused us a great deal of stress. His welcome to the world was very different from Trent's, whom I cuddled in the rocking chair all night. Troy remained on oxygen around the clock for four months to help dry out his lungs. Happily, he turned out to be a suitable match for Trent's boundless energy.

For the last few years, just about every morning, Troy comes into our bedroom at four o'clock to snuggle with us. Troy is one of the cutest little boys on the planet, and Jean and I have to remember that this routine won't last long. When he climbs into our bed, he slips under the covers right next to me and does this little wiggle as he gets cozy. I'll wake up as he settles in and hear his little voice say, "I love you, Daddy." It's the best feeling in the world … and it reminds me that I'm finally home.

14

Who Would Have Thunk It?

My first big job after college was working in the paper industry. I eventually worked for a division of International Paper, a global giant in the field of paper and packaging products. I was in sales and found myself on a fast track climbing the corporate ladder—not that that was a goal of mine. After a relatively short time on the team, the plant manager took me to lunch at a fancy French restaurant in Berkeley, California, where he offered me a top position with a six-figure salary. I was given several days to consider my decision, which, on the surface, seemed to be a no-brainer.

As a newly married man, things were looking up.

Little did I know that a phone call from an old buddy, who was working with Dr. James Dobson and Focus on the Family, would change my life. He asked me if I would be interested in working in the nonprofit arena, specifically with Focus on the Family's mission to strengthen marriage and families. I had to make a quick decision about my pending promotion at International Paper, and so I took the next plane to Los Angeles for an interview.

Jean and I were big fans of the Focus on the Family broadcast and appreciated Dr. Dobson's insights, so we were somewhat familiar with their mission already. After a day of intense meetings, I was offered a position for one-third of what I was about to make in the paper business. Clearly, money would not be the reason to take this job. Once again, God whispered and, thankfully, my wife and I listened. The decision to work at Focus on the Family placed us on one of the most exciting adventures we could have dreamed of.

My first assignment at Focus on the Family was serving as assistant to the president, Dr. James Dobson. My job was to meet with donors of the ministry around the country to personally thank them for their support and give them an update on the various projects we were undertaking. This was an easy task considering how much I respected the life and work of Dr. Dobson. I have never been around a more gifted individual than Dr. Dobson. He has a keen intellect, loves and is a champion of children of all ages, has incredible integrity, and is deeply committed to his faith in Jesus Christ. Working for him has made my life so much richer.

One of my best experiences was a trip to New York where I met with several players on the Buffalo Bills football team. I had breakfast with free safety Mark Kelso, tight end Pete Metzelaars, and quarterback Frank Reich. I had a great time talking with them about the challenges of playing in the NFL and balancing family life, and thanking them for their support.

Then, for lunch, I was scheduled to meet with a couple who had supported the ministry for a number of years. I called and offered to stop by and pick up sandwiches from a local deli. With lunch in hand, I started out to find their home in a modest neighborhood. As I pulled up, I noticed a ramp leading up to the door. As it turned out, both the husband and wife had been schoolteachers, but several years prior the husband had been in a motorcycle accident and was now confined to a wheelchair.

Over lunch they told us about how they appreciated the work of Focus on the Family and wanted to increase their giving. Up to that point, they had not received any insurance settlement from the accident and gave from what the woman made as a schoolteacher. For me, the day was a picture of how God has wonderful people from all walks of life supporting us. Some are well-known people like the football players, while others are the unsung heroes simply living their lives faithfully and, to the best of their ability, giving to help others.

In 1992, Focus on the Family launched an international division. Because of my studies in Japan, Peb Jackson, then senior vice president over public affairs, felt it would be good to have me assist him, along with a couple of other colleagues, in establishing the new international effort. Dr. Dobson was very concerned about falling into the trap of being too much the ugly American in our work outside of the United States. He wasn't sure the content we created for families would be relevant for our friends overseas and would often remind us not to "push" our way into a country. We were there to serve *if* our resources were a fit.

Peb was a genius at laying out the right approach for the work of the international division. "Only go where local folks have invited us to come and join them," he said. Our first task was to follow up with people who contacted us from places such as South Africa, Australia, New Zealand, Europe, Japan, Korea, Malaysia, and China.

My first exploratory trip to Africa was unforgettable. The people we met were so warm and welcoming. Of particular significance was a lunch with Dr. Lillian Wahome, who was trained in psychology from Kenyatta University in Nairobi, Kenya, and was very familiar with Focus on the Family. As we sat for lunch, I said, "Lillian, do you think our message will resonate with folks in Africa and around the world?"

With a wry smile, she said, "It's just like Americans to think you invented families, because you invent everything! But, if you talk to people about keeping their marriages together and raising healthy kids, you will be relevant in every culture because every culture deals with these issues." She gave us the confirmation we were looking for and her assessment has proven to be true. We now broadcast in over 150 countries and work with dozens of partners around the world.

In 1996, I was promoted to vice president of our international division and, shortly thereafter, became vice president of marketing, concurrently with the international role. I was wearing two hats and working hard. Jean was finishing up her degree in biology/chemistry, and I was completing my masters of business administration. Our household was as busy as a beehive even though the boys hadn't been born yet.

During those years I was struck by the fact that Focus on the Family had an extraordinary amount of great content on a wide range of family-oriented subjects. My challenge was to make families aware of this content. From there, I was promoted into a new role as group vice president and, soon after, became the chief operations officer under Focus on the Family's then-president, Don Hodel, a great man of faith who was the secretary of interior and energy under President Ronald Reagan. Working with Don was a highlight. He's such a gifted person, a man I respect deeply.

He exemplified what it means to be a servant leader and was indispensable in assisting Dr. Dobson as he began the journey transitioning from day-to-day management of Focus on the Family to concentrating on the creative aspect of his work. I was stunned, then, when I learned that Don was stepping down as president of the ministry. I was at a loss for words when Don approached me about filling the role of president.

YOU'VE GOT THE WRONG GUY

In the summer of 2004, Don took me aside and said, "You know, Jim, I've given this a lot of thought and I've talked with members of the board. We think that you just might be the guy to lead Focus once I step down. Let's see what the Lord does." There was no way this was going to go anywhere, I thought. I mean, I was the guy with no family tree—no grandparents, aunts, uncles, or cousins—and they think I'm the right person to lead a ministry to strengthen families? I don't recall even mentioning the idea to Jean. I do remember saying to the Lord, "Whatever you want to do, that's fine with me. But I just want to continue moving forward in my role serving the best way I know how."

That fall, Don came back to me and said, "Jim, both the board and Dr. Dobson are definitely serious about handing the leadership of the ministry to you. We think it's a great fit." At that point I thought I'd better talk more seriously to Jean about this and we needed to pray.

I came home after work and found Jean doing the dishes at the sink. I'll never forget her reaction when I broke the news to her. She stopped loading the dishes into the dishwasher and said, "Who would have thunk it?" Without skipping a beat, she added a humorous touch by saying, "Can you take out the garbage now?" She has a way of keeping my feet on the ground.

That evening we prayed about what this promotion would mean, especially since at that point we had the two boys to consider. Thankfully, Dr. Dobson shared our concern. He said, "Listen, Jim, your number-one priority is those boys. We've got to make sure if we do this that they are not negatively impacted."

In January 2005, Don and his wife, Barbara, took a much-needed and well-deserved two-week vacation to Hawaii. I remember receiving a phone call from Don on January 10. He explained that he was thinking June would be the right time to announce the transition. The board would be meeting then and formalizing the promotion. He wanted to know if I was comfortable with that timing. "June would be great," I said.

I could almost hear Don smile across the miles when he said, "Well, if June is great, how about the February board meeting?" I felt my heart jump. "Don," I said, "that's like six weeks away!" He said, "Once we make this decision, we've got to just do it because people will start coming to you. Making the move sooner would be cleaner." The rest was history.

On the night before the official "investiture" ceremony in late February, I was restless. I never sought the office of president and I was being asked to fill some rather large shoes. The board wisely divided the responsibilities between the future radio voice and the administrative duties, concluding that it would be difficult to find someone who could juggle both. My primary role would be on the administrative side of the organization. I don't know how Dr. Dobson carried such a heavy load for more than two decades.

You can imagine the doubts I felt when faced with the reality of this new opportunity. Did I have what it took to do the job? Certainly there was nothing in my personal background to suggest I was capable of the position. I didn't come from generations of a strong Christian family tree. I was born into a troubled situation with two alcoholic parents and a father who loved to gamble. My parents' marriage ended in divorce. Why would Dr. Dobson and the board think I could handle so much responsibility?

I remembered Dr. Dobson talking about his grandfather who prayed for him every day even before he was born. Dr. Dobson's father had a remarkable prayer life, too. He was known as the guy who wore out the toes of his shoes before the soles because he was on his knees praying so much. Talk about a rich heritage. I couldn't remember a time when my father prayed.

Dr. Dobson's mother also played an incredible role in his life. He says that many of the parenting and discipline techniques he wrote about in *Dare to Discipline* and *The Strong-Willed Child* weren't from the University of Southern California's Child Development Department from where he graduated. Rather, they came from his mother and what he gleaned from her wisdom over the years, as well as what he'd learned from Scripture.

Humanly speaking, it seemed to me that the right guy for the job should have a similar background. While my own mother did the best she could in raising us, she didn't know God until the end of her life and, therefore, wasn't incorporating the wealth of knowledge that comes from the Bible in her parenting. Yet, she did convey the importance of honesty and treating people right.

With all of these observations churning away in my mind, sleep was difficult. About two o'clock in the morning, I lay in bed and thought, *Lord, You have got the wrong guy. There's been a mistake. My story is on the other end of this continuum. I've experienced so much dysfunction and pain. What do I possibly have to offer?*

I remember the Lord answering me in the quiet of the night. He impressed an amazing message upon my heart: "Jim, get the focus off you because I own it all. This promotion is not about you. As long as you seek Me, I'm in it all. I'll use what was healthy and unhealthy in your life in ways you cannot imagine. Trust Me." That was a profound night for me. And I can honestly say that since then I've felt His presence every step of the way on this exciting journey.

Allow me to offer one other thought. While working on this book, I traveled to Costa Rica to visit the Focus office in the capital city, San Jose. Someone on that trip talking to a large group observed, "The Bible is honest about its heroes. More often than not, it's the brokenhearted people that God uses." There was something in his statement that resonated with me. I'm not suggesting that I'm a hero—rather, that a broken heart is vital to God's work in our lives. You and I can grow and experience good things from God even when we encounter adversity and pain if we are honest about our brokenness.

On my way back from that trip, as I reflected on this unexpected turn of events in my life, I was struck by something I had read in the Bible. Time and again, God uses the foolish things of this world to confound the wise. Here's the nugget in my view. In spite of how desperate one's circumstances are, God is still in the business of healing our brokenness and, like a gifted surgeon, He takes the pieces of our lives and makes us whole once again.

I am convinced that no matter how torn up the road has already been, or how pothole-infested the road may look ahead, nothing—*nothing*—is impossible for God. In the words of Jesus, "With man this is impossible, but with God all things are possible" (Matthew 19:26).

I know. I'm living proof.

15

Reflections on Faith and Family

I have a confession to make.

There are a host of "life lessons" that I could offer to you based upon my journey: living with Dad and Mom, their divorce, Mom's remarriage, her death, Hank's leaving, becoming an orphan, living with the Reils, reuniting with Dad, his death, and my coming to faith thanks to the role of a godly mentor in my life. So much could be said.

However, I'm not entirely comfortable giving advice, primarily because I see myself as a fellow traveler, not an "expert" on family life. My hesitation comes from the recognition that my story is just that—my story. The details are different from yours. I don't want to put God into a box by suggesting that He will work the same way in your life as He has in mine. What I *can* say with certainty is that *God is near to those who hurt.* As King David, who had his share of distress, wrote in the Psalms, "The LORD is close to the brokenhearted and saves those who are crushed in spirit" (34:18).

Being broken is very real to me. I think it's a good state for the human heart to be in—at least for a season. I've found that when I am broken, I can finally understand how totally dependent I am on

God. Sometimes I wonder whether we make a mistake when we try to save others or ourselves from experiencing brokenness—as if having a broken spirit was like having the plague. Our culture is bent on experiencing "happiness" and being "pain-free" no matter what the cost. In fact, if the truth were known, billions of dollars are spent annually just medicating pain in our society.

Certainly it's tempting to mask our pain—whether physical, relational, emotional, or spiritual—through distractions: entertainment, work, and sports. Pain hurts, and who wants that? Yet, in spite of our best efforts to avoid brokenness, for many people, it seems to be a prerequisite for coming to a relationship with God. I know that was the case for me.

What's more, the purpose of pain is often to develop our character, yet we run from it because pain is the gift that nobody wants. I believe that we rarely understand or perhaps overlook the benefits that pain can bring, not the least of which are the qualities of patience, obedience, and dependence on God.

Which is why I've set aside the airbrush. I've wanted to be open with you about the failures, shortcomings, and trials I've encountered as well as the amazing way God redeemed my trail of brokenness. Truly, He has fashioned the splintered pieces of my life into a remarkable mosaic. It is my prayer, then, that you come away from my story with a picture of hope ... even when your circumstances look bleak. As Paul, another follower of Jesus, wrote, "And we know that in all things God works for the good of those who love him" (Romans 8:28).

That said, before passing along a few observations about faith and family, let me be clear about one other thing: I didn't relate the details of my story to elicit sympathy. I know I'm not the only person who has lived and suffered under the same roof with alcoholic parents—nor will I be the last. Our mailbag at Focus on the Family yields letters every day from those whose stories are just as compelling as mine—if not more so. Stories where the sting of hurt and feelings of betrayal run deep, and where hope has run dry.

Every time I read one of those letters, I want to pick up the phone and say, "I understand a little of what you may be feeling." I want to remind those who are living in desperate circumstances that their file hasn't blown off God's desk. Their marriages may be on the rocks, their kids may be out of control, but He still knows where they live. He cares for them in spite of what they may think at the moment.

God has both the power to quiet our storms and the ability to give our lives new meaning and purpose. Again, those are not empty words. I've lived them and know that nothing is impossible for God. As the prophet Jeremiah wrote, "I am the LORD, the God of all mankind. Is anything too hard for me?" (32:27).

I've had several decades to process the events of my life, and believe there are a few nuggets of truth you may find beneficial. Probably a good place to start is by sharing an important observation that I've only recently grasped: When I was born, I had no control over who my parents would be or over the choices they'd make. In other words, *I'm not responsible for the behavior of my parents.*

I could have been born into a home where my parents were wealthy or poor. My dad and mom could have been the king and queen of some faraway land. Dad could have been the governor of California, or a window washer in New York City. It was liberating when I realized that my parents were who they were and I had nothing to do with their lot in life. I wasn't even born when they chose to turn to alcohol for comfort.

What's more, I had no control over what occurred in my parents' history. I had nothing to do with the influences, the friends, the circumstances, or the choices that shaped them into the mother and father they became. Their ideas of parenting and discipline, spending and saving, fidelity and integrity, financial management and debt, were all shaped long before I arrived on the scene.

That's profound. Why?

Once again, *I'm not responsible for the behavior of my parents.* I know this now as an adult. When I was young, however, such insight flew way over my head as it typically does for children. Far too many of the problems we struggle with as adults can be traced back to the thought that we were somehow responsible for the actions of our parents. If they divorced, we tend to blame ourselves. If they drank to excess, we think we must have done something to cause them to medicate with alcohol.

Nothing could be further from the truth.

When I say that I am not responsible for my parents' behavior, that's not to say that I'm unaffected by their choices. I was … and I am. At the same time, as I've said, God owns it all. While I may not understand what I experienced as a result of how my parents acted, He knows what's going on and He cares. Nothing that happened in my life took Him by surprise.

Put another way, to paraphrase one of my favorite verses in the Bible: Right now we see through the glass dimly. We see in part. We know in part. But we press on because one day all will become clear (1 Corinthians 13:12). I don't know the big picture. I don't have all of the facts. God is at work—for good—even when I cannot make sense out of life's circumstances. If I fail to grasp this, it's easy for me to think of myself as a *victim* of what my parents did instead of a *vessel* loved by God.

My desire is to be God's vessel, to be used by Him as He sees fit. God allowed me to grow up in a home where my dad was betting the farm on the ponies and addicted to the bottle, as well as a household where my mother was a single-parent recovering alcoholic struggling to raise five kids. Why? I can't say for sure. Meanwhile, I've decided to resist the temptation to play the part of a victim and, instead, seek to be His vessel.

When I say vessel, I mean someone who chooses to allow God to use their pain for His glory, for His purposes, for what He knows is best. Will I ever be a "perfect" vessel? No, not even close. This side of heaven the warts and wrinkles of life are part of the experience. But, with His help I can become more like Him.

PROMISES, PROMISES

One of the more poignant examples of the pain I felt as a result of my dad's poor choices was the day he promised to bring me a baseball mitt and didn't follow through. His failure has had a profound impact on me. Yes, I was saddened and hurt by his choice. I wish my memories of that exchange had a happy ending. I'd like to think that my dad had a perfectly good reason for failing to keep such a big promise to his seven-year-old son.

But he didn't.

On a positive note, his failure taught me, now that I'm a dad, to be extra careful with the promises I make to the boys. Allow me a personal example. Several months ago I was feeling a great deal of pressure. Things at the office were intense. The ministry was going through a restructuring to better serve our constituents. The changes were needed but sometimes tricky to implement without stepping on toes during the shuffle.

Meanwhile, Jean and I were moving across town to give the boys a little more leg room to climb trees and play in the dirt. With the sale of one home, the purchase of another, packing fifteen years of stuff, not to mention the responsibilities at work, I was feeling a lot of stress. Not to make excuses, but living out of boxes and eating fast food off paper plates, while trying to juggle the rest of life, shortened my fuse day by day.

Conditions were right for the perfect storm, and it hit.

In meltdown moments like these, I confess I can lose my cool as fast as the next guy—especially when the kids go haywire. Jean is such a gift. She privately and lovingly pointed out that my barking at the kids wasn't the best way to deal with their misbehavior. She was right. If I wasn't careful, my words and my tone could pound away on my kids with the same damaging forcefulness as the ball-peen hammer my father used that night at the "hammer house." Bellowing out orders, demanding obedience, and speaking in strident tones can just as easily wound the spirit of my children as the rants of a raving drunk.

By God's grace, I decided the hammering would stop here with me. Since my tone was clearly affecting Trent, our five-year-old, I sat with him in his bedroom and said, "Trent, I love you and I want to make you a promise."

That got his attention.

You see, the boys and I had talked on a previous occasion about the topic of promise keeping. I've pointed them to what Jesus said in Matthew 5:37: "Simply let your 'Yes' be 'Yes,' and your 'No,' 'No.'" In other words, I explained, we're supposed to stand by our promises; we're to say what we mean and mean what we say. While they don't know about the story of my dad's failure to keep his promise, my boys knew by my direct look and tone of voice that making a *promise* was a big deal.

I asked, "Trenton, are you ready?" He nodded. "My promise, Trent, is that I'm not going to speak with anger toward you. It's a tough promise to make and I know I'll feel angry in spite of my efforts to stick to that promise. So, here's the deal. When I start to get angry, I want you to hold me accountable and remind me of my promise. Will you?"

He thought about that for a moment, and then said, "Sure, Dad." Of course, as part of our little talk, I walked through the difference between being *stern* and being *angry*, but committing to throttle my anger was an attempt to connect with him and build trust between us. I believe it helped him grasp the importance of making, and keeping, a promise.

Sometime later, Trent was giving his mother a difficult time. Frankly, the infraction was probably some silly thing that boys find funny but adults find annoying. I took him aside to the living room and said, "Trent, I need you to make a promise to me. I need you to promise that you'll treat Mommy better today when she speaks to you, okay?"

There was an extended silence as Trent considered the commitment he was being asked to make. After a moment, he looked at me and said, "Okay, Dad. I'll make you that promise." Remembering stories like these gives me hope when I begin to doubt myself and wonder how anything good could possibly come from the kind of messed-up childhood I experienced.

I've been keeping a beautiful, leather-bound journal for each of my boys. My first entry predated their births. I plan to give them their personal journal when they turn sixteen. Not only have I written thoughts and observations about their unique lives, I've included maps from all over the world where I've traveled, and taped in money from foreign countries. Photos from their early life and, most importantly, observations about their spiritual journey round out the journal.

For example, in an entry dated March 26, 2006, in Trent's book, I recorded a touching moment when Trent, Troy, and I were kicking a beach ball around in a large, darkened room. Troy, who was three at the time, announced, "Daddy, I'm afraid of the dark." Without hesitation, five-year-old Trent put his arm around his younger brother and said, "Just get closer to God, Troy, and you won't be afraid of the dark."

The tenderness of Trent's heart as well as his love of God displayed in that precious exchange are further evidence that God's Spirit is restoring my past. He is redeeming those days of brokenness for His purposes right now as well as for the benefit of generations to come.

LET 'EM EAT CAKE

You and I have a choice to make and a message to send. We can repeat the mistakes made by our parents or we can take the best of what we've learned from them, reject the baggage, and choose to set a new course for ourselves and for our families. Each day the decisions you and I make can communicate to those we love that there's nothing we'd rather do than to *be there* for them.

That's so important for me, as a dad, to remember. I'll admit it's easy to slip into the role of the House Disciplinarian—you know, Keeper of the Peace, and Enforcer of the Rules. It's much more difficult for a tapped-out parent to dream up hands-on, creative ways to encourage horseplay and laughter in the home. Yet, like rain and sunshine, both discipline and play are needed for our kids to thrive and to know that we're crazy about them.

As I learned from my mother, laughter is one of the best ways of communicating love, affection, and nurturing a sense of well-being. She found endless ways of lifting our spirits in spite of our circumstances. Thanks to her easygoing example, I've learned to take life as it comes. I really don't stress out about things. In fact, I usually find humor to be good medicine for the soul.

Speaking of creating a festive mood in the home, I've heard of a family that every Friday evening conducts what they call "Barbarian Night." Typically, something really messy is served—like spaghetti and meatballs with plenty of sauce. The plates, silverware, and napkins are locked away. Everyone, including Mom and Dad, must eat barbarian-style: that's *fingers only* and right off of the plastic tablecloth.

Their kids absolutely love it. The laughter and downright ridiculous memories created by that weekly mess far outweigh the extra cleanup involved. Maybe an idea like that appeals to you. Then again, you might opt for something less messy, like "Upside-down Day" where dinner and breakfast trade places. I know that Jean and I want to do whatever we can to make our house a home where there's no shortage of good times, surprises, and laughter.

For those of us with children, I really believe that *now* is the time to start filling the memory banks of our kids with generous deposits of fun, love, and screams of joy. And, whether or not you have kids, consider the youth in your neighborhood who may not have a mom or dad. Maybe find a creative way to put a smile on their face too.

I think I might just stop by the store tonight in time for dinner to pick up some spaghetti and meatballs ... and serve them barbarian-style.

The boys will be thrilled!

GOD IS STILL IN CONTROL

There are a number of people in my life whom I could harbor tremendous bitterness toward, including my dad, Hank, and Mr. Reil. However, if I were to take what they did to me and drag it around like a ball and chain of resentment, guess who would still be in jail? Me. But, as I forgive them and when I don't attempt to "own" any of the destructive decisions or actions they made toward me, then I'm free. I don't have to live my life peering into the rearview mirror. In fact, I feel stronger when I release what was done to me. How? The space in my heart that had been preoccupied with anger or hurt can be set aside to make room for a joy and a peace that makes no sense whatsoever—because God promises that gift to the brokenhearted.

In addition to the fact that I am not responsible for the behavior of my parents, that I have a choice to be a victim or a vessel, that God owns it all, that keeping promises is so important, and making my home a place where love and laughter are celebrated, there's another key insight worth mentioning. You might think what I'm about to say is obvious. However, so often we lose sight of the simple truth that the world we live in is a broken place: *This life is not always the way God intended life to be.*

Far too often, we maintain expectations that are unrealistic for a fallen world. We forget that life is not perfect, and we become surprised, even hurt and disillusioned, when things don't work out perfectly. We're stunned when they don't work out at all. We make the mistake of buying into the concept that, if we do certain things, then God, like a cosmic genie, will bless us or make our situation more comfortable, painless, or acceptable as defined by our misguided standards.

Unfortunately, living in the United States tends to give us a distorted picture of life. Most of us *are* blessed with creature comforts. We have food to eat. Cars to drive. A roof over our heads. The idea that we must eliminate all pain is unrealistic, yet we continue to set the bar so high that we forget that life is tough for everyone at some point. Trials will come and we need clarity in order to face them.

The death of my mother, for instance, was one of the most difficult watershed moments in my life. Looking back, I wish someone had taken me aside, put their arm around me, and given me some honest perspective about the brokenness of this fallen world. Maybe something along these lines:

Jimmy, difficult things like the death of a parent happen to all of us. When we lose someone we love, the pain and despair we feel can be overwhelming at times. No matter what you encounter in life, remember that this life isn't the end. There's a new heaven and a new earth ahead awaiting you. That's what God promises. In the meantime, don't let sadness or bitterness consume you. If, when you wake up all you can do is put one foot in front of the other, then do that much. Trust God for the courage to face the new day and to lead the way.

At least that's what I, as a nine-year-old, needed to hear.

At times, I still need those words.

Perhaps, in times of trials, the most realistic thing you and I can do is to pray, "Lord, just help me to keep standing at the end of all this mess."

I was driving to work the other day reflecting on these thoughts when the song "Cry Out to Jesus," by the Christian music group Third Day, filled the speakers. I immediately resonated with the honesty and perspective of their lyrics. They sang:

When you're lonely, and it feels like
the whole world is falling on you.
You just reach out, you just cry out to Jesus.
Cry to Jesus

> To the widow who suffers from being alone
> Wipin' the tears from her eyes
> And for the children around who are without a home
> Say a prayer tonight
> There is hope for the hopeless, rest for the weary
> And love for the broken heart
> There is grace and forgiveness, mercy and healing
> He'll meet you wherever you are

Yes, life is hard. There is adversity. While seasons of smooth sailing do occur, more often than not, life feels like it's coming apart at the seams. Rather than hide our pain in order to preserve our pride, I believe it's time to take off our masks and be open with one another about the brokenness that we all experience. After all, isn't that the example Jesus Himself set for us as He faced the prospect of dying on the cross?

Hours before Jesus was betrayed by one of His close friends to be crucified, He was praying and weeping and baring His soul to God the Father. Jesus, who lived a sinless life was, in that moment, faced with the prospect of carrying our sins while being mocked and vilified by a horde of bloodthirsty Roman soldiers and hypocritical religious leaders. More than that, He knew when the sins of the world were placed upon His shoulders, God the Father would have to break fellowship with Him for a season.

No wonder Jesus asked the question: "My God, My God, why have you forsaken me?" (Mark 15:34).

You see, throughout His earthly life, Jesus experienced a daily intimacy with God that eclipses our ability to fathom. Given that Jesus was both fully God and fully man, the prospect of a separation from God would literally tear apart His heart. Believe it or not, this is encouraging to me. Why? Because of the suffering of Jesus, I can be 100 percent positive that He understands exactly what you and I feel when we reach the end of our rope.

If Jesus wasn't afraid to ask, "My God, why have You left me?" then you and I are free to be boldly honest and broken before a God who understands what we're experiencing. God isn't insecure. He won't run into the next room fuming about being misunderstood by His children. Rather, He promises to be a friend to the brokenhearted.

Incidentally, this was a big reason I agreed to share my life with you in this book. When we are transparent, we're in the best position to encourage one another to experience the richness and depth of the life God has for us. When we allow God to be involved in our pain, He has this uncanny ability to make sure none of it is wasted.

Acknowledgments

There are so many people who have helped me catch the meaning of the events that shaped my life. At the front of the line are my siblings, Mike, Dave, Dee Dee, and Kim, who each in their own way provided balance in my unbalanced world. Thank you. To Jean, my wife, who has stood with me for more than twenty years as my better half. You have taught me many things about kindness and love. And to my boys, Trent and Troy, although still young, you provide me lessons every day about life and the joy of being a father.

To my colleagues at Focus on the Family, you are the arms around so many hurting people each day. Well done! Dr. James Dobson, thank you for showing me what it means to be a man who stands up for those who cannot stand for themselves. You are a father to so many wounded sons and daughters.

To Cris Doornbos, Andrea Christian, and the entire team at David C. Cook, thank you for believing this story might help someone find meaning, hope, and salvation in Jesus Christ. Your faith and confidence in my story completes a journey that started so many years ago.

Bob DeMoss, my friend for twenty years, I want to thank you for the many hours trying to get the story just right. Your talent has made this book far better than it would have been. And to Greg Johnson, my agent, someone who knows the quiet pain of a wounded spirit, your help has been immeasurable.

To those who read the manuscript and provided invaluable insight into how the story flowed. These friends include Glenn and Natalie Williams, Dan and Susie Rieple, Gillian Sanguinetti, Becky Wilson, Dr. and Mrs. DeMoss, and Leticia DeMoss.

To the countless people who showed me kindness along the way.

Often it was someone with a word of encouragement or a hug. Especially, to my teachers and coaches that modeled what is good and true in those early years. Thank you for caring!

Finally, to the Lord who promised to be a father to the fatherless. Thank you for taking the broken pieces of my life and weaving them into an amazing picture of Your grace.

After pursuing careers in sales and international business, Jim Daly became a member of the Focus on the Family team in 1989. Since then he has risen through the organization until becoming president and CEO in 2005. He lives with his wife of twenty years, Jean, and their two sons, in Colorado Springs.

For more information about Focus on the Family's resources, visit www.Family.org, or call toll free: 1-800-A-FAMILY (800-232-6459).

STRONGER

Trading Brokenness for **Unbreakable Strength**

JIM DALY

WITH JAMES LUND

chapter excerpt

Chapter 1

When I Am Weak

This isn't how it works in the movies.

On a chilly Sunday morning in December, David Works and his family—his wife, Marie, and daughters Stephanie, Laurie, Rachel, and Grace—finish worshipping at New Life Church in Colorado Springs. As usual, they stay after the service to enjoy conversation with friends. On their way to the exit, David announces that lunch will be at a nearby hamburger restaurant called Good Times. The members of the Works family pull their coats tighter and step into a brisk breeze, shuffling carefully across patches of snow in the parking lot.

As the family approaches its white Toyota Sienna van, Laurie heads for the left-side sliding door.

"No, no—you have to sit in the back on the other side," Rachel says.

It is a Works family tradition that everyone keeps the same seat for both parts of a trip. Laurie rode to church in the rear right seat of the van, and Rachel intends to continue the custom.

"Okay, okay," Laurie says.

She walks around the back of the van, enters through the rightside sliding door, and takes her place in the back seat. Rachel, behind Laurie, pauses in front of the open right-side door to look for something in her purse.

That is when it starts.

David, sitting in the front passenger seat and in the process of buckling his seat belt, hears a sharp metallic sound. What was that?

He lets go of the seat belt and swivels his head to the right, surveying the parking lot. To his shock, a young man dressed in black stands just twenty yards away. He's pointing a large assault rifle at the Toyota.

What in the world?

Another shot rings out.

"Get down! Get down! There's a shooter out there! He's shooting at us!" David screams. He curls up in the van's footwell, trying to get as low as possible. He hears the sound of more gunshots mixed with his family's screams. The sound of the shots changes; David understands the shooter is on the move.

Wait a minute—where is Rachel?

She'd been just outside the van when the shooting started. David twists to look behind him. His sixteen-year-old daughter is still standing next to the Toyota, a dazed look on her face. Her burnt-orange T-shirt has a hole in it at the level of her lower-right rib cage.

"Rachel!" David cries.

"I think I've been shot," Rachel says. Suddenly, she collapses, falling backward onto the blacktop.

David jerks his door handle and jumps out. The instant his feet hit the ground, another volley of bullets whizz past his head. He turns; the gunman is no more than ten yards away, rifle pointed directly at him. Before he can move, David feels pain on his right side, just above his waist. He too falls to the pavement. The shots continue.

"Gracie, get down and play dead! He's still here!" David orders. His youngest daughter, eleven years old, had been moving from the backseat to help her sister.

The firing stops momentarily, then resumes, but the sound is more distant and muffled. David realizes the gunman has gone into the church.

David has been shot in the abdomen and groin. He stretches his arm in Rachel's direction, willing his body to move. His daughter needs her father—*her protector*—yet David can't even crawl. Through tears, he says, "I'm so sorry, honey. I can't reach you."

"That's okay, Daddy," Rachel whispers.[1]

On this horrifying, heartwrenching day, David Works would give anything to turn into a Hollywood action hero. If this were a movie, he would be Superman, leaping in front of his daughter and watching bullets bounce harmlessly off his chest. With his super strength, he would pick up the van and fly his family to safety, then return to catch the bad guy before he could hurt anyone else.

But this isn't a movie.

David Works has no super strength. He is lying in a church parking lot, weak, helpless, and bleeding, and watching the life ebb from his beloved daughter.

Panic Attacks

Let's leave this traumatic scene for the moment and visit the mother of a different family. Lori Mangrum is a pastor's wife. She and her husband, John, have two children. But Lori isn't thinking about her family right now. She's slumped in a chair at home. The curtains are drawn. For months, she hasn't slept or eaten well.

Lori grew up in a Christian home and learned to smile and appear joyful no matter what was going on around her. Like any family, she and her parents and siblings had their share of troubles, but Lori didn't want to burden her parents with her own fears and worries. She became the "sunshine" for her family, always working to cheer up others but rarely addressing her own emotional needs.

Years later, after marrying John, having kids, and moving to a new home, Lori started experiencing panic attacks. Without warning, feelings of terror overwhelmed her. She felt a crushing weight in her chest and became nauseous, dizzy, and disoriented. She thought she would die. The attacks increased to the point that Lori couldn't drive a car or go into a grocery store.

One day, after a series of tests, a physician explained to Lori that she had a benign heart condition that could cause some of the symptoms of panic attacks. *Finally!* Lori thought. *I knew they would find something!*

But the doctor wasn't finished.

"You have another problem," he said gently. "I believe this problem manifested itself because of some psychological problems. I want you to see a psychiatrist."

Lori couldn't believe it. *I don't have any stress,* she told herself, *and what stress I do have I handle better than many others!*

Now, sitting in the dark at home for week upon week, Lori is depressed. Friends have told her, "Pray harder, get yourself together, and stop this!" Yet she doesn't even have the energy to talk, eat, or take a shower. Lori is disgusted with herself. She would give anything to change her circumstances, but emotionally, she feels weak and helpless.[2]

Those Uncomfortable Feelings

You may never have faced a crazed gunman or dealt with debilitating depression, but I'm guessing that at some point in life—perhaps many times—you've experienced some of the same feelings that David Works and Lori Mangrum went through in the incidents described above.

Weak. Helpless. Useless. Vulnerable.

Some pretty uncomfortable feelings, right?

We all do our best to avoid situations that expose our failings and fragility. But whether it's a life-or-death crisis or the challenge of simply getting through another day, sooner or later we each confront the undesired sense of being powerless, worthless, feeble, disabled, and dependent on others.

And we don't like it.

Most of us, especially in America, grow up with the idea that we can shape our own destinies. This, after all, is the land of opportunity. This is a place where dreams come true. We see ourselves as rugged individualists, fully capable of taking control of our lives and rising to the top.

And the weak? "Those people" are not us. Most of us profess to have empathy for the struggling and more helpless members of our society. But many of us are also conditioned to feel, deep down, a certain amount of disdain for the unfortunate few. You're homeless? That's too bad—but maybe you need to work harder at finding a job. You're depressed? Yeah, I get discouraged sometimes too—but enough of feeling sorry for yourself; it's time to get yourself together.

Part of the problem is that the weak and helpless are all around us, and when we see others having problems, it reminds us that we're vulnerable too. Some of us cope by closing our eyes and shutting our ears to troubles. I will confess that this can be my attitude at times. But no matter how hard we try to ignore the trials of others, they rise to our attention like steam from a teapot. We think we've guarded our minds and hearts, and suddenly we're faced with:

- The distraught mother who watches her teenage son storm out of the house in anger, not knowing what to say or do and wondering when or if she'll see him again.
- The discouraged father of four who has lost his job, has been evicted from their home, and is so deeply in debt that he doesn't see a way out.

- The terrified little girl who is sexually molested by her "uncle" when Mom isn't home and is told to keep quiet about it "or else."
- The lonely wife who thought she was marrying a soul mate and is desperate because she can't get her husband to talk to her.
- The sullen fourth-grader who repeatedly gets teased and bullied by a sixth-grader on the way home from school.
- The worried single mom whose son is being recruited by a neighborhood gang.
- The shocked fifty-year-old who has just been diagnosed with terminal cancer.
- The young woman who feels paralyzed by depression and guilt over an abortion.
- The husband who can't forgive himself for an affair.
- The despairing grandmother who is watching her children and grandchildren destroy their lives with alcohol and drugs, yet doesn't know what to do about it.

It's hard enough to put aside the struggles and weaknesses of family, friends, coworkers, and neighbors. It's harder still when the hurting wife, husband, mother, father, little girl, young man, or grandmother is us.

Do you know what I'm talking about? Are there times when you feel utterly incapable of dealing with the skyscraper-sized obstacle in your path? When you wish you didn't feel more helpless than a bug on your back? When you wish you were Superman or Wonder Woman instead of plain old pint-sized "me"?

If so, I understand at least some of what you're experiencing. One of my earliest memories, from when I was four years old, is of a man suddenly bursting through our front door one night as my brothers and sisters and I were watching TV. The man looked like a monster. His eyes were puffy, red, and glassy. His face was unshaven. He carried an oak-handled, ball-peen hammer in one hand and a jug of Gallo burgundy wine in the other.

The half man, half monster was my father, and he was looking for my mother. When he realized she wasn't there, he roared, "This is what I'm going to do to your mother!" He swung the hammer and bashed a giant hole in the wall. I spent the rest of that night in my bedroom, cowering under a blanket, even after the police arrived and took my dad away.

Up to that point, I'd enjoyed a fairly typical childhood. I was more worried about missing favorite TV shows like *Batman* than whether I would make it to the age of five. But everything changed for me that night. Although I couldn't have put it into words at the time, I suddenly learned just how vulnerable and helpless I really was.

It was a pretty awful feeling.

The feeling grew worse when my parents got divorced, Mom remarried, and we moved to an apartment complex in Compton, California. One night soon after, someone was murdered ten feet away from my ground-floor bedroom window. The rumor was that the killer used a shotgun. Knowing that only four inches of stucco and drywall separated me from whatever was out there left me distinctly scared.

I felt exposed. Defenseless. *Weak.*

The final blow occurred the next year. I understood that my mom was sick. She seemed to get more and more tired and eventually stayed in bed all the time. My stepfather, Hank, was so overprotective that he wouldn't even let us kids talk to her. Weeks later, when my mom went to the hospital, I still just thought she was really sick. It never occurred to me that she might be dying. When my brother Mike told me that Mom was dead, I was shocked. I squeezed Mike's arm so hard that I left fingernail marks. In some strange way I felt that hanging onto Mike would keep me from losing my mother.

My dad was out of my life. My stepfather left the family the day of Mom's funeral and had no real interest in or relationship with my siblings and me. My mother was gone. I felt completely alone—and more helpless than ever.

How I wished it could be different. I wanted something then that I simply did not possess. I wanted *strength*.

A Different Kind of Strength

Most of us admire strength in its many forms. We all want to be strong. But the word *strong* conjures up a variety of meanings and images in our minds. For some, it means sheer physical power. We might think of bulging muscles and the ability to handle the next bad guy who crosses our path. For others, strength is about having the persistence to do what we set out to do—such as taking the lead on a difficult project at work or potty training our children. Some may think of strength of intellect— an ability to outsmart any person or problem. For still others, being strong means appearing immune to any irritations or challenges that threaten to disrupt daily life. Some like the idea of being emotionally detached, to embody a "James Bond" approach to life. Whatever comes up, we'll take care of it, and we'll do it with style.

Think of the figures portrayed so prominently in the media today: politicians such as our current president; technology gurus such as Bill Gates or Steve Jobs; athletes such as Peyton Manning or LeBron James; actors and actresses such as George Clooney or Nicole Kidman; media moguls such as Oprah Winfrey.

Each of these people possesses strengths that the public appreciates. It might be physical strength, emotional strength, talent, intellectual capacity, or influence, but the world admires these folks for what they have that the rest of us don't. They seem to have it together. They appear *strong*.

But I want to talk with you about an entirely different kind of strength. It's a quality of strength that David Works and Lori Mangrum discovered. It is so powerful that it overshadows every other kind of strength, like a Himalayan mountain towering over a molehill. It wasn't the strength that David and Lori were looking for in their moment of crisis, darkness, and greatest weakness. In some ways, it was the furthest thing from their minds. But it was exactly the strength they needed most.

I think it's just what the rest of us need too.

We're Going Through

In the instant after David Works was shot that December day in 2007, he realized he was in a situation that was beyond him. He didn't have the power or strength to control the events around him. He was helpless to protect himself or his family. So he turned to the only one left who did have the power and strength to change matters.

God, what's going on here? he thought. *This is crazy. We're supposed to be a missionary family getting ready to go around the world for You. What's this all about? It doesn't make any sense.*

David sensed an immediate answer. It wasn't audible, but it left a deep impression on him nevertheless: *We're going THROUGH. We're not going OVER or going AROUND this. We're going THROUGH.*

Most of us would be thrilled to receive a message from the Lord. Under the circumstances, however, that message wasn't what David wanted to hear.

David survived the attack on his life that morning. His daughter Rachel and his oldest daughter, eighteen-year-old Stephanie, did not. Stephanie was struck by a bullet while sitting in one of the van's middle seats. She died at the scene. Rachel died a few hours later at the same

Colorado Springs hospital where David was treated. The gunman was a twenty-four-year-old who had also killed two people earlier that day at another ministry facility. Inside New Life Church, he'd been shot dead by a security guard before he could claim any more victims.

As the father of two boys, I can only imagine the physical and emotional anguish that David and his family endured in the hours, days, and weeks that followed the shooting and loss of two precious daughters and sisters. I can also imagine that they would have been tempted to curse God for what occurred that day, even to turn away from Him for apparently not intervening when they needed Him most. But that's not what happened.

That first night, lying alone in a hospital bed, overwhelmed by shock and grief, David tried to make sense of the tragedy. He took it straight to God.

Lord, I don't understand You at all right now. I don't get it. How could we lose two kids in one day? You're not making any sense.

But somehow, I trust You in this situation. Obviously I don't have any better ideas. I'm not going anywhere. I will stick with You, Lord, because You have the words of eternal life. I need You tonight more than ever.

From that humble beginning, David found a strength he didn't know he had. After just nine days, he was discharged from the hospital. Gradually, and with persistent effort, he recovered from his physical wounds.

What is more incredible was David's emotional and spiritual recovery. At times the grief and despair overwhelmed him; at one point he was out of control, thrashing, wailing, and sobbing until his voice was hoarse. Yet he was able to attend his daughters' burial and memorial service, where he read the Twenty-third Psalm and thanked God for allowing him to heal quickly enough to be there. A few days after Christmas, he addressed a crowd of 350 people and talked about how, through the nightmare of the previous three weeks, God had never left his family.

Most amazing was that when the New Life pastor asked if David and his family would like to meet with the parents of the gunman, they took a day to think about it, then agreed. And when they met, there was no hesitation. David stretched his arms out and encircled another grieving father and mother in a long embrace, followed by the hugs from the rest of his family. Through tears, he and his family repeated, "It's okay. We forgive you."[3]

Lori Mangrum experienced her own amazing emotional and spiritual renewal. In the midst of her depression, she too turned to God. Though He seemed distant, she began reading Scripture with a new interest and curiosity. She read about the Lord's relationships with sinful men and women and saw how He loved them despite their weaknesses.

One afternoon, while driving home from a session with a therapist, Lori cried out to God, "I can't do this alone. It's too hard. If You're really there, then show me, and I will trust You!"

Lori sensed an answer in the stillness.

Trust Me first—then I will show you.

Starting with small steps, Lori began to relinquish control of her life to the Lord. She focused more on pleasing Him instead of everyone else. It helped her to say no to some requests—and to speak up when she felt upset, angry, hurt, or scared. She began sharing her fears and feelings with her husband. And when a panic attack did strike, she faced it head-on, reassuring herself that she didn't have to cooperate with what her body was trying to tell her.[4]

The grace and courage demonstrated by David Works and Lori Mangrum blows me away. Could I have faced and forgiven the parents of a man who murdered my children? Honestly, I don't know, and I don't want to find out. Could I take the brave steps to surrender to the Lord and allow Him to lift me out of a disabling depression? Again, I'm not sure, and I'd prefer not to take that test.

But am I attracted to what David and Lori have? You'd better believe it. Because what they have demonstrated is not simply physical, emotional, or intellectual strength. It's something far deeper, far more powerful, and far more lasting.

Something spiritual.

Something holy.

David and Lori took the worst that life could throw at them. Did it hurt? *Of course.* Did it bring them to their knees, both figuratively and literally? *Yes.* Did they find themselves utterly weak and helpless? *Absolutely.*

Yet somehow, through that weakness and their connection to a merciful God, David and Lori were transformed. They didn't just survive. They didn't just "get by."

They got *stronger.*

That's the kind of strength I want: a strength that never leaves, a strength that actually magnifies during the tough times, a strength that isn't dependent on me but resides in a power that can't be stopped.

How about you?

I don't presume to have all the answers to life. But I know who does, and I know who provides the greatest strength of all. It is a strength that I believe is found and forged *only* through weakness. It's what the apostle Paul meant in his message to the members of the fledgling Corinthian church: "For when I am weak, then I am strong" (2 Cor. 12:10).

Let's talk about it.

1. David and Marie Works, *Gone in a Heartbeat* (Carol Stream, IL: Tyndale House, 2009).

2. Lori Mangrum, "I Was Panic-Stricken," *Today's Christian Woman*, http://www.christianity-today.com/tcw/1997/sepoct/7w5050.html.

3. Works, *Gone in a Heartbeat.*

4. Mangrum, "I Was Panic-Stricken."

Praise for
mom energy

*"**Mom Energy** offers a great gift to moms everywhere—tools to help end our exhaustion! Ashley and Kathy offer real-life tips and strategies for developing self-replenishing energy and balance. Thanks, ladies!"*

— **Cindy Crawford**

*"**Mom Energy** is a must-read—not just for all moms, but for all women. This book will change not only your energy but your life."*

— **KaDee Strickland**, actress, ABC's hit series *Private Practice*

*"A superb book! **Mom Energy** combines cutting-edge science with common sense. Far surpassing the norm for 'how-to' books, Koff and Kaehler combine forces to deliver a book that truly integrates effective dietary and lifestyle programs for better health. I'd recommend it to any mom who is perpetually running on fumes; this book may be her ticket to revitalization."*

— **Gerard E. Mullin, M.D.**, associate professor of medicine, Johns Hopkins University School of Medicine and author of *The Inside Tract*

*"Read this book. I wish I had it when my girls were young . . . it's inspiring! Tune in to your **Mom Energy.**"*

— **Mariel Hemingway**, actress and author

*"I am so glad I read **Mom Energy** as a soon-to-be-mom! I encourage moms with children of all ages—and expectant moms, too—to pick up this book. Really, any woman will benefit, because what woman doesn't need more energy in her life? This book is the answer to all of your energy needs!"*

— **Emily Deschanel**, actress, FOX's hit series *Bones*

*"**Mom Energy** recognizes that health is all about balance. This book will help fuel our world's most precious resource—moms!"*

— **Rachel Lincoln Sarnoff**, executive director/CEO of Healthy Child Healthy World

*"**Mom Energy** is every mother's dream: a true time-saver, body-saver, and life-saver! Brava! From one especially grateful mom."*

— **Mayim Bialik, Ph.D.**, actress, CBS's hit series *The Big Bang Theory*

"As a working mother constantly on the go, I applaud Koff and Kaehler for providing timeless nutrition tips and fitness workouts that I can immediately incorporate into my daily routines."

— **Melissa Rivers**, host, author, and mom

mom energy

ALSO BY ASHLEY KOFF, R.D.

Recipes for IBS: Great-Tasting Recipes and
Tips Customized for Your Symptoms

ALSO BY KATHY KAEHLER

Books

Fit and Sexy For Life:
The Hormone-Free Plan for Staying Slim, Strong,
and Fabulous in Your Forties, Fifties, and Beyond

Kathy Kaehler's Celebrity Workouts:
How to Get a Hollywood Body in Just 30 Minutes a Day

Teenage Fitness: Get Fit, Look Good, and Feel Great!

Real-World Fitness: Fun and Innovative Ways to Help You
Sneak in Activity at Home, at Work, and with the Kids

Primetime Pregnancy: The Proven Program for Staying
in Shape Before and After Your Baby Is Born

Videos

Kathy Kaehler: Total Body Workout

Kathy Kaehler Basics: Total Fitness Workout

Kathy Kaehler Basics: Workout Class

Your Best Body: Target & Tone

The Kathy Kaehler Fitness System

mom energy

A SIMPLE PLAN TO LIVE FULLY CHARGED

From the Experts Who Coach
Hollywood's Most Celebrated Moms

ASHLEY KOFF, R.D.
KATHY KAEHLER

HAY HOUSE, INC.
Carlsbad, California • New York City
London • Sydney • Johannesburg
Vancouver • Hong Kong • New Delhi

Published and distributed in the United States by: Hay House, Inc.: www.hay house.com • *Published and distributed in Australia by:* Hay House Australia Pty. Ltd.: www.hayhouse.com.au • *Published and distributed in the United Kingdom by:* Hay House UK, Ltd.: www.hayhouse.co.uk • *Published and distributed in the Republic of South Africa by:* Hay House SA (Pty), Ltd.: www.hayhouse.co.za • *Distributed in Canada by:* Raincoast: www.raincoast.com • *Published in India by:* Hay House Publishers India: www.hayhouse.co.in

Cover design: Lisa Fyfe • *Interior design:* Charles McStravick

Library of Congress Cataloging-in-Publication Data

Koff, Ashley.
  Mom energy : a simple plan to live fully charged / Ashley Koff and Kathy Kaehler. -- 1st ed.
      p. cm.
  ISBN 978-1-4019-3151-3 (hardback) -- ISBN 978-1-4019-3153-7 (digital) 1. Women--Health and hygiene. 2. Physical fitness. 3. Motherhood. I. Kaehler, Kathy. II. Title.
  RA778.K72237 2011
  613'.04244--dc23
                              2011019362

Tradepaper ISBN: 978-1-4019-3152-0
Digital ISBN: 978-1-4019-3153-7

15 14 13 12   5 4 3 2
1st edition, September 2011
2nd edition, September 2012

Printed in the United States of America

TO MOTHERS

EVERYWHERE

In the 21st century the energy crisis is getting personal.
It's not only about the environment. Just ask any mom!
The most precious and scarcest resource of all is
"mom energy." We're committed to helping
women turn this energy crisis around—
one mom at a time.

— ASHLEY AND KATHY

CONTENTS

Solving the Real Energy Crisis of the 21st Century

mom (mäm): n. the woman for whom energy demands consistently exceed her reserves.

en–er–gy ('en-ər-jē): n. the strength and vitality required for life.

Mom En–er–gy: n. the solution to "mom depletion."

It's nearly midnight and you're still in the kitchen getting ready for tomorrow; in the back of your mind is the urge to log back on to the computer to deal with e-mails marked high-priority (!), a few RSVPs you've been avoiding (!!), and late bills (!!!). The house is finally quiet but you know that the morning alarm will ring soon enough. Too soon, in fact. If a genie were to emerge and grant you three wishes, they'd all be the same: more energy, more energy, more energy. (Okay, so maybe losing 15 pounds and your crow's-feet are also on that list, but we'll get to that.)

Never before has balancing the competing demands of workplace, home, and health been more grueling—or more essential. And, let's face it, we don't know any mother who isn't taking on more than she ever intended to when she said "I do" to having children. Every mom we know has more to do in a day than the time in which to do it.

From the very second you got pregnant, your baby took energy from you, and you've had to share that energy ever since. Now you're the CEO of a family that needs and relies on you, that expects you to be superhuman and somehow conjure the energy to do anything and everything. Your own expectations of yourself are even more rigorous and demanding because you really do want to be the EveryMom—the woman who conquers all with aplomb.

But a big part of you yearns for the magic potion that will infuse you with an eternal source of high, natural, and radiant energy. All year long you've been reading about the latest recovery idea for the economy, and you wonder, *Where's my recovery?*

Well, here's your stimulus package. And this one will last a lot longer than any getting doled out in Washington, D.C.

Two Women on a Mission

But before we lay out the details of our plan, let us tell you a little about ourselves. We've been working in the trenches of fitness and nutrition for years, pretty much our entire professional lives; and between us, we cover every angle of the mom-depletion phenomenon. We've worked with hundreds of women—celebrity and civilian alike—and we see the ravages of mom depletion every day. Clients and industry experts have long urged us to combine our wisdom to create a scientific and practical program that targets moms specifically. So this is just what we've done.

Ashley Koff, a registered dietitian and the founder of her own nutrition counseling and consulting company, brings smart nutrition ideas on turning energy zappers into energy sustainers to *Mom Energy*. Ashley was the expert dietitian behind *The Huffington Post Living's* "Total Energy Makeover with Ashley Koff RD," the CW's *Shedding for the Wedding*, and Lifetime's *Love Handles*. She's also the resident dietitian for ESPN's newest outlet—espnW—and a contributing editor for *Natural Health* magazine.

Three years ago, Ashley launched Ashley Koff Approved (AKA)—a service to audit foods, supplements, and beauty products and the services that incorporate them to determine if they deliver on being part of a healthy lifestyle. To date, she has audited more than 10,000 products and services to decide whether or not they will get the coveted tagline "AKA can't be bought, it's earned." Obviously, Ashley knows a thing or two about energy.

Kathy, the other half of our team, has been a household name in the fitness and health industry for longer than she'd like to admit. Not only was she a regular fitness correspondent on the *Today* show for 13 years and an inductee in the National Fitness Hall of Fame, but she's also worked with stars such as Julia Roberts, Michelle Pfeiffer, Cindy Crawford, Jennifer Aniston, Drew Barrymore, Claudia Schiffer, Kim Basinger, and Angie Harmon—many of whom were excited to let us share their secrets in this book. Oh, and did we mention that Kathy's got three rambunctious school-aged boys (two of whom are teenage twins)? So as a full-time mom and a full-time trainer, Kathy continues to shape the bodies and inspire the lives of millions around the world. And in *Mom Energy*, she shares her energy-enhancing fitness secrets and teaches you how to easily fit healthy activity into your already busy lives.

So suffice it to say, we've been tireless crusaders of health and well-being for a long time, and now we're here to help you get the energy you want by giving you straightforward and effective energy-optimizing techniques that you don't normally find elsewhere. So no, there are no secrets. It's not magic. And we are not genies who will simply give you your three energy wishes. We are realists—practical Midwesterners at the core. We believe in basic and doable, but we also believe in effort.

ENERGY AND HEALTH

Vis viva is Latin for "living force"—it's that internal part of us that makes us feel alive and energetic. And it may be the ultimate marker of optimal health. Poor energy levels don't just mean that you won't get everything done; they are also warning signs that your health has declined, that your body's systems aren't operating at their best.

The body is an energetic force—it's dynamic and can be viewed as a collection of intricate energy equations (don't worry, there won't be any math). If one of those equations isn't balanced, the whole system starts to falter. Like a crack in a window that changes the climate of the entire house. One of the chief goals of this book is to help you understand how the core concepts of physiologic energy relate to your individual body and sense of well-being.

> Lack of energy is one of the top five complaints doctors hear from patients. Unfortunately,
> you can't buy energy, but once you learn how
> to achieve mom energy, it lasts forever.

And when you focus on balancing your energy equations and accelerating your energy levels naturally—as we will show you—everything else begins to fall into place. You'll lose unwanted weight. You'll boost your immune system and have fewer colds each year. You'll sleep like a baby at night. Your skin will glow and your wrinkles will go. You'll ignite your relationships (and sex life!). You'll enhance your productivity and ability to get things done. You'll know how to have that cake and eat it, too, without it sabotaging anything. You'll be able to manage stress better and cope with whatever life throws you (or takes away from you). You'll experience greater happiness and well-being. And you'll automatically find the motivation to keep moving forward with optimism and fortitude. We can't guarantee that we'll cure disease or make special health challenges go away, but we're pretty certain that if you can follow at least some of the guidelines and suggestions in this book, you'll start to notice a better you. You'll sense that sustained, good energy levels make previously difficult health issues weaker and less bothersome.

Energy for Sale

If you could put energy in a bottle, you'd be rich. Maybe that's why the "energy industry" is still booming despite the economy. PowerBar. Red Bull. Amp. Venom. Accelerade. Super Energizer. Energice. SoBe Adrenaline Rush. The number of drinks, herbs, bars, and even goo that sell energy continues to climb. Sales of these quick fixes have more than quadrupled in the last decade.

But even if you buy into this market, you know that caffeine and quick sugar fixes can only go so far to boost your energy in the short-term. These tactics can, in fact, trip a vicious cycle that spirals downward into the pits of total energy depletion. That's right: every time you pick up a can of soda or energy bar, you could be downshifting your body into reverse. Yes, these products do give you that initial jolt, but in doing so they can trigger a cascade that ends in energy exhaustion. In other words, most of those energy blasts are responsible for creating energy imbalances that result in feelings of being tired, worn, sapped, unwell, and, quite frankly, useless.

So if the energy industry can't sell us the cure for this energy crisis, what can we do? The answer: adopt lifestyle habits that naturally infuse you with energy. And that means coming to terms with the economics of your own energy equation so you can then manage it effectively. That's what *Mom Energy* is all about.

We've put together a three-part strategy that entails Reorganizing your time and eating patterns, Rehabilitating your physical body, and Recharging through attention to exercise, sleep, and play. We'll start the book, however, with some groundwork. In Part I ("Before You Get Started") we'll take you on a revealing tour of how our body's energy equations function to either keep us fully charged or leave us depleted; plus we'll offer a series of self-tests that you can take to gauge where you are on the energy spectrum, as well as determine your unique energy profile. This will set you up for embarking on your own personalized energy makeover in the remaining chapters, which are laid out in the order of your three-part strategy: Reorganize, Rehabilitate, and Recharge.

You'll know how to tailor specific goals to the suggestions detailed in Parts II through IV, and instigate slight shifts attuned to your lifestyle.

Because many of the chapters are chock-full of information and ideas, we've made it really simple by adding a section titled "Mom Up: Jump-Start Your Transformation" that gives you a simple and concrete takeaway to try and execute in your life that day or week. We understand that it can take time to implement all the strategies in this book. Sometimes, it helps to just start with one technique, one actionable step. So that's why we'll give you just that and avoid overwhelming you with too much to do. After all, you already have plenty on your plate!

STOP "LIFESTYLE CYCLING"

We all fall into the trap of believing that there's a one-stop solution to the mom-energy problem. If we didn't believe in magic or "secrets" to looking and feeling great, then we wouldn't consume so much content from the magazines that shout out something new to try every month or, in some cases, every day. Admit it: you've heeded countless pieces of advice dispensed from a magazine, blog, or article to give yourself a boost. You manage to stick to a new regimen for a while, but then life—and that probably includes your kids—gets in the way of your efforts.

Over and over again we watch women cycle through one lifestyle trend to another, always ending back where they started and more energy-depleted.

So there must be (and there is) an alternative. You can learn how to stop cycling for good, to live a life that naturally infuses you with energy for the long term. It's about being the best that you can be. It's also about choosing where to put your efforts in the hopes of gaining some benefit in your health and well-being. By educating you to find your individual *vis viva,* we empower you to succeed via your own choices, not another's dogma.

Health is dynamic; energy is dynamic; the body is dynamic. Neither energy nor health is something you get to achieve and cross off your list like purchased groceries or an accomplished task. Just as becoming a mom means you're a mom forever, you'll also never be done with seeking optimal health. The intensity of it will ebb and flow throughout your life, but that's just life! So let's make the most of it.

Help for All Moms

Celebrities may have more money and get more attention, but that doesn't make them more innately energetic or able to feel as good as the public photos and interviews let on. Whether the call comes in for us to fine-tune an actress's diet and exercise routine or put her through a major overhaul, there's a common thread in their "cure": getting results means learning how to make the most effective and efficient choices for them and their families too. They still have to do the work, even though someone else may be footing the bill, and their job rarely allows them to sit there looking good. These ladies are on the move, so they need a total energy solution—not just a quick-fix diet and tone-up plan. They want to have the zip to get through a long day and not feel like a truck has run them over by the end of it.

Take Julia Roberts, for example. Before she was married with kids she filmed *America's Sweethearts* with Catherine Zeta-Jones in Las Vegas. It wasn't all that demanding of a role physically (it wasn't an action film filled with crazy stunts), but with any movie schedule you have to be on and ready at all times. So the days can go on and on, and there's a real need to have an underlying level of energy that you can draw from at any given time. Now Julia has entered another dimension with three kids and a husband, and you'll hear about some of her tricks in later chapters.

Another example is Michelle Pfeiffer. When she played Catwoman in *Batman Returns*, she had to be up at 4 A.M. so she could get a workout in and be on the set by 6 A.M. The days would wear on into the evening past seven o'clock sometimes. This film did have a lot of action, and you'll recall Michelle donned a skin-tight catsuit. But for her the request was: "I need to be able to get through the day on little sleep; I'm up early and the shooting days are long and grueling. Help!"

Even if you're not on a set slugging out 16-hour days, you've got your own version of that grueling job. You've got your own set of shifts from being a mom to being a wife, a daughter, a sister, an employee or boss of your own company, a friend, and back to being a mom again, over and over again. Women today are redefining the workforce and changing all the rules. Now that 51 percent of the workforce is comprised of women—and the majority of those women are moms—it's time that they got their own personal guide.

We all can agree that moms shoulder a whole different set of challenges than our male counterparts. We don't know any mothers who aren't up at the crack of dawn and still awake long after they should have gone to bed. The time has come for them to get some serious attention and lifesaving tips attuned to their sense and sensibilities.

GET READY TO REV

The good news is becoming fully charged doesn't require a complete shift in your lifestyle or denying yourself things you really enjoy. And the best news is it doesn't have to cost more or take more time. This book is for all of us who have ever looked in the mirror and wished we could hit reboot.

PART I

BEFORE YOU GET STARTED

Master Your Body's Native Energy Language

*Women can have so much more than they realize.
I feel very lucky that I've had the opportunity to try to grasp as
much as I can in my life. So, I do have a family, and I do
have a husband, and I do have a career. And not at one time
do I feel that I'm 100 percent in any one [of them].
That means that every day it's a navigation . . .*

— B R O O K E   S H I E L D S

"I can't lose my belly fat. The words *vibrant* and *well rested* are no longer part of my vocabulary. Feeling stressed out and overstimulated is my life. Don't tell me to give up my caffeine, wine, bread, and sugar. I don't remember the last time I went on a diet that worked. They never work! I dream of looking and feeling younger, but have no idea how to without making unrealistic changes that ain't ever gonna happen. I hate being tired all the time. I hate feeling like roadkill. I don't remember the last time I felt sexy and desirable."

Do any of these statements sound familiar? You'd think the word *mom* stands for "Missing Our Mojo." Yet losing your mojo isn't what you signed up for, and it doesn't have to be your reality. Even if you're the most health conscious of moms, if you're like any of the people we counsel, you still find yourself blinking in disbelief and feeling wiped out in ways you never expected and can't rebound from. You can seemingly be doing everything "right" but still sputter on low ebb and low energy (unable to lose those last 10 to 20 pounds or fit into your skinny jeans without fasting for a month).

In this chapter, we're going to take you on a quick tour of your body's energy physiology, and help you begin to see where you might be going wrong, and where there's room for improvement.

THE PHYSIOLOGY OF ENERGY

The word *energy* is quite loaded these days, and you're probably more apt to think about energy in terms of oil or electricity than biology. But the physiology of energy is very real, and more tied into your health than anything else. In fact, if you picked up this book thinking you'd find better secrets to weight loss, or to sleep better, lower your risk for disease, and manage chronic conditions, then look no further than your own energy physiology to help you with all that and much more. It's a shame that we seem to focus so intently on one single area, such as stubborn belly fat or insomnia, when we can help all the important areas in our lives if we just focus on the dynamics of our body's energy. So we want to begin by asking the question: what does energy mean to you? More succinctly, what does energy imbalance mean to you?

When we asked a few fantastic moms to speak about the meaning of an "energy imbalance," we were delightfully surprised by some of the answers we got:

> Energy imbalance is one of the main causes for most of our health issues here in America. To me, energy imbalance means that people are not naturally creating or using energy throughout the day, which causes more exaggerated highs and lows of energy.

Energy imbalance could very well be the number one issue of our time. Most women wear far more hats than they should. Mothers often act as breadwinners, chefs, chauffeurs, the cleaning service, secretary, accountant, and, oh yes, family psychologist. All the while attempting to love herself, which is often the very last thing she has the time or energy for.

I feel better when the energy that I access in my work on a daily basis—i.e., my mind—is balanced by the energy that I access for exercise—my body. By balancing the two of them, I feel I can access the energy that nourishes my spirit.

Energy imbalance means a deficiency in one or more of the following: nutrition, exercise, sleep, and "me time." If any of these are not at an optimum level, it lowers my productivity, immune system, and positive family dynamics.

[E]nergy problems stem from a poor diet, lack of exercise, and allowing ourselves to be stretched too thin. As caregivers, we often forget to take care of ourselves.

Now that's a set of some seriously smart responses! But it's true: there's plenty of science to help explain how energy imbalance lies at the root of many health problems, which we'll get to shortly. Put simply, when you focus on optimizing your energy levels (naturally, not with stimulants that can temporarily give the illusion of energy), you support optimal health. Energy = Health. And when you have health, you have energy. In other words, you feel great.

THE ECONOMICS OF YOUR BODY'S ENERGY METABOLISM

Although every aspect of your life depends on energy, the concept of energy from a biological standpoint can be difficult to grasp. Energy, after all, cannot be seen or touched. It manifests in various forms, including thermal, mechanical, electrical, and chemical energy. And obviously we're not just talking about energy in terms of engineering and the universe at large à la New-tonian physics. It gets much simpler and down-to-earth than that! In the body, thermal energy helps us to maintain a constant body temperature, mechanical energy helps us to move, and electrical energy sends nerve impulses and fires signals to and from our brains. Energy is stored in foods and in the body as chemical energy.

The body is an energetic force—it's dynamic, and its operations can be viewed as a collection of basic, interlocking energy equations. Those equations are what make up our metabolism, which is the total sum of all the reactions that the body uses to obtain or expend energy from what we consume. If any one of those equations isn't fully functional, the whole system is impacted, and with sufficient disruption the system itself can start to falter. When that happens you can kiss being energized good-bye.

There is no better and no more reliable barometer of your over-all health than your perceived energy level. Yep. Very low-tech but as accurate a diagnostic tool in determining general health as you'll find. If you're feeling low on energy, that's an extremely reliable indicator that there's a systemic health problem or issue that needs attending—your interlocking "equations" are not humming. That's why doctors recognize chronic exhaustion and low energy as a red flag signaling a potentially serious decline in health; it's a cue that the body's operations are falling apart. Persistent fatigue, for instance, is one of the most commonly experienced cancer symptoms. It's also usually the case that the more fatigue, the more advanced the cancer—both malignant and benign. Cancer is a prime example of a disease state whereby the body is not performing at 100 percent as it creates unhealthy cells that further disrupt other systems. The mere presence of cancer can increase your body's need for energy, weaken your muscles, and alter your hormones—all of which lead to fatigue. Needless to say, add any treatments like chemotherapy on top of that and you can see why cancer patients feel chronically tired. This isn't to say that being low on energy means you have cancer; we mention this link because it clearly illustrates—to the extreme—the association between true health and energy. And it points to the fact that taking control of your health (and so much more!) hinges on addressing energy levels.

Before moving forward, we want to be clear that "mom energy" is not about "high energy." It's unrealistic to think you won't ever have days when your energy is below average. Life happens, and energy can wane for a variety of reasons—not all of them necessarily bad. What we want to show you, however, is how to work toward having sustained energy and how to respond to inevitable fluctuations in your energy so you can avoid pitfalls and long-term consequences. You can also avoid putting yourself at a higher risk for disease and, yes, even ailments as serious as cancer. Also bear in mind that being low on energy or having an off day is not synonymous with a bad mood.

When it comes to this concept of having and actually feeling energy, we're not just talking about your perceived energy and sense of whether or not you can withstand walking a mile uphill today with your kids in tow. We're referring to a very real and critically important set of reactions and processes in the body that ultimately do determine how energetic you feel. And it all boils down to energy metabolism—the biochemical processes that occur within a living organism to maintain life.

Energy Metabolism 101

The science of metabolism is staggering, and we don't expect you to understand the biology in a way that a doctor or even your high-school science teacher would. It won't help you to maximize your energy, or your metabolism for that matter.

The nutrients in particular that the body breaks down into basic units are carbohydrates, fats, and proteins. From carbohydrates come glucose, your body's—especially the brain's—primary form of fuel; from fats we get glycerol and fatty acids, many of which are essential ingredients in hormones and the protective sheath in our brain that covers communicating neurons; and from proteins we get amino acids, which are the building blocks to lots of structures, including our blood, muscle, skin, organs, antibodies, hair, and fingernails.

Each of these nutrients travels down a different pathway, but all can eventually fuel the body's production of ATP (adenosine triphosphate), which is essentially our bodies' ultimate energy currency. ATP is a high-energy compound that fuels biochemical reactions in the cells. It's responsible for charging our metabolic engines, allowing our muscles to move and our brains to think, and supplying our enzymes with the energy they need to catalyze chemical reactions. ATP is produced continuously throughout the day using the energy from the breakdown of foods. Clearly, what you choose to eat will affect your body's production of ATP, and how you choose to move will also affect your body's use—and need for—adequate ATP. A mom who gets up before dawn to run five miles before the kids get up will have a radically different ATP-producing machine than a mom who sleeps in and has a pancake breakfast with her little ones. That said, each mom's different routine has its own mom-energy merits, and you'll soon come to understand the difference.

The energy-creating centers in our bodies are mitochondria—tiny organelles found inside all of your cells. Your mitochondria are probably the most important structures in your cells. Most cells in the human body contain somewhere between 500 and 2,000 mitochondria, and they make up as much as 60 percent of the volume of muscle cells. Not only do your mitochondria convert the stored energy in fat, protein, and carbohydrates into ATP, but they are involved in almost every energy-intensive process in the cell. Many diseases that deal with energy balances, from diabetes to muscle wasting as one ages, can be traced back to defects in a cell's mitochondria. In fact, mitochondria have their own DNA, so they don't have to depend on the nucleus to repair or replace themselves.

Mitochondria convert calories and oxygen into energy the body can use: adenosine triphosphate (ATP). Your cells contain about 100,000 trillion mitochondria, which consume 90 percent of the oxygen you breathe. This oxygen is necessary to burn the calories we eat in food.

Your body's metabolism is constantly in motion, even as you sleep or sit on a couch zoned out while watching TV. The body will seek resources it needs from the raw materials you feed it. And when those raw materials run low, the body will work its magic to create its own source wherever possible. Case in point: Most cells can produce glycogen, which is a stored form of glucose. But the liver and muscle cells store the greatest amounts. After you eat, liver cells obtain the glucose from the blood and convert it to glycogen. Between meals, when blood glucose levels fall, the reaction is reversed, and glucose is released into the blood. This ensures that cells will have a continual supply of glucose to support life. When you take in more carbs than your body can store as glycogen or are needed for normal activities, all that extra glucose becomes fat and is then deposited into your fat cells. The body has an almost unlimited capacity to do this type of conversion, which is why chronic overeating usually leads to obesity.

CAUSE AND EFFECT

One of the easiest ways to understand the dynamics of the body is to consider what can happen when something gets out of whack, or when there is too much of one ingredient and not enough of another. This is true not just for moms, but for their brood as well. In 2009, reports emerged about a rise in kids getting kidney stones, which may seem unusual but not when you consider the huge amounts of processed foods that our kids are eating these days. Eating too much salt, coupled with not eating enough water-rich foods or drinking enough water to help counter that salt, can result in excess calcium in the urine, which sets up conditions for kidney stones to develop.

Johns Hopkins Children's Center in Baltimore, a referral center for children with kidney stones, used to treat one or two youngsters annually 15 or so years ago. Now it tracks new cases every week. Virtually all hospitals across the country have noticed an increase, puzzling some doctors but confirming to others the repercussions of a high-salt diet—even in children. Unfortunately, convenience foods marketed to kids and their busy parents (ahem!) are often high on the salt meter and low on the water meter. Some examples: chicken nuggets, finger foods such as little sausages and pickles, hot dogs, ramen noodles, canned spaghetti, packaged deli meats, and candy bars.

Whether the rise in kidney stones among kids can be wholly blamed on a salty diet is still up for debate. A metabolic problem also may be in play, but the message is clear: too much salt has a profound effect on the body at any age, and can exacerbate existing problems. You have probably heard about gallstones, which affect up to 20 million Americans and are twice as common among women. This is another example of what can happen when there's an imbalance in the body, as gallstone formation is thought to be due to an imbalance of bile salts and minerals, dehydration, toxins, and excess cholesterol in the bile. The condition is also associated with a high-fat, low-fiber diet and pregnancy. When the delicate ratio that keeps bile in liquid form is imbalanced, crystals ("stones") form from some of those bile components. They can be a real medical problem, blocking the flow of bile from the liver and gallbladder, and sometimes obstructing the pancreas and intestines as well.

Another case of biological cause-and-effect is found in the balance of calcium and magnesium. When we consume more calcium and not enough magnesium, the body notes this excess by failing to sufficiently relax when it should. Due to food processing and a lack of whole grains and legumes in the diet, we see a several-fold decline in magnesium while calcium intake from food and supplements stays steady, thus often resulting in a "conditional deficiency" of magnesium. Since magnesium turns off the body's stress response (inside the cells) and allows for muscle relaxation, this cause-and-effect relationship can cause a very stressful, tight, constipated effect from head to toe, most often affecting one's ability to fall and stay asleep.

We'll give you another example that most people can relate to: sleep. If you don't get enough sleep to keep your body's engine humming, you'll start to throw your appetite hormones out of whack. Sleep is not a luxury.

The two digestive hormones that control your feelings of hunger and appetite are ghrelin and leptin. As with many hormones, these two are paired together but have opposing functions. One says "go" and the other says "stop." Ghrelin (your "go" hormone) gets secreted by the stomach when it's empty and increases your appetite. It sends a message to your brain that you need to eat. When your stomach is full, fat cells usher out leptin (your "stop" hormone) so your brain gets the message that you are full and need to stop eating. A bad night's sleep—or just not enough sleep—creates an imbalance of both ghrelin and leptin. Studies now prove that when people are allowed just four hours of sleep a night for two nights, they experience a 20 percent drop in leptin and an increase in ghrelin. They also have a marked increase (about 24 percent) in hunger and appetite. And what do they gravitate toward? Calorie-dense, high-carbohydrate foods like sweets, salty snacks, and starchy foods. Sleep loss essentially disconnects your brain from your stomach, leading to mindless eating. It deceives your body into believing it's hungry (when it's not), and it also tricks you into craving foods that can sabotage a healthy diet.

Poor sleep catches up to most moms. It also sets moms up for entering a vicious cycle whereby they plunge into deeper sleep deprivation (and reel from its numerous negative effects), and avoid healthy behaviors that can counter the bad mood, such as exercise and eating right. So even if you say you're okay on four or five hours, you should take a good look at your sleep habits if you are unhappy with your energy, not to mention your looks and your weight. See what happens when you force yourself to get more sleep. You just might force yourself to lose unwanted weight and achieve a more beautiful, energetic you. We'll be going into much more detail about sleep in Chapter 9.

A THREE-DIMENSIONAL PICTURE

When thinking about how to simplify the complex mechanics of the human body's energy-manufacturing processes and the seemingly dazzling feats made by the body to sustain life, we thought it helpful to consider three unique dimensions to your overall energy equation. We'll take a quick look at each of these factors here and, throughout the book, come to see how all of these merge together to determine whether you're running on renewable sources of energy or perpetually struggling to find a charging station.

The First Dimension: Your Body's Composition

The three main components in your body are water, muscle, and fat. We're taking some liberties here—our bodies are much more complex than that—but let's focus for a moment on these three big components that do, in fact, contribute largely to the puzzle of our energetic lives.

Waterworks: If you were listening in high-school biology class, then you already know that we are watery creatures. Our bodies are about 75 percent water, so water is a huge factor in your energy, not to mention your survival. Water helps keep your overall metabolism and all other bodily processes functioning properly. Our body's water needs are so critical that if the water content in our blood drops below normal, muscle cells will leach water to support the flow necessary in the blood. When this happens, we become dehydrated. Diets that severely restrict carbohydrates may give people the illusion of sudden weight loss, but here's why: cutting off carbohydrates forces the body to find other sources of energy. It likely turns to glycogen, which is stored carbohydrates on reserve in your muscles and liver. Once glycogen storages are tapped, water gets released. So someone who cuts back on carbohydrates and notices sudden weight loss could be shedding just water weight rather than real fat weight. This could then prompt further dehydration and undeniable hunger.

There's another aspect to this water equation. Not only do fat cells need water to convert fat to usable forms of energy, but your muscles also need water to perform. So when you increase your physical activity, your muscles will store more glycogen with water to meet the demands you're placing on them. Likewise, your bloodstream will carry more water, upping the amount of blood traveling through your system to deliver much-needed oxygen to your muscles. All of this action means a higher level of energy efficiency and a bigger capacity to burn calories—and, in turn, burn fat. It's not a surprise that people who can burn fat easily are using energy more efficiently; as a result, they also feel more energetic as well. The proverbial couch potato will be less efficient and, subsequently, feel less energetic.

The Muscle Factor: People forget how valuable muscle mass is to quality of life, longevity, and the ability to maximize energy. Certainly genetics and special conditions, such as thyroid issues, can come into play, but the overriding factor in both weight gain and metabolic rate is muscle mass.

Unlike fat, muscle is a high-maintenance tissue. It's in constant use by the body, and as such it requires a lot of energy to keep it in good working order. This helps explain why lean, more muscular people have an easier time burning calories at rest than do people with higher proportions of body fat. Muscle burns calories, whereas fat just stores them. Calories, by the way, are units of energy. Your basal metabolic rate is the energy—measured in

Don't confuse "energy density" with food that
will infuse you with "high energy." In a nutshell,
energy density refers to the number of calories in
a particular volume or weight of food. High-energy-
density foods, such as an apple fritter, pack a lot
of calories per bite; conversely, low-energy-density
foods, such as a regular apple, contain fewer calories per bite. Bite for bite, or ounce for ounce,
you'll consume more calories—not all of which
will be necessary to sustain your body's needs
and keep your energy running on high. In other
words, high-energy-density foods can sabotage
your efforts to optimize your energy. Don't panic:
if this sounds confusing, you'll soon understand
what we're talking about. For now, bear in mind
that low-calorie foods (low-energy-density) that
can infuse you with real energy do exist. We'll be
showing you exactly that in Chapter 5.

calories—that your body needs daily for your cells to function properly and to stay alive. It's what you burn without exerting any effort. Most women need a daily average of 1,500 to 1,800 calories. Of course, this depends on activity levels, body size, and body type. To lose a pound of fat, you have to burn 3,500 more calories than you consume. For example, if you cut back on calories and increase your exercise so that you create a 500-calorie daily deficit, you'd burn enough extra fat to lose a pound in a week.

We get asked all the time: isn't a calorie the same in all foods? In theory, yes, but not when you consider how the body responds to calories from different sources. A chocolate chip muffin, for example, can be chock-full of calories coming from sugars that will likely get stored in your fat cells. This happens due to the spike in insulin that occurs when you eat that tasty muffin. The insulin tells your body to store the extra—what the body doesn't need for immediate energy—as fat. Eating a deli sandwich on one slice of whole-grain bread with organic turkey, bell peppers, and avocado, on the other hand, won't cause the same surge in insulin and, in fact, requires time and an expenditure of energy to break down its proteins, healthy fats, and carbohydrates. The sandwich will keep your energy sustained and balanced.

> People who go to extremes to lose weight quickly often impair their fat metabolism by cutting too far back on calories, which forces the body into starvation mode. When this happens, the body holds on tightly to fat and burns up muscle tissue for energy—two counterproductive events to fat loss, energy conservation, and overall health.

People whose muscle-to-fat ratio is high feel more energized and motivated to stay active. And it's not just about the muscle fibers that allow us to move and exercise. Involuntary muscle activities are going on continuously to keep you alive. Your heart, which itself is a muscle, pumps oxygen and nutrients to cells; muscle action pumps lymph through your lymphatic system as part of your immune system; breathing depends on muscles to deliver oxygen; and muscle activity in the skin allows you to sweat and maintain your temperature.

Every year after age 25, our body's composition begins to shift quite dramatically. We gain, on average, about one pound of body weight each year and lose a third to a half pound of muscle. As a result, our resting metabolism decreases approximately 0.5 percent annually. So unless you downshift your caloric intake as your metabolism slows down, you'll experience frustrating weight gain, which can then inhibit optimal energy metabolism.

Although losing a fraction of muscle mass each year may seem minuscule, it adds up to be quite significant—translating to about a 1 to 2 percent loss of strength each year. With this loss of muscle strength, we tend to spontaneously become less active because daily activities become more difficult and exhausting to perform. We, in effect, lose energy more easily just like an old car that hasn't been serviced in a while will use up more gas than a new, efficient model.

Women have special challenges in the fat vs. muscle department. Because on average we don't have as much testosterone as men, it's harder for us to build and maintain muscle mass. This partly explains why recent research suggests that we'll lose muscle mass twice as fast as men of the same age. Add to that any hormonal challenges or conditions like diabetes and you can see why women have a harder time losing weight and keeping it off than men do.

In this book, we're going to challenge you to pay closer attention to your muscle mass than your fat mass. It's not that we wouldn't want you to lose excess fat, but when you put the focus on muscle—a positive, energy-grabbing tissue—then you will automatically tip the scales in favor of muscle and effortlessly gain more energy. And yes, this will include a bow to physical fitness as well as nutritional sense. *Fitness* is really a word that means fit to metabolize energy efficiently. When you're fit, you can create energy optimally. A fit person is an energetic person.

The Truth about Fat: In the past decade, scientists have uncovered a wealth of knowledge about types of body fat. Like cholesterol, there are good and bad types. Just last year researchers discovered an alarming difference between brown, or "good," fat and the more predominant "bad" fat, which tends to be white or yellow and collects around the waistline. Brown fat, which actually has a brownish tint to it, is stored mostly around the neck and under the collarbone (so, to a large extent, it's invisible). This fat encourages the body to burn calories to generate body heat (ahem: energy!), and plays an important role in keeping infants warm (infants, as we all know, have fatty necks). Until very recently we believed that this fat was either gone or no longer active by adulthood. Much to the contrary, it may have a huge role in our ability to stay lean as adults. These recent studies found that lean people have far more brown fat than overweight and obese people, especially among older folks. Unlike its bad-fat counterpart, brown fat burns far more calories and generates more body heat when people are in a cooler environment. Women are more likely to have it than men, and women's fat deposits are larger and more active.

The unhealthy fat that collects around the waistline is often referred to as visceral fat, because it collects around the "viscera"— your vital organs such as your heart, liver, and lungs. And it doesn't just sit there. Visceral fat is metabolically active, but instead of burning lots of calories, it prefers to release chemicals that affect your metabolism—negatively. Put simply, it can impact the balance of your body's interlocking equations. Excess calories stored as body fat generate hormones that can cause weight gain while preventing the production of healthy substances that can lead to weight loss. We are just beginning to understand how visceral fat can change the body's chemistry and work against any attempts to lose weight and fight disease—or to sustain energy, for that matter.

Visceral fat is an age maker and energy depleter—it wreaks havoc on the liver and has been linked to a slew of health problems, including heart disease, diabetes, some forms of cancer, and a cluster of risk factors called metabolic syndrome, which increases the chance of developing these diseases. It should come as no surprise that the more visceral fat you have, the lower the amount of energy your body can create. Visceral fat is not a problem just for overweight or obese people. You can be thin and still have visceral fat if you're not fit. Because visceral fat is the most dangerous kind of fat, doctors have grown more concerned about waist size than the number on the scale, which can be very deceiving. While abdominal fat is usually visible, visceral fat can be hidden deep inside an outwardly "thin" person. The same holds true for fat that can line blood vessels, restrict blood flow, and damage the cardiovascular system.

The Second Dimension: Hormones

Is there any mom who isn't familiar with the power of hormones? Since the time you hit puberty you've been under the spell of raging hormones at least once a month. And certainly anyone who's been through pregnancy and childbirth definitely has a love-hate relationship with these powerful chemicals.

Because everything in the body is connected, shifts in hormones through the years can have profound effects on the body's energy system. From a physiological standpoint, hormones help control how you feel, such as hungry, thirsty, tired, hot, cold, horny, and down in the dumps. They also command where we are on life's continuum, from our childless days to our postmenopausal years when our bodies try to thrive on a totally different concentration of hormones.

Briefly, hormones are simply chemical messengers that travel in the body's blood vessels to target areas where they have an intended effect. These chemical messages, which are tiny in volume, have many large and important jobs, such as regulating metabolism, growth and development, tissue function, and even your mood. The body's hormonal system includes the sex glands (testes in men, ovaries in women), the kidneys, pancreas, hypothalamus, pituitary, pineal, parathyroid, thyroid, and adrenal glands. There are many hormones in the body. In addition to estrogen, the most familiar ones include progesterone, cortisol, adrenaline, and androgens such as testosterone. Every organ has certain hormones, and many hormones have multiple functions that overlap. When all hormones are balanced, the body works as it should, organs function properly, tissues are supple and resilient, and your energy-packing metabolism runs smoothly. Conversely, the smallest variation in hormone levels can cause great, sometimes catastrophic effects all over the body, including the systems that generate energy and make you feel energetic.

Exactly how our hormones ebb and flow quite automatically within us can take up a whole semester in biochemistry. In brief, when stress hits, cortisol tells our brains that we are hungry, so we then seek out food. "Stress," by the way, doesn't have to be the kind we experience while traversing a highway to make our exit. Eating a box of chocolates or a pint of premium ice cream when you're sad, frustrated, angry, and moody—all of which the body can interpret as being stressed—has its reasoning. Fatigue born out of sleep deprivation and a caffeine addiction also causes the body to cry out for energy. These cries come first for carbohydrates, the body's preferred source of energy, thanks to cortisol's message to our brain that demands sugary, fatty foods—all the wrong foods for stopping the cycle. Rich, sugary foods don't do much for us but contribute to insulin swings, poor blood-sugar balance, as well as extra pounds, potbellies, worse moods . . . and do we need to mention low energy?

What's more, the usual culprits—chips, cookies, quesadillas, bread and butter, my kid's ice cream—register in our brain's reward center in ways that make us crave them even more. When we give in, what we ingest dictates how the body will respond from there. We usually (1) don't choose well, and (2) overconsume when we are seeking carbs for energy. If we choose a sugary carb with fat, the combo can actually override our brain's satiety mechanism and we will keep eating (think ice cream, chips and guacamole, or cupcakes with icing). If we overconsume carbs, we get more energy than the body can use, and two things happen: (1) the extra gets stored as fat, and (2) we have more energy which then keeps us awake (if we are eating at night) or sets us up for another energy drop (what goes up must come down). This is what we call the carb hangover.

Another way to think of this cycle of carbohydrate overload is to consider each serving as a building block. When we have more than one block or have one without the balancing effect of other necessary blocks (ahem: healthy fats and proteins), then while our energy rises it also crashes. Some people may even get shaky due to hypoglycemia or other health conditions, or as a result of drinking caffeine at the same time. As you begin to worry about being able to function on low energy and fatigue sets in, the body will call out for sugar (that is, carbs) for energy. If you give in to this demand, which is primal, you'll awaken the body but create yet another vicious cycle—especially if you choose a low-quality form of carbohydrate. As we saw earlier, an imbalance of appetite hormones brought on by sleep deprivation alone can trigger an intense craving for foods high in fat, salt, and sugar. Recent research on the brain shows just how lethal this mix can be on the body, encouraging what's called conditioned hypereating, which short-circuits the body's self-regulating mechanisms, leading to chronic body chaos and energy loss.

We can tell ourselves that we're tired and acknowledge a deep hunger for "cheap" carbs, but then telling ourselves to avoid them can be extremely hard to do, if not impossible. Unfortunately, many of us remember feeling moody, low energy, or just darn deprived from the low- and no-carb diets that may have even worked, albeit temporarily. It isn't about carbohydrate avoidance; it's about learning to balance them, along with portion control and choosing better quality. While this may seem daunting or not like a "program" at all, it is indeed the energy solution that allows you to sustain energy and manage highs and lows that occur when life inevitably happens.

There's also new evidence to show that ingredients in some foods can disrupt your metabolism and your hormonal system, which impacts how well your body processes and burns energy. A class of natural and synthetic chemicals known as endocrine-disrupting chemicals (EDCs), also gaining the name "obesogens," can act in a variety of ways to make and keep you fat: by mimicking human hormones such as estrogen, by misprogramming stem cells to become fat cells, and, researchers think, by altering the function of genes. They enter our bodies through a variety of ways: from natural hormones found in foods, from hormones administered to animals, from plastics in some food and beverage packaging, from ingredients added to processed foods, and from pesticides sprayed on produce. The lesson: when you eat organic whole foods, your body recognizes them and you help stoke your body's metabolism. Translation: fat loss, sustained energy. (We'll be going into more details on this topic later.)

Suffice it to say that the amount of stress your body endures, both physical and psychological, profoundly affects your energy level. In Chapter 10 we'll share nuggets of wisdom about managing stress. We'll also reiterate throughout the book ways in which you can calm the storm of certain stress hormones that work against every effort to sustain energy—and health.

The hormones that control our blood chemistry stability, and insulin in particular, deserve our attention. We already mentioned insulin briefly, but later on we'll look deeper into how insulin commands so much of our energy metabolism. So many moms today, for example, try to operate with insulin resistance, a condition in which the cells become ineffective at using energy efficiently. Which brings us to the third dimension to the overall energy equation.

The Third Dimension: Health Conditions

In Chapter 6, we're going to give you the scoop on health conditions that could be undermining any efforts to gain better energy. From thyroid issues to anemia and plain old digestive disorders like constipation and irritable bowel, the state of your health in every system of your body will dictate the state of your energy level. As we've been covering, when there's a bleep in an organ, tissue, system, or group of cells, there's a misfire that culminates in an inefficient metabolism. Just one minor deficiency or miscue happening in the body can trigger a cascade of troubles that results in energy depletion. Conversely, it's hard, in fact, to be low on energy if your body is operating efficiently and there are no hidden health challenges. It's simple: if you don't give the body the excuse to downshift, it won't. But when there's a health issue to address and the body needs to fight a germ or make up for a dysfunction somewhere in the whole system, then you will certainly feel it. Your energy will be limited as your body uses all it can to heal, protect, and consolidate its resources, so the ones that are required to keep you alive are still available no matter what. The body doesn't necessarily care, for instance, that you feel energetic. It just wants to maintain its non-negotiable systems of survival such as your heart and lungs.

One condition in particular that you've no doubt heard about is called inflammation, and it has everything to do with energy. Inflammation is the common denominator to virtually all medical conditions. At this writing, a Google search on inflammation turns up about 114.8 million hits—and there will be many more by the time this book is in your hands. It's practically a celebrity on its own. We're all familiar with the kind of inflammation that accompanies cuts and bruises on our skin—that pain, swelling, and redness that emerges. If you suffer from allergies or arthritis you're also tuned in to what inflammation feels like. But inflammation goes much deeper than that and can happen in your organs and systems without you even knowing it—without you really feeling it per se.

Although inflammation is part of our bodies' natural defense mechanisms against foreign invaders such as bad bacteria, viruses, and toxins, too much inflammation can be harmful. When inflammation runs rampant or goes awry it can disrupt your immune system and lead to chronic problems and/or disease. It's like having your furnace turned on to keep you warm and comfortable; if that furnace doesn't turn off once a certain temperature is reached, then your environment is going to get hot, uncomfortable, and dangerous. Soon enough, things in that environment will start to become adversely affected.

Inflammation may not seem remotely related to energy but, in fact, volumes of international research prove just how insidious chronic inflammation can be on the body. Researchers are now discovering bridges between certain kinds of inflammation and our most pernicious degenerative diseases today, including heart disease, Alzheimer's disease, cancer, autoimmune diseases, diabetes, and accelerated aging in general. Virtually all chronic conditions have been linked to inflammation, which, put simply, creates an imbalance in your body that stimulates negative effects on your health and, as such, your energy.

At the center of inflammation is the concept of oxidative stress—"rusting," if you will, of your organs and tissues. This can happen both on the outside, causing wrinkles and premature aging, and on the inside where it can stiffen our blood vessels, damage cell membranes, and essentially wreak havoc. Oxidation happens everywhere in nature and is a normal part of our biology; it occurs during the natural process of metabolism, which again is simply the body's means of turning calories (energy) from food and oxygen from the air into energy usable by the body. Oxidation, then, is very much a part of our being, but when it begins to run amok or there's too much oxidation without a balance of antioxidant action, it can become harmful. "Oxidation," of course, entails oxygen, but not the kind we breathe. The form of oxygen that's the culprit here is simply "O" because it's not paired with another oxygen molecule (O_2).

> Think of oxidation as a combustion process, and the exhaust is made up of by-products called free radicals that need to be controlled. A biologist at UC Berkeley estimates that free radicals damage the DNA inside one of our cells some 10,000 times a day.

You've also no doubt heard about free radicals by now. These are molecules that have lost an electron. Normally electrons spin around in pairs, but forces such as stress, pollution, ultraviolet light from the sun, and ordinary body activities (even breathing) can make one of them break off. When that happens, the molecule loses all sense of propriety and starts ricocheting around, trying to steal electrons from other molecules. This commotion is the oxidation process itself, a chain of events that attacks cells and kicks off inflammation, which creates more free radicals. Because oxidized tissues and cells don't function normally, the whole destructive process sets you up for a bevy of health challenges, from saggy skin and a low metabolism to obesity, heart disease, cancer, dementia, and other diseases. And as we've been covering, all of these resulting effects equate with low energy as the body is trying to constantly heal itself and repair DNA damage. It's no wonder that people with high levels of oxidation have an extensive list of symptoms: fatigue, brain fog, low resistance to infection, muscle weakness, joint pain, anxiety, headaches, depression, irritability, allergies . . . the list goes on and on.

As you can imagine, anything that reduces oxidation reduces the bad, chronic types of inflammation, and anything that reduces harmful inflammation reduces oxidation. That's partly why antioxidants are so important. These unselfish nutrients (including vitamins C, A, and E) donate electrons to free radicals, which interrupts the chain reaction and helps prevent the damage free radicals do. Historically, we ate food rich in antioxidants, such as plants, berries, and nuts. In the last century, the advent of advanced food manufacturing has radically changed how we eat. In the early 1900s, the processing and packaging of foods became an enormous growth industry; today, it's the largest industry in the world. Unfortunately, it's an industry that processes a lot of nutrients out of our diets that are sorely needed for optimal health and energy metabolism. Our bodies are equipped with their own antioxidants to protect us, but they are easily overwhelmed by poor diet.

While a detailed discussion of inflammation is beyond the scope of this book, we want you to keep in mind that the lifestyle you choose dictates the extent to which you experience inflammation. What you choose to eat for nourishment, for example, factors into this equation as much as the level of toxins you're exposed to or how much you engage in physical activity and reduce your stress. Foods high in processed sugars and unhealthy fats, for instance, can exacerbate inflammation. This, in turn, antagonizes energy metabolism and puts you at a higher risk for weight gain among a host of other health problems. It also sets in motion a vicious cycle that leads to more and more inflammation. The strategies in this book will point you in a direction toward the things you should be doing to support the natural structure and functions of your body so it maintains a healthy balance, limits inflammation, and ushers in optimal energy.

Speaking Your Body's Language

Now that you have a general idea about how the body makes and uses energy, you can better understand the steps that need to be taken to balance your energy equation. You now speak the language of your body, which puts you way ahead of the game in the quest for energy.

The way most people think about "healthy eating" and "healthy lifestyle," based on the popular theories and headlines, is exactly the opposite of how our bodies actually work—and specifically how the body reacts and interacts with what we put in it and the environment around it. Topping the charts is our continuing obsession with counting calories, prioritizing carbs vs. protein vs. fat, and silly, overgeneralized nutritional recommendations for every body (one size fits all never works, especially when it comes to nutrition!). The diet business is a multibillion-dollar industry but the bottom line is: what it dishes out doesn't work.

Nevertheless, millions of people remain desperate to get healthy, feel energetic, and lose excess pounds, so they rededicate themselves to the same old strategies but will be doomed once more to disappointment in the long run. It is a telling benchmark of where things are that we devour advice that counsels healthy eating by swapping out your daily Whopper with cheese for a Big Mac. We can and must do better than that! But we often don't, or we think we're doing something right when it's actually a giant misstep that leads us in the wrong direction.

So, what do people use to live healthfully and feel energetic? We often hear about the tendency to have coffee in the morning, an energy bar in the afternoon, and a drink (or two) after work. In between these planned "energy boosts" there's the consumption of foods that must be unwrapped and which contain long lists of ingredients; and perhaps there's also a "master cleanse" once a year to clear everything out (and maybe drop a few pounds). The people who live like this believe they're doing the right thing. They're not eating huge meals or taking in excessive calories, and they believe their annual detox is sufficient. But are they really making the grade? Unfortunately, we think not.

As we mentioned before, sales of quick fixes—from ubiquitous energy bars and "health" drinks to odd-sounding powders, pills, extracts, and elixirs lining the aisles at popular health-food stores—have more than quadrupled in the last decade. The number of foods and beverages sold in packages with "natural" ingredients promising to do wondrous things to your health and longevity also has skyrocketed. In fact, as we write this, the makers of a popular drink, advertised as an antiaging dream-come-true that can lead to a "30 percent decrease in arterial plaque" and "17 percent improved blood flow," is being sued by the Federal Trade Commission for making false and unsubstantiated claims. Food health claims abound, and until the government clamps down on ads that tout specific health benefits, we must do a lot of the decoding ourselves. Even though on some level we want the pill or drink that does miracles, especially after experiencing the miracle of creating life, we know that life is more complex, and it's a gift—one that shouldn't be sold for $9.95 at a superstore or on QVC.

Despite what marketers would have you believe, there isn't one pill or drink that will work miracles. Yes, they do give you that jolt and the perception that they are doing something good for you, but here's the surprising truth: most of those energy blasts are responsible for creating energy imbalances! How does that happen?

To better understand this, let's look at body balance related to something all of us mothers remember: pregnancy. When you are pregnant, the body goes into a special mode to develop and protect the growing fetus. It gives the fetus total priority! Your immune system, for example, ticks down a notch to prevent your body from attacking your wondrous creation. And if your baby doesn't get the nutrients he or she needs in the womb, it will borrow from you IOU style—only it doesn't send a reminder for you to restock your stores. The reason you need extra calcium during pregnancy, for instance, is because your baby will take all the calcium from you and your food that it needs to grow. Any deficiencies you experience during pregnancy are more likely to harm the "host"—you!—over the long term. This type of exchange depletes energy reserves during pregnancy, which can affect your system all the way through grandmotherhood and beyond. The body will make sure there is calcium in the blood without worrying about taking it from the bone.

Caffeine, which is arguably the most commonly used (and abused) form of an energy blast, works in much the same way. While it may appear to aid or enable energy on some level, it throws energy off on other levels. Your heart, for instance, will tick a little faster in response to the caffeine, your liver will work a little harder to process the caffeine, and your kidneys will filter more fluid due to caffeine's diuretic effect. It's well documented that caffeine enhances performance, so you'll likely work a little harder and burn more energy while under the influence of caffeine, which can result in energy depletion, sleep deprivation, and perhaps a caffeine withdrawal headache once it's all gone. You've essentially robbed your long-term energy stores to get a short-term jolt, and the energy debt will be felt as low mood, exhaustion, and yes . . . less energy!

Don't get us wrong: there can be a time and place for caffeine, but you need to be aware of its hidden consequences. And as we'll see in Part II, the same can be said for other energy Band-Aids that offer an artificial boost.

Keep in mind that there is no single approach to optimizing energy, and neither diet nor exercise alone will balance your body's massive and complex energy equation. As this book clearly highlights, the combination of various habits, from how you stock your kitchen to how you manage stress, achieve restful sleep, cope with chronic conditions, and schedule exercise, are just a few of the important players in your energy level. Without a doubt, they also play into your health, happiness, and looks as well. It would be impossible to say which of these factors is more important. They all bear weight, and perhaps which one carries the most depends on your uniqueness, especially as they relate to your genetics and other lifestyle choices.

The Kickback Effect: energy can neither be created nor destroyed. That's basic physics. It helps to think of the body in these simple terms as well. When we burn lots of energy, we ask our bodies to work harder at creating more sources of energy.

Something else to keep in mind: we don't want to put too much energy in reserve (i.e., fat cells), because the body doesn't efficiently go to those cells when it needs energy. Instead, it calls out for more "new" energy, triggering that hankering for carbs, and typically low-quality carbs at that. It's like when your kids have plenty of school supplies, clothes, and toys but they still cry out for new ones.

CHAPTER 2

Determine Your Profile: Put Your Energy to the Test

The face you have at age 25
is the face God gave you,
but the face you have after 50
is the face you earned.

— CINDY CRAWFORD,
channeling Coco Chanel

It helps to have a general idea of where your overall energy stands today so you can maximize your journey forward and identify where you could be paying closer attention. This chapter presents two distinct tests. First you're going to find out how severe your energy lack is from a general standpoint, and then we'll help you identify which profile you fit so you can then customize the recommendations in this book to your life.

Quiz #1: How Low Is It?

Following is a brief quiz we've put together to help you gauge your level of energy—from the inside out. It's unlike other typical tests in the health category that you may have taken because we won't ask about your cholesterol level or number on the scale. Be honest with yourself as you answer these questions. You don't have to share your responses with anyone. We encourage you to revisit this quiz whenever you want, to see if any of your answers have changed for the better. You can always come back to this quiz as a way of checking in with yourself and see how you're doing.

1) I have caffeine (e.g., soda, coffee, tea, energy drinks):

    a. Never

    b. Only in the morning, to get me going

    c. Throughout the day; I should own stock in Coke

2) At 7 P.M. I feel:

    a. Hungry and tired

    b. Depressed

    c. Relaxed

3) I feel refreshed when I wake up in the morning:

    a. Most days

    b. Rarely, perhaps when on vacation

    c. Never—you've got to be joking

4) One glass of wine makes me:

    a. Chatty and relaxed in a good way

    b. Hungry and apt to indulge in high-carb or fatty foods

    c. Sleepy and oftentimes grumpy

5) I experience digestive issues (e.g., gas, bloating, constipation, acid reflux/heartburn, and/or diarrhea):

    a.   Once a month, if that

    b.   Once a week or more; check out my medicine cabinet

    c.   Once in a blue moon

6) I crave sweets:

    a.   Daily, usually midafternoon or at night

    b.   When I'm stressed or during my period

    c.   Rarely—I don't have a sweet tooth

7) I've been on a diet:

    a.   Never

    b.   Within the last year

    c.   Since I was a teenager

8) The last time I initiated sex was:

    a.   Last week—it was great

    b.   Last year, I think

    c.   I can't remember—who has the energy for that?

9) I can walk a mile in less than 14 minutes:

    a.   Yes, I'm in great shape

    b.   Are you kidding me? No, and I wish exercise weren't so important

    c.   I have no clue

10) My kids and family typically:

    a.   Come first and I schedule time for myself around their schedule(s)

    b.   Adjust to my needs when I take time for myself

    c.   Never let me take a break; I can't even seem to put my foot down and schedule more time for myself

11) My sleep life is:

    a.   Dreamy: I love my sleep and get lots of it

    b.   So-so: Sometimes I sleep well, other times I don't

    c.   A nightmare: I rely on sleep aids frequently

12) My co-worker or friend would describe my energy as:

    a.   Nonexistent: I don't have a pulse

    b.   Hot and cold: I experience highs and lows

    c.   Pretty good: My energy is mostly consistent throughout the day

Answer yes or no to the following questions:

13) I buy products (e.g., bars, drinks, supplements) that promote their "energy" value.

    Yes/No

14) I suffer from anxiety, restlessness, and/or depression (not necessarily diagnosed by my doctor).

    Yes/No

15) I have an immediate family member who has one or more metabolic disease(s) or symptom(s): high blood sugar, high cholesterol, high waist circumference, high blood pressure, etc.

    Yes/No

Scoring:

1. a (3 points); b (1 point); c (0 points)

2. a (1 point); b (0 points); c (3 points)

3. a (3 points); b (1 point); c (0 points)

4. a (3 points); b (1 point); c (0 points)

5. a (2 points); b (0 points); c (3 points)

6. a (0 points); b (2 points); c (3 points)

7. a (1 point); b (0 points); c (1 point)

8. a (3 points); b (1 point); c (0 points)

9. a (3 points); b (1 point); c (0 points)

10. a (0 points); b (3 points); c (1 point)

11. a (3 points); b (2 points); c (0 points)

12. a (0 points); b (1 point); c (3 points)

13. yes (1 points); no (3 points)

14. yes (0 points); no (3 points)

15. yes (0 points); no (3 points)

The lower your score, the less energy you have. Conversely, the higher your score, the more energy you have in your life.

If you scored below 10 points: You're barely holding on, and you know that you are laying the groundwork for some serious health consequences, too. You don't feel in control of your world, and you're never on your own priority list. The thought of exercising more, eating better, and focusing more on yourself sounds daunting and downright energy draining. The word *energy* makes you look around as if it's something you can buy (case in point: you bought this book!). We're guessing you hide the extent of the chaos pretty well from friends and family, but you know that if you don't get a handle on things soon, you're going to crack. *Energetic* is not a word you use very often.

You can't remember the last time you felt youthful and truly happy. You don't know what's good for you anymore because you've gotten so lost. And the dread of living like this for another year, let alone another day, is practically unbearable.

You have work to do and you know it, but the good news is one little step can result in a giant leap forward. We're here to help you catch your breath. It may take you time initially to get used to living by a new set of strategies and from a new perspective; but through the ideas presented in this book, you'll be able to shift how you live your life and learn to never let living low on energy steal your well-being again.

If you scored between 11 and 20 points: Your life needs a makeover, too, but you've seemingly got a better grip on things. You know you need to take action today or risk falling much further down the hole. You do try hard to keep all the balls in the air, but your juggling often leaves you exhausted emotionally and physically. The fatigue still lingers, the stress still accumulates like fat around your waist, and the mind still wanders down depressive paths when there's finally time. More than likely, energy highs and lows are a constant in your life because you reach for quick fixes and proverbial Band-Aids all the time. Despite knowing what's good for you deep down, you still struggle with gaining control over what's important in your life, and avoiding or limiting the things that you know bring your energy levels down. You have good, energetic days and you have days when your energy is so low you want to send your kids to someone else's house so you don't have to deal with them. Other people can easily suck your energy reserves, and you've never gotten good at saying no. And when it comes to your kids, they rule. But you're aware of this, which is why a little bit more effort and focus can propel you to where you really want to be: happier and more energetic every day.

If you scored above 20 points: You get the gold star. You're lucky to be part of a small but growing group of moms who work hard at maintaining balance in your lives with plenty of energy on reserve for those unexpected moments that require more out of you. But that work requires constant vigilance and attention. You know how easy it can be to slip up and then have to pay the consequences—physically, mentally, emotionally, and even spiritually. You still have moments of feeling guilty for taking time for yourself, or not being there for your children (or others in general) due to work, but you sense that your priorities are in some semblance of order because you don't feel that bad about yourself and your life. For you, this book will be a welcome reminder, and its fresh tips can help you to further fine-tune the good habits that keep you balanced and energetic on all levels.

The ultimate question: If there was a pill for Mom Energy, but to get it you would have to do one of the following, which would you choose? (1) give up your child(ren) for six months; (2) break up with your partner; (3) move to an island with a book, a lover, and your favorite foods but no communication with the outside world; (4) run a Mom Energy weekly support group in addition to your current commitments; or (5) none of the above, I'd pass on the pill and deal with less energy.

QUIZ #2: IDENTIFY YOUR PROFILE: WHAT IS YOUR #1 ENERGY THIEF?

Now, let's see what type of energy makeover you need. The quiz below will help you to tailor the strategies in this book to your unique profile. We'll give you the focal points you need to maximize your journey forward.

We have found that there are typically five types of moms dealing with different challenges, and you can certainly have characteristics of more than one. Below are five checkboxes, each with questions that will help you to pinpoint your energy profile. Don't worry about checking more than one box, but see if you can relate to one of these profiles more so than the others. This mini quiz will identify your biggest issues and help you to personalize the ideas in this book to your life. Following the quiz are recommendations specific to each profile. You can read through them all if you like, and get out a highlighter and mark anything that resonates with you. Then, as you begin to make slight shifts in what you do each day, pay particular attention to what you highlighted and the suggestions specific to your profile.

Once you finish the quiz, make sure to remember which profile you identify with. While all parts of this book are helpful to all moms, there are some passages that will benefit people who fall in specific profiles more. As you're reading through, keep your eye out for the profile alert boxes that will draw your attention to specific sections. If your profile is listed in the profile alert, be sure to read those pages extra carefully. They should offer you specific solutions to your unique challenges.

❏ Do you suffer from a chronic condition such as irritable bowel, migraines, diabetes, fibromyalgia, depression, low thyroid, or any other medical conditions that have you taking (or contemplating) medication? Do you get sick a lot? Are you going through perimenopause or menopause?

» If you answered Yes, then Profile 1 is for you.

❏ Would you consider yourself an insomniac? Do you have trouble falling asleep and staying asleep? Do you wake up feeling as if you never slept?

» If you answered Yes, then Profile 2 is for you.

❏ Do you burn the candle at both ends? Are you

overloaded with To Dos, either at work, at home, or both? Would you consider yourself an emotional wreck?

» If you answered Yes, then Profile 3 is for you.

❑ Are you trying to lose weight? Have you been on a diet in the last year in an attempt to drop a few pounds? Are you on a diet now?

» If you answered Yes, then Profile 4 is for you.

❑ Do you feel stuck in a bad rut? Did you pick up this book because you feel as if you're struggling with every problem under the sun and need to break a vicious cycle of unhealthy habits that robs your energy . . . but you don't know where to start?

» If you answered Yes, then Profile 5 is for you.

Profile 1: The Medicine Cabinet

You may not have a medical diagnosis, but you do find yourself seeking relief from countless over-the-counter medications to keep up with chronic symptoms. It may be a lingering headache or a full-blown migraine. It may be an upset stomach or diarrhea. It may be premenstrual syndrome, perimenopause, or hot flashes from the real thing. It may be another backache (from playing with your toddler), or just a bad day working through a flare-up from your arthritis, fibromyalgia, or raging hormones. Suffering from a chronic condition leaves most people low or limited on energy. You feel awful with good reason, and your body chemistry isn't helping, especially if it's having to fight an illness, a shift in hormones, or just a passing cold.

Focal Points: Getting to the bottom of health conditions that could be affecting your energy is a must. Then, seeking proper treatment to help manage or, in some cases, cure your condition is also a must. Sometimes, however, treatments can entail medications that go against your energy reserves. In Chapter 6 we'll give you the information you need to make sense of some underlying medical aspects to energy—and energy depletion. This will help you to have the right conversation with your doctor. You may not, however, have to resort to drugs in all cases. It may just be that you need to focus on a few lifestyle changes to transform your health status and kick your condition to the curb. We can't promise any miracles here, but we've seen plenty of people change their health for the better and experience a surge in energy like never before, and which helps them to further manage or live with any irreversible condition.

Profile 2: The Mom Zombie

We get nearly an hour less sleep a day than we did 40 years ago. Juggling work and family seems to be the primary sleep thief. Medical conditions may also be at play. If you're going through menopause or are close to it, night sweats could be waking you up repeatedly. Or you could be lacking sleep due to the realities of a newborn baby, staying up to ensure your teenager makes it home safely, or paying bills late at night because 24 hours just isn't enough time. Or perhaps you can't turn off your mind to welcome sleep. And if you do, in fact, log a decent amount of sleep but it's not restful, then you could be suffering from a sleep disorder such as sleep apnea (which is actually quite treatable!). Whatever the cause, you've got a sleep deficit that's outstripped the national debt. And worrying about being tired adds to your anxiety and energy drain.

Given the problems we have with sleep lately, it's no wonder so many moms roam around like the walking dead during the day, alternating endless cups of coffee with cans of soda.

It's fine to consume caffeine in reasonable amounts (hey, it does serve a purpose and can deliver some beautifying antioxidants), but if you start living off the stuff, it can perpetuate an endless—sleepless—cycle that results in total energy depletion.

Focal Points: For you, getting a handle on your sleep will be your top priority (Chapter 9). This will likely entail rethinking your schedule and budgeting your time better (Chapter 3), how much caffeine you drink, and whether or not you really need to own stock in Starbucks. It's amazing how much one small shift, such as getting a good night's sleep on a consistent basis, can do to your overall health and energy levels. You might find, for example, that becoming a sound sleeper helps solve so many other challenges you've faced and makes it easier to deal with the kinds of adversity a mother encounters.

Profile 3: The Overworked and Overscheduled (and Overtired)

Moms who fit this profile are trying to do too much day and night. You can't seem to wean yourself from work—or your kids—enough to take any time for yourself. You might think that watching television late at night once the house is quiet with a tub of ice cream and/or a glass of wine is relaxing, but your body might be crying anything but. You're ripe for burnout, but the adrenaline that constantly fires through you somehow keeps you going. Deep down, though, you're probably suffering from some serious stress that could be sabotaging your health, from weight-loss goals to even your risk for things such as heart disease and cancer. Any energy you have is mostly fictitious—conjured by coffees and Cokes all day long.

Focal Points: Mom, you need to restructure your life! For you, getting a handle on your priorities and bringing your life—and your body—a semblance of balance will be key. Don't skip Chapter 3. No, you cannot do it all, but you can learn what your body needs most and how to provide for its optimal wellness. Even if you sleep pretty well, you probably burn through a lot of extra energy during the day unnecessarily. When you learn how to allocate your time and energy better, you won't crash into bed every night feeling like roadkill.

Profile 4: The Chronic Dieter

Chronic dieters are chronically energy depleted. In brief: traditional dieting typically revolves around restrictions and deprivations. Rather than a constant flow of energy, you experience highs and lows. And when you can't stand avoiding sugar any longer, you eat an entire box of cookies, sending your body's innate energy equations into a biological tailspin. Chronic dieters rarely make good examples for their children, either. You likely find yourself talking about weight ("I'm so fat!") in front of your kids without realizing it, and without knowing what that could be doing to their own sense of self and body-image issues.

Focal Points: If you're on a diet right now, stop! See if you can incorporate the strategies in this book without feeling as if you're on a traditional diet. You would do well to pay attention to all the chapters in this book, but pay closer attention to the nutritional aspects, especially Part II, which covers ideas on managing what you consume. Make it a goal to stop searching for hard and fast rules to what you should and shouldn't do, and instead, learn what you need as well as how to make the right choices for *you*. We won't demonize sugar, or any foods for that matter, but we will teach you how to enjoy all foods responsibly so none inflicts too much energy-depleting harm.

Profile 5: The Dead Battery

You go through the motions every day, clawing at every tip you read to feel better—and better about yourself—but nothing has worked. Maybe you're going through a divorce, or you've remarried and become a blended family with stubborn stepkids, or you have a capricious, explosive boss. . . . Whatever is going on, your energy (and confidence and self-esteem) has plummeted to the point that everyday irritants you'd normally blow off are getting to you at an alarming rate. Conversations with loved ones turn into arguments. You still say yes to too much, and harbor lots of resentment for doing so. Your diet is dead. Your attempts to exercise are dead. The person you thought you'd be as an amazing mom is dead. The only thing keeping you going is a big flood of stress hormones, but even that is not enough to recharge your battery.

Focal Points: For you, everything in this book will be helpful. Taking baby steps will be key so you don't give up entirely. Choose just one thing to do differently this week, then choose something else next week. Don't try to incorporate too many changes all at once. Take it slow. Rather than beat yourself up over "bad" habits, focus on creating new habits so there's no more room for the old ones. Focus on getting charged one day at a time versus being fully charged today with Band-Aid solutions. By learning which behaviors are the biggest energy detractors and how to exchange them for energy-gaining solutions, you will get charged and stay that way.

Most of us fit into one or more of these five mom profiles. As moms, we all get stuck in similar ruts at various times in our lives, and recognizing them for what they are makes it easier to combat them. Remember your profile and focal points because these will help you to maximize the ideas in the book for optimal results.

PART II

REORGANIZE

CHAPTER 3

Time Warp:
Get More Done
in Less Time

With great precision, I plan everything in advance:
who's dropping off, who's picking up. We have charts,
maps, and lists on the fridge, all over the house.
I sometimes feel like I'm in the CIA.

— KATE WINSLET,
on the question of balancing work and raising two kids

Good time management can change your life. If you've heard it once, you've heard it a million times—but there's good reason. One of the biggest energy drainers that moms fail to address is poor time management. And this can have a serious impact on your energy. Planning your meals, grocery shopping, basic errands, personal time, and house cleaning—just generally keeping everything afloat—takes a lot of effort. Is there an ideal way to map out a week? We think so, and it doesn't have to resemble your mother's cookie-cutter plans or any other mother's for that matter. It just has to match your habits, lifetstyle, and personal needs.

Years ago, Stephen R. Covey was made famous for his quadrant theory on what makes a highly effective individual, which became a cornerstone in his *First Things First* and *The 7 Habits of Highly Effective People* bestsellers. He revolutionized the business world, changing how executives, managers, and even everyday people allocate their time and accomplish goals. Covey created his masterpiece long before we had the Internet at our fingertips, chronic e-mails blasting through to us and competing for brain space, and more digital junk than we know what to do with. His Time Management Matrix is undoubtedly more relevant today than ever.

Well, we've taken Covey's matrix and modified it so it's attuned to a mother's needs and demands. We're calling it the Energy Matrix. Where you see yourself in this matrix says a lot about your energy woes—and how to fix them.

> **Profile Alert!** Although the information in this chapter will benefit all the profile types, people who saw themselves as fitting Profile 2 (The Mom Zombie), Profile 3 (The Overworked and Overscheduled), and Profile 5 (The Dead Battery) should pay particular attention here.

THE ENERGY MATRIX

Which Quadrant defines the kind of life you're living? Ask yourself where your priorities are. When something comes across your desk as "urgent," how do you respond? What brings you stress and feelings of being overwhelmed? Are you a master at excuses, a proactive leader in your life, or just dead in the water? Let's find out.

Which of the following sets of descriptions best relates to you?

Quadrant I: Urgent and Important

If you're living in Quadrant I, everything seems urgent and important. Your life is about crisis, pressing problems, and deadline-driven projects.

How many of the following boxes can you check?

☐ I respond immediately to everyone and everything, and am constantly putting out fires.

☐ I live with extreme energy highs and lows, and feel anxious all the time—I'm constantly in crisis mode.

☐ I don't make To Do lists and have never been good with priorities.

Examples of life in Quad I: Ringing phone, crying child, last-minute bill paying, backloading (eating the majority of your calories in the back half of the day), trying every fad diet but getting no results, and abusing short-term energy fillers such as caffeine and sugar.

Symptoms of too much living in Quad I: Overwhelming stress, extreme energy highs and lows, weight gain, anxiety, sleeplessness, fatigue, mood swings, arguments with others, carb cravings, high blood pressure, high anxiety, heart palpitations, digestive problems, headaches, no major accomplishments, nonexistent sex life, no time to do anything you love, grabbing the bottle of wine before happy hour ("Hey, it's happy hour somewhere"), canceling your personal appointments that make you feel like a woman, unhappiness, dissatisfaction.

Bottom line: You're *reactive* rather than *proactive*.

Quadrant II: Not Urgent but Important

A mom in Quadrant II works hard at self-development and health maintenance. She also works at building her relationships and planning smartly for the future. This is the sweet-spot Quadrant where life feels relatively balanced and rarely are there issues about lack of energy.

How many of the following boxes can you check?

☐ I'm a pretty good planner and map out my days—even my future years—carefully. I'm also good about planning my meals and "me" time, so that I get what I need to get done, eat well, and find peace with myself.

☐ I rarely feel deprived because I take responsibility for my choices and practice discipline.

☐ I share deep connections with others, feel energetic most of the time, and enjoy the thrill of learning something new.

Examples of life in Quad II: Exercise, recreation, learning about nutrition and what feeds you, fulfillment, education/developing new skills, planning meals, scheduling events and personal time-outs, date night, weekly dinner with friends, vacations, hobbies, setting goals for future, relaxation techniques, playing with the kids, crafting, meditation, magazine time, physical contact with others (massage, facial, acupuncture, reflexology), making choices so you don't feel deprived (e.g., you might choose to have dessert at one point, or wine, etc. but you're at energy harmony so your choices are coming from what you know is best, whether it's indulging or choosing not to).

The blissful signs of living in Quad II: Balance, discipline, hope for the future, deep connections with others, an ideal weight, feeling energetic and well rested, in control of one's life, happiness, feeling that life is good.

Bottom line: You're *proactive* and life is good.

Quadrant III: Urgent but Not Important

You know what it's like to live in Quadrant III if you let everything steal your attention and walk over you even if it's not necessarily important. Interruptions and unscheduled phone calls are the norm. You let trivial mail and pointless meetings distract you. You constantly address things that can wait, and feel depleted on a regular basis for doing so.

How many of the following boxes can you check?

☐ I stay up late catching up on important tasks that I didn't accomplish during the day because of all the "busy work."

☐ I have an endless texting plan and use up my minutes every month.

☐ I hate myself for failing at another diet and blame my demanding kids and boss for not letting me succeed.

Examples of life in Quad III: Responding to e-mails that can wait, accepting/making phone calls that can wait, going to every single PTA or community meeting, saying yes to things you really don't care about or can delegate to someone else, saying yes because you feel guilty, comparing yourself to others, not making priorities, chronic dieting, excuses galore.

Symptoms of too much living in Quad III: Feeling victimized, out of control, unmotivated, and deprived. You sense that goals and plans are worthless because you never get the results you want.

Bottom line: You're *reactive* but rather than a victim of immediate pressing circumstances, you're just not being strategic enough for your needs. You're not thinking long term, and you lack focus. Everything feels too hard, too difficult. There are *a lot of excuses* in this category.

Quadrant IV: Not Urgent and Not Important

Do you fall into the trap of doing busywork? The hallmarks of Quad IV include a lot of time wasters that don't enhance your life (or your energy). Maybe it's the pull of the television or Internet, or the addiction to shopping for no apparent reason (and without a list). Or maybe it's an obsession with your smartphone, as you check e-mail and messages as if you're in the midst of a serious crisis, and you cannot go a day without texting. Routines and schedules are not your thing, and you have no idea where to begin to prioritize your life because it's become such a shapeless blob of craziness.

How many of the following boxes can you check?

- [ ] I take care of things when I feel like it, even if that means someone else suffers, a bill is late getting paid, or I have to lose a night of sleep and eat crap because I haven't gone to the grocery store.

- [ ] Stuff tends to pile up quickly at home, but I'm not motivated to clear it out.

- [ ] I feel emotionally bankrupt, have wondered if I'm depressed, and have no idea what to expect of myself in the future.

Examples of life in Quad IV: Endless/mindless TV watching (and channel surfing) or Internet surfing, late-night e-mailing and Web browsing/blog reading, reading junk mail/e-mail, goalless shopping, engaging in conversation with toxic people, doing the dishes/cleaning house after your preferred bedtime.

Symptoms of too much living in Quad IV: Lacking a routine, unconscious eating and food obsessions, disconnectedness with yourself and others. You let yourself go and feel emotionally empty. You lack a sense of responsibility and are unable to meet bigger, long-term goals for you and your family.

Bottom line: You're *inactive*. Inert. Indifferent. You watch the exercise video or *The Biggest Loser* TV show but you're not connected to yourself enough to take action. You're living outside your own body. Your kids (and spouse) want to fire you!

The Mom Energy Matrix

Quad I: Urgent and Important

- Living in crisis mode
- Pressing problems
- Deadline-driven projects

You respond to everything in the moment and live on stimulants such as caffeine and sugar. You seek quick fixes but never get the results you want in any area of your life. To say you run low on energy all the time is an understatement.

You're *reactive* rather than *proactive*.

Quad II: Not Urgent but Important

- Focusing on self-development and health maintenance
- Relationship building
- Planning the future

You're in control of your life and have energy harmony. Even in the face of unexpected challenges and energy suckers, you find a way to maintain balance because you're well prepared.

You're *proactive* and life is good.

Quad III: Urgent but Not Important

- Interruptions, unscheduled phone calls
- Distracting mail and meetings
- Things that can wait

You struggle with goals and agendas. Everything seems high-priority and you let it take over your life. When something fails, you find an excuse to cover for it. Your life lacks structure. Keeping all the balls in the air—especially ones you shouldn't be carrying—are constantly draining your energy. Finding new excuses is also depleting.

You're *reactive* and full of excuses. You lack focus and structure.

Quad IV: Not Urgent and Not Important

- Busywork
- Time wasters
- Addictions and obsessions

You are the quintessential mom who has let herself go. Nothing takes priority, not even you when you need it most. You are running on empty—and don't have a clue where to begin. You can't acknowledge your nonexistent energy because you're out of touch and can't read the signals your body is telling you.

You're *inactive*. Inert. Indifferent. If you knew how bad it was, you'd fire yourself.

In which category did you find yourself? Are you playing the victim (Quad I), living in reactive mode (Quad III), acting as if you're dead (Quad IV), or really being proactive (Quad II)? If you've got energy issues, then we doubt you're living a proactive life today. Our guess is that most of you are hanging out in Quad I, III, or IV and wishing you were in Quad II. It's perfectly normal to find yourself hovering somewhere between Quadrants and see yourself with a mix of descriptors from all categories. Hybrids of these Quads are possible, and if there's one common denominator for those living mostly in Quad I, III, or IV, it's a lack of prioritizing and creating realistic To Do lists attuned to your true vision and needs.

Take a deep breath. We don't expect any mom to feel as if she has to always thrive in Quad II. That's unrealistic. All of us inhabit each of these Quads in the real world. Life happens. Kids get sick, and you get tired. The difference between what's "urgent" or "important" can be fuzzy or can suddenly change. The goal is to learn to recognize where you are within these Quadrants, and with that awareness, optimize your situation so you don't have to let the circumstances or consequences affect you as much. In other words, don't let yourself remain a victim or be inactive for too long. If you're stuck in Quad I, III, or IV for whatever reason, make it a goal to shift out quicker than the last time you inhabited that place. By the same token, we know it's not fair to tell a new mom, a menopausal woman, or a mom with three teens that she has to plan everything or focus on relationship building. But we want to show you how to avoid being totally unprepared and blindsided by the serious repercussions of not taking control of your time. There will be moments when you need to put a relationship in a holding pattern, and that's okay. At the end of the day, we're shooting for your health and your energy—no one else's!

No matter who you are—whether you're a working or stay-at-home mom—there's never enough time to finish all the To Dos.

Everyone has a list of things to do that exceeds the physical limitations of time and boundless energy. The concept of free time just doesn't exist for anyone these days. But here's another way to look at it. You say you don't have time, but considering that lacking energy prevents us from capitalizing on our time, imagine all the time you'll magically create by just getting this one area in your life under control.

Time is no longer something I have anymore.
I realized to live the lifestyle and have the profession I have,
I needed to prioritize how I get my energy and use it wisely. . . .
I have a huge problem doing two things at once and getting
either one done fully. Now that I am a mom, I find it almost
a necessity to be able to do two things at the same time
to get anything done. How do I do that?

— J E S S I C A   M E N D O Z A ,
professional softball player, Women's Sports Foundation
president, and ESPN commentator

The Secrets to Sanity

Shifting into Quadrant II won't happen overnight. It will take patience, consistency, and a shift in thinking as much as a shift in lifestyle. We don't know any mom who isn't time-crunched and on the verge of burnout, but it doesn't have to be that way.

The solution? Develop a system for organizing your life according to what needs to get done now, what can wait until later, and what can wait until much later. Use this system for everything that demands your attention during the day, whether it's a phone call, an unhappy child, or a piece of mail. Prioritize your tasks by creating To Dos marked "now," "later," and "can wait." Set standards for dealing with important monthly stuff, such as bills, by designating every other Sunday to address the unpaid bills or mail that requires your attention within a certain time period.

If you're the reactive type who's easily distracted, then you may want to create boundaries for yourself by checking e-mail, watching television, and turning on your cell-phone ringer during only certain hours of the day. For some people, mornings before ten o'clock can be an incredibly efficient pocket of time for taking care of important tasks. This may be when you choose to catch up with your sister, or complete urgent or routine tasks such as tidying up your living quarters or balancing your checkbook.

The following strategies can help you make the shift into living in Quad II. Incorporate as many as you can into your life. Take them one at a time if you need to, adding more strategies each week or month as necessary.

Track your life: There are lots of habits that people get into without realizing it. Take a few days—or even a week—at a time to record everything you do. Keep track of what time you go to bed and when you wake up. Also include how many times you wake up in the night. Do you get up? Why do you get up? How long do you stay awake? Do you have lots of electronic lights on in the room? Do noises keep you awake? What clothes do you wear to bed? Do you watch TV before falling asleep? The answers to these questions may ultimately relate to your energy shortages.

Keep a chart for your exercise workouts and the duration of each one. See how consistent you are with keeping a routine, as this plays a huge role in your energy. This is a good exercise for moms in any Quad. We all have lows in energy during the day, and it's important to know when that low arrives and what you habitually do about it. Tracking your life to know where your time goes—down to every last minute—will help you to implement other strategies for organizing your life and planning accordingly.

Take inventory of your Band-Aids: This is also a good exercise for any mom. Examine your diet and medicine cabinet for the culprits: fast food, energy bars, mochaccinos, pain and headache medication, acid reflux/digestive medication, prepackaged foods, soda, and sleeping pills. Try to manage these better. You may need some of these once in a while, but not every day. Highly reactive and inactive people tend to rely on medications and exterior sources of "energy" to keep going.

Distinguish between urgent and important: Anyone who found herself in Quad I or III should do this on everything, from your son's principal calling to your husband's pleas for attention. "Urgent" refers to things that truly have an immediate impact on you and your family's health and life, such as a sick child. However, consider that the urgent shouldn't always take precedence over the important. It's easy to let emergencies or the latest crisis run your day, and if you don't develop the skill of knowing when the important trumps the urgent, you won't ever be in control—because you'll be chasing after the urgent and ignoring what's important. Identify those tasks that truly need your attention first, and don't allow yourself to be distracted. Just because someone puts one of those high-priority flags on their e-mail doesn't automatically make it so. Prioritize. Prioritize. Prioritize and manage your day accordingly.

I try to be aware and stay on top of all my challenges one day and sometimes one hour at a time. I take it one thing at a time, first things first, and then go from there.

— CHAKA KHAN,

ten-time Grammy Award–winning singer, songwriter, philanthropist, mother, and grandmother

---

Structure your day and take control of every minute: Don't let incoming work control you. It bears repeating: set boundaries—specific time periods during which certain tasks get completed while other, less important tasks wait. If you're prone to distractions such as e-mail, phone, or the television, put a system in place for blocking out these intrusions and addressing them only during certain times of the day. This may mean checking e-mail only once every four hours, or allowing the television to be on during specified time periods. While moms in all Quads would do well to follow this advice, inhabitants of Quad IV should pay particular attention. Structure will help you to manage your busywork and place importance on things that are indeed important. Structure will also give you the motivation and inspiration to take charge in ways that will pull you out of a miserably inactive, inert, and indifferent life. You'll begin to feel happier and more in control, too.

Get control of your paperwork: Create a mail center, where all mail goes and gets dealt with. In this same place, set up a message center containing a calendar marked with important dates. Hang a whiteboard to jot down important lists, To Dos, or that thought you don't want to lose. Try a corkboard, too, to pin those circulars, notices, or invitations that you don't want to forget.

Assign a specific day to prioritize and plan: This gets you into the habit of scheduling food and workouts around non-negotiable commitments; maybe you can get other family members involved and divvy up responsibilities. Set a time and day for laundry, food shopping, meal planning, house cleanup, and so on. Typically a Sunday is the ultimate day to prioritize. Make sure that you spend some time looking ahead at what's coming so you can prep yourself. Note the pitfalls: the two-hour parent-teacher night that tends to last three hours; the regular Thursday staff meeting; the 85 unanswered e-mails that could consume the entire morning. Every day has its molehills, but if you're prepared and limit the time you give them, they won't turn into mountains. Know your appointments and commitments, but look at them in terms of where you're going to schedule workouts, "me" time, and obligations you want to keep for yourself. For example, Tuesdays and Fridays could be your 5:30 A.M. workouts while Wednesdays are the day you'll exercise after the kids go to bed. When you have a realistic plan in your head and on your calendar, chances are you'll follow it closely. You'll feel in control and manage to fit everything in *and* have room for the unexpected. You may, for instance, hit a week where you realize that there are three nights that you cannot make dinner for your family. Knowing this in advance allows you to plan accordingly; maybe that first night will be Crock-Pot dinner, with leftovers the next night.

At first I thought I could not give as much energy as was demanded. It was overwhelming . . . but then I adapted . . . I had to adjust and learn to prioritize my time . . . start my day with silence to find my balance and end it with a little R & R to regain my sanity. One must stay focused and delegate time to different projects as needed. When I start my day in silence, this gives me the focus I need to organize the rest of my day efficiently.

— MARIEL HEMINGWAY,

mother, author, yogi, and spokesperson for green living

Go online: Pay your bills and monitor your financial accounts online wherever you can. For help with all things organization, try Google Calendar. Experiment with online grocery shopping. Some major chains now offer free delivery, and once you have a trusty list of staples, you can double-click your way to a full, healthy kitchen. Imagine the time saved! You can spend that extra time on just *you.*

Practice IKEA-style cooking (i.e., some assembly required): While we'll discuss more of the specifics of food choice in the upcoming chapters, one big part of time management focuses on cooking and shopping, so we have to mention this strategy here. Keep healthy ingredients on hand that can be assembled into a variety of delicious dishes. Aside from your usual shopping routine, schedule a trip to the grocery store once every three or four months when you can spend some time investigating labels or to check out a new market—farmers' or regular. This trial-and-error time will help you comfortably expand and maximize your future time.

Don't let your kids be enablers: We've hinted at it before and we'll stress this again, because it's one of the most pervasive problems facing moms today. Kids afford moms the perfect excuse to buy all kinds of junk and, let's face it, avoid exercise. We watch so many moms go through the motions of a day like this: being "good" in the morning by limiting calories with coffee and/or a diet-conscious smoothie or bar for breakfast, then a salad with chicken for lunch, which then progresses to nibbling on the kids' after-school snacks and cookies, skipping a workout to tidy up the house and perform chores, downing mac and cheese, pasta, or fast food with the kids for dinner . . . and then letting loose in the kitchen late at night once the kids have gone to bed. Sound familiar?

Don't feed the cycle: When TV, bills, and Internet call late at night, a mom can easily wind up feeling revved up with enough anxiety and a rush of sugar from that last bowl of ice cream to avert bedtime. So what does she do? Pop a sleep aid and then feel guilty about staying up too late, which then affects her energy the following day. The vicious cycle continues. A mom in reactive mode (Quad I or III) can find herself in this cycle at any given time. Be aware of it. See what you can do to seize control of it.

Make big goals smaller: Listen up, moms in Quad IV, who feel so overwhelmed by everything that you're seemingly paralyzed and inactive! If you can't seem to ever get anything done, maybe your goals are just too big or unrealistic. Persistently pursuing a big dream is great when you're getting somewhere. But if you're not, it's the energy-draining pits. Repeatedly hitting dead ends can also make your levels of CRP—C-reactive protein, a marker of inflammation—rise. Since inflammation has been linked to depressive symptoms, stewing over going nowhere may add to your blues. Instead, let go of what's not working and replace it with smaller, newer, more reachable goals.

Take a 10-minute mind-trip: Remember the last time you were on vacation and it embodied every definition of that word? You can go there any time you like—and reap the relaxing rewards—using your imagination. All it takes is a quiet spot, an easy chair or place to lie down, and 10 to 15 uninterrupted minutes. Eyes closed, bring to your mind an image of the place where you felt peaceful and happy. Now scan the scene from top to bottom, left to right and "see" little details—the way the sun reflected off the water or the appearance of a decadent dinner. What sounds did you hear? How did the air smell? Relive as many things as you can. Feel the pure pleasure of being in that space and time. You'll soon feel as relaxed as if you'd actually been there. You can then open your eyes and be prepared to maximize your time and energy better. Moms who live in Quad II already know how to enjoy their mental time-outs, and anyone seeking to join them can master this technique as well.

I really think that television is a total energy suck. Sometimes it's great to just veg out and give in to that, but I think it should be something that we look forward to once in a while—rather than every day. Even if you just have it on in the background, the sound and visual movement on TV interrupts the kind of focus you need to foster in order to get things done as a mom. We have enough little energy suckers running around, let's limit the ones we can turn off!

— RACHEL LINCOLN SARNOFF,

executive director and CEO of Healthy Child Healthy World, founder of www.EcoStiletto.com, and mom of three, on secrets to energy success

---

Listen to your body: It sounds cliché, but it's true. Listening to your body can do wonders, and you know what kind of listening we're talking about. It's the kind that dictates a mother's instincts. It's also the kind that allows you to be really honest with yourself and your needs, avoiding excuses, external messages or influences that can block your ability to hear yourself. When you're contemplating exercise, for instance, you can say, "C'mon, are you just feeling lazy and sorry for yourself? Overwhelmed? That's when you need to pull yourself up by your bootstraps and go! You'll get so much from it." We know how to listen to our bodies. We are women. We've been listening since our training bras. We're far better at this than men. Don't fool yourself or use excuses.

Becoming a master of time management takes more than practice. It also takes a commitment every single day to navigating competing demands and constantly asking yourself where you should be putting your energy first, second, third, and so on. Most of us let our time-management skills fall by the wayside once in a while, even those of us who think we're living in Quad II. It's inevitable. We intuitively know what's really urgent and what's not but we feel compelled to respond to everything. And there's no end to the amount of information we increasingly find ourselves bombarded with through e-mail, snail mail, texts, IM, the television, and so on.

Just having a good sense of where your weaknesses are and keeping practical strategies on hand will help you to get through your days with efficiency, and hopefully some energy left over. We hope the lessons in this chapter will prepare you for the advice coming up in the next two chapters on making "energy exchanges" in your dietary choices. We don't know any mother who doesn't waste precious time trying to keep up with all the myriad choices we have now in the marketplace. Between the promotional machines and the sheer number of options in the grocery stores, it can get downright confusing and exhausting. So, in addition to reorganizing your time and priorities, let's now turn to how you can rethink your grocery shopping and, in turn, reorganize your kitchen, pantries, and entire eating patterns.

MOM UP! JUMP-START
YOUR TRANSFORMATION

Regardless of which Quadrant you're in, see if you can up your level of productivity and overall energy just doing the following: go on a media purge for one week. This means being brutal with the time you spend on the Internet, e-mail, and television. Set very clear boundaries, such as not checking e-mail or doing anything digitally related until after 10 A.M. On the other end of the day, disconnect yourself from electronics at 6 P.M. to spend quality time with the family. Try to avoid reading too many headlines as well. Author Timothy Ferriss writes about going on such a purge in his best-selling book *The 4-Hour Workweek* (if only motherhood held such a promise!), and he proves how enormously transformative it can be to a person's overall ability to get things done (with energy to spare). So see if you can last for one full week on a media purge and take note of how you feel (better) and what you're able to accomplish (more). This is like giving your body a time-management "reboot"—you'll emerge out of the purge with a new perspective on what's really important and be able to better prioritize and manage your life. You'll lose the fat (life in Quads I, III, and IV) and gain the fitness (life in Quad II).

CHAPTER 4

The Energy Exchange Part 1: Ditch Energy Drainers in Your Diet

Motherhood has a very humanizing effect.
Everything gets reduced to essentials.

— MERYL STREEP

We live in an age where dietary advice comes at us from every portal of our daily lives. Some of these new advancements fall under the high-tech category, such as keeping a food journal on our phones or scanning a bar code for additional info or ratings on food products. Other high-tech advancements fall into the arena of food technology. Food product developers can now make seemingly healthier versions of our favorite foods by adding artificial scents and tastes that remind us of the original thing. They can also use chemicals such as artificial preservatives and additives, as well as pesticides and genetic engineering of plant and possibly animal DNA.

We've gone from living in a primal forest where our food was picked directly from the ground or plucked from trees to living in a technologically advanced Jetsons-style society where even our "natural" foods are engineered. To think we can engineer animals now, such as salmon, to "create" fish that are twice the size in half the time is amazing on the one hand, but on the other raises questions. Is this a good thing? What does eating a genetically modified fish do to our bodies?

If we think that speeding up the growth process could have any positive merits, then let's think about what else involves sped-up cells: cancer and premature aging, anyone? And what does it mean for developmental stages among consumers of genetically modified foods that may (or may not) adversely affect our biology? When we take shortcuts, there are usually trade-offs to consider. And when it comes to genetically modified foods, we just don't know yet what repercussions could be brewing. Eating foods that look normal on the outside could be telling another story on the inside. Added hormones in the food chain have already been blamed for some of the trends in adolescents whereby girls reach puberty much sooner than girls in previous generations.

So while all this food technology makes our food prettier and bigger, it also departs from nature. These foods don't necessarily speak our bodies' native language, which means they can throw our energy equations off balance. When it comes to foods, consider the watchful phrase "just because they can doesn't mean we should."

As much as the world around us has vastly changed, our bodies still speak the same basic language they have always and forever known. But now the ingredients listed on the packaging of foods often sound more like an advanced chemistry lesson than a simple snack. And just as these words sound foreign to us, our bodies aren't naturally programmed to understand "monosodium glutamate," either. When we lived in the state of nature, there was a perfect fit between our physiology and our food supply. What we ate was perfectly suited to our physical needs—and as a result we "hummed." Chronic low energy and a sedentary baseline would have been completely unknown to our primitive ancestors. Obviously, we are not recommending that we all don loincloths and try to recapture the primeval lifestyle, but we could learn a lot from our cavewoman ancestors. Think about it: without lights they went to bed and rose with the sun. Energy wasn't an option; it was a means of survival.

PREPARE TO END BODY CHAOS: GO BACK TO HIGH SCHOOL

You remember the days when life was relatively easy. You got up, went to school, probably did something fun afterward, and then sat down to do homework before going to bed to rest up for another day. Your choices in snacks were probably healthier than they are today, too, by virtue of the fact we didn't have so many processed options back then. Thoughts about the "real world" and having children were farther away than your dreams. The kind of math you were trying to understand was something along the lines of $a + b = c$.

You may have forgotten algebra now that you are, in fact, in the real world, but the beauty and simplicity with which algebra allows us to make certain calculations can be applied to our biology. Metaphorically speaking, that is. When you treat your body in simple, straightforward terms, it will respond by maximizing functionality and energy production. When you feed it "fake" ingredients, suddenly $a + b$ no longer equals c. Instead, we get $a 1 + b + 2 = c1 + 2$. Body chaos ensues. The energy equation breaks down. This is what lays the foundation for chronic disease and blocks energy.

Nutritional medicine is a rapidly growing area of research that will continue to gain momentum as we learn more and more about the connections between nutrition and health—not just for general health, but for all kinds of health concerns. In fact, the link between nutrition and diseases such as obesity, diabetes, cancer, and cardiovascular disease are well documented. Gaining the upper hand on oxidative stress, inflammation, and, to a lesser extent, genetics, is key because they are the chief agers in our bodies that spur chronic conditions that wear us down. And if diet can help this in any way, then we should be paying attention.

Anything that goes against the natural design of our body's most basic and elemental needs will invariably sabotage efforts to maximize energy. For example, that diet soda or latte may work as a (very) short-term fix, but it will only exacerbate the problems that are underlying your energy shortage. Similarly, if you're conscientiously following a diet program that isn't operating in sync with your body's true needs, then no matter how "good" you're being or how saintly your intent, you are not going to see the results you are working so hard to obtain.

We realize that you may have heard (and tried) to "avoid processed foods" in the past to drop a few pounds or get healthier. But your efforts eventually failed. We agree, it can be daunting and ultimately unsatisfying, as well as unrealistic. We live in the 21st century, and there's something to be said for having access to quick and great-tasting food. We're not asking you to nix everything that hails from a factory or comes in a package. We're just asking you to manage the energy drainers in your life by (1) recognizing where they are, and (2) being more mindful of how much you choose to pick from the energy-giving plate versus the energy-sapping one. And therein lies the challenge: knowing the difference between what you think you're eating and what you really are. Today's marketing dynamics are just as much to blame in perpetuating body chaos as we are to blame for favoring processed foods over wholesome, natural ones.

Modifying the way you eat and buy goods may take some time to get used to. We won't sugarcoat the reality: if you've been eating processed, packaged foods regularly for years, shifting how you eat won't happen overnight. And that's okay. Make it a goal to just upgrade at a pace that's doable and with choices that give you the biggest nutritional bang for your food buck. If you can't imagine changing your breakfast or lunch staples, then what about adding organic vegetables to them? What about swapping out a less-healthy fat for a healthier one in your dressing? What about splitting your meal in half and having the second part three hours later for better energy balance? What if these evolutions, not revolutions, resulted in more energy, looser-fitting clothes, and an internally healthier you? We can confidently say they can and will. We've found the weight-loss factor in particular to be enormously motivating for women. In fact, both of us have witnessed women who simply stopped using coffee creamers and artificially flavored beverages (sold under the guise of "light" or "diet" items) and achieved significant results in just a week's time. And they far outpace those who go back to consuming artificial ingredients in their weight-loss efforts. Keep it simple, and the body gets it and has an easier time getting rid of excess fat, not to mention toxins that go with it.

If the thought of depriving yourself of the foods you currently enjoy doesn't sit well with you, then simply pick up more fresh fruits and vegetables at the market and don't change anything else. Make additions rather than deletions to your lifestyle at the start. You can and will wean yourself from the stuff the real energy is not made of once you begin to incorporate nutrient-dense, energy-supporting alternatives into your life. Over time, when you aren't operating from a self-deprivation strategy, you will notice that your taste buds have changed and you'll find yourself obsessing less over the displays at the bakery and more over what you can do with the colorful array of goods in the produce section of a market. Or as one mom-energy model shared with me: "We get a delivery now once a week of organic vegetables so we've had to get creative about how to use them. I love the recipes they send, but I have also started swapping with some friends on Facebook who get the same vegetable box." As with anything, as you become comfortable with it, your priorities change and you begin to instinctively make different choices. (Does this remind you of other big changes you've already gone through in your life as a mom?) You'll start to order food differently in a restaurant and be more conscious about reading labels and asking questions about how your meals are prepared.

MANAGE MARKETING MAYHEM

In recent years, we learned to "skip the center and shop the perimeter" of the food market, but as we learned and changed our shopping behaviors, so did the stores and the companies. Today, the perimeter often has as much poor-quality food on display as the healthy stuff. If we can't trust the package and we can't shop the perimeter, does this mean there are no shortcuts to healthy shopping and hence healthy eating? Does shopping have to be a new skill that we must study to achieve successfully? Well, yes and no. Before you close the book and shudder at the thought of more to do, exhale and read on to our list of shortcuts—but also note that changing habits and learning new things does require a commitment. But just like you don't run a mile the first day you decide to exercise, you can start by walking—and walking through the grocery store means taking a list based on the ideas and examples in this book and trying to replace the items that you would have bought before with healthier versions to see how it goes. It may feel boring or limiting, but it will be safe. It will save you time. It will get you results. And then as you succeed, you can start to increase your speed, add hills, run for longer—or the equivalent in the grocery store by trying to modify old favorites.

One prominent food manufacturer once promoted its brand by challenging children to recite the ingredients in a popular product. The kids who read the label could clearly state—and understand—the words, such as *eggs* and *milk*. The kids who read the competition stumbled over long, convoluted ingredients that sounded like a chemistry set. The lesson: if you can easily pronounce the words on a list of ingredients, nine times out of ten you're eating something close to nature. That's a pretty good barometer to use.

When you walk into the fresh produce department of a grocery store, you're not likely to find "high in vitamin C" on an orange, or "a great source of healthy fats" on an avocado. Instead, these claims are trumpeted from boxed, processed, and packaged goods.

Whenever a processed product boasts such a claim, you should question why. Food manufacturers want to control what matters to you. Every single food and food product in the store has a marketing team working hard to promote the brand. The net effect: when you walk down a grocery aisle, it's like hundreds of voices talking to you at one time (and you thought a household with two to five voices could get crazy). It's overstimulation, and we need to take our brains back! Let's look at some considerations:

- Even if a manufacturer has added something to a food to achieve a higher nutritional level than what exists in nature, it begs the question: is the form of what's added absorbable? Can we absorb that much? Should we? What's the rationale?

- Just because manufacturers can and do add nutrients to a food product, does that action have other consequences, such as competing with what's naturally in the food? For example, increasingly higher calcium in the absence of magnesium can create an imbalance of these two minerals that ultimately detracts from your body's energy-making machine.

- If we give too much attention to one vitamin, can it create a "conditional deficiency" of another? (Ask your kids: if you give more attention to one, how does the other feel?) B vitamins work best together, so if we over support one B vitamin, we can create a condition whereby the lack of others at the same level creates unhealthy by-products and dysenergy—dysfunctional energy—issues in the body. Whom do we trust to meet our nutrient needs: Mother Manufacturer or Mother Nature?

- What about getting 100 percent (or more) of your daily needs in one food—is that a smart goal? At first it seems great because it means we don't have to think about getting any more throughout the day, but we should think about consuming nutrients all day long, especially from whole-food sources. A glass of OJ at breakfast with 100 percent of your daily vitamin C needs doesn't mean you should shun a real orange or other vitamin C–packed whole fruit later on as part of a snack.

- And what about ingredients added to foods that naturally wouldn't contain them? For example, our yogurt may not supply us with a lot of fiber, but it gives us high-quality protein plus pre- and probiotics—the ingredients to support lean body mass, a healthy balance of hormones, digestive wellness, and heightened immunity. We can increase fiber by adding fresh fruit or ground flaxseed on top. Yogurts that add synthetic or processed fibers may be less than ideal, but moreover, they are unnecessary when you rely on nature's fiber sources.

> Don't judge a book by its cover: The front of all
> packaged goods simply reflects what you told the
> food manufacturers you want. Yes, we all want a
> high-fiber, low-sugar, low-fat, delicious combination
> of ingredients that will cure cancer, provide energy,
> and help us fit into our skinny clothes. But always
> be sure to check the nutrition facts and ingredients.
> Just because the front of the package says so,
> doesn't mean the contents can or will deliver.

Marketing terms are regulated but to date, unfortunately, not very well enforced, and again, these terms aren't typically a complete nutrition thought. For example, "Naturally fat free" could distract us from the fact the product is loaded with sugar. Deceptive claims abound: low-fat, high-fiber, light, no sugar added. Some brands have become more healthful. But many manufacturers are promoting a product's healthful ingredients while playing down its less nutritional qualities. Last year, the FDA sent warning letters to 17 food manufacturers, many of which were household names, insisting they change the wording on their labels. Even First Lady Michelle Obama and the White House Task Force on Childhood Obesity have recommended that labeling on food packages be more clearly defined, yet they believe it should come from the companies regulating themselves. Companies respond to consumer demand, so in order for them to self-regulate we need to demand that change by buying differently. In 2010, the Center for Science in the Public Interest, a nonprofit health-advocacy organization, published an alarming report called "Food Labeling Chaos" about just that—the confusion over what labels claim. The changes currently being lobbied about in Washington, D.C., could take years to go into effect. Until then, be wary of the words and phrases you're reading in the grocery aisles. Here's our cheat sheet to the marketing mayhem.

Natural or organic: One is legally regulated, the other is a marketing concept with no definition. A company can use the term *natural* to mean just about anything. Consumers often assume it implies organic, but that's not the case. The U.S. Department of Agriculture has strict guidelines for a company to meet before it can label a food organic, but the organic versus nonorganic conversation can sometimes get confusing. (We'll discuss more on the term *organic* later.)

Made with whole wheat: If it does not say 100 percent whole wheat or 100 percent whole grain, then be wary. The food may contain only a trivial amount of whole grain. Example: one popular brand of English muffins lists "unbleached enriched wheat flour" as its primary ingredient. That is just a fancy phrase for ordinary white flour.

Healthy: To use the word *healthy,* companies must meet certain FDA regulations per serving size. Some companies have been accused of increasing the number of serving sizes per product, rather than change the ingredients. If a person eats the entire jar or drinks the whole bottle, it would not meet the regulations. Manipulating the serving size is, by some experts, the most dangerous problem in food-labeling confusion. We've all eaten an entire can of soup thinking it's all one serving. But if you look closely, the nutrition label on the back might say otherwise—and it may even list a strange 2.5 servings for two and a half people. So at the end of the can, you've downed more than twice the number of calories and probably maxed out your sodium needs for the entire day—not a good thing for balance and energy. Remember, a food shouldn't have to tell you what it is—as in "healthy" or "food"—so if it does, then it likely isn't telling you the whole story, but rather telling you *their* story. It should be illegal for companies to use words such as *healthy*, *lean*, or *light* unless those foods adhere to a clear set of nutrition principles. In England, for example, food manufacturers aren't allowed to use the term *superfood* without meeting certain science-based criteria. Clearly, such terms have a lot of marketing power.

Supports or a source of: These are loose terms that insinuate the food helps protect against a popular health concern. The latest trend is a lack of vitamin D, because of concerns that a deficiency in vitamin D may play a role in a host of health conditions, from obesity to dementia and even autism. If a food says it is an "excellent source of vitamin D," it may only mean that it will provide a percentage of the current RDA, which is 600 IU (International Units). However, most experts agree the current RDA is extremely low for general health, as well as completely insufficient to replenish those who are clinically low in vitamin D. Moreover, you could be getting it in a form that isn't well absorbed. D is a fat-soluble vitamin, so it helps to have some healthy fat nearby to ensure optimal absorption.

High in fiber: Dietary fiber is critical to a healthy diet and the proper functioning of our bodies. It helps our bodies absorb carbohydrates efficiently; it help us feel full; it aids digestion both by adding bulk to stool and by scraping the lining of the digestive tract (our built-in cleaning system); it aids heart health; and as a prebiotic, it promotes a hospitable environment for probiotics, the healthy bacteria that help our digestion and support our immune system. Although fiber is not technically a nutrient, its role in managing the nutrients in your body—and its energy equations—is so essential to your health and metabolism that we might as well call it a nutrient.

Fiber is naturally found in the skins of fruits and vegetables, legumes, sprouts, and grains (especially whole grains). Most people don't get enough fiber, which is in the orbit of at least 25 grams per day for women. Our consumption of highly processed foods and beverages (other than pure water) has decreased the average amount of fiber in our collective diet; as a result, numerous synthetic fibers are sold as supplements and added into food products. Is the fiber found in a processed box of sugary cereal the same as what drops from an apple tree? Not nearly.

Many foods contain "isolated fibers" to boost the fiber content. But it is unlikely these isolated fibers, usually inulin, polydextrose, and maltodextrin, provide the same health benefits as "intact fibers," such as those found in whole beans or oats. Fiber One Oats & Chocolate bars, for instance, provide 35 percent of daily fiber, but the fiber comes mainly from chicory root extract, which contains inulin, and which incidentally can cause bloating and gas in many when they consume significant quantities at one time.

While these additives may add bulk and provide some of fiber's benefits, they don't necessarily include the phytonutrients, vitamins, and minerals found in nature's fiber sources. Add whole foods into your diet first, and then carefully incorporate fiber-added products only as needed. Try to include some fiber at every meal. If you have food allergies or intolerances, it's important for you to include other natural sources of fiber (rice bran, chia bran, and flaxseeds are excellent sources) to make up for the fiber in the foods you avoid. And watch out for fiber added to foods that are high in sugar. Froot Loops, for example, says it "now provides fiber." But the 12 grams of sugar in each 1 cup serving of the cereal could have far more negative effects than any benefit from the slim amount of added fiber.

Zero trans fat: In 2003 the FDA announced that trans fat was a contributing factor to coronary heart disease. If a product says it contains few or zero grams of trans fat, look at the nutrition label. Often it will be loaded with saturated fat, which can be just as unhealthful as trans fat. Example: One popular frozen snack makes the "zero trans fat" claim on the front of the label, but the nutrition facts panel shows it has 17 grams of saturated fat, 80 percent of the daily value of fat a person should consume.

Naturally fruit flavored: Some snacks display fresh fruit on the front label and state they are "naturally fruit flavored!" But often the real fruit contained in the package comes from a small amount of pear juice concentrate, a highly sugared form of fruit. Example: Betty Crocker Strawberry Splash Fruit Gushers are made primarily from pear concentrate and contain about 12 grams of added sugar. Also watch out for the label "made with real fruit." Most of these products have little nutrition as compared to their authentic fruit counterparts. Manufacturers put a drop of juice into the product, even though added sugar outweighs the fruit. When Ashley Koff Approved (AKA) was asked to "approve" a product developed by two moms that is USDA certified organic, AKA was appalled at the first three ingredients on the label—various forms of sugar and juice concentrate. A fruit snack? This was candy—albeit organic candy. Had they marketed it as such, AKA could have approved of these products for occasional consumption and with a portion control note. But as a fruit snack? That's absurd, organic or not.

> "Rich in calcium!" "Lower in sugar!" "High in vitamin C!"
> If it has to say it, it's likely not your best option.
> This is especially true about energy promises (or
> over-promises). Plain and simple, real food provides
> energy. It's just absurd that marketers promote their
> products with promises of more energy or better
> energy than food found in nature. After all, it isn't
> just the food's inherent energy but how the body
> uses it for energy that provides net energy results.

Contains antioxidants, contains vitamins, contains omega-3s: Sometimes foods and beverages are fortified with nutrients, such as "functional" soda pops or cereals with added vitamins and minerals. But fortifying a junk food does not undo its junkiness. Every year there is a new "it" ingredient among food manufacturers, which then gets media coverage. Soon after, we're looking for it in every food we eat. This poses nutrition issues as opposed to resolving them. First of all, a product with added nutrients from isolated forms is unlikely to benefit you the same way that those nutrients would when consumed in their natural form.

Second, it's possible to get too much of a single nutrient when it's added to a food product, and more isn't necessarily better.

The same holds true when it comes to the omega fatty acids. In the last 15 years or so we've been isolating a few omegas and concentrating them down to add to foods and supplements. But when you consider natural food sources that contain omegas, we often find a whole host of other healthy fats that we need but don't get when we consume isolated omega-3. Could we potentially see deficiencies of omega-5, -7, or -9 in the general population down the road if we continue to focus on supplementing omega-3 at a high dosage? Something to think about.

> **Profile Alert!** Did you see yourself as Profile 4 (The Chronic Dieter)? If so, pay attention to the following section.

DIET DETOX

We are what we eat. Though that statement is cliché, it's really true. If you performed a complete chemical analysis of your body, the report would list materials similar to those in foods: water, fat molecules, carbohydrates, protein complexes, and vitamins and minerals that help you to metabolize food and generate the energy you need to live. Think of the body as a self-maintaining factory; it is constantly regenerating itself down to every cell. Each month we renew our skin, every six weeks we have a new liver, and every three months we have new bones. To renew and rebuild these organs and tissues, we need to supply our bodies with the elements that have been lost as a result of constant use, degeneration, or aging. We also need to manage the imposters and substitutes that vandalize our normal functions. Let us explain.

In Dr. Mark Hyman's *UltraMetabolism: The Simple Plan for Automatic Weight Loss*, he calls for detoxifying the liver as a critical step to weight loss. His reasoning: a healthy functioning liver makes for a healthy functioning metabolism that can properly process foods.

He underscores the fact that toxins from both within our bodies and our environment can contribute to obesity. Hence, eliminating toxins and boosting your natural detoxification system is an essential component of long-term weight loss and a healthy metabolism.

> Carrying excess fat isn't an issue of appearance per se.
> We know it plays a role in serious metabolic changes
> that interfere with the body's core systems and organs.
> Excess fat is a signal—an important one at that.
> It shouldn't be ignored.

We couldn't agree with him more. It's another vicious cycle that results in low energy: the more fat you have, the more toxins you retain, and the more toxins you retain, the harder it becomes to sustain a healthy metabolism to support ideal weight and energy production.

Too much fat can also slow down the time it takes for you to feel full, so you overconsume and fuel the cycle again. This is possible due to the hormones involved with fat metabolism. When faced with toxicity, our bodies respond by retaining water in an effort to dilute water-soluble toxins; our bodies also retain fat, to try and dilute fat-soluble toxins. Science has now proven that toxins in the blood can make a direct hit on our resting metabolic rates. Moreover, the same studies have determined that toxins affect the production of the thyroid hormones, which play a major role in your body's metabolism.

For 30 years now we've known that toxins can hinder our fat-burning engines by upward of 20 percent. Contrary to what you might think, fat cells are not inactive. Fat generates a multitude of biomolecules, including enzymes, hormones, and chemical messengers that tell our bodies what to do, which in turn affects how we look and feel. It has been said that our total body fat mass represents our largest endocrine (hormonal) organ since it is much larger than our pituitary, adrenal, thyroid, and sex glands.

Many of these molecules, such as estrogen, cortisol, and leptin, can promote more fat storage. The aromatase enzyme in fat, for example, converts testosterone into estrogen and further promotes fat storage. In fact, much of what fat does is continually signal the body to make more fat cells and store more energy via fat. In this process toxins are stored in fat as well, which aggravate the situation even more by promoting more fat storage. These toxins essentially mess with the proper signaling we need for maintaining a good ratio of fat to muscle.

Other factors can also contribute to the chaotic signaling. In our 24/7 lives where the lights are always on, we sleep rarely (and poorly), and we have an abundance of refined sugar available to keep us artificially charged, exacerbate the imbalance we experience in our body's internal workings. So again, it's a vicious cycle.

Toxins typically travel with the other impersonators found in our diets. Below is a list of common ingredients to avoid, followed by a few tips to cleaning up your environment. If you avoid these imposters, you'll automatically detoxify your kitchen and fuel your energy-producing power.

High-fructose corn syrup: It is NOT "just fruit plus corn." High-fructose corn syrup is a man-made ingredient that the body works harder to break down. When we eat this stuff, the result is digestive slowdown and increased risk of disease. Moreover, high-fructose corn syrup contains genetically modified (GMO) corn, so it's got unnatural ingredients in the corn that could create allergies and irritation, and have a negative impact on the body's energy. Stick to eating fruit and eating corn—your body gets them because they are real food. Watch out for high-*maltose* corn syrup too. As people begin to avoid high-fructose corn syrup, the food manufacturers are getting crafty with new variations on the same theme. Maltose is just another type of sugar that's often man-made. (For more about "real" versus "natural," see the box on page 80.)

Processed or added sugar: The sugar in a carrot is not the same as the sugar in a slice of carrot cake. The carrot has 30 calories and is loaded with beta-carotene, fiber, water, and potassium. The piece of cake is just a 300-calorie land mine of sugar and fat. It's the added sugars that are the problem in our diets today—not the natural sugar in foods untouched by man. Food manufacturers have used this added-sugar versus natural-sugar issue to their advantage, deceiving us into thinking their foods are made with real ingredients. Some have tried to pass high-fructose corn syrup off as natural, when in fact it's far from it. Others suggest that high-fructose corn syrup is fine in moderation, but the average American consumes 30 teaspoons of sugar daily—19 more teaspoons than advised by the World Health Organization. Clearly there is no moderation.

You can still go for sugar, even in excess once in a while, but do so knowingly (and use the cheat sheet in the box on page 80 as a guide). Everyone has a slightly different sensitivity to sugar. The more sensitive your moods and cravings are to sugar, the bigger bang for your buck you'll get by cutting back. So yes, you can have your cake and eat it too, but know that the effects of sugar in the system can last a few days. Highly processed, sugary items are the ultimate dead-battery food, such as regular ketchup, barbecue sauce, and peanut butter, for instance.

Keep organic fresh fruit and veggies cut up in the fridge; make smoothies using fresh fruits such as bananas, berries, and orange juice; or buy frozen, plain smoothie packs and then customize.

Artificial sweeteners (aspartame, saccharine, sucralose, acesulfame potassium, and cyclamate): These are hundreds to thousands of times sweeter than Mother Nature's sugar, and as such they can prevent you from feeling any sweet satisfaction from real food. If you get used to these little packets (or low-fat, sugar-free packaged goods that contain artificial sweeteners), suddenly fruit and sugar from our Mother doesn't taste so sweet. Studies prove that these sugars can trigger you to overeat. One Purdue study in particular found that even though these sweeteners don't contain calories, they cause weight gain in animals. The researchers speculate that the intense sweetness tricks the

Navigating the Sugar Minefield: Is it real or fake? A diamond or a cubic zirconia? Unfortunately, nutrition labels don't have to say where the sugar came from; they just have to provide total sugar content. To sleuth out the truth, read the ingredients list. All of the following are code words for added sugar:

Brown sugar	Fruit juice concentrates	Molasses
Corn sweetener	Glucose	Raw sugar
Corn syrup	High-fructose corn syrup	Rice syrup
Crystalline fructose	Honey	Sucrose
Dextrose	Invert sugar	Sugar
Evaporated cane juice	Malt syrup	Syrup
Fructose	Maltose	

Also, bear in mind that a food's contents must be listed on the label in descending order from most to least. The closer to the top of the list, the more of an ingredient is in the food. Aim to avoid or limit foods that contain any of the above-mentioned sugar aliases in the top three ingredients. If you focus on limiting the biggest offenders—soda, fruit drinks, candy, sweet baked goods, and ice cream—you'll do your body's energy metabolism well. More than 75 percent of our sugar comes from these items. Here's another way to look at it: if you eliminate just these five categories of foods from your diet for a year, you could save 78,000 calories and drop 20 pounds!

brain into thinking that calories are on their way when they aren't! The body gets confused, slows metabolism, and ramps up appetite. This imbalance in regulating calories leads to overeating. Also, artificial sweeteners are often found in combination with sugar alcohols such as maltitol, sorbitol, glycerol, and mannitol, among others. Sugar alcohols, which offer sweetness but do not get absorbed, are designed to replace table sugar. Because these molecules technically are not digested, they can linger in the digestive tract for a longer period of time and cause stomach upset in people with sensitive tummies or who consume excessive sugar alcohols.

Better alternatives: Use natural forms of sweetness such as organic honey, organic sugar, organic coconut palm sugar, maple syrup, molasses, and natural sweeteners such as organic stevia and erythritol in moderation.

Hydrogenated and partially-hydrogenated oils (ahem: trans fats): You know these clog your arteries already from all their media exposure, hence the halo over monounsaturated options such as extra-virgin olive oil. As we just noted, nature provides a balance of fats in many whole-food forms, so the key is to consume most of your fats in the whole-food form. When consuming products with fats in them, look to see if they contain a variety so you're not consuming just one type of saturated fat and zero monounsaturated fat. Limit your intake of the polyunsaturated from these vegetable oils (e.g., corn, sunflower, safflower, soy, and cottonseed), and use extra-virgin olive oil more often to replace these. Olive oil is heat-stable at low temperatures for cooking, which is the healthier way to cook anyway. Or, use other fats such as omega-3-rich chia and flaxseed oils, or blends such as an omega-3, -6, -9 mix or hempseed oil. As we'll see in Chapter 5, you'll want to eat more oily fish (salmon, sardines, herring, mackerel, and black cod) and use a variety of nuts and seeds such as walnuts, chia, hemp, and flaxseeds; as well as omega-3 fortified organic eggs to ensure you get sufficient omega-3 fatty acids for optimal health.

Enriched and bleached flour: After the refining process strips this flour of dozens of nutrients, it's then "enriched" through the addition of just four nutrients (B1, B2, niacin, and iron, in a synthetic form). Don't be fooled by the "enriched" name. You're not getting any richer. You're losing out on energy-fueling ingredients naturally found in these foods before man got a hold of them in the processing plant.

Monosodium glutamate (MSG): MSG should stand for "something that my body hates." Okay, maybe that's harsh, but for many people their reaction to it is just that—severe. For the rest, what we need to know is that MSG irritates our digestive tract, which is a big negative for optimal energy. For a list of MSG hideouts, see the following table.

MSG HIDEOUTS		
Foods always contain monosodium glutamate if any of these are in the ingredients list:		
Autolyzed plant protein	Glutamic acid	Sodium caseinate
Autolyzed yeast	Hydrolyzed plant protein	Textured protein
Calcium caseinate	Hydrolyzed vegetable protein	Yeast extract
Gelatin	Monopotassium glutamate	Yeast food or nutrient
Glutamate	Monosodium glutamate (MSG)	

Foods often contain MSG if any of these are in the ingredients list:		
Annatto	Flavoring seasonings (most assume this means salt and pepper or herbs and spices, which it sometimes is)	Protein-fortified anything
Barley malt	Flowing agents	Protein fortified milk
Bouillon	Gums	Rice or brown rice, syrup
Broth	Lipolyzed butter fat	Soy protein
Caramel flavoring (coloring)	Low or no fat items	Soy protein isolate or concentrate
Carrageenan	Malt extract or flavoring	Soy sauce or concentrate
Citric acid (when processed from corn)	Malted barley (flavor)	Soy sauce or extract
Corn syrup and corn syrup solids (partly depends upon process used)	Maltodextrin	Spice
Cornstarch	Milk powder	Stock
Dough conditioners	Modified food (or corn) starch	Ultra-pasteurized anything
Dry milk solids	Natural chicken	Vitamin enriched
Enriched	Pectin	Whey protein isolate

The mind, mouth, and reward system love the one-two salt-sugar punch. If we have salty food, do we crave sweet soon after? Often. So skip the soy sauce with sushi and perhaps an orange as dessert will satisfy you, versus needing ice cream or frozen yogurt.

A better alternative: Instead of using salt, season your meals with herbs, such as basil, oregano, and rosemary. These have anti-inflammatory properties, so they act like little energy optimizers in your body. Some ideas to have on hand in your kitchen:

- Fresh lemons

- Vinegar (balsamic, red-wine, apple-cider, etc.)

- Mustard

- Chiles

- Pepper

- Garlic

- Coarse sea salt or sesame salt

- A collection of fresh or dried herbs
  (e.g., basil, thyme, oregano, rosemary)

Look out for canned and packaged foods; they often contain way too much salt. Rather than using salt, cook with foods that naturally contain sodium, such as beets and their greens, kelp powder and other seaweeds, celery, chard, parsley, spinach, and kale.

Colorings known as red 3, yellow 6, blue 1, blue 2, and green 3: Nature created colorful fruits and vegetables so they'd be attractive to us. They help with our hearts, our eyes, our skin, our digestive tract, and provide antioxidant benefits. The colors created in a lab with numbers on them are made to look pretty, but they are imposters and may exacerbate behavioral reactions in people with sensitivities. As this book was going to press, the FDA commenced an investigation into a potential link between food dyes and attention deficit hyperactivity disorder (ADHD) in children. Pretty soon, we could see these ingredients totally banned!

Salt: We all need a little salt (sodium) in our diets for the healthy function of nerves and muscles, including the heart. Salt is also essential for counteracting toxins in the body, for strengthening digestion, and for helping with the balance of acid-forming foods or acidic conditions created by nutritious foods such as beans, peas, grains, and meats. Although every cell in your body needs salt to work properly, we consume far more than we need. Your chance of being deficient is nil. That's why when we take in extra salt, we require extra water to reduce the sodium concentration to an optimal level, which results in excess water retention throughout the body that can tax our systems and drag our energy metabolism down. What's more, not all salt is created equal. Salts should have minerals, and they should be used in the cooking stage or ingredient combining—not as an additive and not as an extra preservative.

REDUCING ENERGY-DEPLETING TOXINS FROM NON-FOODS

It's not just about the foods that impart energy-depleting chemicals. Although it's impossible to avoid all the toxins in our world, there are a number of easy, practical things you can do to minimize your exposure. Some of them:

- Remove your shoes when entering your home, so you don't track germs and pollutants inside.

- Use air filters or commit to proper ventilation: HEPA/ULPA filters and ionizers can be helpful in reducing dust, molds, and airborne chemical compounds.

- Drink filtered water: use reverse osmosis systems or carbon filters. (Brita and Pur water systems allow you to fill up pitchers from your sink to filter and keep chilled in the fridge; you can also buy filters that go right onto your main tap in the kitchen.)

- Clean and monitor your heating system: this will reduce carbon-dioxide emissions that can literally poison you.

- Keep houseplants: live plants filter the air and add oxygen. Fill your home with spider plants, aloe vera, chrysanthemum, Gerber daisies, Boston fern, English ivy, and philodendrons.

- Purchase environmentally friendly cleaning products (baking soda and distilled vinegar products are relatively harmless).

- Avoid excess exposure to environmental petrochemicals, such as those found in gardening supplies, dry-cleaning fumes (air out your clothes when they come back from the cleaners), car exhaust, and secondhand smoke.

- Reduce or eliminate plastics, nonstick wares (i.e., Teflon-coated), and aluminums when you store (and, for that matter, cook) foods. Use nonplastic wares, containers, and wrappings, such as ceramic, porcelain, glass, and natural parchment paper.

- Use products with organic ingredients.

- Keep a tidy house (just the sight of a clean house can be energizing).

Don't look at this list and feel overwhelmed. You're not expected to change the way you live overnight. Just pick one thing to focus on for the week or month and then add more To Dos over time. Give yourself permission to modify your home and possessions in a relaxed and time-conscious manner.

I like to think of my body and my family's bodies more scientifically when grocery shopping, and I don't prepare meals with the thought that they're only pleasure feasts. I prepare great-tasting gourmet meals for them with the thought of refueling similar to a high-performance car: the higher the octane (i.e., organic and local nonprocessed), the more superior the output. I find when my kids eat balanced nutritious meals, they listen better, play together better, and are in better moods, which makes my energy level higher.

—DANIELLE DIETZ-LIVOLSI,

founder and president of JagRma LLC (the NuttZo brand),
mom of 3, and grandmother of 1,
on secrets to energy success

PUTTING THE "OH" IN ORGANIC

It's got to be one of the top questions we get these days: do organic foods deserve a halo for goodness or a warning sign for hype?

First, the most important point to remember is that organic food means food. Period. Anything else is food plus chemicals. It provides us food sans the genetically modified seeds, without the use of pesticides, and with an optimal nutrient load (i.e., that which a plant or animal develops naturally). In that regard, it deserves more halos than many other halos dished out today in the food court, such as the terms *superfoods*, *all-natural*, and *healthy*.

In a general sense, eating organic food is more likely to satisfy you because it forces you to find foods close to Mother Nature. You're also likely to consume more plant-based nutrients that include phytochemicals for disease and wrinkle prevention, and to energize as nature intended.

But there's a caveat emptor to consider. While organic is healthier than chemically produced food, it cannot be the only deciding factor. Organic does not mean calorie appropriate, low sodium, low sugar, higher fiber, or nutrient balanced. You still have to evaluate organic products for these and other nutrition principles. Eating organic does not give you permission to ignore sensible portion control and achieving a balance of nutrients. So if you choose to have a helping of organic Oreos, for example (they do exist: "made from organic flour and sugar"), you still must take into consideration their fat and carbohydrate content and try to consume some healthy protein as well to get a better balance of nutrition.

BEWARE OF GENETICALLY MODIFIED FOODS

Nearly 60 percent of all manufactured food products in the United States today include soy—but not the soy you might affiliate with a healthy Asian diet or the natural bean, a sacred grain dating back thousands of years. Estimates suggest that 80 percent of the soy production in the United States is genetically modified. Initially, farmers planted GM soybeans in the weakened fields during crop rotations to rejuvenate the soil. Then they would discard the soybeans with the tilling of the field. But when the big business of today's commercial farming and food industries realized they could sell this mature crop rather than throw it away, they decided to find some uses for it. This move has created an industry worth billions, similar to that of the corn industry, which gives us high-fructose corn syrup.

Over half of the corn planted in the United States has been genetically modified using biotechnology, and the jury is still out on what this could mean for human health and the environment. We do know that one of the largest groups of diseases (autoimmune) as well as an exponential increase in emergency room visits for allergies all share a common theme: the body is intolerant to, irritated by, and being confused into attacking itself by something it's consistently exposed to. That GMOs permeate the list of foods and products (soy, corn, gluten) that are problematic for many people further helps connect the dots to the potential impact of GMOs. This seems to be enough evidence for at least 30 other countries to enforce significant restrictions or ban genetically modified versions of these foods entirely because they are not considered safe. In late 2010,

To keep abreast of all the latest science when it comes to food (and the chemistry of food), check out The Center for Science in the Public Interest (CSPI) at www.cspinet.org. The CSPI is a consumer advocacy organization whose twin missions are to conduct innovative research and advocacy programs in health and nutrition, and to provide consumers with current, useful information about their health and well-being. You can access reports and alerts, as well as stay current with what's going on at the federal level to ensure food education and safety.
Other resourceful organizations include the Non-GMO Project (www.nongmoproject.org), the Environmental Working Group (www.ewg.org), and the Organic Center (www.organic-center.org).

when the news hit about the genetically modified salmon we mentioned earlier—the one that grows twice the size in half the time—the war about how to label this "Frankenfood" began. Until we know more about how GM foods affect us and our energy metabolisms, we would do well to avoid or limit them and stick to the foods nature gave us. Because we don't know the long-term effect, or even short-term consequences, anyone consuming GMOs is, in effect, a guinea pig in a very large experiment.

MOM UP! JUMP-START YOUR TRANSFORMATION

It's really true: fast food is key to mom energy. And by that we mean food that's easy to assemble or prepare, that can be picked up or packaged for on-the-go, and that's above all, balanced. Traditional fast food that clogs our highway rest stops (and our arteries) is the true speed trap to our energy; it should be renamed "junk food." If you need to do just one thing differently this week, given all the information we've given you in this chapter, then let it be this: see if you can move one baby step away from relying on any speed trap set up by a fast-food chain or food manufacturer whose product reeks of ingredients that we've called out as those to avoid. Spend ten minutes checking out the labels in your pantry and refrigerator. Find at least three products you use consistently and find a healthier substitute for them. For example, replace your ketchup made with high-fructose corn syrup with one that's made with real tomatoes and organic sugar. Or swap out your peanut butter that contains added sugar for a jar of another made with just 100 percent nuts. The ingredients should say "100 percent peanuts" and nothing more.

CHAPTER 5

The Energy Exchange Part 2: Choose Energy Solutions in the Marketplace

Many people worry so much about managing their careers,
but rarely spend half that much energy managing their LIVES.
I want to make my life, not just my job, the best it can be.
The rest will work itself out.

— REESE WITHERSPOON

Clearly, avoiding the Frankenfoods and managing the marketing mayhem relies heavily on the choices made about what to eat (rather than what not to eat). All the tools our bodies need to function optimally and efficiently (read: produce and utilize energy) can be found in foods. We need food to live, to maintain the structure and function of our cells, and to support and fuel the systems that keep us going strong—immune, digestive, respiratory, circulatory, and so on. But some foods can have little to none of the nutrients we need, so when we eat nutrient-poor foods, we ask the body to work with fewer resources. When we provide nutrient-poor food *and* chemicals, then we ask the body to not only do its daily work with fewer resources, but we also ask it to combat additional challenges. We are starting to see research that indicates this may be a recipe for disease. Regardless, we know that it's a recipe for imbalanced energy, which tips our metaphorical scale in favor of burnout, premature fatigue, careless mistakes, and confusion. Put another way, when we perpetually consume nutrient-poor foods and beverages filled with harmful impersonators such as hydrogenated trans fats, saturated fats, and refined sugars—topped with preservatives, additives, and artificial flavors and colors—we set ourselves up for downgrading our energy metabolism and, in turn, our health.

The short answer to how this happens is that our bodies lose the capacity to self-heal efficiently as chronic inflammation takes over and our natural sources of "fixer uppers," such as antioxidants, get used up. In addition, without ample supplies nearby and continual replenishment of the nutrients we need to run our systems and natural defense mechanisms, the flames of aging, inflammation, and free-radical pandemonium hit high marks. And when the stress simmers over long periods of time—perhaps years—the entire waterfall effect among hormones, inflammatory chemicals, and free radicals sets the stage for accelerated aging. It also spells a recipe for energy disaster.

We know we're not the first to hawk the idea of everything in moderation, but it's really true that moderation is key to establishing a successful, energy-sustaining relationship with food and eating. We also understand the need for certain comfort foods and sugar on occasion; sometimes we give in to environmental cues that have us indulging in foods that provide more consolation than pure energy. By definition, comfort foods make us feel good, can lift a bad mood, and plain and simple be a form of stress relief. So in that regard sugar can be medicine, too! But there's a difference between a food that provides us immediate comfort and one that provides us lasting comfort. The secret is to combine sugar with other ingredients so it doesn't promote body chaos and send you through swinging highs and lows. If you eat sugar after a meal rich in lean proteins, healthy fats, and carbs, or eat sugar alongside these types of hormone-friendly foods, it won't incite such a huge insulin response as it would on its own.

If you haven't figured it out by now, we are complex beings. There is no magic pill, potion, or formula for guaranteed energy. So many things coalesce in our bodies to produce either the results we want or don't want. You've already gotten a good dose of information about diet choices, hormones, exercise, sleep, and so on. Plenty of scientific research exists about eating certain foods to support your health and energy metabolism, and learning how to balance others that don't necessarily maximize your energy goals. Don't panic: we won't ask you to do anything unrealistic, such as suddenly savoring wheat-grass juice. Our ideas are meant to resonate with your intuitive sense of how to care for yourself, which goes to the core of how you care about others. We're not here to act like overbearing mothers, forcing you to eat your vegetables, clean your plate, evict dessert from your life forever, and enter a zone of deprivation. Living a healthy, energetic life is much easier than that!

As with any healthy-eating guidelines, the goal here is to supply your cells and systems with the raw materials they need to function efficiently and optimally, inside and out. You don't want to give your body any excuse to downshift, so you need to be sure that at any given time it has all the resources it requires to stay alive and nourished to the max.

Before we even get to the details of filling a plate following the Mom Energy plan, though, let's take a quick detour to cover an area relevant to any woman searching for satisfaction in her diet: the food-mood connection.

THE FOOD-MOOD CONNECTION

It's easy to forget or ignore the difference between hunger and appetite. Each one of us is programmed to be hungry when our bodies need nutrients to survive; it's experienced as a drive to find food, and if we don't satisfy that need we'll feel an unpleasant sensation. Appetite, on the other hand, is more of a learned behavior; as the body's different senses trigger a desire for energy (i.e., food), even when we may not need it, over time we can respond to appetite cues that result in eating. This explains how one person can choose to eat poorly while another person chooses nutrient-rich foods when hunger strikes. Put another way, whereas hunger is a physiological need, appetite is a psychological desire. Anyone who has ignored hunger or overresponded to it knows what having an appetite out of control can be like. It's what leads to ingrained eating behaviors that lead to problems with weight.

We can't deny the emotional factor, which often provides the undercurrent to appetite. Our behavior around food is also intimately connected to deep emotional requirements such as the innate need to feel happy and satisfied. What we crave or use for comfort can be rooted in our eating patterns, which have profound psychological significance. This helps explain why you might go to the kitchen when you're unhappy, bored, stressed out, or sad and eat the leftover birthday cake rather than reaching for an apple. Likewise, when you're feeling insecure, you might eat a pastry mindlessly while on the phone with a friend. Or, as you say to yourself, "I am not going to feel sad; I am going to make the kids' lunches," you might then find yourself nibbling on the same treats you include in their bags as you assemble them. The other factor to consider is the circumstances—the context of the eating. You may be emotional, for instance, and then you enter the kitchen. The food is there and your mind goes to places that ultimately result in an override of your body's physiologic cues of true hunger, or lack thereof. Suddenly, your body's fullness gets rebooted and you find room for food no matter what.

Preventing a roller-coaster ride in your bloodstream that leads to a bona fide stress response is all about keeping those blood sugars balanced. This is accomplished by choosing carbohydrates that are filled with fiber, high-quality proteins, and healthy fats—all of which foster a slow and steady digestion. It's like the difference between driving a car in cruise control and putting your foot on and off the gas pedal to drive as fast as possible, dodging other cars and cops. When you set up your cruise control, you're effectively letting the car work the best it can—staying at a constant, doable speed and varying its speed appropriately as needed. The body, like your car, prefers the former approach—much less wear and tear. In doing so, you will be able to avoid those crazy, bingeing moments when you feel so out of control and live in constant reactive mode.

The fact that food can trigger your biological stress response system is significant. Numerous studies have shown that an overactive stress response is associated with overeating, changes in blood chemistry and hormones, and, in particular, a decrease in the amino acid tryptophan. Why is this important? This amino acid is a necessary building block in the mood-regulating neurotransmitter called serotonin. As you know, low levels of serotonin are linked to depression (or simply a depressed mood), insomnia, anxiety, anger, and continued bingeing on sugary, fatty foods. And what you may not know is that low serotonin levels are also associated with overeating, even bingeing, on carbohydrates because of its role in making tryptophan usable in the body as serotonin. All of which can then lead to energy loss and weight gain, especially the most unhealthy kind of all around the midlines and waistlines. Like a drug addict looking for our next hit, we want this serotonin when we attack the kitchen seeking sugary, nutrient-poor carbohydrates. Our brains release a short burst of serotonin when we eat simple sugars and carbohydrates; we feel good for a moment, but soon return to our low-serotonin state, and crash and burn. That's when we crave more sugar and carbohydrates in hopes of feeling that little high again . . . and the downward spiral continues.

Fat is another issue that helps us to prevent binges, and which stabilizes mood-energy. As we mentioned earlier, fat is not as stationary and inactive as a hibernating turtle. It can release hormones and chemical messengers that promote inflammation and will instruct your body to hold onto fat while breaking down components that are pivotal to energy metabolism, such as muscle. In 2005, researchers demonstrated that abdominal fat cells produce cortisol in large amounts. Japanese researchers have found that fat cells can generate free radicals that can then do damage throughout the body. They concluded that excess abdominal fat may bring on system-wide oxidative stress that has profound overall effects. So the lesson is clear: achieving and maintaining an ideal weight and a healthy muscle-to-fat ratio is important. It's also the cornerstone to optimal energy. The diet guidelines in this chapter will help you to accomplish this.

> **Profile Alert!** Once again, attention all Chronic Dieters (Profile 4). The following guidelines don't just speak to moms seeking to keep their energy reserves charged. These rules amount to a way of eating that will end all diets and help you to achieve the body— and constant energy levels—of your dreams.

Break the Rule of the Meal

Too often people get caught up in thinking that a snack is small and fun while a meal is large and happens at set times. But our bodies don't think this way. To employ the car analogy again, our bodies don't want to fill up with 1,800 calories in the morning and then allocate those calories throughout the day similar to how your car operates after you fill it up at the gas station. In fact, it won't know how to allocate all those calories at once, and it will shove a lot of them into fat storage. Your body much prefers to run like a racecar that has periodic pit stops about every three hours. How much we eat at that pit stop depends on a combination of our in-the-moment needs and the availability of food.

Although we will still use the word *meal* in this book, it helps to reconfigure your definition of this word to refer to it as an eating occasion. Forget the old rules of having to eat three meals and two snacks a day, or six small meals plus snacks. That's a pointless piece of advice. Every woman is different and should approach eating as would any other animal: she should eat when her body—and being—needs something. The caveats, of course, are what screw up many moms: (1) you have to recognize your body's internal hunger cues—tuning in to how you feel, what your food preferences are in the moment (and why), and what your goals are; and (2) you have to know how to make the most of those occasions and fill up on high-quality nutrients to satisfy all those needs. Many women fail to do this, resulting in endless grazing all day on mediocrity or storing up hunger and later pigging out on energy-depleting whatever.

Pit Stops versus Fill-ups. For optimal efficiency and to prevent fat storage, we need to refuel with only the amount of energy the body needs and will use about every three hours. Don't let yourself run on empty or backload—which refers to eating lightly all day and getting all your calories at night.

EAT ROUGHLY EVERY THREE HOURS

Less really is more in the energy equation. Give your body less and it will work more efficiently, producing higher energy. Put another way, in order to get the right amount of food without overwhelming the body and forcing it to store energy in the form of fat, you should aim to break up your eating into about three-hour increments. Regular meals spaced about every three to four hours apart help keep the metabolism running in high gear. They also trigger the body to use good calories for fuel and give up the fat. This explains why someone who cuts back on overall calories may struggle to make excess fat go away. The body senses the reduction in calories, goes into survival mode, and holds tightly onto its fat. When food intake is spread throughout the day, however, this tells your body it's getting plenty of energy and can let go of that fat! Simply knowing that you get to eat again in a few hours has hidden benefits; you won't have that last-meal mentality that can lead you to overeat.

So aim to eat roughly every three hours no matter what, starting with a high-quality breakfast within an hour of rising. (Break the fast.) If you struggle with eating breakfast, then consider this: your body needs nutrients to turn it on—to shift from fat-storage mode to energy-using mode. The more you prolong this, the longer your body stays in fat-storage mode. Once you start eating correctly for optimizing your energy, you'll find that your body gets hungry approximately every three hours. You'll get into a rhythm of needing food consistently around that time frame. So even though it may feel strange at first, you'll eventually find yourself in a virtuous cycle of sustained energy.

How many of us have stuffed ourselves to the gills at a buffet-style Sunday brunch and felt lethargic (and guilty) the rest of the day? It sets the tone for the entire afternoon and pretty much disqualifies dinner because you just aren't in the mood or hungry enough. Similarly, we're all familiar with the uncomfortable sensation of being famished. The key to success is finding the middle ground between these two—not overdoing it to produce storage and not running on fumes. Just like when you try to find the balance between showering your kids with things they want and controlling how much you give them so they don't develop a sense of entitlement (not to mention a false sense of reality about money). Eating every three to four hours keeps the body on a relatively even keel. You'll avoid those energy highs and lows that spell metabolic disaster.

Remember, the body can only handle so much of any nutrients at one time, and if you don't need them for fuel (you may feel as if you're running a mom marathon in your mind but your body is not), then those excess calories will be stored as fat. Forcing your body to convert excess calories into fat puts a kink in its efficiency (hence the slow and sluggish feeling after a huge meal). Conversely, if you give your body less, you force it to use all that energy for fuel until you eat again, and you will feel the difference in sustained energy levels and mental clarity. Added bonus: you'll also produce less waste. That's the ultimate sign of an efficient body that makes use of all that you consume without needing to store extra fat. It's kind of like when you make a meal for the family and there's something that everyone likes. There are no leftovers, and cleanup is manageable.

No matter where I am or what I am doing, I have food supplies with me. Whether it be a banana or a Pure Bar, a Ziploc bag of Goldfish or a smoothie, I make sure I am providing my body with proper fuel throughout the day. My life is on the go all the time and sometimes sitting down for a full meal is not an option. But without food I am useless, so I make sure I always have my snacks so I am fueling my body no matter what I am doing.

— **JESSICA MENDOZA,**
professional softball player,
Women's Sports Foundation president,
and ESPN commentator

QUANTITY, QUALITY, AND BALANCE

Aside from feeding your body routinely, becoming a master at knowing what to eat and how much will take practice. Old rules need to be forgotten in this regard, too. You won't necessarily have to eat the same amount at every eating occasion. You might, for example, perform a hard workout on a Sunday afternoon but not feel the need for extra fuel to recover until Monday morning. Or you may be up with a sick child on a Tuesday night and feel like your eating is totally thrown off all day Wednesday. Choosing what to eat and when should be less about rules and more about tuning into what your body—and even your mood—needs. The way that nutrition has been taught historically and how it typically gets explained even today is counter to how the body works. It's not about calorie content, especially when it comes to energy. The body understands three ingredients:

carbs, protein, fat. Period. So yes, please stop counting calories and instead focus on getting the right balance of these three main ingredients to energy, and watch what happens. See if you can shift your focus from calories to nutrient balance. The ideas presented below will help you to do that. It's about becoming a "Qualitarian." This means, first and foremost, that you choose to be the gatekeeper for what goes into your body. That you don't feel deprived but rather empowered when you turn down a veggie burger with genetically engineered ingredients or hexane and enjoy one made from organic quinoa and mushrooms or a wild salmon burger. It also means saying no to a ready-to-eat salad of chemically sprayed lettuces in favor of cooking your own organic broccoli (great to start with frozen, too). And it means taking pride in listening to your own smarts instead of the front of a package or a commercial. Put simply, being a Qualitarian means choosing high-quality foods in the right portions to achieve a balanced meal that satisfies all your needs, from nutritional and physical to emotional. Whether you're a meat lover or a vegan, everyone can be a Qualitarian.

We all know that we need to manage our portions, and it does get confusing about what an ideal portion actually is, whether we're eating a piece of meat or diving into a bowl of gnocchi. But here's something to keep in mind when thinking about the relationship between eating and energy:

1 serving of carb, protein, or healthy fat = 1 hour of energy

So, if at each eating occasion you eat one serving of carbs, one serving of protein, and one serving of healthy fat, your body will have a total of three "power hours"—the first from the immediate energy of the carbs, and the second and third from the protein and fat, which take longer to break down.

Another way of looking at this math is to say that when you consume all of nature's foods—carbs, proteins, and fats—in respectable portions (which we'll get to shortly), you can maximize your energy metabolism over the course of three hours. You won't ever feel famished or stuffed, and your body will love it. Of all the guidelines in this chapter, this tenet—to achieve nutrient balance at every eating occasion—is most important.

General Guidelines

The overall principle of what to eat is simple: you choose one serving from each of the main categories—carbs, protein, and fat—and are allowed an unlimited amount of vegetables (no one is going to gorge on onions or spinach, so you get the point). For most people, this formula works, but there are lots of gray areas to consider. Some moms will have to bump their portions up to two servings of carbs and protein and one of healthy fat if they are exercising more or feeling the need for more. Any mother breastfeeding, for example, will need more carbs. If you're a vegan, you may end up higher on the carb side because your protein sources are often carb based. And some people may have two servings of protein with one carb and one fat because that balance helps their body address carb cravings and energy dips.

Already confused? Don't be intimidated here. Again, learning the ropes to finding your ideal serving of each category will take time and practice. These general guidelines are just that—general guidelines or guiding principles. They are not meant to be hard and fast rules, so don't look at this as a rigid list of exact measurements to be followed at all costs. You will need to improvise in some areas, as well as experiment with foods to address your personal choices and take into consideration social and cultural requirements. We cannot possibly give you a formula that works for every single situation or type of meal. You have to learn how to mix and match, and how to give and take. If you want to have dessert after dinner, but you also love the restaurant's breadbasket, then you may not want to order the lentil soup or hummus. Your carb box is already checked, so you just have to choose a healthy fat and protein for your entrée, and enjoy the vegetables. Use your common sense.

Never forgo carbs entirely at any given meal. One of the biggest mistakes you can make is to skip the carbs or save those carbs for a later feast. This will sabotage your energy equation. If you skip carbs at lunch thinking that you can then indulge in pizza with your kids at dinner, think again: you will more than likely be reaching for a carb-rich food by 3 P.M. to help you deal with the sugar craving you're sure to get. Remember to balance *all three nutrients* at every eating occasion no matter what. You really don't have any excuses to skip carbs given the volume of carb sources available today.

Remember, this is about choice! In fact, it's so much about choice that we encourage you to stop and ask yourself the following questions before you even decide what you're going to eat: *What am I looking for? What does my body crave? What does my inner voice say it wants?* Identify your body's chief needs first, and then decide what you're going to prepare for yourself (or purchase).

The following breakdown of foods in various categories will help you to choose wisely. Food is complex, so each food is listed by the dominant nutrient. Not every food you've ever heard of is on here, and the way in which the foods are listed doesn't mean you have to eat it exactly that way. You can steam or sauté your veggies, for instance. This breakdown is merely to help you begin to track how your meal is designed. Get creative about how you cook and prepare your meal with spices and seasonings. Note that there are two blended categories: one that includes foods that contain both carbs and protein, and another that has foods typically high in protein and fat.

Let us reiterate: don't panic about how to do the 1 + 1 + 1 with mixed categories. You'll get good at building your own eating occasions over time.

CARBS

Grains

Serving size: As indicated or your fist

amaranth; barley; bread, whole-grain, sprouted; buckwheat; bulgur (cracked wheat); crackers, whole-grain; kamut; millet; oatmeal, cooked (¾ cup); oats, whole (⅓ cup); pasta; pita, whole-wheat (½); quinoa; spelt; rice, basmati, brown, wild; teff; tortilla, corn, whole-grain, whole-wheat (½)

Fruit

Serving size: As indicated

apple (1 medium), apricots (3 medium), banana (½), blackberries (1 cup), blueberries (1 cup), cantaloupe (¾ cup), cherries (15), fresh figs (2), grapefruit (1 whole), grapes (15), mango (¾ cup), melon (¾ cup), nectarines (2 small), orange (1 large), papaya (¾ cup), peaches (2 small), pear (1 medium), pineapple (¾ cup), plums (2 small), raspberries (1½ cups), strawberries (1½ cups), tangerines (2 small)

Dairy/Dairy Replacements

Serving size: 6 ounces or as indicated

almond, rice, coconut, and soy milks, unsweetened, plain; coconut water, plain (11 oz); milk, organic; yogurt and kefir, plain, organic

Starchy Vegetables

Serving size: As indicated or your fist

beets; carrots (½ cup cooked or 2 medium raw or 12 baby); corn; peas; sweet potatoes or yams (½ medium baked); vegetable juices: carrot, beet, tomato (6 ounces); winter squash: acorn or butter nut

CARBS & PROTEIN

Beans/Bean-based Foods

Serving size: As indicated or your fist

beans: adzuki, black, cannelloni, edamame, garbanzo, kidney, lentil, lima, mung, navy, pinto, etc.; bean soups (¾ cup); bean dips (¼ cup); soy or veggie burger (4 ounces); tempeh (3 ounces); tofu (fresh: 8 ounces, cube: 3½ ounces)

Grains

Serving size: Your fist

quinoa

Dairy

Serving size: As indicated or your fist

cottage cheese, plain, organic; mozzarella, organic; ricotta, organic; yogurt, plain, Greek, organic (6 ounces)

PROTEIN

Meat, Fish, Poultry & Eggs

Serving size: As indicated or palm of your hand

beef, lean cuts; bison, buffalo, and other game; chicken, breast only; Cornish hen, breast only; eggs (1 whole or 3 egg whites); egg substitute (⅔ cup); fish; lamb, leg; shellfish (3 ounce fresh or ¾ cup canned in water); turkey

FAT & PROTEIN

Nuts & Seeds

Serving size: As indicated

almonds, brazil nuts, cashews, and hazelnuts (10 to 12); peanuts (18); hemp seeds, pistachios, pine nuts, pumpkin seeds, sesame seeds, sunflower seeds (2 tablespoons); nut butters (1 tablespoon)

Dairy

Serving size: 1 ounce

fattier cheeses: blue, Brie, Camembert, cheddar, Colby, Comte, Gorgonzola, gouda, Gruyère, Havarti, Manchego, Monterey Jack, Muenster, provolone, Swiss

FAT

Oils

Serving size: 1 tablespoon

canola, chia, coconut, extra-virgin olive, flax, grapeseed, hemp, olive, sesame, walnut

Nuts & Seeds

Serving size: As indicated

chia seeds (1 tablespoon); macadamia nuts (10); pistachios (¼ cup); walnut and pecan halves (7 to 10)

FAT (continued)
Fruit
Serving size: As indicated
avocado (¼ cup); coconut, shredded, unsweetened (3 tablespoons); olives (8 to 10)
Spreads
Serving size: 1 tablespoon
cream cheese, low-fat, plain; Neufchâtel; pesto; tapenade

NON-STARCHY VEGETABLES
Serving size: Unlimited
artichokes, arugula, asparagus, bamboo shoots, bean sprouts, bell or other peppers, bok choy, broccoli, broccoflower, Brussels sprouts, cabbage (all types), cauliflower, celery, chicory, chives, collard greens, cucumber/dill pickles, eggplant, escarole, garlic, green beans, kale, leeks, lettuces, mushrooms, okra, onion, radicchio, radishes, salsa (sugar free), sea vegetables (kelp, etc.), snow peas, spinach, sprouts, squash (yellow, summer, or spaghetti), Swiss chard, tomatoes, water chestnuts, watercress, zucchini (Italian)

When choosing animal and animal products, choose organic. For fish, there isn't a definition for "organic" so choose sustainable seafood, which includes most wild fish and some select farm-raised seafood.
(For help, visit www.seafoodwatch.org.)

Try Tracking

Now that you know the general formula for your eating occasions, it helps to track what you eat every day for the first week so you can really see how much you're eating from each category and whether or not you're truly getting a good balance. At the end of each day, ask yourself two questions: (1) Did I eat about every three hours? If not, why not? (2) How many servings of carbs did I have at each eating occasion? This is how you may find out that gosh, your breakfast contained six servings of carbs and then you had zero carbs until dinnertime, at which point you gorged on seven servings of them.

If you reduce your portion sizes and still find yourself very hungry, then you've got three options to consider:

- Choose higher fiber foods.

- Eat more veggies.

- Check in with yourself to see if you're actually not hungry, but not stuffed. Many people become so conditioned to big feelings of fullness that they have to reacquaint their bodies to feeling like they've had just enough and will be okay for another couple of hours before they eat again. Remember: your body works best when it's underwhelmed.

Don't let yourself get too hungry. Blood-sugar drops are exhausting and emotionally straining (for your kids too!). I always carry a bag of energy with me that includes a healthy, balanced snack that doesn't skimp on protein. I love my nuts and seeds.

— **MYRA GOODMAN**,

co-founder of Earthbound Farm, cookbook author, and mom

SECRETS TO CREATING MORE ENERGY FROM EATING PROTEINS AND FATS

Due to the attention on carbs over the past decade, many of us have gotten pretty good at knowing the difference between a "good carb" such as whole-grain bread and a "bad" one such as plain white bread stripped of its nutrients and fiber. But all the focus on carbohydrates has left people still confused about proteins and fats. And there's a lot that can be said about these two critical macronutrients our bodies need to create sustained energy. Let's take a look at each of these in turn, followed by some general guidelines for making the most of your eating experience.

Choose an Assortment of Proteins

Proteins are found in both animal and vegetable sources. However, each food source contains differing varieties and amounts of amino acids, which are the individual chemical units that comprise proteins. In other words, amino acids are the building blocks of proteins. The terms *complete protein* or *high-quality protein* are used to refer to those proteins that provide all of the essential amino acids in a proportion needed by the human body. A couple of the essential amino acids play a critical role in feeding the mitochondria, which, you'll recall, are the energy units of cells.

Proteins play an important role in our body. The most well-known is their role in building lean body mass (muscle), but many proteins are also enzymes which mean they are messengers in cellular communication that signal metabolism and immune responses among other core functions. When consumed, your body goes to work breaking down proteins into their amino acids, which then get absorbed and transported by the blood to cells for use. The mere act of breaking down protein burns calories and keeps your blood sugar stabilized. Amino acids can then be converted to glucose and used as energy, or they can form new protein molecules needed by the body.

While the body needs protein daily, it can get too much. The body does not store excess protein and the process for removal requires the liver and kidneys to work hard at removing these larger molecules. These organs are adept at doing so, but if it becomes a longstanding pattern or if they are in a weakened state, this can prove challenging to them and they may signal their displeasure by working less effectively or even going on strike. They can also lose their functionality if the body doesn't get sufficient carbs, in which case it uses protein for energy but creates significant waste.

The word *protein* gets thrown around a lot today. One reason for this is because there are so many sources of protein available now including those from animals and other vegetarian options such as whole grains, beans, nuts, and seeds. But a key energy distinction lies in whether the protein is isolated—which means extracted from the whole food through some processing—or if it remains in the whole-food form. This can make a big difference in nutrient quality and digestibility. When it comes to soy protein, which shows up in so many places such as powders, bars, and shakes, be aware that soy protein isolate can be problematic for some people. This form of soy is produced by removing nutrients from the whole soybean, which may play a role in modifying the hormonal effects of soy—raising concerns for people with thyroid imbalances, certain cancers, and metabolic syndromes like polycystic ovarian syndrome.

Vegetarian sources of protein offer tremendous nutritional profiles, but vegetarian doesn't always mean healthy. There are poor-quality vegetarian proteins sold on the market that can be as energy-sapping as low-quality animal protein.

As already mentioned, wherever possible, seek organic sources of protein, especially from animals (including whey and egg white) and soybeans. This means that no chemicals were given to the animals or sprayed on the plants, and that no genetically modified seeds were used. The choice between animal and vegetable sources of protein should be one of personal preference, ethics, environmental concerns, and taste. We say this because it is a myth that vegetarians and vegans can't get sufficient protein from a plant-based diet. Yes, some plants have components that can block absorption of some proteins, but that doesn't mean one cannot achieve adequate protein intake. It merely means that it requires knowledge and planning.

When it comes to vegetarian sources of protein, try hemp protein (e.g., powder, seeds) for its nutrition profile and ease of digestibility; and several of the pea/quinoa/rice blends are satisfying, healthy options. Quinoa and hemp are naturally complete proteins whereas the others are not, so you would need to consume other sources of amino acids throughout the day to arrive at a more complete profile. A note on hemp: it's made from the seeds of the hemp plant and thus it does not contain THC, the psychoactive component of the marijuana plant. If you feel really good from eating hemp, it's coming from true energy and nutrition and not a drug (this includes the healthy fat source GLA, present only in hemp). Another item to note is that some products will contain sprouted quinoa, grains, nuts, or seeds. Sprouting is an excellent way to improve the availability of the protein; these are great for those with digestive issues where absorption may already be challenged.

ASHLEY'S ENERGY ADVICE:

I get asked all the time about energy bars and shakes. Are they a smart choice? Are they Ashley Koff Approved? Sometimes. But proceed with caution. Many people just grab a bar or whip up a protein shake after dinner. Or they will have two or three during the day because the small size of the bar means they don't register the caloric density they've consumed (some bars can have as many calories and be as nutrient poor as a Caesar salad or slice of pizza), wondering why they find weight loss or maintenance such a challenge.

Two general nutrition concerns apply strongly to the category of ready-made bars and shakes: unnecessary processing and unnecessary use of preserving agents. For example, if you're consuming a bar with nuts and dried fruit, why not just choose an apple with some nuts or nut butter instead? The difference in calories and nutrient balance can be significant. For starters, many bars' carbohydrate content is too much (two to four servings) while its protein content is minimal—not even one serving. Many bars are high on the glycemic index, meaning they will stir a spike in blood sugar, and this is often due to lots of dried fruit—not necessarily added sugar. They often don't give you enough to eat from a practical standpoint. You eat three to five bites quickly and don't register a full signal, so you seek something else to satisfy you, which can then throw your nutrient load overboard. Also, many of these items contain nonorganic versions of fruit that should only be eaten from organic sources. They further may contain processed or chemical ingredients and isolated soy protein (remember: if eating soy, eat the whole non-GMO bean to get the protein, fiber, and healthy fats). The excuse of "a bar is for convenience" has gone too far. How inconvenient is an apple and some nuts? This is what many bars purport to be, but then again, you get fiber and water and phyto-nutrients from the skin of the apple, which you probably won't get in the bar.

Know the distinction between a desire for a bar or shake versus the true need for convenience. Can you take a little extra time and assemble something yourself? If not—and keep in mind I'm a realist who gets how life can demand some quick fixes—make sure to choose a product that doesn't have you trading convenience for optimal health. Look for extra sugar and salt. Count the grams of carbohydrates, proteins, and fats.

Indeed, there is a time and place for bars (e.g., traveling, post-gym, a back-up plan for emergencies), but the whole-food route is always a better option when it's available. And finally, it's important to consider what else is in there aside from artificial ingredients. In an effort to make protein bars, shakes, and powders as powerful—and marketable—as possible, as well as to differentiate their brand, manufacturers routinely add herbs, vitamins, minerals, and other nutrients. As such, a final consideration should be a review of these ingredients, an assessment of their quality, an assessment of any possible contraindications with medications, sleep patterns (if you are having a protein drink or bar at night that has stimulating ingredients it could keep you awake), and individual sensitivities. For example, I recently couldn't figure out why I was having shaky hands and my pulse was racing. Then I realized I had been sampling a sport protein powder for work and it was giving me the same issues that I have with caffeine. The culprit? An intended energizing combo of maca root and other potent stimulant herbs!

Boost Your Brain with Balanced Fat

High-fat fish such as salmon are called brain food for a reason. Fats don't just add cushion and warmth; they are necessary for energy production, and even for your sanity. About two-thirds of our brains are composed of fat, and the protective sheath around communicating neurons is 70 percent fat. So in a sense we need fat to think and to maintain healthy brain function, which in turn help us to feel balanced; in particular, the class of essential fatty acids called the omega-3s and omega-6s play a crucial role in brain function as well as normal growth and development.

Ever heard of mommy brain? Feel that your memory was sharper before kid number one and is gone after number three? There's some nutritional rationale for this, which goes back to the idea that when pregnant, the body preferentially gives our DHA over to the baby to support its brain development. So if we don't replenish, we net at a loss. Since DHA intake doesn't appear to save us in the late stage (once we have dementia, or worse, a cognitive disease such as Alzheimer's), what we do know is that we have to restock our stores all along the way.

The omega-3 fats in salmon as well as other cold-water fish, nuts, seeds, algae, and soybeans have numerous proven health benefits, including those that protect the heart. One omega-3 in particular, docosahexaenoic acid (DHA), is the nervous system's favorite fat. It's the most abundant omega-3 fatty acid in the brain and the retina of the eye. A full 50 percent of the weight of your neurons' plasma membranes are composed of

DHA. Low levels of DHA or a deficiency results in reduction in logical thinking, hormonal changes, poor memory, mental decline, a higher rate of cell death among brain cells, depression, and an increased risk for heart disease. DHA not only provides structure to neurotransmitters and facilitates neurotransmitter activity, but it also increases neurotransmitter receptor density, which allows the brain to make use of serotonin and dopamine signals (good for good moods!). Because of DHA's effects on brain and eye development, many prenatal vitamins for women now include DHA supplements. DHA protects the brain and acts as an anti-inflammatory.

Healthy essential fats such as DHA are at an all-time low in moms' diets, whereas unhealthy fats (e.g., saturated and trans), are at an all-time high. But it's healthy fats that help fat-soluble vitamins such as A, D, E, and K move around the body; create sex hormones; build cell membranes; lower LDL (bad) cholesterol while raising HDL (good) cholesterol; and contribute to the health of skin, eyes, nails, and hair.

In the omega-6 family, gamma-linolenic acid (also known as GLA) is one of the all-stars. Well known as a stress-reducing nutrient, GLA is largely deficient in the standard American diet because it's a rarer oil, found in seed oils such as borage oil, evening primrose oil, black currant oil, and hemp oil.

People are more likely to overdo other omega-6s from sources such as refined vegetable oils, which can increase—not decrease—inflammation. Soybean oil, much of which hails from GMO soybeans, for example, is ubiquitous in fast foods and processed foods; in fact, 20 percent of the calories in the American diet are estimated to come from this single source. This can create an imbalance of too many omega-6s and not enough omega-3s, which is partly being blamed for the rise of myriad diseases from asthma and heart disease to many forms of cancer and autoimmune diseases. The imbalance also may contribute to obesity, depression, dyslexia, and hyperactivity. One study showed that violence in a British prison dropped by 37 percent after omega-3 oils and vitamins were added to the prisoners' diets!

The omegas don't end there. We can't forget about the omega-9s, -5s, and -7s (do you feel as if you're playing cards yet?). Technically, olive oil is an omega-9. Omega-7, known as palmitoleic acid, may appear to have minor status in the world of monounsaturated fats but its health benefits are hardly such. Omega-7 helps regulate fat and blood sugar metabolism (in adipose tissue and in the pancreas). In vitro studies suggest that omega-7 helps improve the function of the insulin-producing beta cells of the pancreas. And when it comes to the skin, omega-7 is no minor leaguer—it's a major fatty acid in epithelial cell membranes. This means skin, blood vessels, and mucous membranes. The presence of omega-7 in the epithelial cell membrane plays a protective role including inhibiting bacterial growth, as well promoting tissue recovery and healing. Research specifically on sea buckthorn oil (which contains 30 to 40 percent omega-7), shows its role in improving eczema, acne, oral and stomach ulcers, and vaginal irritation/dryness. Common dietary sources of omega-7 fatty acids include wild salmon, macadamia nuts, and sea buckthorn berries.

Omega-5, otherwise known as myristoleic acid, is less common in nature—found primarily in the seed oil from plants in the Myristicaceae genus where nutmeg is the most well known; the oil is also extracted from saw palmetto. Myristoleic acid extracted from saw palmetto has been shown to effectively combat cancer cells in prostate and pancreatic cancers. Additionally, omega-5 may play a key role in the inhibition of 5-lipoxygenase, a mediator of inflammation, thus, by acting in this anti-inflammatory capacity it helps to promote appropriate inflammation in the body. Food sources of omega-5, beyond extracting myristoleic acid from the aforementioned plants, include the fat of marine animals (wild Alaskan salmon), beavers, and bovines.

Getting a good balance of these fats is pretty easy. One key takeaway from this omega story is that rather than picking one or two favorites, which Mother Nature doesn't do, think of your omega consumption as an orchestra—all the different omegas playing together make the sweetest music. Whether food or supplement, consider making the choice that provides an array of omega fatty acids. After all, a whole-food approach to nutrition will help ensure you get omega-5, -7 and -3, -6, -9 for optimal health.

As we've already noted, simply reduce your consumption of processed and chemically laden foods; also reduce the use and consumption of polyunsaturated vegetable oils (e.g., corn, sunflower, safflower, soy, and cottonseed). Switch to extra-virgin olive oil as much as possible (it's heat-stable so use it to cook, too). Eat more oily fish (salmon, sardines, herring, mackerel, and black cod) as well as walnuts, flaxseeds, and omega-3 fortified eggs. Consider supplementing with a true fish oil like one from wild salmon, which will deliver all the omegas found in this fish naturally.

NINE WAYS TO PRACTICE A HEALTHY EATING ROUTINE

Below is a collection of ideas to help you maximize the execution of the ideas described in this chapter. See if you can begin to fold these simple ideas and, in some cases, actionable steps into your life.

Watch Out for "Energy" Bars Marketed as Low Sugar or Low Carb

The vast majority of these "diet-friendly" bars contain preservatives and modified ingredients such as sugar alcohols. Sugar alcohols, which we mentioned earlier, are designed to offer a low-carb sugar profile and can present a challenge to the digestive system; they are not meant to be absorbed and as such often cause gas and irritation. So instead of helping your energy level, these sugar alcohols and other preservatives may further irritate your entire system and, put simply, clog your energy flow. Opt instead for soybean in the whole-food form (edamame, tofu, etc.) versus bars and other food products made with isolated soy protein. There are great nutrients in the whole bean, fiber, and omega-3 fatty acids, among others that are lost when the protein is isolated.

Remember, carbohydrates are what the body needs for energy. Ingredients that impersonate carbs for taste but don't provide genuine energy are cheating the body, and the body always catches on to cheats—often resulting in an irritated digestive system.

Stock Your Freezer

With the economy, food-safety issues, and time efficiency on everyone's mind, the freezer offers one of our best tools for nutrition for optimal health. Whether it's fruits, vegetables, or fish, these foods are frozen immediately after they are plucked from a tree or the sea and washed. This means that these foods are literally frozen in time at their peak freshness and don't endure as much exposure to potential contaminants. What's more, stocking your freezer means you always have a healthy option available. With a quick run under hot water or a steam, you can create a truly fresh dish in minutes. What's more, frozen goods last a long time so you get your money's worth. Here are some tips to help you be freezer savvy.

- Buy frozen organic fruits and vegetables, especially when it comes to berries and other fruits that go bad quickly when you buy them fresh. You can use organic frozen berries in yogurts, on top of frozen desserts, or in a smoothie in lieu of ice. When buying frozen vegetables, you can defrost them in the refrigerator overnight and use them the next day. Or place them in the fridge in the morning, and they'll be ready to cook when you arrive home in the evening.

- Order takeout or buy prepared food that can be tweaked at home in seconds for a blast of nutrition. Always have frozen veggies on hand to add to dishes. Spinach, broccoli, and soybeans can be added as a side dish or thrown into pasta sauces and on top of frozen pizzas. Add extra veggies to a dish of beef and broccoli from the Chinese restaurant (ever notice there's way more beef than broccoli in those containers?); correct the imbalance with your own assortment of veggies and extend the dish from four to eight servings.

- Frozen wild or quality farmed fish is another example of better quality and freshness. Pull frozen fish from the freezer and place it in a bowl to defrost in the fridge. When you start to prepare dinner, mix thawed veggies with the fish, place them in a saucepan, and pour vegetable broth (low-sodium please) and spices into the saucepan. Cover and boil or steam for five to seven minutes. Voilà!

- Store individually wrapped, single-serving portions of meat, poultry, and fish in the freezer.

Engage Your Young Kids

Food education starts early. Challenge young kids to weekly contests by asking them to count how many (natural) colors are in the fridge and the freezer. Take them with you to the grocery store once in a while to show them how you shop and why you're choosing one item over another. Kids will appreciate learning about food and its nutritional value. Contrary to what you might think, they don't necessarily want junk food all the time.

The following is a list of top fish to buy,
many of which are rich in healthy fats that you
won't find in other foods to the same degree.
Unless otherwise noted, aim for wild-caught,
sustainably sourced varieties:

Abalone (U.S. farmed)	Herring	Salmon (from Alaska or British Columbia)
Anchovy	Hoki	Sardines
Bigeye (troll or pole caught)	Mackerel	Squid (from California)
Black cod	Mussels (farmed)	White sea bass
Catfish (U.S. farmed)	Oysters (farmed)	Tilapia (U.S. farmed)
Clams (farmed)	Rainbow trout (U.S. farmed)	Tuna (troll or pole caught albacore and yellowfin)
Dungeness crab	Rock lobster	
Halibut	Sablefish (from Alaska or British Columbia)	

For more information about
these fish and others not listed, check out the
Monterey Bay Aquarium's Seafood Watch website
at www.seafoodwatch.org.

Keep It Safe, Keep It Simple

The kitchen should be a safe zone. Don't keep too many treats
lying around or they will get eaten (sooner than you think). You
should go out for treats. Think of it this way: if your excuse is "Oh,

I had the cookies in the house for the kids," and you find yourself consuming them, then you've just let your kids enable your dysenergy.

Also keep it simple. Don't become a short-order chef. Kids need to learn how to eat like adults so you don't spend hours in the kitchen fixing food that fits each member of the household's palate. If you allow this then you must really like your kitchen. Getting your kids to try all kinds of food makes it easy to prepare a regular dinner that everyone enjoys. And by all kinds of food, we're also talking about how it's prepared. Take chicken, for example, and do it every way possible—grilled, broiled, and roasted. We all know we (moms and kids!) need to eat more veggies. Choose two or three per night and try roasting or baking your veggies rather than plain old steaming them. Don't forget that kids love to dip so let them do so with pasta sauce, hummus, or aged balsamic vinegar with a drizzle of olive oil.

Examples of staples to keep around: organic milk, brown rice, organic eggs, whole-grain bread, apples, strawberries, organic cheese, black beans, extra-virgin olive oil, crushed garlic, veggie or chicken broth, frozen organic vegetables (e.g., spinach, soybeans, broccoli, asparagus), organic chicken breasts and fish in your freezer, and tomatoes. You can whip up several dishes using these basics.

Clean Out Your Kitchen Closets

Pantries are overrated. They just encourage you to buy more food that you don't need. And why would you want to have food that keeps for months? That only means it is full of preservatives, additives, and chemicals that you don't want anyway.

Once a season, go through your cupboards (and your refrigerator while you're at it) and check expiration dates. Just as you would revamp your clothing closets at the beginning of each season, do the same for your kitchen. If it's been there since last month (or maybe even last year!), and you haven't eaten it or used it in a recipe, it's time to go. You can do a cupboard exchange with friends—asking them what their secrets are. Ask to take a look in your friends' cupboards and refrigerators to see if they have ideas you can use, too.

Some of our pantry staples: whole-wheat flours, organic white and brown sugar, pure maple syrup, organic hulless popcorn, steel-cut oats, whole-wheat pasta, black beans, kidney beans, garbanzo beans, brown rice, pasta sauce, tomato paste, low-sodium soups and broths, cacao, nuts and seeds, oils, dried fruit, and spices.

Don't Be Fooled

Navigating the supermarket today can be tricky. Supermarkets now place junk food next to healthy food. They also make it easy to grab what they want you to grab by how they place goods and attract your attention through specials and signs. Here's a classic example: you're in the produce department and next to the organic greens is a line of salad dressings. Next to the heads of broccoli is a sauce that can be used when cooking the veggies. But if you were to make an effort to peruse the aisle dedicated to sauces and dressings, you'd be able to find a much better one than those tossed randomly in the produce department. Avoid the samples handed out unless they are of something you love but don't want to have at home. Don't rely on the person doing the demonstration—they mean well, but may not point out any downsides to the product ingredients. Read the label yourself.

Be Careful about Buying in Bulk

Buying in bulk often does not save you money. If you don't read the expiration date and purchase items that expire very soon (and you don't have a family of 15), then it's wasted money. Bear in mind too that if the bulk product was in a bin and is a food that is sensitive to oxygen and light (e.g., nuts, seeds, grains), then you're doing yourself no favors. Most bulk foods come with preservatives and additives—it's what allows it to be sold in bulk! That said, load up on organic frozen fruits and vegetables that your local big-box store sells. Buying in bulk can help you get organic at lower cost. You can also visit company websites to learn new ways to use ingredients you buy in bulk so that you use up the product before the expiration date and get your money's worth.

Health is within everyone's budget. The goal is to realize true savings and avoid buying tons of items no one in the family enjoys (and refuses to eat). Nothing has been saved if no one is happy.

The True Power Lunch

Eating a nutrient-balanced lunch can do more for your P.M. energy than just a high-carb or high-protein one can. Remember, when we get a balance of nutrients and keep it to about one serving of each (carb plus protein plus healthy fat) plus unlimited vegetables, the body gets three power hours. For extra energy, take a B vitamin complex or your multivitamin/mineral supplement with your lunch. It will optimize the metabolism of your food for energy.

Allocate Your Alcohol

You can still have your wine and drink it, too. But be mindful of how much you are consuming. A drink while you cook, then another glass or two at dinner can amount to too much. It will disrupt your sleep cycles and potentially disturb your digestion as well. For most women, one five-ounce glass is plenty. Savor it with your meal and drink sparkling water with a wedge of lemon or orange while you cook.

Is white wine as good as red? There's been a lot of media frenzy over red wine's super-antioxidant resveratrol, but what about whites? According to Drs. Dipak Das and Alberto Bertelli of Connecticut and Milan respectively, white wine derives its cardio-boosting effects from two antioxidants—tyrosol and hydroxytyrosol—which are also found in olive oil. Interestingly, these antioxidants, such as resveratrol, trigger a gene that may slow aging, and have benefits for diabetes prevention and kidney function. So go on, love your whites as much as your reds. If you're like Kim Basinger, you'll take white wine and cut it with sparkling water. To really reduce the amount of sugar (and calories) you're consuming, opt for a dirty martini. Stay away from soda and fruity or creamy drinks. And when you do indulge, count your drink like it's a dessert instead of just a beverage.

THE ENERGY EXCHANGE

Remember, even though you now have all this information about what to eat and what not to eat, healing energy issues is not about displacing or replacing food and beverage consumption with other excesses, such as shopping, over-exercising, drinking too much alcohol, etc. Many women try to mask their symptoms of low energy with something that makes them feel invigorated, albeit superficially. You can spend a small fortune at the mall, for instance, but that doesn't really do anything for you but drain your bank account and your energy due to the stress of going broke. We've met moms who admit they've overspent money on superfluous items because they didn't want to face reality and get to the bottom of why they were sad. So they not only max out their credit cards, but they go home still longing to feel better as they juggle demanding children. The kitchen then calls to them, and they start eating—chips, a carton of ice cream, and liter of soda for the caffeine—and then they usually end up feeling bad about all those calories and money spent. The next day, their physical and emotional energy is really low, and the cycle can repeat itself. And if it's not the mall calling them, it could be the cocktail bar, or engaging in fantasies of living an easier life—or even cheating on a partner to get energy from the excitement of an affair. There's definitely something to be said for the energy derived from behaviors that have a "forbidden" factor or "forget it for a moment" component.

The takeaway here is you don't want to eat around a craving or exchange one energy drain for another. Doing so is called "eating transference," meaning that you go shopping, for example, instead of eating—in essence, you binge at the mall. Or maybe you're the type to use excessive exercise as a way to avoid eating. The human body is smarter than you think. You'll manage to avoid eating what you really want but pay consequences later in other terms. Another example: if you want chocolate but have a salad, lean protein, tea, and berries because your mind tells you that's better, chances are later on you'll have the chocolate anyway, but likely devour it on a greater scale than if you had just chosen chocolate with tea the first time around.

In all of these scenarios, what you're really aching for is permission to just cry, scream, or do *anything* that will take you out of the current moment. The lesson here is clear: even though certain foods and actions can change your spirits or help you forget your stress, these are often Band-Aids at best and energy zappers at worst. In later chapters, we'll provide ideas to help you find other ways to lift your spirits, overcome those emotional low notes, and keep your emotional baggage in check. For now, we just want you to be aware of this all-too-common cycle. Learn to spot it when it begins to surface. Energy will travel wherever you decide to take it.

MOM UP! JUMP-START YOUR TRANSFORMATION

Aim to live by the four tenets: quality, quantity, frequency, and balance. Start slowly. This week, try structuring one eating occasion each day by our balanced 1 + 1 + 1 formula. See how that one tiny shift makes all the energetic difference by the end of the week.

PART III

REHABILITATE

CHAPTER 6

Rehabilitate Your Body: Relieve Advanced Imbalances

It doesn't get any easier, it just gets different.
You respond differently.
You have different needs.

— LISA MARIE PRESLEY
on motherhood with different-aged kids

Congratulations. You've begun to take control of your health. You've started to master the art of choosing the right foods for you and your family. You've taken a few steps to reorganize your life and the foods you bring into your home. Hopefully you've noticed an uptick in the level of your everyday energy. Your stress is reduced. Your body is feeling better. And your mood is happier. Maybe your family members have noticed a difference too (or just a few changes in the kitchen!). But the shifts you need to make don't end there. It's possible that you are still fighting other problems that could be getting in the way of true success. We face the possibility of a lot of additional health concerns that make it nearly impossible to balance our energy equations just by focusing on how we spend our time and what we put into our bodies.

So now we turn to the second part of this book where we look at ways in which we can rehabilitate the body—getting it back to a fully charged state. For some of us, trouble comes from a chronic medical condition that requires routine maintenance, such as irritable bowel or diabetes, while for others it stems from a temporary blip in life such as menopause or an underactive thyroid that needs treatment. In this chapter, we're going to take you on a tour of some of the most common health conditions that will sap any mother's energy, and what you can do about them. Then, in the next chapter, we'll cover when and how to embark on a detox regimen, as well as give guidance on supplementing. Sometimes, we just need to hit "reboot" and take a few days during which we stick to a very specific protocol. This can have the benefit of squelching serious cravings for energy-killing sugar, salt, and fat—helping us to make the changes in our diets that we want permanent. But for now, let's turn to the secrets to nourishing and nurturing a happy body.

MAKING A HAPPY BELLY

Is your belly talking back to you? Does it call out to you in the most awkward moments? Have you been exercising and eating right but your belly hasn't changed shape—or worse it's expanded? Any and all of these are signs that you've got an unhappy belly. And it's time to take matters into your own hands . . . well, almost. It's important that if you have chronic (that means regularly occurring) digestive complaints that you speak to your doctor so that he or she can evaluate you to rule out anything being wrong, functionally speaking. If you are like so many of our clients, you will get the A-OK from your doctor, which can be bittersweet because it's great knowing there is nothing seriously wrong but you also know that your belly's blabbering is seriously causing disturbance in your life (and clothes!). And even if your doctor discovers something and prescribes a treatment protocol, eating right will be a core part of your plan.

Digestive complaints—gas, bloating, reflux, constipation, heartburn, irritable bowel, pain, diarrhea, or a wonderful combination of all or any of these—are signs of imbalances that your body wants you to tune in and correct, like yesterday. Your belly doesn't want to be sluggish, overworked and underpaid, or moving so fast it's out of control and leaves you spinning. Digestive disturbance means that nutrients aren't getting where they should—either to your cells for energy and repair work, or out of the body because they don't belong. So an unhappy belly is something that deserves your attention ASAP.

Don't be ashamed, for you're not alone. More than 80 million people in the United States suffer from digestive disorders, which happens to be the second leading cause of missed work behind the common cold. The role of digestion on energy levels is sorely overlooked, yet it literally could be "the guts" of moms' problems with low energy. An occasional bout of heartburn or constipation is often easy to tolerate and disregard, but these ailments are far too common these days and are doing more energy-depleting damage than we think. It doesn't matter what you take in (how good it is), if your inner machine isn't working, you won't achieve optimal energy. A healthy gut allows energy to flow. It acts as a center of gravity for all things energy related. In fact, your digestive system is way more than a processing plant for food; you'll soon come to learn that it's really the heart and soul of your immune system. It's pretty much the defender of your entire well-being.

First and foremost, digestion is your body's energy packer. It must work for the body to work. The best efforts fail in a compromised digestive system. We increasingly work with clients who forget to consider the health of their digestive system in addition to what they eat and how often they engage in physical activity. It may seem like common sense, but far too often the gut's overall health goes unnoticed until you've got a serious problem on your hands that makes it obvious, such as illness or disease. Although we have many barometers that we can use to tell us when something is wrong, such as blood pressure or heart rate, tummy trouble is a quick and easy telltale sign of the body experiencing an imbalance.

It's the body's way of saying, "Pay attention to what's bugging you!" Many of us can go long without figuring out the culprit to digestive problems, especially if those problems are covered up with frequent use of medications that dull symptoms, but do nothing to address the underlying culprit. What doesn't take long, however, is realizing how the unhappy belly makes us unhappy.

So it's really no surprise that the solution to our energy problems are sometimes as easy as fixing a poorly functioning gut. After all, your gut is arguably the most important ingredient in your overall energy equation. Your gut is also intimately involved in some intensely emotional business that factors into your energy equation: we rely upon our gut instinct to tell us the right thing to do! Who hasn't experienced a gut reaction to people who offend or delight us? Who hasn't felt sick before giving a speech or confronting a superior? We do a gut check when facing a challenge and congratulate ourselves when we display the intestinal fortitude, or guts, to take it on.

This is all for good reason, as your gut is synced up with your brain. Just think about how a bout of intense fear or panic can liquefy your innards—or, more commonly, when a cramp or brief wave of nausea alerts you to a nagging anxiety your mind had been working so hard to suppress. There's a good reason your gut and your brain communicate so seamlessly: every class of neurochemical produced in the first brain is also produced in the second.

Stress hormones present another kind of chemical that acts as the primary go-between for these two brains. When the brain detects any kind of threat—whether an impending layoff or a dustup with your spouse—it shoots stress hormones to your gut. Sensory nerves there respond by adjusting acid secretion and shutting down both appetite and digestion—a throwback to more dangerous times in our past, when we needed to summon all our resources to stand and fight, or flee. The result may be a nagging stomachache or a full-blown bout of gastrointestinal (GI) distress.

Suffice it to say our guts are very complex systems, which play into so much about us and our capacity to feel energetic.

The strategies presented in this chapter help rebuild a sick or malfunctioning digestive system, plus we'll give tips for those with added challenges such as lactose intolerance, acid-reflux, irritable bowel, gluten sensitivity, food allergies, and even migraines. Energy is often a casualty to other underlying conditions as well, such as anemia, thyroid issues, depression, sleep apnea, autoimmune disease, allergies, and diabetes.

Brief disclaimer: We're not here to help you formally diagnose any of these conditions if you do, in fact, suffer from one or more of them. We're here to equip you with the information you need so you can have that conversation with your doctor if you suspect that something else is going on to steal your energy. If you cannot get your energy level up after following the strategies in this book, we encourage you to seek medical help in targeting the problem. All too often hidden medical conditions can be overlooked, yet may have easy and quick remedies under a doctor's care. These strategies can be used in combination with therapies to treat an underlying condition.

Profile Alert! Anyone who identified themselves as Profile 1 (The Medicine Cabinet), should digest every sentence of this chapter. We also think that Profile 2 (The Mom Zombie) and Profile 5 (The Dead Battery) would do well to read through this chapter slowly. Think about your habits, behaviors, and personal conditions that could be the main instigators of your energy woes.

The Guts of the Matter

In the hectic pace of everyday life, the health—and the mechanics—of your digestive system is not on your mind. But it's undoubtedly something that none of us can afford to ignore. Once you've taken your last bite of a meal, you probably don't think about what's going on inside from your brain all the way down to your bowels.

You may have drawn the curtain on your eating for the moment, but the show has just begun for your gut, and it will take between nine hours and a day or two for the food you just ate to be fully digested. During that time, your stomach and small intestine break your food down into molecules that the small intestine's thin lining can absorb, allowing essential nutrients—the energy stream that fuels every cell in your body—to enter your bloodstream. The lower part of your small intestine then wrings out the water remaining in your meal and ushers it into your colon, which funnels it into your bloodstream to help keep you hydrated.

As straightforward as this process sounds, the seemingly simple chore of digestion depends on a finely orchestrated series of muscular contractions, chemical secretions, and electrical signals all along the 30-foot-long gastrointestinal tract. And there's plenty you can do to keep this operation running smoothly.

Digestive health is the center of gravity for all other points of health in the body. When out of balance, sick, or diseased, virtually every other system and organ gets negatively affected, triggering scores of problems you wouldn't normally or intuitively link directly to the digestive tract. As noted earlier, irritable bowel syndrome (IBS), for instance, is one of the most common intestinal disorders, affecting about 10 to 15 percent of people in North America alone. Up to 20 percent of people have symptoms of IBS, such as abdominal pain and altered bowel habits, although less than half of them see a doctor for their symptoms—most of which interfere with normal life and feelings of energy. But what few people talk about is that getting a diagnosis of IBS requires so much energy investment. First, you see your doctor, who then usually wants to run a few tests and he or she may ask you to keep a food journal. You may have to see a specialist if tests don't turn up anything, which then eventually leads to the following: "The good news is there is nothing wrong with you (functionally), so it must be irritable bowel syndrome." And then you will be told to work on stress, diet, lifestyle, and perhaps you'll be given some symptom-relieving recommendations to try, such as fiber, medication for acid reflux, and so on.

A Fine Balance

Generally speaking, we perform two broad physiological functions in charging and running our battery. First, we take in and absorb nutrients, and second we expel waste products of that energy metabolism. It's the yin and yang of energy metabolism, similar to what we do when we cook in the kitchen: first we make a great meal but then we have to clean up. We excrete our body's waste products (clean up our kitchens) mostly when we visit the bathroom, but also to a lesser degree when we breathe, sweat, cut our hair, and trim our nails. Everyday physiological processes such as energy production, digestion, and hormone synthesis create waste products that, if not discarded, interfere with the function of our internal organs.

Most of these wastes are the by-products of the air we breathe and the food we eat. However, our intestinal tracts are full of bacteria and yeast that also produce waste. These bacteria and yeast are often called gut flora or intestinal microbes. Some of these bacteria are highly beneficial. They assist in the digestion of some vitamins and they play a significant role in our immune response. About 100 trillion (three pounds) of these bacteria live in the intestinal tracts of virtually every human on earth. In fact, we have more of these microbes living in our intestinal tract than we have cells in our body (only about 80 trillion). These bacteria are either good for you, bad for you, or neutral.

The good bacteria are often called probiotics (a term that means "for life") because of the role they play in keeping us healthy. These good bacteria produce substances such as acetic acid, which helps to destroy harmful bacteria. Two examples of these good bacteria are *Lactobacillus acidophilus* and *Bifidobacteria bifidum*. We also have bad intestinal flora. Some examples of bad flora are salmonella and *Candida albicans*, a yeast that can cause an infection when it grows out of control. This is the same yeast that causes some of us to get vaginal yeast infections. These bad flora are constantly taking in nutrients and creating wastes in the form of indol, skatol, and methane. Methane is an internally produced toxin that results in gas and bloating. Long-term production of these internal toxins can lead to a weakened immune system, inflammation, and a slower metabolic rate. Obviously, we want the good bacteria to be more prevalent than the bad bacteria. We can't ever eradicate all the bad bacteria—it's a part of life. But if the balance is upset, we see an increased risk for digestive problems, impaired immune system, skin problems (resulting from digestive disturbances—our skin is our other major excretory organ and remember stuff that's meant to get out of the body will find a way to get out!), and other potential health issues.

If you've ever had food poisoning, you know your gut is an uncompromising vigilante. When a nasty microbe hitchhikes a ride into the body on the back of real food, the gut quickly recognizes the interloper and strong-arms it to the nearest exit. To make the ID in the first place, it calls upon a reliable army of sentries, millions of immune system cells residing in its walls.

If the fact that the gut plays a major role in immunity sounds surprising, consider that the whole purpose of the immune system is to differentiate what's you from what's not you. Then consider that every day, you introduce pounds of foreign material—your daily bread—into your gut. The immune system has to decide what's okay to let through and what's not, so it makes sense to headquarter that process right where the food comes in.

This powerful system gears up from day one. A newborn's gastrointestinal tract is entirely germ free, but immediately after birth, pioneering bacteria begin to colonize it. The first few years of life, everyone's gut develops a unique extended family of bacterial species, determined in part by genetics and in part by diet, hygiene, medication use, and the bacteria colonizing those around us. Perhaps bacteria's most important job: stimulating and training the body's immune system and, by its overwhelming presence, crowding out more harmful critters.

The specific microbial mix (your gut contains thousands of species of bacteria) you wind up with has a big impact on your health. Besides making you more resistant to disease, the balance (or lack thereof) of microbes in your gut may lower your risk of obesity or influence your risk of autoimmune disorders such as rheumatoid arthritis, multiple sclerosis, psoriasis, and inflammatory bowel disease. Clearly, this extended family deserves coddling.

Probiotics: Hype or Help?

It's hard to imagine that we each host billions of live bacteria in our digestive tract that colonize by replicating quickly and massively, but it's true. What's even more fascinating is that different bacteria live in different places based on what they desire as a home environment. Think of a native Montanan versus a New York City resident—some like crowds and feed off the energy of the crowd, the noise doesn't bother them, the pollution isn't a major deterrent, and they've adapted to the types of food available, whereas others need wide open space. They preferentially choose pure air and hunting for their food, and they are okay if they only see a crowd on holidays or if they happen to travel. By the same token, a person who lives in Montana will have a different gut flora than someone who lives in New York—or Tokyo—for that matter.

There are many more bacteria in the large intestine versus the small intestine (100,000:1), as it is significantly less acidic; another way of saying this is to remember that your lower GI prefers to be more alkaline. The small intestine contains more digestive enzymes, has more movement (peristalsis), and generates more antimicrobial chemicals (for example probiotics acting on fiber can create an acidic by-product that functions like an antibiotic). Thus, because bacteria have different preferences, what we eat and as a result the environment in each area of our digestive tract will either encourage or discourage the bacteria to inhabit and flourish in their respective geography.

Outside factors, in addition to what we eat, affect bacteria balance ("gut flora"). Antibiotics ("anti" meaning against, and "biotic" meaning bacteria vs. "pro" meaning for, or good) get rid of the good with the bad so even one dose of antibiotics can upset the desirable ratio of bacteria. This doesn't happen immediately, but it does occur exponentially week after week due to how quickly bacteria replicate. So if we don't replenish the good bacteria, the bad can get an advantage right off the bat once the antibiotic's action wears off. Many of us were given antibiotics frequently as children (to treat ear and throat infections) or as young adults for skin problems. It's very common for doctors today to treat adult patients complaining of GI problems and learn that their issues stem from a lifetime of periodic or even chronic antibiotic use that caused an imbalance in their gut flora. This isn't as uncommon as you might think. By the time an individual reaches her late 20s, she can experience digestive problems that are then exacerbated by the inclusion of birth control pills and/or poor dietary choices over the previous decade. What's more, today's food and water technology makes it difficult to avoid getting secondhand exposure to antibiotics by eating animals and even drinking water in some places that have been treated with antibiotics.

As an aside, one key side effect of bacteria imbalance is a tendency to bloat around the middle and gain abdominal weight despite good dietary and activity practices. Additionally, we continue to be intrigued by research exploring the link between bacteria imbalance and obesity, for there is some compelling evidence that deserves further exploration. Imagine being able to control or treat obesity by simply changing the balance of intestinal bacteria, or even the types of bacteria present. Future research will bear this out.

So how do we get the balance back? Probiotics are found in food and in supplement form. Let's discuss the foods first. Before probiotics became the food trend they are today, reliable food sources of probiotics included fermented foods such as kimchi, raw sauerkraut, pickles, miso/natto, cultured vegetables, yogurts, aged cheese, and kefirs. Today, a rapidly growing number of food products (not fermented foods) are marketing themselves as containing probiotics. This raises two issues: (1) can/do they support live bacteria in their product (a lot of them note the amount of live bacteria at the time of manufacture—not at the time of consumption), and (2) do they contain a strain that has proven to be effective? Although we don't need to be eating foods that added probiotics to them—there is no danger, and in fact they could do good if the probiotic is viable (live)—but the question is about need and dietary diversity. We don't need cereals that contain probiotics—our cereals can be our fiber and other nutrient sources and if we want probiotics we can eat some yogurt with the cereal. We can choose from the aforementioned list of foods that naturally contain probiotics. If we are allergic to one and don't like the taste of another, we can move on to a different one on the list.

Some companies are making different versions of foods that naturally contain probiotics. Many of these are worth exploring, especially if dietary preferences or intolerances restrict certain foods (such as dairy). But also be a knowledgeable consumer and be wary of marketing or food trends. For example, of the numerous yogurts being marketed for their probiotics, many contain higher than necessary (and higher than healthy) amounts of added sugar in the name of getting in probiotics. Yogurt comes from milk so it will naturally have milk sugar, but it doesn't need added sugar. Find out how many probiotics are in these specially created probiotic yogurts (many don't say on the label) as opposed to a regular yogurt as opposed to a frozen yogurt marketed for its probiotic content. Per serving, most of them are similar, so make your choice based on what your palate desires and skip the sugar-coated probiotic unless you were going for something sugar-coated anyway! And if you don't want to do all this work—you can refer to the AKA list of approved products at www.AshleyKoffRD.com.

For individuals without the health issues described above and who have never take antibiotics, routine probiotic consumption through food should be sufficient to maintain bacteria balance. However, for those seeking to address health issues impacted by bacteria imbalance, a probiotic supplement will likely have the best therapeutic benefit in addition to dietary modifications. Supplements can guarantee that one gets a probiotic dosage sufficient to address symptoms. The necessary quantity ranges with the type and severity of the health issue.

A word on probiotics in supplement form: they are not all created equal. The type of probiotic, "strain specificity," is critical when it comes to the selection of a probiotic supplement to address a health issue. Clinical research, as well as anecdotal reports from practitioners, helps to validate which strains demonstrate greater effectiveness than others. For example, *B. infantis* is one of a few strains found to improve all symptoms of irritable bowel syndrome. Some strains of *L. bulgaricus* have been shown to aid in lowering cholesterol.

Additionally, supplements, lacking government oversight of probiotic production may not contain what they say they do. Also, the bacteria may not be alive at the time you take the supplement despite it being packaged alive (probiotics are very heat sensitive which is why most require refrigeration). In 2005, *Consumer Reports* found 40 percent of the probiotics tested contained significantly fewer live microbes than the label promised. So caution with product selection is recommended. For a list of brand recommendations, visit www.AshleyKoffRD.com and check out *The Probiotics Revolution* by Gary Huffnagle.

And just because we put the good guys in there, doesn't mean they have what it takes to do battle successfully. What tools do they need? How can we cultivate a friendly environment for good bacteria? More and more we're hearing about prebiotics, which are defined as non-digestible food ingredients that stimulate the growth and/or activity of healthy bacteria in the digestive system. It helps to think of prebiotics as precursors to healthy bacteria—they provide raw materials that the good bacteria prefer to have available in order to thrive. Typically, prebiotics are carbohydrates but they may include noncarbohydrates. The most prevalent forms of prebiotics are nutritionally classed as soluble fiber. Many forms of dietary fiber exhibit some level of prebiotic effect. Examples of foods containing prebiotics include raw chicory root, raw Jerusalem artichoke, raw garlic, raw leeks, raw onions, raw asparagus, raw wheat bran, cooked whole-wheat flour, and raw banana. In addition to including prebiotic fibers in the diet, we can also create a more hospitable environment by focusing on choosing foods and beverages that help promote a more alkaline environment in the intestines (See Chapter 5).

Bottom line: while just adding probiotics may not be the magic bullet or cure-all, they are definitely part of the solution!

> ### Original Sources of Pro- and Prebiotics:
>
> • Probiotics: kimchi, raw sauerkraut, yogurt, dairy kefir, coconut water kefir, fermented soy (tempeh, miso, natto)
>
> • Prebiotics: Jerusalem artichoke (sunchokes), chicory root, asparagus, oats, raw honey, barley, flaxseeds (ground), onions

Common Conditions That Cramp Your Digestive Style

No one gets to 100 percent perfection in anything. Repeat: no one gets 100 percent perfection. This is especially true in the digestive-wellness department. So aim high but not for perfection (let's say 80 to 90 percent most of the time). Digestive wellness isn't something you achieve and then can forget about, quickly reverting back to your old habits. People will say, "So I've been avoiding refined flour products and coffee for three months and feel great; can I have it again, now?" The answer is maybe yes, and you can choose to test the waters to see if you can go back to having something you gave up. However, keep a few things in mind. For most of us, digestive problems didn't develop in just three months—likely they were years in the making (remember your college eating/drinking plan, or after-school outings in junior high?). And while giving something up for forever seems dramatic, equally dramatic is the idea that having something means that you have it every day. When we remove different items as part of therapeutic treatment we are doing so for two reasons: to reduce known irritants and to identify potential intolerances. The latter may never come back into your eating regimen but the former may make their way back—infrequently—once your system is no longer in its irritated state. That said, let's go back to the initial sentence: " . . . and feel great." Why is it that if you feel great, now is the time when you want to make changes or revert back? How great does great feel? Perhaps you don't even need to try an old food source. Maybe it's about trying something new. Instead of the coffee, maybe you try coconut water or herbal tea. Or instead of pasta you try quinoa, kamut, or millet—if these were good enough to make strong bodies of the Greeks, Chinese, and Aztecs, perhaps they will do the same for you, too.

Following is a quick rundown of common conditions that are linked to digestive issues. Use this as a guide to understanding the basics to these energy-killing culprits and discuss your unique concerns and questions with your doctor.

Autoimmune Diseases (e.g., rheumatoid arthritis, fibromyalgia, lupus, multiple sclerosis): Although these are not technically "digestive disorders" we must mention them because not only are they prevalent among millions of women today, but they are conditions that can indeed cramp a digestive style. Anyone who suffers from an autoimmune disorder has a system that, for whatever reason, is attacking itself. Such a hostile environment does not bode well for the digestive tract that aims to achieve nutrient and energy balance. It's common for people with an autoimmune disease to simultaneously suffer from food intolerances and digestive disorders that require unique attention to diet.

Celiac Disease: This condition entails an allergic reaction within the inner lining of the small intestine to proteins (gluten) that are present in wheat, rye, barley, and, to a lesser extent, oats due to cross-contamination in production. The body's immune response causes inflammation that destroys the lining of the small intestine, which then reduces the absorption of dietary nutrients and can lead to symptoms and signs of nutritional, vitamin, and mineral deficiencies.

Some people may not have celiac disease but are still sensitive to gluten. For both the gluten-sensitive or, at the extreme, intolerant person, following a gluten-free nutrition plan is about a lot more than just removing gluten from the diet. To heal the digestive system (and maintain a healthy digestive system), as well as to reduce the risk of other chronic diseases and to maintain a healthy weight, it is critical to consider all aspects of the diet. This means paying attention to quality, quantity, nutrient balance, and frequency—all of which were discussed in Chapter 5. Unfortunately, the surge in "G-free" products has resulted in a glut of options that wouldn't rank high on the nutrient meter and could just trigger other energy imbalances. It's shocking how many G-free products, for instance, contain chemicals, artificial ingredients, and excessive amounts of sugar and unhealthy fats—as if gluten-free automatically means healthy or healthiest. What's more, some of these ingredients can be irritating, so you eliminate one problem (gluten) but haven't addressed the overall health/energy issue fully. For everyone, especially someone who suffers from allergies, autoimmune disease, or other indications that the body is challenged, we need quality food choices—period! Anyone choosing to or having to follow a gluten-free diet should aim to make organic and whole-food choices as often as possible.

Chronic constipation or diarrhea: Both of these ailments are very common yet there are numerous possible reasons causing either one, including IBS, medications, infections, etc. The common denominator here is an imbalance in the body's movement of food through the digestive tract. Somewhere, there's an imbalance and the result is constipation or diarrhea—and in some cases, an alternating of the two. Many moms don't even acknowledge a change in their bowels until they begin to discuss it with girlfriends or watch Dr. Oz.

Gastroesophageal Reflux Disease (GERD): GERD is a condition in which the liquid content of the stomach regurgitates (backs up, or refluxes) into the esophagus. Some people reflux up food or liquids, while others reflux acid, so in truth GERD does not always equal acid reflux. But stomach liquids usually contain stomach acid and the enzyme pepsin, both of which can inflame and damage the lining of the esophagus. The refluxed liquid also may contain bile that has backed up into the stomach from the duodenum, which is the first part of the small intestine that attaches to the stomach. The acid is believed to be the most injurious component of the refluxed liquid, though pepsin and bile also may cause damage. Lots of medications are available today to help combat GERD, both over-the-counter and by prescription.

But if we just turn to a drug, we may be missing something. The body's normal function is not to reflux (unless it is helping us in a moment of trauma to avoid choking or to get rid of something that it detects as bad for us). If you are having reflux routinely it means that the body is seriously trying to tell you something. It could be that you're producing too much stomach acid, but a lot of people actually have too little acid in the stomach. Too much food or eating too quickly? Food intolerances? Gravity working against you (lying down after eating)? As you can see, there are many things that could be factors, and medication addresses just one—reducing the acid. So if it isn't your specific problem or your entire problem, you may not get the full fix. Let's review some ideas to try before or in conjunction with a medication:

- Keep the digestive tract *under*whelmed: eat small, frequent (about every three hours) meals and chew your food well. Let your mouth do some of the work so your esophagus and stomach get what they need, how they need it!

- Incorporate plant-based digestive enzyme supplements with your meals, especially when you eat animal proteins. Plant enzymes can help break down the food.

- Already have esophageal irritation? Add an L-glutamine supplement: this amino acid may aid tissue recovery.

- Get plenty of probiotics naturally from foods (e.g., yogurt with *Lactobacillus* and *Bifidobacterium*) and/or take a high-quality supplement containing live cultures (e.g., Align with Bifantis).

- Shoot for more omega-3s, naturally found in wild cold-water fish or taken as a supplement. Omega-3s may help reduce any inappropriate inflammation of the digestive tract.

- Chew deglycyrrhizinated licorice between meals (we know, it's a mouthful of a word, but it is commonly referred to by the acronym DGL). This can work as an acid-reflux aid. Try mastic gum, which has antibacterial properties.

- Try taking magnesium citrate or glycinate before bed to improve the movement of food and waste through your digestive tract.

- Avoid lying down or going to bed right after eating or drinking. Give yourself a two-to-three-hour window ideally to allow for digestion of food to get it past the stomach.

Insulin insensitivity and resistance: Millions of Americans are increasingly getting diagnosed as insulin insensitive or resistant, a prelude to diabetes as well as a key sign that the body's energy equations are out of balance. Here's the short story on how it happens: If you overconsume refined or poor quality carbs, your glucose level will rise sharply, but soon fall back quickly. (Note: Other issues could also be at play, such as deficiencies of necessary nutrients; not enough chromium, for example, can inhibit insulin absorption.) When this happens, you experience a true energy low. At the same time, you usually experience a craving for more carbohydrates to bring your blood sugar back up, which will offset the general feeling of malaise characterized by shakiness, fatigue, brain fog, and dizziness that go with low blood sugar or hypoglycemia. Habitual energy imbalances like this set off a repetitive pattern of quick rises and drops in blood sugar levels, which can challenge your pancreas and liver. Both of these organs manage insulin—your body's chief energy hormone, which gets released from the pancreas upon eating and escorts glucose out of the blood and into the tissues. As you can imagine, when this pattern repeats itself over time, your whole body's energy metabolism can begin to falter, and soon enough you might find yourself in a prediabetic state on the road to diabetes. The good news about gaining control over this chaos is that it can be as simple as gaining control of your diet and related lifestyle risk factors like excess weight and smoking.

Intolerances: Anyone who has the unfortunate experience of consuming a problematic food knows that it's an energy killer. Food allergies, for instance, are on the rise today, especially among children. The number of kids with food allergies went up 18 percent from 1997 to 2007, according to the U.S. Centers for Disease Control and Prevention. This term can be misconstrued, however. A true food allergy is an abnormal response to food that is triggered by a specific reaction of the immune system and expressed by certain, often characteristic, symptoms. Other kinds of reactions to foods that are not food allergies include food intolerances (such as lactose intolerance), food poisoning, and toxic reactions. Food intolerance is also an abnormal response to food, and its symptoms can resemble those of food allergy. Food intolerance, however, is far more prevalent, occurs in a variety of diseases, and is triggered by several different mechanisms that are distinct from the immunological reaction responsible for food allergy. The most important thing to keep in mind is that the body, when irritated, will appear intolerant to most of that which is presented because it is trying to get our attention. It's irritated to the point that anything that goes in will be seen as an annoyance. So working on digestive wellness overall as opposed to troubleshooting certain intolerances is the prescription. In other words, if you are lactose intolerant and also have other intolerances, just switching to lactose-free products won't necessarily heal your system.

Irritable Bowel Syndrome (IBS): As already noted, IBS is one of the most common ailments of the bowel (intestines). What can be frustrating about IBS is that it's not linked to any structural defects. In other words, it's a functional disorder. If you are personally familiar with IBS, then you know very well how much it can hamper quality of life. Many studies have concluded that the constant intake of food additives and the ingestion of pesticides, chemicals, and dyes can cause irritation to the intestinal tract and/or an imbalance of the intestinal bacteria, resulting in inflammation or symptoms of IBS.

Lactose Intolerance: If you can't digest and absorb the sugar in milk (lactose), you're said to be "lactose intolerant." It makes eating dairy products all the more challenging and painful. Your GI will scream "oh no!" and you'll feel it with gas, bloating, urgent/uncontrolled bowel movements, and general discomfort. The first cure for lactose intolerance is to simply avoid the foods that trigger the problem (ahem, anything containing milk). Depending on the severity of your intolerance, you may be able to consume hard cheeses, fermented dairy, and sheep or goat's milk products versus cow's milk. That said, whenever consuming dairy you want to consume the highest quality. Just because lactose-free products are available, if they have a lot of sugar or artificial ingredients, they may help you with the lactose issue but be poor for overall energy and health. Lactose-free products are widely available today, as are supplements to further help you digest milk-containing foods and beverages. Lots of people don't realize they are lactose intolerant until they no longer want to tolerate its awful side effects and are ready to get to the bottom of their discomfort by zeroing in on the culprit. Half the battle is just coming to terms with being lactose intolerant, and then doing what you can to minimize your exposure to lactose.

Small Intestinal Bacterial Overgrowth (SIBO): SIBO refers to a condition in which abnormally large numbers of bacteria are present in the small intestine and the types of bacteria resemble the kind typically found only in the colon (large intestine). This encroachment of bacteria can cause gas, bloating, cramps, diarrhea, and constipation. SIBO may also contribute to food allergies and nutritional deficiencies. The good news is that it's easy to test for and responds well to proper treatment.

Secrets to a Happy Belly

In addition to any specific prescriptions that a doctor would advise that you follow to heal a sick digestive system, be it a diagnosed problem such as IBS or just chronic constipation with no definitive culprit, all of the following suggestions will help you to maintain as healthy a gut as possible. Also keep in mind that the other things we outline in this book—eating quality food in good proportions, limiting alcohol consumption, getting a good night's sleep, and incorporating regular exercise into your routine—are important to maintaining your happy belly.

Remember: your ultimate goal in soothing a troubled tummy is to get clearer intuitive signals. When something really bugs you, your second brain will let you know loud and clear. Use the following strategies in combination with any of the ones described above to match your unique issues. And again, discuss any protocol with your physician.

Think slow and steady: A rushed meal is out of sync with the creeping pace of the gut. In the last chapter you learned why eating every three hours is good for your energy metabolism, and good for your gut. This approach also helps you to avoid overeating, as your next meal won't be too far away. Our bodies prepare to eat at the mere thought, sight, and smell of good food. The digestive process actually starts before we take our first bite, as our brains send signals to our stomachs and salivary glands to secrete chemicals that will help break down food. Chew your food well so your gut doesn't have to work as hard to break it down. Eat slowly to avoid gulping air, which will make you gassy, bloated and—thanks to the mind's payback to the body—irritable.

Mind your manners: Chewing gum, smoking, drinking through a straw, and talking while you're eating can all cause you to swallow excess air, leaving you bloated and uncomfortable.

Find your inner balance: Gut-friendly bacteria use fiber as their main food source, hence the recommendation to eat plenty of fruits, vegetables, and whole grains, such as oats, barley, whole wheat, and popcorn. Fiber also aids the passage of food and waste through the gut. Aim for over 20 grams of fiber a day. But again, go slowly: increasing your fiber intake too quickly can cause gas and bloating.

In the next chapter, we'll offer some ideas on how to do a detox correctly—one that supports your digestive health rather than hinders it. Many of today's detox diets, or colonic cleaners, will wipe out the good bacteria and cause an overgrowth of the bad bacteria.

Don't be too sweet: Keep this in mind the next time you go for a treat. Sugars, dried fruit, sweeteners, and juice are treats that are not friendly for many digestive systems. Carbonated drinks on top of excess sugar such as sodas can make your stomach puffy, bloated, and distended. Keep it simple—stick to water with lemon, added organic frozen fruit, and herbal teas.

Follow the rules of the restroom: Unfortunately, toilet seats recline us back because they are too high for most of us. Solution: lean forward and rest your chest on your lap as if you're trying to read a newspaper on the floor (you can also place something to read on the floor if that helps). This avoids pushing or straining to have a bowel movement, and puts your body into a more squatlike position. In a squatting position, the abdominal wall and the bowels are fully supported for more complete elimination.

Turn a digestive frown upside down: Having a bad belly day? Cooked fruits and vegetables, such as a baked apple, steamed spinach, etc., may work better than raw. Avoid known gastric irritants. Lower your intake of animal fats (dairy, beef, etc.) and replace it with plant fats such as hemp seeds, hemp oil, chia, or flaxseed oil. Eat smaller portions, and try digestive enzymes. Also some people do better with purees and liquids on these days—just make sure you still make nutrient-dense and nutrient-balanced choices.

Spice things up: Spices don't just make your food taste good, they're important for your overall health, too. Ginger and turmeric have anti-inflammatory properties, while caraway, cumin, and cinnamon play a role in digestion and can help with weight management. Adding different spices to your meals and snacks can help spice things up . . . the right way.

Respect what your gut has to say: Even the most finely tuned machine has its quirks—if certain foods trigger GI problems for you, avoid them. Common heartburn culprits: acidic, spicy, and fatty foods; caffeinated and carbonated drinks; chocolate; and onions. Make it a goal to replace known gastric irritants with gastric healers, so you're not just getting rid of irritants.

Notorious gas producers include beans, onions, and cruciferous vegetables such as cauliflower, cabbage, and radishes. (These veggies are loaded with vital nutrients, so don't shun them altogether, but enjoy them in small doses.) The same goes for packaged low-carb treats and other foods containing artificial sweeteners—especially the sweetener sorbitol.

Bust the bloat: A probiotic can help you get rid of stomach bloating and make your middle area look smaller. It also will help the body process carbs and support the immune system.

Breathe into your belly: Meditation, yoga, deep breathing, and other practices that encourage mindful relaxation encourage the body to be less sensitive to stress. Plus these practices force more oxygen into your body, which will amp up your energy metabolism and streamline your systems. Deep breathing, using the muscles of your diaphragm (you should feel your belly expand and deflate with each inhale and exhale), can also help calm your mind and release tension in your abdominal muscles, easing indigestion. It will also further help flush toxins and inflammatory molecules from your body. Another way to calm the body's autonomic nervous system—which regulates digestion, among other things—is through progressive muscle relaxation, tightening and then relaxing small groups of muscles beginning in your toes and working your way up to your face. (More ideas on this will be presented in Part IV.)

Balance your pH: An overly acidic system can wreak havoc not just on your digestive system but also your bones and skin. How so? Bad bacteria and viruses thrive in an acidic environment, and in order for the body to maintain its preferred pH of about 7.4, it will remove calcium from the bone to alkalinize itself. So while our body needs acid in the stomach, the rest of the digestive tract and resulting urine is meant to be alkaline for optimal health.

Things that contribute to excess acidity:

- Excess animal protein: if you eat animal protein, exercise portion control and make sure to balance the protein with plenty of alkaline food choices (see page 152).

- Chronic stress, lack of sleep, dehydration, unresolved anger, overall depletion: tough times happen, but learning to relax and replenish the system is critical.

- Artificial additives: sweeteners and preservatives can add extra hydrogen or acidic ions to the system, producing inappropriate acidity in the body.

- Unnaturally white foods: white sugar and white flour are acid forming.

You can help alkalinize your system by reducing the acidifiers and increasing your alkalinizers. Here are some ideas:

- Add lemon to your water: a weak acid, lemon can actually alkalinize.

- Go green: include more vegetables in your diet, such as parsley, seaweeds, kale, celery, and spinach.

- Choose whole and sprouted grains (even more alkaline forming): standouts include quinoa, millet, and amaranth.

- Play around with incorporating these potent alkalinizers: sesame seeds (great source of calcium), fresh coconut, almonds, apple-cider vinegar, sea salt, cayenne, and watermelon.

Go Pro, and Avoid the Anti: Look for yogurts and plain kefir, as well as other fermented foods that contain strains of *Lactobacillus* and *Bifidobacteria*. In addition to protecting against colds and flu and promoting healthful bacteria, probiotics can help relieve diarrhea caused by infection or antibiotics, irritable bowel syndrome, or Crohn's disease. Watch out for antibiotics. Though you may need these on occasion to treat an infection, overusing antibiotics can disrupt your gut's microflora. They kill not only the pathogens causing your ailment but also good bacteria.

Avoid inflammatory foods: While avoiding inflammatory foods is always a good idea, it's especially important if you're trying to heal an unhappy belly. Use the table on the next page as a quick guide to what you should buy. Eating in this manner will reduce inflammation and help your belly get back to normal.

Consume as often as possible:	Avoid as much as possible:
Foods that can be found in nature	Food products (no trans fats, partially hydrogenated oils, high-fructose corn syrup, dyes)
Foods with recognizable ingredients	Foods with ingredients you cannot define
Whole, high-quality foods	Completely ready-to-eat meals from poor-quality ingredients, preservatives
New foods daily and on a seasonal basis	Same thing every day
Whole fruits and vegetables—skin, pulp, and cells are packed with nutrients	Fruit products, including juices
Vegetable sources of protein—good sources of fiber and valuable nutrients	Animal proteins exclusively as a way to avoid carbs (quality carbs are an essential part of any healthy nutritional plan)
Vegetables at meals and snacks to satisfy hunger	More animal protein or fat to feel full

Meals full of natural colors	One color or colorless meals
Fruits and vegetables with dark-colored flesh or leaves	Vegetables without color (e.g., iceberg lettuce, white potatoes)
Fresh and frozen organic fruits and vegetables	Canned, dried, and processed conventional fruits and vegetables
A variety of whole grains	Refined grains (flours, white bread, crackers, etc.) or flour-based carbohydrates at every meal
Wheat-free grains such as quinoa, amaranth, teff, buckwheat, oats, rice, and wild rice	Wheat every time you want a grain
Organic, locally grown, hormone-free, preservative-free foods	Chemicals
Water, herbal teas, healing tonics	Nutrient-poor, high-calorie, or artificially sweetened beverages
Dishes that are inherently flavorful by cooking with spices and herbs	Foods hidden beneath sauces of unknown origin

ADDITIONAL HEALTH CONSIDERATIONS

Just about any medical condition can cause a major disruption in your energy metabolism, but for us to address each one individually would take up an entire library of books. However, we didn't want to ignore that medical conditions—and what you're doing to treat them—can seriously affect your energy. Below is a snapshot of some strategies to consider if the advice in this book doesn't enhance your energy or if you know you are dealing with a larger medical condition.

Mind the medications: Virtually all medications, whether they are over-the-counter or prescribed, can change your body's natural energy metabolism. Common energy-depleting culprits include proton pump inhibitors (e.g., Prilosec, Nexium, Prevacid, etc.), birth control, antibiotics, sleep medications such as Ambien, SSRIs for depression (e.g., Prozac, Zoloft, Paxil, etc.), allergy medications, pain relievers, and drugs to boost bone density. Even cosmetic injections and treatments for skin conditions such as acne and psoriasis can be energy depleting. Be sure to discuss your concerns about medication affecting your energy levels with your physician. It's possible that another medication can be prescribed that won't affect your energy as much.

Heed hormonal hang-ups: The get-help message applies here, too. We'll explore how stress does a number on our hormones in Chapter 10, but take note: if you cannot regulate your hormones—from digestive ones to those that control your mood, menstruation, metabolism, and even your perceived level of stress—then you cannot regulate your energy. As women, we worry so much about the illnesses related to hormonal imbalances rather than considering what could be *influencing* the hormones to begin with. Remember, hormones are our body's main couriers. They send messages back and forth, so everything about energy is wrapped around hormones. Like pain, when hormones are off, it's relatively easy to go into a "crazy mode" (i.e., *I feel like I'm having an* *out-of-body experience!*); or a sad and frustrated mode (i.e., *I feel like I am doing everything right but not getting results!*). Either mode can make us susceptible to grabbing at proverbial straws—emptying our wallets in front of infomercials, trying new plans touted in magazines or among friends, and so on. Having an open conversation about your hormones with your doctor is critical, and you need to keep these conversations going. All of the strategies in this book will help you to optimize your body's main hormonal cycles. Some cycles may require calling in heavier artillery in the form of hormone-replacement therapy, which is a decision you have to make with your doctor's help. Just as there can be no rhyme or reason to experiencing hormonal hang-ups, there's really no definitive cure for hormonal challenges. It must entail a combination of therapies that include diet, exercise, and sometimes supplements and medication. (For more, see Kathy's Energy Advice on page 157.)

Test your thyroid: Your thyroid is your master metabolism hormone. If it's out of balance, guess what: so are you. Your metabolism will be running amok and taking your energy with it. An underperforming thyroid (hypothyroidism) is one of the most underdiagnosed conditions in America, yet it's incredibly common—especially among women. Common symptoms include depression, muscle cramps, joint pain, dry skin, thinning hair, low sex drive, menstrual problems, weight gain or difficulty losing weight, constipation, a "foggy" mind, and of course fatigue. Although all of these symptoms may be blamed on the aging process itself, a low-functioning thyroid can also be at play. It's believed that 20 percent of all women have a lazy thyroid, but only half of women get diagnosed. More bad news: there is no single symptom or test that can properly diagnose hypothyroidism. To arrive at a trustworthy diagnosis, you'll need to look at your symptoms in addition to blood tests. And to fix a thyroid problem you'll also need to look at the whole picture. This means making sure you get key nutrients needed for your thyroid to function, including vitamins and minerals such as selenium, iodine, zinc, vitamins A and D, and the omega-3 fats. It also means supporting your adrenal glands by reducing your stress load. And it may mean going on some type of thyroid hormone-replacement therapy. Your doctor will be able to tailor a protocol specific to you.

Don't dodge a diagnosis: If you have any inkling that something else is going on with your body beyond a condition remedied through traditional diet and lifestyle choices, speak up!

Plan a visit with your doctor and have that conversation. If you don't know what you're dealing with, you can't begin to take proper action. Energy woes can be blamed on conditions as straightforward as anemia (low red blood cells that provide much-needed, energy-infusing oxygen) to those as complex as fibromyalgia, rheumatoid arthritis, or menopause. If you suffer from migraines, do what you can to manage them with attention to dietary triggers, sufficient sleep, and medication when necessary. If you're an insomniac (and Chapter 9 isn't enough to cure you), then ask your doctor about visiting a sleep lab. You may have sleep apnea, which can be easily treated and which will allow you to get your life—and energy—back! In sum: get help.

THE BOTTOM LINE: PHYSIOLOGY FIRST

It's pretty simple: if the body doesn't have what it needs to function, it won't do so or it won't do so optimally. Depending on your unique physiological needs and concerns, you may require a medication to treat an underlying condition. Or you may just need to overhaul your diet and exercise more. Either way, it's important to deal with your energy issues—large or small—as these indicate a problem with your overall health.

If you're experiencing the pain and discomfort of a chronic or acute condition, don't let it lead you astray in the energy-saving realm. When we are in pain, we may eat poorly and forgo exercise—the very ingredients needed for our bodies to heal. If it gets to this point, you should talk with your doctor about what options there are for you.

And if you do reach for help in the form of a medication it should only be temporary, as medication can perpetuate a cycle that promotes the pain and drains the energy. And bear in mind that when you do take medications, you are asking your body to rely on that medication rather than its own tools. Drugs can oftentimes stimulate other conditions. You don't want to trade one problem for another. If you take iron supplements to treat anemia, for example, the iron can trigger constipation and require another set of medications or nonpharmaceutical strategies to avoid the constipation.

A disease or symptom is a flashing sign that energy equations have been disrupted beneath. If we only give medications to make the body "correct" again, then we may miss looking at the core issue causing the problem. And we may miss the ultimate solution. For example, if you have diabetes, you can use insulin or sugar-free foods to correct your blood sugar, but what about eating better quality foods to begin with? What about getting key nutrients found in whole, natural foods?

Diabetes isn't just about too much sugar in the blood or about not enough insulin; these are symptomatic of the deeper problem of chronic inflammation, which is a risk factor for so many diseases. So if you reduce your sugar by exchanging sugary foods and beverages for sugar-free ones, but don't address the quality of your overall diet, you still have risk factors for cancer and other diseases.

So when dealing with larger medical conditions, be sure to explore all of your options and address the lifestyle pieces that you can before you choose medicine. In many cases, there are better choices that can keep the medications at bay and tip the energy scales in your favor.

Feeling better and alleviating one problem usually has a domino effect and leads to other benefits. Curing sleep apnea, for example, will infuse you with more energy because the body will be so happy to have continuous oxygen. This in turn will motivate you to get up in the morning and exercise, which has its own host of benefits that will come back to boost your health and energy. Remember, there's no magic bullet to managing or curing illness or dysfunction.

MOM UP! JUMP-START YOUR TRANSFORMATION

When was the last time you had a heart to heart with your doctor about your health and any medical conditions that you may be treating? If it's been a while since your last checkup, now is the time to schedule a new one. Take inventory of all your medications, vitamins, and supplements. Bring them with you and ask about how your daily doses could be affecting your energy levels, and if there are any alternatives to consider. You might be surprised to find that you don't really need to be taking some of your medication anymore, or that another, newer version of a certain drug has emerged on the market that has fewer side effects. Diagnosing and managing medical conditions often requires a team effort—you and your doctor, dietitian, trainer, therapist, and so on.

CHAPTER 7

Reboot:
Cleanse and Supplement

*I feel pure and happy and much lighter.
I dropped the extra pounds that I had gained during a majorly fun
and delicious "relax-and-enjoy-life phase" about a month ago.*

— GWYNETH PALTROW,
on her detox diet

Detox diets have gained popularity in the last few years, no doubt spurred by Hollywood's fixation on them like a sparkly accessory. But are they safe? Do they work? Which kind is best?

You may lose weight sipping lemon water with cayenne pepper for days, but radical fasting detoxes and master cleanses such as these, especially when done for rapid weight loss, can challenge the body much more than your current daily routine. They can deny your body of nutrients it needs, downshift your metabolism, and leave you more sensitive to foods, beverages, and your normal daily chaos when you return to your precleanse eating habits. Not to mention they are a metabolic recipe for energy loss. During a fast the body slows its systems and workload to compensate for a perceived lack of nutrients. To this end, if your cleanse doesn't supply sufficient nutrients (the range of nutri-ents—carbs, proteins, healthy fats) it's likely that the body may alter its metabolic functions in a way that prevents sustainable results and may compromise short-term energy and immune function. Not a good thing for your health or your energy.

For a true detox that will have lasting results, you needn't look further than the ideas already presented in this book. Eating a bal-anced, clean diet per the guidelines in Part II, coupled with adequate physical activity is more than enough to keep your body mean, lean, and clean—and does so without any of the side effects of an extreme detox. When people come to us for the secrets to detox-ing the body, it usually means they've been indulging in their own "relax and enjoy life" phase of being less mindful of their dietary choices or they haven't been engaging in regular exercise and think a detox will help jump-start their efforts. They find themselves feel-ing low on energy and thicker around the waist thanks to eating lots of processed and classic junk food, and washing it down with enough wine to make a desperate housewife look good. What they really seek in a detox program is motivation to go back to basics and evict all the things that tax their body's optimal functioning.

In some instances, someone may ask about a detox program as they are recovering from treatments or battling with digestive or immune-related issues. They wonder if a detox will clear out whatever is disagreeing with their body. This is actually the worst time for a detox, as the body is in a weaker state and needs nutri-ent support. The body should be given the resources it requires to attend to its physiologic needs.

While the word *detoxification* may conjure images of drugged-out celebrities in rehab for substance abuse, from a scientific per-spective it actually refers primarily to the body's natural methods of self-cleansing—of ridding waste that are the by-products of its normal function, and dealing with potentially harmful invaders such as bacteria, viruses, or toxic chemicals. Detoxification is a constant bodily process. We are continually eliminating excess toxins through our digestive, urinary, skin, circulatory, respira-tory, and lymphatic systems and processes.

Rather than thinking of detoxification as a way of eliminating energy-depleting elements from your body, think of detoxification as a way of giving your body the equipment it needs to effectively act as its own shield against energy-depleting ingredients and incoming toxins, some of which we just cannot circumvent today. Detoxification helps fuel the engines that will literally clean up your body on a cellular level and support its natural operations. It also can physically re-boot your body so you can begin to make those small but transformational shifts in your lifestyle that will help you to live a more energetic life.

Earlier we paid homage to Dr. Mark Hyman's *UltraMetabolism*, in which he calls for detoxifying the liver as a critical step to weight loss, pointing to the fact a healthy functioning liver makes for a healthy functioning metabolism that can properly process sugars and fats. He underscores the fact that toxins from within our bodies and from our environment both contribute to obesity. So getting rid of toxins and boosting the natural detoxification system is an essential component of long-term weight loss and a healthy—energy-generating—metabolism.

We don't want to sound any alarms or scare you about the fact that we all live in a toxic world today. We have become a society where we no longer have to worry so much about things such as plague, famine, and poor sanitation. We now suffer from the products and by-products of our own technological advancements that provoke poor health and chronic illness. Myriad products we meet daily can harbor toxic substances that our bodies absorb little by little over time—from mattresses and mouthwash to carpets, clothing, and cosmetics.

And a lot resides in our food where preservatives, additives, coloring agents, pesticides, and other chemical residues hide. It's been argued that the reason fat cells bear the brunt of storing toxins is because our bodies were never designed to protect themselves from these toxins. So instead of the body being able to efficiently eliminate them, it throws them into fat cells much like you throw clutter in the garage or basement to deal with later. You're not quite sure what to do with it, so you store it somewhere that's out of sight (and temporarily out of mind). But as the toxins accumulate, they begin to have nasty effects on your body's functioning. You can begin to experience health problems, from minor ones such as allergies and endless colds, to serious illnesses such as cancer and brain disease. Lack of energy will be just the tip of the iceberg.

Skin Deep: Your skin is your largest organ. Keeping it healthy and red-carpet glowy goes way beyond the right facial or access to a cosmetic dermatologist. It begins at home—with a healthy digestive system, proper hydration, and regular exercise. The secrets to great-looking skin aren't all that secret by now. They originate in the diet:

- *Go Pro:* Add probiotics to your diet.

- *Animal Exchange:* Choose vegetarian fats and proteins rather than animal fats and proteins (e.g., scoop up nuts and seeds, and spread their oils and butters; and swap your steak for quinoa).

- *Don't Have a Cow:* Skip dairy in favor of healthy vegetarian sources of protein, such as quinoa and hemp seeds (e.g., pass on cheese, but pass the organic eggs). Or opt for organic dairy in limited amounts.

- *Get Green and Yellow:* Get your organic greens in several times daily to help with detoxification and use lemons and limes, which provide alkalinizing benefits in the digestive tract.

And any attempt at healthy skin must include a regular fitness routine that gets the circulation going, blood pumping, and your skin sweating. Try the following quick remedies for spot treatments:

- Slather the body with organic coconut oil after a shower.

- Dry-brush to improve lymphatic circulation and minimize cellulite (you can find dry-skin brushes at most beauty-supply stores).

- Stretch before and after your workout.

- Run with a sweatshirt on. Ever wonder how those got their name? They help to get you to sweat more if you wear them during your workout (Rocky Balboa style).

- Schedule a spa day with a friend and sit in the sauna and/or steam bath for a long, sweaty soak.

After all, who doesn't feel energized when they have great skin?

Another way to look at this is to consider what happens when the body tries to process toxins that the liver cannot easily break down. The toxins that are fat soluble will be sent to your fat cells, so the more toxins you have to store away, the more fat tissue your body needs to store them (and use precious energy to do so). And the fatter you become. This largely explains why detox programs ultimately help people to lose weight—and gain energy. Their body is able to release these stored toxins from the fat cells, rendering the fat cell empty.

They lose the need for the extra fat to begin with, and more energy can thus be conserved.

Avoiding the fat-soluble toxins may sound like a solution, but that's difficult to do today. We have considerable exposure to fat-soluble, carbon-containing, toxic chemicals used as solvents, glues, and paints. Common cleaning products, formaldehyde, toluene, and benzene are all solvents (meaning they are capable of dissolving other substances) we can typically encounter in daily life when we pump gas, shop for clothes, buy a new car, and pick up laundry. These fat-soluble chemicals collect in the fatty tissues of the body rather than being excreted quickly. They are particularly damaging to those who are deficient in essential fatty acids, because a body deprived of essential fats is a body that will grab on to oily substances—even if that includes toxic substances such as diesel fuel—similar to how a dry sponge readily soaks up water.

It's unrealistic to think we can totally eliminate all the potentially harmful substances in the world, their risk factors, and their energy-depleting effects. The best we can do is limit and manage our exposure—without driving ourselves crazy. If you've already begun to employ the ideas in the previous chapters, then you're well on your way to naturally detoxifying your system and making room for more energy. Adopting a healthy lifestyle for some people, though, is a challenge. It helps to go through a more specific protocol that sets the tone and gives you a much-needed launching pad.

Well, let this chapter be your starting point then. We're going to give you two step-by-step action plans for making our strategies come alive. Try either the 8-Day Deep Cleanse or the 3-Day Quick Cleanse and see how you feel. If you're really feeling ambitious, start with the 3-Day Cleanse and transition to the 8-Day Deep Cleanse. We bet you come out looking and feeling more energized, and it will show through your skin, too.

The 8-Day Deep Cleanse

This is about doing an energy-boosting cleanse that works with your body rather than against it. It's really simple: skip processed and packaged foods, chemicals, sugar, alcohol, and caffeine, and replace them with organic vegetables, whole grains, and healthy fats . . . and you've got yourself a cleanse that will work with the body. If you're (mostly) already doing this or looking for a jump start, you can also do a liquid cleanse of pureed organic vegetables, a little fruit, and vegetarian sources of protein, which will relax the body. (Because liquids don't require engaging the digestive process as much, the body can get to some of its deeper cleaning at this time.)

On each day, you must also engage in something physically demanding for at least 30 minutes. Examples: power walk in a hilly neighborhood, use a piece of gym equipment and spend time at an intensity that's slightly uncomfortable, attend a group class, perform at least five of the exercises showcased in the appendix, etc.

Note that you can choose to do all eight strategies at once starting on day one and continuing through all eight days. Or add one component at a time, one day after the other.

Day 1: Clean Up

Get rid of any packaged foods containing high-fructose corn syrup, hydrogenated oils, colors with pound signs (#) by them (e.g., blue lake #3), and artificial ingredients such as MSG (monosodium glutamate) or autolyzed yeast. You can have the kids help you out but be sure to check everything—you will be surprised what so-called healthy options may not be as healthy as they seem.

Day 2: Color Play

Aim to eat one serving of each of these colors (Skittles and Froot Loops don't count): red, blue, green, purple, and orange. Extra credit: choose organic (frozen organic is a great option).

Day 2 Hint: Stock your kitchen with colorful antioxidants. Plants offer the best source of antioxidants—the crusaders against free radicals. Eating up antioxidants will eat up those free radicals, preventing damage and ultimately boosting energy metabolism. While citrus fruits and berries are the most plentiful sources of antioxidants, all fruits and vegetables provide good supplies of antioxidants. The deeper and brighter the color of the food, the more densely packed with vitamins it is. Buy the most vividly colored fruits and veggies you can find. Make sure to keep some of the following all-star antioxidants in your kitchen as much as possible:

- Blueberries, raspberries, and strawberries

- Pomegranates, blackberries, and açai

- Vitamin A sources: carrots, mangoes

- Vitamin C sources: kiwis, mangoes, papayas, black currants, camu camu berries

- Vitamin E sources: nuts, seeds, whole grains, dark green leafy vegetables

Day 3: Some Assembly Required

Eat one to two (one for weight loss or if your physical activity is low) servings of carbohydrates and proteins, and one of healthy fat per eating occasion. Still hungry? Serve up some unlimited vegetables. Examples: apple + 1 tablespoon almond butter; palm-sized wild salmon + sauteed garlic spinach + fist-sized portion of rice; bowl of organic berries + drizzle of chocolate sauce.

Day 4: Beverage Patrol

Drink one cup of coffee or tea max for the day. For maximum metabolic and fat-burning advantages, go for green tea and oolong. Go decaf the rest of the day and no beverages with sugar—even if they promote their product as just a little sweet or no sugar added.

Day 4 Hint: Veto the vitamin water. Water isn't meant to be a source of vitamins. Yes, you need both vitamins and water, but not in a beverage with additives often including sugar; additionally, these vitamins aren't typically as easy for the body to use as the vitamins we get from quality food sources. Some water naturally contains minerals, but vitamins? Really? For the same grams of carbs in the water, you can eat a small banana, which is naturally rich in energy-revving B vitamins and potassium, and whose nutrients are likely much more bioavailable (ahem, easily absorbed).

Day 5: Treat Yourself

Remind yourself how great nonfood gifts can be to give and receive. Book a massage, get a manicure/pedicure, do something with a friend, or indulge in a long night out with your husband while the kids are well taken care of by a babysitter.

Day 6: Exchange—Part 1

Swap an animal for a vegetarian source of protein today. Ideas: organic nut butter on an apple. A veggie burger. Hemp granola or hemp seeds with a bowl of organic berries. Hummus and veggies. A bowl of quinoa with chopped walnuts, ground flaxseed, cinnamon, and ginger.

Day 6 Hint: For a list of AKA-approved brands, go to www.AshleyKoffRD.com.

Day 7: Exchange—Part 2

Swap high-fat dairy and less healthy animal fats for vegetarian sources (e.g., hemp, flax, olive, avocado, coconut) and wild fish (e.g., sardines, cod, salmon), or choose organic lower fat dairy options including goat and sheep sources. Try different cultured veggies or tempeh. Exchanging organic and antibiotic-free dairy as well as adding fermented foods will decrease antibiotics and increase probiotics.

Day 7 Hint: For a list of AKA-approved brands, go to www.AshleyKoffRD.com.

Day 8: Flavor from Nature

Spice up your cooking by using cardamom, oregano, thyme, ginger, cinnamon, and fennel seeds.

> ## ASHLEY'S ENERGY ADVICE
>
> I recently had a *Shedding for the Wedding* cast member ask me after months of massive changes and the resulting weight loss and health gains, "Do I need a cleanse?" And I said, "My dear, you've been on a cleanse for months—no sodas, no artificial ingredients, lots of exercise, lots of veggies, super good quality foods, not much red meat, etc. . . ." Skip the packaged deal you saw at the market and stay the course!

THE 3-DAY QUICK CLEANSE

For those who need to be handheld through a quick cleanse, try the following 12-step program every day for three full days.

1. On waking, take a probiotic with hot tea or hot water with lemon.

2. Stretch, do some exercise. You may feel hungry or slightly lightheaded so adjust your pace/duration accordingly but even 15 minutes will net some fat-burning effects.

3. Make a protein-greens drink with water (or coconut water) and a healthy fat like avocado. See www.AshleyKoffRD.com for brand ideas and recipes. Drink slowly and take a vitamin D_3 supplement.

4. Sip on hot beverages (herbal tea, water with lemon) throughout the morning. If starving, add almond or rice milk (organic, plain).

5. Midmorning: have a snack of 1 cup organic applesauce and 1 tablespoon flaxseeds or chia seeds.

6. Midday: this is your best time for an eating occasion. Try organic veggies or veggie soup (pureed, no dairy) with vinegars or hempseeds, herbs, and spices. Roasted and sautéed veggies are great too if done with a healthy organic oil.

7. Midafternoon: perhaps a self-made tea latte, unless you have a place that does organic almond or rice milk and *no* sweetener. Most commercial coffee shops making tea lattes use both sugar-based tea powders and sweeteners or sweetened soy milk, so make sure you ask. Add some veggies or cultured veggies with hemp seeds, spices, and dressing, or a small cup of soup or real seaweed salad (not the neon green sweet one at the store). If you're not into all the "fancy stuff," cut up some cucumber, jicama, and celery and mix it with cayenne and lime to make a great crunchy snack option.

8. Before 7 P.M.: blend up a smoothie but skip the added greens if you have trouble sleeping.

Note: all of these eating occasions are interchangeable, so if you go out to dinner, get an organic greens salad and soup (maybe bring your hemp seeds or dressing or just opt for lemon juice). Or if you have a morning meeting, have your drink and get sautéed veggies at the meeting.

9. About 1 hour before bed take a magnesium citrate supplement that aids sleep and stress reduction. (Magnesium citrate prodcuts are available as an organic powdered form.) Dosage should reflect your regularity—if you are having regular bowel movements go with 1 to 2 teaspoons.

10. Consider dry brushing the skin, a hot bath or shower, coconut oil on wet skin, a facial mask for 20 minutes, and using a roller to roll out your muscles.

11. If you can, during the cleanse wear minimal or no makeup or nail polish and let the body air itself out.

12. Get regular exercise (yes, you want to sweat), schedule a massage and infrared sauna sessions, practice yoga, take long (hilly!) walks, and find time to sit in silence.

EXIT GRACEFULLY

When followed properly, a quality cleanse can work effectively to help us shift seasons, to get out of a mental or physical fog, or to jump-start weight-loss goals and live a more health-conscious life.

You want to ease your body back into a healthier diet. Start by eating foods easily digested, such as lightly cooked vegetables. Then move to fruit and whole grains. Pay attention to portion control and frequency of eating occasions. Eat vegetable protein before animal protein, and avoid known gastric irritants. Continue to consume water and liquids for hydration. Keep a food-mood journal and notice how a reintroduction of certain foods makes you feel. If you had given something up, assess why you feel you need to return to it. For example, if you were used to drinking a glass of wine nightly or coffee at your break, what has it been like to avoid that? This doesn't mean you can't have it, but it helps to look at the why. And be sure to get your rest. You may be done with the cleanse, but your body is working through changes. Let it.

SUPPLEMENT SMARTLY

With so many supplements on the market today, one frequently asked question is does the form of the vitamin—tablet, capsule, liquid, powder, spray—matter? YES! And is there a particular set of supplements you should be taking? YES! You have to supplement smartly.

The type of nutrient in a supplement matters a great deal—for example, d-alpha tocopherol (as a vitamin E source) is not identical to dl-alpha tocopherol. That one extra letter spells the difference between natural and synthetic, as in nut versus photo paper. Yup, you read that right—photo paper! And what about magnesium oxide versus magnesium citrate? There is a major difference in absorption. And oftentimes minerals—not necessarily vitamins—can be a much bigger issue when it comes to optimizing energy.

Even the best, healthiest eater can benefit from supplements today. It's simply a fact of life given our habits and stress levels (both of which can strip our bodies of nutrients). Certain health challenges can also be a factor. If you've recently had surgery, take medication on a regular basis, or are in the throes of menopause—these can change your body's needs and supplies of the ingredients it requires to run like a champion. If you've ever had problems with digestion after taking supplements, try taking them in the middle of a meal. Never take supplements on an empty stomach unless instructed to do so by your doctor. Following are some more guidelines to consider:

Multivitamin and mineral supplement. Remember the movie *Jerry Maguire*? In one of the movie's most memorable scenes, Tom Cruise's character says to Renée Zellweger's character, "You complete me." That's exactly what you're going for when it comes to taking a daily multivitamin. Even if you eat well, you're bound to run low on a few nutrients due to the realities of life (hey, no one can eat perfectly all the time). So select a comprehensive and balanced formula containing all the major vitamins, minerals, and trace minerals; select an iron-free formula if you are postmenopausal. Look for high-quality, organic forms of the ingredients. For example, the fact that vitamin E works at the mitochondrial rather than cellular level, and does not work at the blood level, is proof that synthetic vitamin E ("dl-alpha tocopherol") is an ineffective form; you'll want to take d-alpha tocopherol, which is vitamin E in its natural form. Ideally, go for gluten-free; and if you've got a history of digestive issues, try a food-based liquid vitamin to ensure bioavailability of nutrients and optimal absorption.

Magnesium. Make sure that you are getting sufficient magnesium to counterbalance supplemental and food intake of calcium. Seek a magnesium citrate supplement, which will absorb better than magnesium oxide. Magnesium creates the calm—whether it's mental or physical; it turns off our stress response, allows our muscles to relax (which means all muscles: especially our digestive tract muscles), and is critical for strong bones along with its partner calcium. Magnesium is responsible for more than 300 metabolic reactions in our body, and it's thought that over 50 percent of the U.S. population is deficient in magnesium. Our current decline in adequate magnesium is partly due to a combination of food processing (white flour has 60 to 80 percent less magnesium than whole-wheat grain), an avoidance of magnesium-rich carbs in general, and a decrease of this mineral in our soils due to chemical farming versus organic. Magnesium-rich foods include whole grains, artichoke, beans, nuts and seeds, dark leafy greens, and even some chocolate. It's practically pointless to get plenty of calcium if you're not getting your magnesium as well, because they work in tandem.

B Complex. You'll find plenty of B vitamins in a variety of foods (chiefly brewer's yeast, wheat germ, whole grains, beans, dark green vegetables, low-fat and nonfat dairy, fish, eggs, and poultry), but to ensure that you get an adequate daily supply, it's best to supplement with a B complex every day that covers all eight Bs—thiamine (B_1), riboflavin (B_2), niacin (B_3), pantothenic acid (B_5), pyridoxine (B_6), biotin (B_7), folic acid (B_9), and cyanocobalamin (B_{12}). These gems are important to energy metabolism and can easily be stripped from the body as a result of stress and certain medicines. Women who take the birth-control pill, for example, have been shown to have low blood levels of B vitamins, which may then trigger migraines.

Essential fatty acid supplements. There are certain fatty acids (omega-3s and -6s) that the body doesn't make, so it's necessary that we get these from the food we eat. Like our multivitamins, which provide foundational support for vitamins and minerals, essential fatty acid supplements can provide these nutrients to ensure we meet our required daily intake. For optimal energy and health, we recommend dietary supplements from whole food forms. This may be in the form of fish oil (especially from wild salmon), flaxseed, chia, and hempseed oils. Vegetarians or those not eating fish or taking fish oil supplements can also choose micro-algae-derived DHA and EPA supplements. Shoot for at least 500 mg of omega-3.

Supplements for bone health. While recommendations used to be for just calcium, we know today that bone health requires a mixture of nutrients including vitamins D and K and minerals like calcium and magnesium, as well as other trace minerals. An evaluation of your diet, your bone-building efforts, and any bone health risks with your doctor can help determine the best supplementation plan for you to achieve your healthy-bone goal.

Vitamin D. Vitamin D has gained a lot of attention in recent years due to an enormous body of research confirming its role in human health and the fact that we don't get enough of it. It's not just a result of us working indoors all day and protecting ourselves from the sun's damaging rays, but it's also a consequence of geography. The vast majority of people who live in North America can't get the same amount of sunlight as those closer to the equator. It's easy for the body to manufacture plenty of vitamin D from brief exposure to UVB radiation a few times a week, but it's very hard to get that same amount of vitamin D from diet alone. Why is this vitamin so important? It's actually a hormone critical to survival because it has a role in numerous communications. A number of studies have found that higher vitamin D, which the body makes when sunlight hits the skin, protects against some cancers and illnesses such as rickets, bone-thinning osteoporosis, and diabetes. It also helps the body's immune system work properly; reduces inflammation; and plays a role in muscle, cardiac, immune, and neurological functions. If you're not casually exposed to sunlight for brief periods a few days a week ("brief" meaning 10 to 15 minutes and long before you'd begin to burn), consider adding a vitamin D supplement that has at least 1,000 IU to your daily regimen.

Antioxidants. If your multivitamin also contains a blend of antioxidants, more power to you. In addition to the usual suspects (vitamins A, C, E), you might also find others, such as alpha lipoic acid, citrus bioflavonoids, extracts from teas and grapes, milk thistle, n-acetyl cysteine, quercetin, curcumin (turmeric), selenium, and coenzyme Q10. Note: While some antioxidants have a recommended daily allowance, such as vitamins A, C, and E, most do not. Instead of trying to count milligrams of your antioxidant intake, just try to get as many of these into your diet from colorful organic fruits and vegetables as possible.

Iron alert. Before you consider supplementing iron, get tested for iron-deficiency anemia. You don't want excess iron in your system, especially post-menopausal women who don't lose iron through blood loss regularly, as excess iron can function as an unwanted prooxidant (the opposite of antioxidant). Additionally, iron supplementation can cause or exacerbate constipation. That said, if you're still in your reproductive years and menstruate regularly, you lose iron each month. Unless it's replaced in your diet or with the combination of diet and supplements, you could suffer some of the unpleasant symptoms of iron-deficiency anemia—chronic exhaustion being one of them.

STAYING TRUE TO FORM

If you're on a diet or detoxing, what do your children think when you don't eat with them at the table or nibble on something strange that they'd never eat? What kind of messages are you giving them? Staying true to yourself and your role as mom is critical.

Many of you don't really start to think about yourself as a "role model" until your children are conscious of you and your habits. That's when it becomes imperative to pay closer attention to your actions. If you don't eat like your kids, what message are you sending? Kids learn through watching and attempting to mimic their parents. Think about where you learned your habits—both good and bad. Remember, your kids are watching you as much or more than they are listening to you. Don't expect your child to love being active if you're not. If they ask where you are going and you say, "I have to go work out; I have to use my muscles," they will begin to understand the importance of exercise. They need to know that you spent part of your day in a workout.

The same holds true with eating. Let them be curious and ask questions about your diet choices. If you eat a salad with the dressing on the side, share with them why it's much easier to control how much unhealthy fat you're consuming so you can ultimately have more energy for them. When you're enjoying a side of French fries with your broccoli and chicken, you can discuss balance. Teach them the difference between an occasional treat and unlimited indulgence. Most moms want to demonstrate a healthy and active lifestyle for kids; it sets them up for a lifetime of healthy habits. This message should also ring loud and clear for grandmothers, too. It's common for grandmothers to indulge grandchildren with treats and splurges. But grandmothers can set good examples as much as mothers can by cooking healthy meals and engaging in physical activities with their grandchildren. Parents who eat differently than their kids can unwittingly do damage that can then be difficult to change. For example, picture the mom who orders a salad while her kids get the Whopper. Or she eats a Lean Cuisine and orders a pizza for her kids. Given the rising rates of obesity among children today, we need to rethink how we fuel our families. Similarly, if mom goes to an exercise class while the kids stay home and watch TV or play video games, this pattern over time can spell trouble. Think about ways in which you can include all of your family members in your whole journey and mission to be a healthy, energetic mother. Otherwise, your life will backfire and the challenges that surface will do nothing but take away your energy and any hope of recovering it. Besides, to be a fully engaged mother and feel fulfilled in your role, it helps to participate in your kids' lives as much as possible—at the table, on the playing field, and in their day-to-day choices. Kids will eat what's put in front of them. They will copy a parent who shows enthusiasm for regular exercise. They will come to admire the fact that you make healthy choices to maximize your energy reserves for their benefit.

Something else to keep in mind: marketers would have you believe that kids should eat separately. They'd like nothing more than to encourage you to buy two types of dinners—one for your kids and another for you. It shouldn't be that way. If the kids are having chicken fingers, then so should you. It bears repeating: Bring your kids into the conversation about health early. Let them help you decide what you're having for dinner as a family. Remember, you're teaching a lifestyle. There's nothing more unappealing than an adult who doesn't eat vegetables and whose favorite food is chicken fingers, mac and cheese, and pizza. You're not a parent on some days of the week or during certain hours of the day. You're a parent 24/7, so be a role model every minute of the day as well. Let that responsibility inform all of your decisions and your kids will love you for it. Being true to form all the time is what will allow you to really maximize your entire energetic life. As this next part shows, you'll optimize your time, capitalize on your sleep, and make the most out of the stressors that compete with your energy.

MOM UP! JUMP-START YOUR TRANSFORMATION

If the thought of removing certain foods to do a detox as outlined in this chapter just isn't your thing, then start by slowly adding the supplements that were discussed. If you don't already take a multivitamin, start with this. Go to your local health-food store and ask about which brands are recommended. Whole Foods, for example, has its own "whole body" section with a designated person there who is well versed in all the varieties they sell. If you already take a multivitamin daily but nothing else, then aim to add another supplement or two to your daily regimen. Soon you'll be getting just what you need to fill in any blanks. Bring a list based on the guidelines we've given and ask the store representative for help in purchasing the highest-quality supplements possible for you. (Alternatively, you can visit our websites at www.kathykaehler.net and www.AshleyKoffRD.com for our own lists of brands we recommend.)

PART IV

RECHARGE

CHAPTER 8

Make Magic
with Movement:
Bring Exercise into Your Day

*Positivity is energy. Always leave the party when you are having fun.
And when I can remember to count my blessings,
balance is naturally restored.*

— SARAH SCHLEPER DE GAXIOLA,
Olympic skier, mother

Julia Roberts perhaps said it best when she declared, "Don't tell me I look tired. Just tell me I look like a mom!"

When moviegoers watched a ravishing Julia emerge bikini-clad out of a swimming pool in the 2007 movie *Charlie Wilson's War*, women everywhere wondered how she did it at four months pregnant with twins. Later, for her role in *Eat Pray Love*, Julia focused her attention again on getting in shape to handle the rigors of moviemaking, which took place around the world and back as she juggled three kids under age ten. At the film's New York premiere, she was photographed on the red carpet wearing a feminine tuxedo in short shorts. Her long, toned legs looked endless. Once more, the questions circled: How did she get those legs? What does she do?

To the dismay of some moms, who wish the secret were a new trick they hadn't heard of yet, Julia's secret weapon was none less than a classic step workout. It may scream circa 1990, but it worked magic and could be used just about anywhere. She'd go up and down on it for 40 minutes and mix her workouts up with other beloved traditions such as yoga and running. If there's anything "unusual" about her step workouts, though, it's that she often adds a friend to the routine. Even at the crack of dawn she'd make it fun by inviting someone to join her so they could talk and kill the time with laughter, movement, and a sharing of ideas. The topics would run the gamut, from better ways to recycle, recipes, and the kids' sleep habits, to gossip. Though a slight departure from what most people would call a "workout," it's a workout nonetheless. And with obvious results.

The moral of this story is that you don't have to close everything off and focus on just the exercise to get a fat-defying, energizing workout. Most moms can agree that exercise has to fit into your life and the business of your household. Granted, Julia has always been good at consistency, which is another key to keeping the body up to speed and which can be a challenge for moms who aren't exacting with their priorities and schedules. But of all the "secrets" we hear about when it comes to sculpting the body and maintaining fitness, we often don't think about the bonus of nurturing friendships at the same time. Julia can't get sick of her workouts if she's simultaneously chatting with a friend and connecting with another mother. As women, we have an innate need to identify with other women, especially moms who share the same struggles of raising children. And for Julia, her workouts can be as much about the mental therapy of good conversation as they are about the body therapy of good exercise. It's as easy as that.

Here's something else to consider: Most of us ache to engage in lively, engrossing conversations. We rarely get the opportunity given the time constraints of motherhood and the dynamics of a typical day. Most of us have highly fragmented days—our minds are ricocheting from one crisis or commitment to the next faster than we are simultaneously transporting ourselves (and our brood) from one place to another. It's a recipe for energy loss. A mother's life does not dovetail the way we are designed to converse with other human beings where one topic is allowed to flow seamlessly into the next. When's the last time you engaged in an endless stream of thoughts with an old friend without having to think or worry about anything else? Imagine how that experience would add up to a big infusion of stress-relieving energy.

We're not saying that you have to exercise with friends every day, but the point is clear: it helps to view exercise as an opportunity to tune out your "real" world as an overscheduled mother and just be in the moment with your body. It's where you are allowed to finish a sentence. It's where you give yourself permission to have no interruptions and to focus on just yourself and perhaps another human being. Your body may be working hard, but your mind is relaxed. You don't feel exasperated. There's nothing more energy-building than that. Far too often we see women treat exercise as yet another chore, another To Do. It's boring. It's hard. It's exhausting. It's not fun, but it doesn't have to be that way. Far from it!

The message here isn't so much about what Julia does specifically to stay in shape, because any activity that gets you moving and your heart beating is enough to do the job. But it's how she goes about her activity that makes a difference. With the goal of losing herself among thoughts, friends, and a body in sweaty motion, she gets results that go farther than a nice pair of legs, or set of abs, or whatever. And that's probably the ultimate key to success in staying active and fit. Without that component you won't be motivated to do anything.

> **Profile Alert!** All the profile types can benefit from the recommendations and information in this chapter. Whether you're The Medicine Cabinet (Profile 1), The Mom Zombie (Profile 2), The Overworked and Overscheduled (and Overtired) (Profile 3), The Chronic Dieter (Profile 4), or The Dead Battery (Profile 5), finding movement in your day is key to your well-being.

The Electric Power of Exercise

We usually think of exercise as leading to fatigue but a significant body of evidence shows that the immediate effect of exercise is increased energy. You've probably heard the mantra about exercise being good for you many times before (even in this book). But if there's one magic bullet for enhancing your energy and the amount you can keep on reserve, not to mention boost your looks, your mood, and your life in general, it's exercise. The science is well documented: exercise fights the onset of age-related disease, promotes a positive sense of well-being, increases your lung capacity so you can take in more oxygen, boosts circulation to deliver nutrients to cells, lowers inflammation, and for many is said to be the ultimate stress reducer.

Physically and mentally, exercise has profound effects on the body. All the intertwined biochemical activities that accompany exercise, from the release of anti-inflammatory endorphins that counteract the stress hormone cortisol to the increased circulation and deeper breathing, are a recipe for stress reduction and energy creation. That healthy glow you get after a great workout (rosy cheeks indicative of the increased circulation that is nourishing all those facial cells and tissues) isn't just for show.

As we stated in the first chapter, the more lean muscle mass you have, and the more oxygen you can deliver to your body's tissues, the bigger your battery is. It's as simple as that. These two critical goals—more lean muscle mass and increased capacity to deliver oxygen throughout the body—are achieved through regular exercise. Recall, too, what we said about your most important energy packagers in the body: your mitochondria. The majority of the functions of mitochondria are to convert the energy in food into ATP—the molecule that provides energy for physiological processes. It's your body's energy currency.

The age and efficiency of your mitochondria have a direct correlation with your metabolic health. Because they are a center of gravity for your physiology, they are direct targets for cellular damage. Think about it: they charge your physiology but in doing so expose themselves to your physiology's by-products, including

Working the body physically lights up the energy powers from within, and sweating is physical evidence that you're powering up your battery. Do we need to remind you about the advantages of exercise that have long been reported and proven? All of the following benefits circle back to having a positive influence on your energy and the ability to sustain an optimal metabolism:

- Increased stamina

- Increased flexibility

- Increased blood circulation

- Increased oxygen supply to cells and tissues

- More restful, sound sleep

- Decreased stress

- Increased self-esteem and sense of well-being

- Increased muscle strength, tone, and endurance

- Increased levels of brain chemicals called endorphins that act as natural mood lifters and pain relievers

- Decreased food cravings

- Decreased blood-sugar levels, and risk for diabetes

- Improved weight distribution and maintenance

those pesky free radicals that can inflict harm and clog the very system designed to create and sustain your energy. In fact, the specialized energy conversion functions that the mitochondria perform make them and their DNA more susceptible to mutation than the normal DNA of the cell, which lies protected inside the nucleus of most cells. Those nasty free radicals will unwittingly attack the mitochondrial membranes and DNA—making them less efficient over time. For this reason, mitochondria have been called the Achilles' heel of the cell in aging.

And here's where we bring in the beauty about exercise. No doubt what you eat and what you expose yourself to in your environment affects the extent to which your mitochondria function and how much damage they endure, but people forget the influence that exercise has in this regard. Moderate intensity aerobic exercise for just 15 to 20 minutes, three to four times a week has been shown to increase the number of mitochondria in your muscle cells by 40 to 50 percent. That's not very much exercise for a huge increase in your energy metabolism (and ability to burn fat).

PUTTING THE ENERGY IN EXERCISE

Exercise physiology has come a long way in the last 20 years. We know so much more about the mechanics of the human body through laboratory and clinical tests that show us exactly what's going on when we decide to charge up a hill or train for a marathon. Entire new fields of medicine have been created, such as metabolomics, which is a form of metabolic profiling that aims to find patterns in people that either spell disease or lower their risk for certain illnesses. Out of this new field has come the confirmation that the fitter you are, the more benefit for your metabolism. This is due to metabolic changes that occur during exercise. In a study done by a team from Mass General, the Broad Institute of MIT, and Harvard, fit people were found to have greater increases in a metabolite called niacinamide than unfit people. Niacinamide is a nutrient by-product that's involved with blood-sugar control. In fact, this team found more than 20 metabolites that change during exercise. These are naturally produced compounds involved in burning calories and fat, and improving blood-sugar control. Some weren't known until now to be involved with exercise. Some revved up during exercise, such as those involved in processing fat. Others involved with cellular stress decreased with exercise.

Another recent discovery relates to the classic "runner's high"—the state of euphoria associated with prolonged exercise (talk about high energy!). It's no longer explained solely by the adrenaline and endorphin hypothesis. Scientists now believe that the physical and psychological well-being experienced by many endurance athletes is due to the exercise-induced activation of cannabinoids—lipids, in fact—in the body whose actions resemble those of the active ingredients of marijuana. These cannabinoids can suppress pain; they inhibit swelling and inflammation; and dilate blood vessels and make breathing easier. The phenomenon of exercise addiction is largely due to these powerful chemicals naturally produced in the body.

There's no end to the number of studies that prove the energy connection in relation to exercise. In 2009 another study emerged clearly showing that exercise causes your brain to turn up production of certain brain chemicals known to have antidepressant effects. Anything that helps us stave off depression and lift our spirits is good for energy. The researchers also found that exercise excited a gene for a nerve growth factor called VGF. VGFs are small proteins critical to the development and maintenance of nerve cells. Even more fascinating is the fact the study brought to light 33 VGFs that show altered activity with exercise, the majority of which had never been identified before.

With all this new information, there's been plenty of confusing and seemingly conflicting data. It's been proven, for example, that just 10 minutes of brisk walking (now that's low-tech!) enhances energy levels for up to 90 minutes thereafter. This is partly due to the discoveries just made about exercise triggering metabolic changes that last at least an hour—especially for those who are already in shape. But this isn't enough to keep us in shape. It's also been shown that moderate exercise at least five days a week for 30 minutes a pop will not result in long-term weight loss and maintenance. So how do we rectify all the competing information?

If you work out for an hour at a moderate level, you will burn and recharge only so much depending on where you are physically. Many people casually work on the StairMaster or the elliptical, for example, and count the minutes as they go by just to say, "I did 30 minutes today." When they complain of not getting the results they want, we have to remind them that their battery demands to be challenged in the exercise department. You can't just move more in daily life; you have to up the ante. This entails going hard in a workout a few days a week to stress your aerobic capacity and to put pressure on your bones so they are forced to stay strong. It could mean the difference between looking okay but not feeling great.

People forget the effects that aging has on the body and the ability to maintain a strong energy metabolism. In addition to the muscle loss and strength that we experience naturally alongside the inevitable slowdown of our metabolisms over time, we fail to consider the practical reasons for weight gain and energy depletion: we have a tendency to become more sedentary yet don't change our eating habits. Hormonal changes put more nails in the coffin, exacerbating an already troubled energy metabolism. This is why a study released in 2010 and published in the *Journal of the American Medical Association* stated clearly that the 2008 U.S. guidelines urging about a half hour of exercise five days a week won't stop weight gain while getting older without cutting calories. Put another way, it takes more to lose more as you age more. According to this latest study, older women at a healthy weight need to engage in moderate activity for at least an hour a day if they want to maintain their weight without changing their diets. The research is more sobering for those who are already overweight: even more exercise is called for to avoid gaining weight without eating less.

KATHY'S ENERGY ADVICE

Since hitting the onset of menopause, I've had to seriously crank up the intensity of my workouts. I went through a year of being achy, feeling bad, and gaining weight no matter what I did. My body was in a standstill. One day, exasperated but determined to find something that worked, I decided to test the limits of my physicality and charge up a hill on my mountain bike like a madwoman. It shocked my system, but it's exactly what I needed. I had to get my heart rate up so high that my body was forced to respond. Since then, everything has changed. I feel far more in control now. I have this energy that's very reliable. Rather than feed my body excuses like "I can't get out of bed," I remind myself that I can rise at 5 A.M., I can do 17 loads of laundry (if I need to!), and I no longer spend hours at night facing racing thoughts and anxiety. I sleep like a baby.

Reaching the inevitable hormonal shifts had its hidden benefits. It compelled me to stop and think about the choices I was making. It demanded that I go back to basics—to really look at calorie expenditure and how hard I was pushing myself physically. For me, that meant finding an activity that burns hundreds of calories and gets me outside. It's imperative for you to have something that allows you to jack up that heart rate, cover yourself in sweat, and reach a point where you're panting. Right away, you'll feel this rush of "Oh my gosh!" That's your energy tap. Open that up. Foods do play a huge role, but the physical part of exercise is also where it's at. Think of it this way: We're not churning the butter. We're not putting our clothes on the line, washing our cars, or doing any physical labor like we used to. You've got to do something else if you don't want to take this other route of reluctantly succumbing to changes in your body. Walk or bike ride up a steep hill, or climb stadium stairs. Get a trainer to make you work out harder. Find a friend who is more fit than you and tag along. Make goals for yourself. Don't let the excuses pile on. You can find something!

The Fountain of Youth

Energy is often equated with youth. When you're young, you have more energy, feel more energetic, and look the part, too. This isn't just a sensation. Our age can be seen in our genes, and we can also see the difference that physical activity makes.

The idea that exercise can "reverse" aging is no longer proven by anecdotal evidence alone. It's been an area of intense and exciting research worldwide. In 2008, for example, a team of Canadian and American researchers showed that exercise can partially help reverse the aging process at the cellular level. They looked at the effects of six months of strength training in elderly volunteers aged 65 and older. They took small biopsies of thigh-muscle cells from the seniors before and after the six-month period, then compared them with muscle cells from 26 young volunteers whose average age was 22. The scientists expected to find evidence that the program improved the seniors' strength, which it did by 50 percent. But they never expected what else they witnessed: dramatic changes at the genetic level. The genetic fingerprint of those elderly volunteers who'd gone through the strength-training program was reversed nearly to that of younger people. In other words, their genetic profile resembled that of a younger group.

How did they measure this change and difference? At the beginning of the six-month period, researchers found significant differences between the older and younger participants in the expression of 600 genes, indicating that these genes become either more or less active with age. By the end of the exercise phase, the expression of a third of those genes had changed, and upon closer observation they realized that the ones that changed were the genes involved in the functioning of mitochondria. That's right: it all goes back to your mitochondria, your cells' chief generators where ATP gets created to process nutrients into energy.

Giving you a detailed exercise program is not the goal of this chapter. Instead, we're going to present a few ideas to consider in pursuit of establishing your own unique routine. The goal is to inspire exercise for energy, and to show how the "what we do" becomes the "how much E we have" in the day. Put another way, when you know how to find the right balance of testing and respecting your body's limits from a physical standpoint, you can achieve that Holy Grail of optimizing your energy.

(For those dying for a list of best exercises you can do just about anywhere, we invite you to flip to the appendix. There, you'll find The Whole-Body List that includes basic step-by-step instructions.

THE ESSENTIALS TO THE ENERGY EQUATION

The type of activity you do is not nearly as important as how often you do it and how long you do it. Because exercise lowers stress for up to 24 hours, it's important to avoid being the "weekend warrior" and make it a goal of keeping a semi-daily routine. Remember, consistency is key. It's also critical that you match your body to where it's at physically, and even emotionally. If it's having to use its resources elsewhere, say to fight a cold or breastfeed a baby, then your personal exercise program won't be the same as someone else's. One great question to ask yourself is: What exercise will address what my mind and body need? If you are mad at work, for example, you may need to work it out aggressively on a hard run or dance class so you don't take that negative energy home. But if your kid was up sick all night and you got little sleep, you may just need a simple walk and a nap.

Ultimately, we want to make sure that we don't ask too much of the body, while at the same time encourage it to test its limits once in a while in order to get stronger and build endurance—the kind of endurance every mother needs.

When Angie Harmon tried to get back into shape for a new series after having her third child, she still looked fabulous. But her physical shape told a different story in the gym. Angie battled serious back problems stemming from the pregnancy that traveled down to her legs, for which lots of stretch-and-hold exercises (for 30 to 60 seconds) came to the rescue. To boost her endurance, which also had hit an all-time low, cardio and weight training helped get her back into the game.

Ideally, a well-rounded and comprehensive exercise program that optimizes your energy metabolism includes cardio work, strength training, and stretching. Each of these activities affords you unique benefits that your body needs to achieve and maintain peak performance. Cardio work, which gets your heart rate up for an extended period of time, will burn calories, lower body fat, and strengthen both your heart and lungs. Strength training (use of weights or elastic bands, or even your own body weight as resistance in some cases) will keep your bones strong and prevent that loss of lean muscle mass. Stretching will keep you flexible and less susceptible to joint pain.

Also don't forget that the benefits of exercise are cumulative. Another fact science has proven is that short exercise bouts throughout the day are just as effective as one long workout and may be even better. So you don't have to sweat it out on a treadmill for a full 60 minutes all in a row. You can do 10 minutes here, 20 minutes there. The reason for this is twofold. First, interval training that really gets your heart and lungs thumping trumps the slow-and-steady exercise routine. The essence of interval training is going hard for a short period of time, then backing off for a few minutes before resuming a higher level of intensity again for another short interval. You can do this in virtually any type of exercise, from walking to utilizing equipment in a gym. Varying your speed, adding weights, or increasing the incline on, say, a walk outdoors on hills, are all ways in which you can create your own interval-training routine. Those bursts of high-intensity intervals will equate with bursts of high-intensity energy! If you're not the type to zone out for an hour in a workout like Julia Roberts, then sprinkle pockets of workout times into your day—at lunch, after dinner, or in the 15 minutes right after you get up and the house is still quiet.

Consistency can be too idealistic. Life with kids is dynamic, sporadic, and ever changing. Understand what your possibilities are. If you really want to work out, you have to take advantage of when you know you have the opportunities. When kids are napping or at school, seize the moment and do it. But if it gets away from you, there might be another window that could open up later on that you did not anticipate. We can't feel like if we miss a workout, it's the end of the world. Just shut down earlier and wake up earlier the next day to get it done. Sleep in workout clothes or have them next to the bed. Accept that you won't get it done and it's okay, but use that energy to plan the next day.

— A N G I E   H A R M O N ,
actress and mother of three

Cut to the Chase

The second explanation behind the benefits of "burst" activity—spreading your workouts throughout the day into short bursts—is that it helps prevent you from the ravages that sitting down all day can do to you. We hope you're not sitting down while reading this. No joke: as we were putting together our materials for this book, researchers at the American Cancer Society released a study published in the *American Journal of Epidemiology* that pretty much said sitting down for extended periods poses a health risk as insidious as smoking or overexposure to the sun. A second study at the International Diabetes Institute in Melbourne concluded that even two hours of exercise a day would not compensate for "spending 22 hours sitting on your rear end."

While several studies support a link between sitting time and obesity, type 2 diabetes, risk factors for cardiovascular disease, and unhealthy dietary patterns in children and adults, very few studies have examined time spent sitting in relation to total mortality. This latest study makes a stunning case for the strong association between continually sitting down (as many of us do nowadays at desks, on the couch, and in our cars) and disease. The shocker: women seem to be more affected by spending time on their derrieres. In the study, women who reported more than six hours per day of sitting (outside of work) were 37 percent more likely to die during the time period studied than those who sat fewer than three hours a day. Men who sat more than six hours a day (also outside of work) were 18 percent more likely to die than those who sat fewer than three hours per day. The association remained virtually unchanged after adjusting for physical-activity level. The people in the study were followed from 1993 to 2006; researchers examined the participants' amount of time spent sitting and physical activity in relation to mortality over the 13-year period.

The act of sitting itself is not the culprit here. It's the biological effects that sitting triggers in the body that are a game changer. And by that we mean sitting's metabolic impact. Prolonged time spent sitting, independent of physical activity, has been shown to have significant metabolic consequences, negatively influencing levels of things such as triglycerides, high-density lipoprotein (the "good" cholesterol), blood sugar, resting blood pressure, and the appetite hormone leptin, all of which are biomarkers of obesity and cardiovascular and other chronic diseases.

The message is clear: you must move—and move frequently—to maintain health. It's not just a matter of energy. It's a matter of life and longevity. Even people who just break up their sitting time by walking to a friend's house rather than e-mailing her, for instance, have a lower risk of diabetes.

Whether it's a structured class at a gym, power walking with friends in the morning, dancing, or renting DVDs with the latest from fitness trainers, there are lots of options today. Get creative and have fun with your activity. Don't make it a chore, and don't make yourself miserable by doing something you hate.

Exercise should be enjoyable, something you look forward to every day. And remember, many forms of exercise can involve

KATHY'S ENERGY ADVICE

What exercises can I do with my kids? I get this question a lot, because traditional forms of exercise typically exclude children unless you're playing with them in the park or at a jungle gym. However, there are lots of things you can do to engage your kids in a workout that has the added benefit of demonstrating to them the importance of leading a physically active life and making exercise a priority. You can also begin to teach them about taking care of their bodies and making them strong and fit.

The first thing I like to recommend is letting your kids do a workout DVD with you. They love to copy Mom—it makes them feel grown-up. Then I remind moms to take active vacations and schedule active family nights where you plan to do something physical together like bowl, go to the batting cages, dance, play Frisbee at the park, or just walk the dog after dinner. Finally, you might want to check out the use of a trampoline, which is not something just for kids. I've used these with Jennifer Lopez as well as Kim Basinger. Kim bought one for her daughter but then realized from my workout that it's a great way to get your heart rate up. You can play all kinds of games with your kids using a small trampoline that will fit in most dens or living rooms. Take turns jumping on it and challenge each other with how many jumps you can make with your toes pointed, tucking your knees, and so on. The fun will just be getting started when you realize that your hearts are pumping like mad and you're connecting with your kids in ways you never have before.

your family and friends, which can be very motivating and offer an added benefit—especially psychologically. Of course, giving yourself consistent recovery days is also part of a well-rounded workout routine, and in Chapters 9 and 10 we'll be going into the details of finding time to relax and settle your mind in ways that don't entail pumping your heart.

No matter which form or type of exercise you choose to do, its positive impact on your energy level—and looks and health—cannot be underestimated. Do you know any fit mother who doesn't look amazing and say she feels younger than she did ten years ago?

GETTING STARTED

Still don't know where to start? Are you sitting down reading this, terrified that you've cut your life short by staying on your butt all day long—yet the thought of exercise scares you?

If you're a true beginner, check out your local gym. Cardio classes are great if you need someone else to push you, and the energy of the other people in the class is sure to motivate you. Most gyms offer lots of choices, including step class, boot camps, indoor cycling, kickboxing, cardio dance class, and more. While you're there, check out the cardio equipment. But note: your body can adapt to these easily so the results you get in the first few months will no longer impress you. Keep changing it up. The recumbent bikes and the sit-up bikes are great for your legs and butt. The elliptical is awesome especially if you can crank the arms as well. Combining a workout with three different cardio machines is also a great way to kick up your heart rate as you know you will be moving on shortly. And if you're feeling intimidated, then have a trainer at your facility take you through a workout. Signing up for a short series of training sessions is not a bad idea as this will get you more familiar with the equipment and you'll feel more confident when it comes time for you to be on your own.

Here are a few more tips to make your move into working out regularly be as easy and effective as possible:

- **Pay attention to how you feel.** As you exercise, ask yourself: *Can I push harder? How am I breathing?* To have fun is to make your workouts a challenge.

- **Get meditative about it.** Find workouts that take you away. Listen to music that has a beat and rhythm to it that synchs with your workout. Create a playlist with songs that have a certain number of beats-per-minute depending on the type of workout you want to have. It's hard to pick up your pace if you're listening to Frank Sinatra.

- **Get a mentor or group of mentors.** Remember, group classes can help keep you stimulated and focused. Or get a friend who is in better shape than you and work out with her.

- **Hire a trainer.** We've said it before, but here it is again. A trainer can help keep you focused, busy, and motivated. You may need only one session to learn a comprehensive routine that you can repeat, modify, and improvise as you move forward.

- **Think whole body.** Visualize what your body parts do. Arms lift, push, pull, press, swing. So find machines that do those motions. Watch other people in the gym. Using the individual machines that focus on a particular body part is sometimes the best way to start. You want to hit arms, back, shoulders, chest, abs, legs (front and back), calves, and core.

- **Take a strength class.** A class where the instructor uses weights can help you learn positioning and how the exercise is supposed to feel as well as know what muscle you are working. This way when you get in the gym by yourself you will feel very comfortable picking up the free weights.

- **Try the kettlebells.** These are all the rage today but form and style are imperative to make this type of exercise effective. If your gym offers these classes, take one!

- **Go for new gadgets**. Gyms are typically filled with odd-looking gadgets—exercise balls, rubber tubing, ropes, jump ropes, foam rollers, etc.—that will add so much to your workouts. Before testing them out on your own, ask a trainer for help or check out the schedule for classes that teach you how to use them.

On a personal level, I feel better when the energy that I access in my work on a daily basis—i.e., my mind—is balanced by the energy that I access for exercise—my body. By balancing the two of them, I feel I can access the energy that nourishes my spirit.

After I became a mom, I needed exercise in so much more of a crucial way. Whereas I used to use exercise for the physical effects, I found that as a mother I looked to it for the mental benefits. Especially when you have three kids in the house at one time (!), it becomes difficult to feel like you're completing a task—let alone the 20 that you set out for yourself each day. I found that if I took an hour to walk the baby in the stroller and did a few sets of squats along the way, I felt a sense of accomplishment throughout the day that helped me battle postpartum blues and, later, just general mom-frustration!

— R A C H E L   L I N C O L N   S A R N O F F,
executive director and CEO of Healthy Child Healthy World
and founder of www.EcoStiletto.com

Unexpected Energy Benefits

Admit it: at some time or another, you've made the following declaration: "I'm so fat!" Maybe even in front of your kids without realizing it. It's hard to get away from the topic of weight in our society today. From endlessly hearing about the obesity epidemic to the latest trends in losing weight and hiding fat with fashion, the subject of weight just won't quit. It's pervasive and do we need to say it's also energy depleting? Hopefully this chapter has given you some ideas on ways in which you can rev your physical engine through exercise. But if the scientific benefits of exercise aren't enough to motivate you, then consider the other benefits: those that entail your commitment to your children and your positive self-image. Here's what we mean by that.

Obsessively thinking about weight seems to be par for the course these days among women. It's just too easy to slip into those thoughts even when we know deep down that they are not good for us, nor helpful. Consider the shallowness of that statement as you look at your child—your creation that was born from your amazing body. Every time the "I feel fat" statement zips through your brain, think of your beautiful children and learn to accept the body that has resulted. Granted, this doesn't imply that you cannot change your body and work toward having the body of your dreams. But don't let low-hanging comments like "I'm fat" derail your good intentions and psyche.

You have to look at the big picture—through your children's eyes or through your own ability—and rise above the lameness of statements like that. Instead, move in a direction of "I'm just going to do the best I can and be honest with what 'the best I can' means for me." How much will you let your muffin top really bother you? If you feel fabulous but cannot fit into size-2 jeans, isn't that okay? Having a skinny body isn't the goal—having a fully-functioning, vibrant body is.

Don't lose sight of your physical body. When you do there's a big disconnect from your neck down, and the types of problems that begin to present themselves at a very accelerated pace could be anything from knee problems to back problems to sleep issues, anxiety, overeating, boredom, and mood fluctuations. It's an over-used analogy, but looking at the body as a vehicle helps you to see why TLC is important. If you rely on your car to get you places, you are going to pay attention to its service. Similarly, the body is very resilient but there's only so much it can withstand without proper maintenance. And as you age, it will inevitably start to fall apart quicker.

There's energy in acceptance. Our youth-obsessed culture has us believing that younger is better. Giving in to that belief is draining. When you cannot accept who you are and where you are on your own spectrum of personal transformation, you cannot maximize your energy. And you cannot be the role model that your children deserve.

Mom Up! Jump-Start Your Transformation

Getting into shape starts with just one mile. You can do this on a treadmill or take your GPS-equipped phone with you on a walk outside (or the old-fashioned method of mapping out a mile from your car's odometer so you know when to turn around). Alternatively, you can find a track at your local high school and walk around it four times. If you're on a treadmill, try putting your speed at 4.0 (four miles per hour) and see if you can keep up with that. If not, slow down. See how long it takes for you to do a full mile. Can you reach a mile in under 15 minutes? Make it a goal of just walking one mile at the start and then as you increase your speed, watch your time drop off. This is an indication that you're getting more fit. Ideally, a great walking workout is to walk three miles in fewer than 45 minutes. Don't hesitate to add intensity to your walks with handheld weights, hills (inclines and declines), stairs, and intervals of taking it up a notch and cranking hard for 10 minutes here and there.

CHAPTER 9

Refuel:
Bring Sleep into Your Night

Life as a mom is a shapeless blob of happy chaos.

— J U L I A   R·O B E R T S

What your body does from the time it slips into bed to the time it wakes you up might have more to do with your energy metabolism than you realize. New findings in sleep medicine are currently revolutionizing how we think about the value sleep brings to our lives.

For so many moms we interviewed for this book, sleep ranked high on the list of priorities. Chaka Khan calls sleep "the key to a great energy balance"; Julia Roberts admits that any extra sleep she can get helps counterbalance the "mom struggle" that naturally accompanies having time thieves running around her house. Most of us just don't get the sleep we need. Sleep deprivation is epidemic. And let's face it: when we're sleep-deprived, moody, and things don't go our way, we can begin to go down that dreaded path that ends in depressive thoughts or a full-blown depression.

Moms in particular are starved for sleep, evidenced by the National Sleep Foundation's annual poll. The average woman aged 30 to 60 sleeps only six hours and 41 minutes per night during the workweek (less than the optimal eight to nine hours for health and wellness). On average, we get an hour less sleep per day than we did 40 years ago, and roughly two-thirds of us complain that sleep deprivation cuts into our life and well-being. In fact, sleep may have a greater influence on your ability to enjoy your day than household income and even marital status. One study found that an extra hour of sleep had more of an impact on how a group of women felt throughout the day than earning more money per year.

Without adequate sleep, not only does your entire body reel from its repercussions, but one system in particular—the endocrine, the center of gravity for a woman's energy levels—starts to malfunction. This can lead to everything from appetite and fat-storing hormones running amok to bona fide infertility.

Cutting-edge science now shows how critical sleep is to our ability to stay focused, learn new things and remember old things, lose fat and keep excess weight off, and generally lower the risks for a slew of health problems such as heart disease, obesity, and cerebrovascular disease. It also recharges us (duh!). But moms everywhere are burning the candle at both ends and leaving sleep last on their list. What's more, millions of moms struggle with chronic pain, high anxiety, or full-blown depression, and many become addicted to pain soothers such as alcohol or prescription pills, all of which further drain energy—including the energy required to get well.

Profile Alert! Wake up, Mom Zombie (Profile 2)! The information and ideas in this chapter should speak directly to you. Of course, we recommend that all the profile types heed this advice, but anyone who struggles to get a good night's sleep on a regular basis should really take this chapter to heart (and bed).

Today sleep medicine is a highly respected field of study that continues to provide alarming insights into the power of sleep in the support of health and energy. Sleep can dictate whether you can fight off infections, and how well you can cope with stress. We've already covered how sleep deprivation creates an imbalance of hormones that control your appetite and how your body burns energy. That's just the tip of the proverbial iceberg when it comes to associations between sleep and well-being.

Sleep is not a state of inactivity. It's not as if our bodies press pause for a few hours during the dark. Much to the contrary, a lot goes on during sleep at the cellular level to ensure that we can live another day. Clearly, a night of poor sleep or no sleep at all won't kill you, but prolonged sleep deprivation can have unintended consequences, not to mention putting you at high risk for an accident.

There's something to be said for looking refreshed and feeling smarter upon waking from a good night's sleep or a nap. Seemingly magical events happen when you're sleeping that just cannot happen during wakeful hours, and which help keep you energized and quick-witted. Proof of sleep's profound role in our lives also has been demonstrated over and over again in laboratory and clinical studies. It keeps you sharp, creative, and able to process information in an instant. Losing as few as one and a half hours for just one night reduces daytime alertness by about a third. And among the many side effects of poor sleep habits are hypertension, confusion, memory loss, the inability to learn new things, weight gain, obesity, cardiovascular disease, and depression.

One underappreciated aspect to sleep that is especially influential to our sense of well-being is its control of our hormonal cycles. Everyone has a biological, internal clock called a circadian rhythm (yes, even men can say they have a biological clock). It's the pattern of repeated activity associated with the environmental cycles of day and night—rhythms that repeat roughly every 24 hours. Examples include the sleep-wake cycle, the ebb and flow of hormones, the rise and fall of body temperature, and other subtle rhythms that mesh with the 24-hour solar day. When your rhythm is not in sync with the 24-hour solar day, you will feel (and probably look) it. Anyone who has traveled across time zones and felt off-kilter for a few days can understand this.

So much of our circadian rhythm revolves around our sleep habits. A healthy day-night cycle is tied into our normal hormonal secretion patterns, from those associated with our eating patterns to those that relate to stress and cellular recovery. Cortisol, for example, should be highest in the morning and progressively decrease throughout the day, with the lowest levels occurring after 11 P.M. With (hopefully) low evening cortisol levels, melatonin levels rise. This is the hormone that tells you it's time to sleep; it helps regulate your 24-hour circadian rhythm, alerting your brain that it's dark outside. Once released, it slows body function, lowers blood pressure, and, in turn, core body temperature so you're prepared to sleep. Higher melatonin levels will allow for more deep sleep, which helps maintain healthy levels of growth hormone, thyroid hormone, and sex hormones. All good things for keeping up appearances and energy levels.

> If you've ever had a tough time winding down at night due to stress, you may be secreting too much cortisol, which competes with the sleep-enhancing melatonin.

Why You Need to Go Deep

Lots of hormones are associated with sleep, some of which rely on sleep to get released. As soon as you hit deep sleep, about 20 to 30 minutes after you first close your eyes, and then a couple more times throughout the night in your sleep cycle, your pituitary gland at the base of your brain releases high levels of growth hormone (GH)—the most it's going to secrete in 24 hours.

Growth hormone does more than just stimulate growth and cell reproduction; it also refreshes cells, restores skin's elasticity, and enhances the movement of amino acids through cell membranes. Growth hormone aids in your ability to maintain an ideal weight, too, effectively telling your cells to back off on using carbs for energy and use fat instead. Without adequate sleep, GH stays locked up in the pituitary, which negatively affects your proportions of fat to muscle. Over time, low GH levels are associated with high fat and low lean muscle.

Growth hormone affects almost every cell in the body, renewing the skin and bones; regenerating the heart, liver, lungs, and kidneys; and bringing back organ and tissue function to more youthful levels. Growth hormone also revitalizes the immune system, lowers the risk factors of heart attack and stroke, improves oxygen uptake, and even helps prevent osteoporosis.

Sleep on this: The trouble with running up sleep shortages day after day is that it's very hard to make up the loss unless you're going on vacation. What's more, when sleep is skimpy, your cortisol levels don't drop as much as they're supposed to at night, and growth hormone doesn't rise as much as it should, which can undermine muscle strength. Remember, you need a daily dose of growth hormone, which gets secreted during deep sleep, to refresh your cells and prepare you for the next day. It not only stimulates cellular growth and reproduction, but it also has strong anti-inflammatory, antifat, and anticortisol effects—all good things for energy (not to mention weight maintenance!).

How Does Sleep Happen?

It's one of those fundamental questions that have plagued scientists for a very long time. As we were writing this book yet another study emerged to help explain how the body knows to flip the switch and go from wakefulness to a sleep state. It turns out that those fundamental molecules of energy that literally charge our cells—ATP—take center stage. Washington State University researchers documented how active brain cells release ATP to start the events leading to sleep. The ATP then binds to a receptor responsible for cell processing and the release of cytokines, small signaling proteins involved in sleep regulation. By charting the link between ATP and the sleep-regulatory substances, the researchers found the way in which the brain keeps track of activity and ultimately switches from a wakeful to sleeping state. For example, learning and memory depend on changing the connections between brain cells. The study shows that ATP is the signal behind those changes. Pretty cool stuff, and once again a reminder that energy has as much to do with how we feel during our waking minutes as it does with how well we sleep at night and prepare for another active day.

THE MAGIC NUMBER

It's a myth that there's a magic number of hours the body requires to sleep. Everyone has a different sleep need. The eight-hour rule is general, but not necessarily the ideal number for you. Most people need seven to nine hours, and chances are you know what your number is. If you feel like a drag after a six-hour night, then clearly you need to aim for more sleep. Think of the last time you went on vacation and slept like a baby for more hours a night than usual. That is probably your perfect number. Poor sleep catches up to most of us, and it's practically impossible to make up a sleep loss because life keeps moving forward and demanding more of us. Despite what many people attempt to do, shifting your sleep habits on the weekends to catch up can sabotage a healthy circadian rhythm.

Not surprisingly, stress and staying up too late are the two big culprits to poor sleep, which is why it's important to establish what's called a healthy "sleep hygiene"—the habits that make for a restful night's sleep regardless of factors such as age and underlying medical conditions that can disrupt sleep. The goal is to minimize those factors' effects on us so we can welcome peaceful sleep.

12 PATHS TO PERFECT SLEEP

1. **Get on a schedule.** Go to bed and wake up at the same time seven days a week, weekends included. Try not to fall into a cycle of burning the midnight oil on Sunday night in preparation for Monday, letting your sleep debt pile up for the week and then attempt to catch up on sleep over the weekend. It won't work. Stick to the same schedule seven days a week. Your body and energy levels will love it.

2. **Unplug to recharge.** Set aside at least 30 minutes before bedtime to unwind and prepare for sleep. Avoid stimulating activities (e.g., work, cleaning, being on the computer, watching TV dramas that get your adrenaline running). Try soaking in a warm bath or engaging in some light stretching. Once you're in bed, do some light reading and push any anxieties aside.

3. **Don't let your To Do list or worries take control.** Early in the evening—say, right after dinner—write out tasks you have yet to complete that week (not tonight!) and prioritize them realistically. Add any particular worries you might have. If these notes begin to talk to you when you're trying to go to sleep, tell yourself it's time to focus on sleep. Everything will be okay. You're tired and will have a productive day tomorrow. You're relaxed and at peace. The body needs to sleep and is ready for it.

4. **Create a restful refuge.** Reserve the bedroom for sleep (and sex) only. Remove distracting electronics and gadgets and keep it clean, cool, and dark.

5. **Nix the fix and cut the caffeine.** Stop drinking caffeinated beverages about eight hours before bedtime. Due to caffeine's half-life (how long it takes for caffeine to lose half of its punch in your body), you'll need all that time to let your body process all the caffeine so it won't infringe upon restful sleep. If you cannot go cold turkey on the caffeine in the afternoon, then switch to drinks with less caffeine, such as teas.

6. **Don't sweat it.** Watch out if you exercise within three hours of bedtime. For some people, exercise can be stimulating to the point it affects getting to bed on time and falling asleep easily. This is when tracking your sleep experiences and what you do beforehand can help you to pinpoint your own unique culprits to restless sleep. If your body's reaction to exercise is stealing your sleep, then shift your exercise to earlier in the day.

7. **Limit your libations.** Be cautious about alcohol intake in the evening hours. If you use a glass of wine as a way to unwind after the kids have gone to bed, which is how many moms decompress at the end of the day, be mindful of how that glass (or two) could be influencing the quality of your sleep. You might want to test out avoiding this routine and see if it changes how refreshed you feel the next day.

8. **Ditch digestive distractions.** Keep in mind that heavy foods too close to bedtime can upset your sleep as much as they upset your stomach. The best bedtime snack is nothing. Eating provides energy and that runs counter to prepping the body for rest. If you

need to take a medication or if you are breastfeeding and up during the night, then maybe a liquid such as plain coconut water will satisfy you. This requires no extra digestive work; it's a diluted amount of carbohydrates that also provides potassium for hydration, which will help the body with recovery. To balance it out, you could have 10 to 15 nuts with it.

9. **Focus on relaxing.** Try valerian herbal tea or a chamomile blend before bedtime. Take your magnesium supplement in the evening hours to help relax muscles for better sleep and regularity.

10. **Practice aromatherapy.** Keep a sachet of lavender by your bed and take a whiff before hitting the pillow. Lavender has known sleep-inducing effects. Other aromas widely considered to be relaxing are rose, vanilla, and lemongrass—but different ones work for different people. For you, maybe lavender is stimulating and rose is not. Scented lotions can also be effective.

11. **Take a d-e-e-p breath . . . and release.** On your back with your eyes closed and your body stretched out, hands by your sides, palms facing up, begin to squeeze and release your muscles, starting with your head and face and working down to your toes. Breathe in deeply and slowly, telling yourself, *I will fall asleep. I am going to sleep.*

12. **Get out of the bedroom.** We all think that if we lie in bed long enough, sleep will come. Instead, our minds tend to get busier and our muscles tenser as we stress over being awake. Give it a rest. If you can't get to sleep within 20 minutes, slip out of bed and go to a safe haven—a place that's comfy, has dim lighting, and no distractions. Just sit comfortably.

Or do your breathing exercises. Or read. No e-mail,
TV, or other electronics though. The point is to give
your mind-body a respite from trying so hard to
nod off. After 20 minutes or so, go back to bed and
see what happens when you're more relaxed. Repeat
once or twice if necessary.

Do sleep aids aid? There are plenty of pill pushers these days
in the sleep department. From over-the-counter remedies to prescriptions marketed as nonaddictive and safe, sleep aids are a
gigantic industry. Choosing to go that route is totally up to you,
but be aware of the potential downsides, including those related
to energy metabolism. Modern sleep medications are not all they
are cracked up to be. They may not be as chemically addicting
as earlier generations of sleep drugs, but they can be psychologically addicting. What's more, they can prevent you from reaching the furthest reaches of deep sleep for long enough to reap all
of its rewards. They may also make you groggy or feel hungover
the next day.

You'll be amazed by the power of sleep when it comes naturally just by regulating your sleep habits. You body will respond
and adapt to the sleep cycle you put it on. If your body clock is
truly off, try getting some natural morning sunlight on you, do
some exercise during the day, don't stay up until the wee hours
of the morning cleaning house, and set aside time to wind down
before bedtime. Yes, it's as simple as that!

GOT TOO MUCH NEGATIVE ENERGY?

One more note before moving on: sometimes our sleep troubles are hiding more profound problems which surface late at
night, stirring insomnia. Let's call it negative energy, and this
can entail any number of loaded guns—body-image issues, feeling inadequate as a mother or wife, health concerns, failures
in your relationships, disappointments at work, worries about

money and financial strife, struggles with juggling your parents' health and raising your own children, etc. Go ahead and think of what keeps you up at night. We all have our lists. And they can be long.

Don't think for a minute that these matters don't play into our energy equation. They will pull down any bit of good energy and sabotage it into a very dark and negative place. They can bleed into every part of your being—your relationships with your kids, spouse, friends, job, yourself. Letting these dilemmas simmer in our minds is so worthless, and it gets us nowhere. It also eventually leads us to degrade ourselves. And our bodies hear it, immediately downshifting to preserve precious energy.

In the next and final chapter, we'll delve into the secrets to managing stress, which will play into your ability to get a good night's rest. When you do find yourself churning awful thoughts, turn it around and say something positive about yourself and your commitment to make positive change. For every negative thing you say about yourself and any "predicament" you might find yourself in, say three positive things. I hate my legs. I love my elbows. I love my chin. I love my hair. I hate my job. I love my children. I love my courage. I love my strength. Self-esteem and self-confidence are very powerful. They are also very energizing.

MOM UP! JUMP-START YOUR TRANSFORMATION

Of all the ideas we've given to help you get a good night's sleep, one of the most essential (and least followed) is the one about setting aside time to wind down before bedtime. Far too often, moms find themselves doing last-minute chores and tasks long after the day should have been declared over. Once the kids go to bed, don't give yourself permission to use the rest of the night to catch up on everything else at the expense of a full night's sleep. So if you want just one thing to do differently, see if you can—for one week, hopefully longer—allocate *one hour* before your bedtime during which you don't engage in any stimulating activities such as e-mail, Internet surfing, or even watching television. Instead, opt for a hot soak in your bathtub, reading, or spending time with your spouse. If one hour is unrealistic, then try it for a few days and then cut it back to 30 minutes. But no less! This is You Time, and you'll notice a difference in the quality of your sleep.

CHAPTER 10

Have Fun:
Learn the Power of Play

I feel there are two people inside me—me and my intuition.
If I go against her, she'll screw me every time, and if I follow her,
we get along quite nicely.

— KIM BASINGER

Kim Basinger is by far the one who adheres to the utmost perfect nutrition and a regular exercise routine no matter what's going on in her life. She lives with pure dedication. No sidetracks. It's a mind-set for her that never wavers. "You decide this is the way I'm going to live my life and you stick with it," she says. "You live it, you breathe it, and you do it."

Not everyone can adhere to Kim's stoic way of living, but she affords us a role model by which to compare values and priorities. Too many women let motherhood prevent them from taking care of themselves. In this final chapter we drive home the power of play—giving yourself regular permission to put yourself first and routinely pamper yourself. Only then can you recharge maximally and amplify your capacity to fulfill that role as Mommy. After all, the body needs playtime. It's what nature intended.

Playtime is what ultimately allows us to manage our biggest, and most wily, adversary in our pursuit of more energy: stress. We could have easily based the whole book around the effects stress can have on our energy, but decided to save this topic for last. By now, you've already gained a tremendous amount of information about the body's chemistry and energy metabolism. We hope you've already turned the volume down on your stress level just by incorporating some of our strategies. But we need to expand on stress's far-reaching implications that can do way more than just sap your energy from a superficial standpoint. For some of you, this chapter's ideas could very well be your starting point for change. Why? Because the secret to getting more energy could very well begin with simply admitting that you don't have any energy, for which starting with recovery (ahem: relaxation) first is required. Alcoholics who participate in the classic 12-step program have to admit the problem, which is their first baby step to a sober life. So it's something to consider: achieving an energetic life might start just with taking the sting out of your stress.

Profile Alert! The Overscheduled and the Dead Battery will want to read this chapter twice. That's right: if you're Profile 3 or 5, chances are you never find a spare moment to play. And it's about time that you did.

A COMMON DENOMINATOR TO LACK OF ENERGY

Stress's impact on all things physiological, mental, psychological, and spiritual are well documented. And remarkable. Innumerable studies have shown a direct link between stress and weight gain, for instance; stress can drain your energy simply by taxing your metabolism and flooding the body with stress hormones that weaken your whole energy equation. In studies, more than 70 percent of those who undereat or overeat during a stressful period admit to snacking on foods that are nutrient poor. Fats and sugars seem to fit the bill during times of stress.

New research from Germany shows that people who had heart attacks were three times more likely than not to have been sitting in traffic an hour before their symptoms began. And for some strange reason not identified yet, a woman's risk of heart attack is five times higher within an hour of being in traffic.

This scenario, coupled with our society's increasing financial troubles, has a far-reaching domino effect. To make more money to pay for living expenses, we are working longer hours. Stay-at-home moms don't get a free pass, either. In fact, the mother who devotes all of her time to caring for the needs of her children may be shouldering more stress than the mom who can escape to an office. Unfortunately, stay-at-home moms often don't feel they have the right to be stressed, or that somehow their stress isn't validated so therefore doesn't count.

Suffice it to say, whether you're a working mother or not, we are accepting an unprecedented level of stress in our lives. All of this has put a great strain on our health and well-being, especially because the vast majority of Americans are barely keeping up. So it's not surprising that over the past few years doctors in all fields of medicine have seen a dramatic change in their patients' stress levels. Stress is at the top of the metaphorical food chain—tripping a cascade of events that can lead to thicker waistlines, dour moods, poor sleep, chronic inflammation, and oxidative stress, and, as a result, an unhealthy body and energy level.

On the positive side, if stress is such an influential cast member in our world, and we can learn how to control it with the help of our lifestyle choices, then we may be able to champion the balancing act so we achieve peak health and energy. And that's exactly what we're going to do. Let's take a quick tour of your body's stress-response system and then see how we can lighten the load.

> Stress is an issue, but *the* issue is our inability to relax—to learn to turn *off* the stress.

THE SCIENCE OF STRESS

From an evolutionary and survivalist perspective, stress is a good thing. It's supposed to prime the body for battle and get us out of harm's way. The problem, though, is that our physical reaction is the same every time we sense a potential threat, whether it's real and coming from something truly life-threatening, or just the To Do list and screaming kids.

First, the brain signals to the adrenal glands to release epinephrine, better known as adrenaline. This is what causes your heart to pick up speed as blood rushes to your muscles in case you need to make a run for it. That adrenaline, by the way, steals blood from the skin and face to allocate it toward your muscles, which is why you can suddenly look pale as a ghost or become white with fear.

As soon as the threat passes, your body returns to normal. If the threat doesn't pass and your stress response gets stronger, then a whole wave of stress hormones gets released in a series of events along the hypothalamic-pituitary-adrenal (HPA) axis. The hypothalamus, a region of the brain, first releases a stress coordinator called corticotropin-releasing hormone (CRH). The hypothalamus is frequently referred to as the seat of our emotions. It's our chief leader in emotional processing. The split second you feel anxious, deeply worried, scared, or simply concerned that you can't pay a bill, the hypothalamus secretes CRH to start a domino effect ending in cortisol rushing into your bloodstream.

We've already mentioned cortisol—it's the body's chief stress hormone, aiding in that famous fight-or-flight response. It also controls how your body processes carbs, fats, and proteins, and helps it to reduce inflammation. Because it's the hormone responsible for protecting you, its actions increase your appetite, tell your body to stock up on more fat, and break down materials that can be used for quick forms of energy, including muscle. Not all that you'd like to happen, but when your body senses stress (even when you know it's not the kind that will physically kill you in ten seconds or less), it thinks you won't see food again for a while—or it may need an ample supply of fuel to camp out on during a famine or use to make a mad dash. In other words, cortisol causes tissues to break down, including muscle, skin, and collagen, while at the same time assembling fat.

For this reason, excessive cortisol levels can wreak havoc on the body, making it hard to lose weight, replenish cells, encourage the growth of new cells, and form new youth-building collagen. Excess cortisol over time can lead to increased abdominal fat, irritability and full-blown depression, bone loss, a suppressed immune system, fatigue, and an increased risk for insulin resistance, diabetes, and heart disease just to name a few things. Everything takes a hit, including blood vessels that become more fragile and can't keep meeting demands. Cortisol does, however, serve a positive role. It helps immune cells attack infectious invaders and tells the brain when those invaders have been taken care of. And another way to look at its effects in mobilizing fat and upping your appetite is that it builds up energy reserves (calories) that your muscles may need soon. But for the most part, you don't need those energy reserves because you're not in dire straits. You're just overreacting to a trivial stressor that your body interprets as something serious. But it has a profound impact on you regardless.

The scientific study of the impact of stress on the body from the inside out, and even the outside in, has made tremendous advances in the past decade. In 1998, doctors from Harvard University conducted a joint study with several Boston-area hospitals designed to examine the connections and interactions between the mind and the body, specifically the skin. They dubbed their findings the NICE network, which stands for neuro-immuno-cutaneous-endocrine. In plain speak, it's a network consisting of your nervous system, immune system, skin, and endocrine (hormonal) system. All of these are intimately connected through a dialogue of shared interactive chemicals. Like a giant wireless network, when one phone rings, the others can hear it and respond.

The Boston researchers studied how various external forces affect our state of mind, from massage and aromatherapy to depression and isolation. What they discovered confirmed what we had already known anecdotally for centuries: our state of mind has a definite impact on our health and even our looks. People suffering from depression, for example, look older and less healthy, and not because they've let themselves go and aren't grooming themselves as rigorously as their happier counterparts. But they actually are older than happier comrades who are the same biological age. The stress of living with depression has accelerated the aging process and damaged their health.

Depression is not something to take lightly. One of the more troubling pieces of news to come out recently is the fact that depression will have a huge impact on our world in the future. The World Health Organization has estimated that by the year 2020, depression will be the second leading disability-causing disease in the world. In many developed countries, such as the United States, depression is already among the top causes in terms of disability and excess mortality.

Take time for yourself. Don't let yourself go. Exercise, eat well, and get a manicure or pedicure once in a while. Stay connected to what is important to you. Make time for your marriage or with your partner, make time for each other without discussing work or your kids—it's a chance to grow closer.

Being a mother never ends. It's a gift that we are given to learn about who we are and how we show up in the world.

— MARIEL HEMINGWAY,

mother of two, author, yogi, and spokesperson for green living

---

Ways to Relax and Rev Energy

You already know in your heart that taking care of yourself sets the tone of your life and health. It sounds almost cliché to say you need to relax because it will reduce stress, since this is like telling someone not to breathe (or check e-mail). Stress will always be a part of our life—and our livelihood. The key is to keep certain sources of unnecessary stress at bay so they don't affect us like a charging rhino. Easier said than done, but here are some strategies to consider.

Be brutal about boundaries. We talked a lot about boundaries throughout this book, but how well have you been able to live up to our recommendations? Can you set a time each day after which you turn off your electronics and don't respond to nonemergency calls, e-mails, text messages, and so on? Can you create a bedtime routine that prepares you for sleep 30 to 60 minutes prior to lights out? Can you plan your days better so you're not as harried? When you create (and stick to) boundaries that help you to achieve better health, you'll increase your chances at optimizing your energy. You can make boundaries for yourself in all areas of your life, from what time you choose to get up (or, on the other side of the day, go to bed) to what you buy in the supermarket and how many days you'll let go by without exercising.

Find your inner scribe. Okay, so maybe you're not a writer, a blogger, or someone who keeps a journal. We're not asking you to be any of those, but you'd be surprised by what taking just three to five minutes at the end or start of your day can do. Use it to evaluate how you feel and what you're thinking at a subconscious level and watch what it does to your sense of well-being, peace of mind, and even your capacity to dream big, set realistic goals for the future, and realize optimal energy. So few of us take the time anymore during our days serving and caring for others to turn the volume down on everyone and everything else and just think in our own creative space and quietude.

Self-care begins with self-discovery. And committing your thoughts and ideas to paper can make a huge difference. It affords you a record from which to look back in the future and simultaneously offers accountability. It also gives you a chance to adjust your attitudes if need be and set a new course that moves you closer to where you want to be. Find a comfortable spot (or just do this exercise while sitting in bed) and consider playing some relaxing music.

You may find it helpful to keep more than one journal. Have one that you use to write down the more mundane tasks you need to get done, such as picking up clothes from the cleaners, grocery shopping, or organizing a birthday party. Have another that keeps track of your diet choices and physical activities. Yet another journal, a so-called worry journal, can be very handy for people who have a hard time getting to sleep at night as stressful thoughts intrude and steal much-needed sleep time. A worry journal by your bedside can act as a mental depository of your anxieties. Once you write them down, you close the book and tell yourself that you will deal with them tomorrow. Sometimes you'll find that the act of writing down a worry will lead to solutions that you never thought of before. And all of these exercises will subconsciously give you hope for your future.

Last but certainly not least, keep a positive-note journal that tracks all the good things you've accomplished. At the end of even the most stressful days, stop to reflect on what went right. What are you grateful for? What good things came out of the day, even if they were unplanned or unexpected? Sometimes, on the worst of days, we can just be thankful that we got through it, and soon we can embrace a whole new day with happy, promising thoughts and intentions.

Sounds ridiculous, but take a walk. I always found that getting outside my house when I was in almost any mood made for more energy and creativity. Even if it was around the block. Studies prove it, but anecdotally it is true. It is also hard to be sad or unhappy when strolling outside in nature. All the while the residual effects strengthen bones, burn calories, and boost feelings of happiness, so walk on! In addition—have a snack in your purse. My body tends to need fuel every two hours, so I found keeping a small snack with me helps energy levels stay even, which in turn kept me from unnecessarily yelling at my child.

— L O R I   C O R B I N

ABC7 Los Angeles' Food and Fitness Coach,
and host of Live Well HD's *Custom Fit*

Try something new. Remember how exciting that first day of school was back when you were entering the third or fourth grade? It's thrilling to enter a new environment, meet new people, and learn something different. Women trying to keep up with their everyday obligations rarely give themselves permission to act like schoolgirls again, but doing so can have some surprising benefits. In addition to expanding your horizons and exposing yourself to a new hobby or skill, trying something new can take you just far enough away from your established and routine commitments to give you the feeling that you're on vacation, that you're allowed to goof off and replenish the kid in you again that's unencumbered by the banalities of everyday life.

Think about your current hobbies or one you'd like to try, and see if you can find a club, group, or class nearby in which to participate. This can be any number of things, including cooking class, a writing class, a pottery workshop, a photo club, a class for learning a new language, or a book club. And if you can't find anything attuned to your interests, then start your own club or group and invite your friends.

Trying something new can also mean seeking a new setting. Go for a walk and call a friend you haven't spoken with in a long while, get on a bicycle, take an exercise class, jump rope for a solid minute or get 100 revolutions without missing, make a pot of green tea and then sit by a window and flip through a magazine, take a cat nap in the sun. Do something that gets you out of your normal routine.

Take (a few) deep breaths. Deep breathing techniques can yank you out of a blue mood quickly. Slow, controlled breathing is the foundation for many Eastern practices such as yoga, qigong, tai chi, and classic meditation—all of which aim to plunge the body (and mind, clearly) into a balanced, stress-free state. One of the reasons why deep breathing is so helpful is that it triggers a parasympathetic nerve response, as opposed to a sympathetic nerve response, the latter of which is sensitive to stress and anxiety. At the onset of stress, the sympathetic nervous system springs into action and is largely responsible for those oft-damaging spikes in the stress hormones cortisol and adrenaline. The parasympathetic nervous system, on the other hand, can trigger a relaxation response, and deep breathing is the quickest means of getting these two systems to communicate. You can flip the switch from high alert to low in seconds as your heart rate slows, muscles relax, and blood pressure lowers.

Meditation, which entails deep breathing, also has mind-altering benefits. The practice casts the human brain back to its pre-neocortex state, allowing us to be freed of our analytical selves. In this blissful state, one is aware of senses, feelings, and state of mind—without the negativity. We lead very scatterbrained lives, wrapped up in the frenzied competition that is our society—and momhood. We rarely take the time to sit and concentrate on ourselves without the dramas of being a mother affecting us. No wonder meditation is so effective just by virtue of its permission to let us be mindful, centered, and focused. It appears that meditation is truly exercise for the brain, as if it helps grow stronger "muscles" in the areas used.

The Breath of Fire. Can you take a recess for some deep breathing or meditation when problems present themselves and your mind starts to race? Problems can easily swell into unmanageable portion sizes for our consciousness and bring us down. Then they get out of control and look worse than they really are. Deep breathing or meditation will help you to gain perspective and reclaim sanity again. The following exercise is adapted from a yogic breathing technique. Its aim is to raise vital energy and increase alertness, and can be done anytime you need to feel rejuvenated in less than 60 seconds.

1. Inhale and exhale rapidly through your nose, keeping your mouth closed but relaxed. Your breaths in and out should be equal in duration, but as short as possible. This is a noisy breathing exercise.

2. Do not do for more than 15 seconds on your first try. Each time you practice the Breath of Fire, you can increase your time by 5 seconds or so, until you reach a full minute.

3. If done properly, you will feel invigorated, comparable to the heightened awareness you feel after a good workout. You should feel the effort at the back of the neck, the diaphragm, the chest, and the abdomen. Try this breathing exercise the next time you need an energy boost and feel yourself reaching for a cup of coffee.

Recent studies have shown that yoga and meditation, practiced for three months, reduced waist circumference, systolic blood pressure, and fasting blood sugar and triglyceride levels. It also increased levels of high-density lipoprotein (the good fats). In addition, at the end of the study periods, feelings of anxiety, stress, and depression were significantly decreased, and optimism was significantly increased. That all spells more energy. The researchers concluded that yoga not only helps in prevention of lifestyle diseases, but can also be a powerful adjunct therapy when diseases occur.

Deep breathing can be done anywhere, anytime. Sit comfortably in a chair or lie down.

Close your eyes and make sure your body is relaxed, releasing all tension in your neck, arms, legs, and back. Inhale through your nose for as long as you can, feeling your diaphragm and abdomen rise as your stomach moves outward. Sip in a little more air when you think you've reached the top of your lungs. Slowly exhale to a count of 20, pushing every breath of air from your lungs. Continue for at least five rounds of deep breaths.

Plan your personal days, even if it's just for ten minutes. When you map out your week in advance, figure out when you'll be able to set aside time for just you—no kids, no demands, no work. Be brutal with your time and make it happen no matter what. You never know, you just might find a full extra hour to treat yourself to a massage or another therapeutic treatment of your choice. When you plan, extra time finds you. Use it for just you.

Remember, we're people with lives independent from our kids, and we need to put ourselves first on a regular basis so we can enjoy (and not resent) the wonderful families we are lucky enough to be a part of. A day of golf, lunch and a movie with friends, a weekend trip to visit a college buddy—whatever! You have to trust that the world goes on without you and it's okay for your husband and kids to cover for you.

Grab the great outdoors. Enjoy the calming effects that only nature can provide. So few of us spend time outdoors anymore. We live and work indoors, often chained to electronics, meetings, and chores. But being outdoors and among plants and other living things can enhance feelings of health and well-being. This is partly why going for walks and hikes, or sailing, skiing, cycling— doing anything in the open air—can be so invigorating. Don't forget to bring the outdoors in, too. Park a big, live plant in the room where you spend the most time each day (philodendrons are nearly impossible to kill). Set up a reading chair beside a window where you can observe trees and birds.

Soak in a dose of morning light. Our body clocks don't exactly match the day's 24-hour-day clock, which makes us want to sleep about 12 minutes longer every day and stay up later every night. What helps? Getting out of bed at the same time every morning and sitting in a sunny spot for breakfast, or exercising outdoors, or just turning on lots of lights. A dose of brightness in the morning helps synch up your internal clock with the 24-hour day. Which also helps you get on a regular, saner schedule.

Ask for help. Trade babysitting nights with family or friends. Ask your spouse to pick up more slack. Single moms need to be even more vigilant with their time and energy, and not hesitate to call on friends and family for help. Nearly half of working mothers are heavily stressed every day. It takes a village to raise children, but many parents are doing it solo. Do what you need to do in order to have more *you* time.

By the same token, don't play "helicopter" parent. Start your children at an early age performing age-related tasks that make life easier. Get them to make their own breakfast, clean their rooms, and place their things in proper spots. Less chaos is helpful for everyone. Shower them with love, but send them to bed on their own after second grade. The bedtime situation is usually challenging.

Be attentive to the state of your health at all times.
Paying attention to my self-care informs everything I do.
If I'm not taking care of myself, how can I take care of others?
And by taking care of yourself you set an example for your
children on how important self-care is.

— SHEL PINK,
mother and founder of SpaRitual

Share the vibe. Schedule a dinner club once a month with your friends—people with whom you share deep connections. Setting aside time with those who can help us relax and move away from the limelight of stress is important for our emotional and physical health. As we mentioned earlier, it's important for us as women to get together and talk, share stories and advice, and laugh. It's a great way to decompress. Once a month, plan your outings with your friends (where, when, who is hosting, who is cooking, etc.) and don't let a month go by without one of these get-togethers. Maybe you'll just sit around playing Bunko or listening to music and drinking wine. However the night plays itself out, you'll come to enjoy these times together—and so will your body's energy-making machine. Warning: talking on the phone doesn't count here. Even though we have more gadgets now than ever to connect with others, we also have a higher number of people complaining of loneliness and feelings of disconnectedness. It seems like the more connections we make on the surface, the more we lose out on opportunities to nourish and renew those much deeper and rewarding connections in person.

Be your own cheerleader. Before you have to take care of anyone else in your day, take care of you first by giving yourself a morning pep talk while you're in front of the mirror. It may seem silly, but saying a few positive affirmations, such as "I'm going to have a fabulous day; I'm full of untapped energy and health, and it's up to me to make great things happen" has hidden benefits. Even if you don't quite believe yourself, it's still effective. Research has shown that over time, a daily rah-rah builds resilience, which can fortify you against stress.

Laugh more. Even if you have to force yourself to laugh, it's worth it. The health benefits of laughter are proven and plentiful, ranging from strengthening the immune system to reducing stress and food cravings to increasing one's threshold for pain. Hormones, of course, are the reason. Health-promoting endorphins and neurotransmitters get released during a good laugh, and the number of antibody-producing cells and the effectiveness of certain immune cells also increase. An emerging therapeutic field known as humor therapy aims to help people heal more quickly with laughter.

Give back. Have you ever signed up to volunteer in community events? Have you ever offered your time and expertise to a local youth club or adult-education center? Have you ever joined a mentorship program that matches you with another individual who wants to learn your skills? Have you ever watched a group of volunteers cleaning up a park or beach and wished you could join them? There are dozens of ways you can give back. Though the media likes to focus on how giving back is the practical way in which each one of us can have an impact in the world and effect global change, think about what it gives the person who is doing the giving back: a chance to forge new friendships, to squelch feelings of isolation and stress, and to enjoy the act of making a difference that will surely make a difference on a much smaller—yes, energetic—level.

Don't have time to volunteer? Then try this: adopt a sister from around the world through an organization such as Women for Women International.

Get out of your world. Maybe it's planting succulents in funky pots or shopping for vintage clothing. If you're like one of us, perhaps it's buying *Country Living* magazine to find ideas for rearranging furniture and creating new sitting areas in your home. Find a crafty, silly activity that takes you out of your world. Make it a ritual as often as you can. Denise Richards loves to volunteer at animal shelters. For her, it's a relaxing diversion and removes her from the rigors of daily life. Best of all, it doesn't require any money and involves physical work. And that's key. See if you can find a hobby that pushes you a little past your comfort zone, engages your creativity, costs little or nothing, and challenges you to try something different for a change. It could be as simple as flipping through a stack of favorite photographs. Can't think of anything? Then just try this: after the kids have gone to bed, fill the bathtub, light candles, and slowly sip a cup of hot tea or glass of wine as you read a book for an hour. See how that makes you feel. Experiment with activities that cleanse your mood, from aromatherapy to visualization.

Dare to disconnect. There's a strange duality to being attached to machines that allow us to connect with others around the world in an instant. From cell phones to social networks that can transmit what you're doing right now in fractions of a second, communication these days is quick, easy, and, to a large degree, isolating. When you resort to electronic transmissions of information rather than speaking to someone in person or even over the phone, you lose a human touch to the experience. You also have a tendency to lose focus, as those transmissions become rapid-fire, frequent, distracting, and intrusive. We admire people who make a choice to carve out time once or twice a week when they put down their smartphones and don't check their e-mail. It can be incredibly invigorating and stress-reducing to disconnect yourself occasionally from the digital world. See if you can designate a single day a week, perhaps a whole weekend from time to time, when you let the voice mail and the e-mail pile up. Detach yourself from the need to keep checking and responding to the constant, chattering influx—much of which is not important, not urgent, and not helpful to your health and well-being.

You can always find 30 to 60 seconds. Thirty to 60 seconds of deep breathing while concentrating on following your breath is a quick but very restorative meditation. Same for a short stretch. And if you can take 15 minutes for a power nap, the world looks different. Hug your kids, husband, and friends a lot. And pay 100 percent attention when you do. At the end of the day, write a list of anything you need to get done in the near future that weighs on your mind, put it aside, and then think of all you enjoyed and accomplished that day. Gratitude is a great antidote to frustration and upset.

— MYRA GOODMAN,

co-founder of Earthbound Farm,
cookbook author, and mom

Move more. The power of exercise in reducing stress is well known. But here's something you might not have known: exercise makes your blood circulate more quickly, transporting the stress hormone (and fat-friendly) cortisol to your kidneys and flushing it out of your system. Remember, cortisol encourages your body to store fat—especially visceral fat—that releases fatty acids into your blood, raising cholesterol and insulin levels and paving the way for heart disease and diabetes. One study found that 18 minutes of walking three times per week can quickly lower the hormone's levels by 15 percent!

Be still. For most of us, life is so scheduled, speedy, and "on" that we never do absolutely nothing. It's rare to set aside time to simply be—no agenda, no demands, no plan. So find a comfortable, quiet spot to sit for five to ten minutes every day, stop all your hustling and bustling . . . and simply, by yourself, be still. Slowing down in this way, if you do it every day, helps create a sense of spaciousness in your life, a break in the old routine. It can open the door to new perceptions, new solutions to old problems, and new possibilities. It gives your brain, your psyche, your whole being a break. Like one long peaceful sigh.

Bust a bad day. Having a really bad day? End it! Sometimes we can't fix a day that's gone really bad. The sooner you can end it, the sooner you can leave it behind and start afresh again. And if it's too early to end it, then try a nap to reboot yourself—and your day. Be careful how your bad day is affecting your decisions (e.g., what you eat, how you behave in front of your children, and so on). Don't trade one bandage for another, such as soothing your bad day with an outrageous shopping spree that sinks your bank account. Continue to make informed decisions that feed your energy tank so you don't feel like a victim but you also don't feel deprived. Don't be afraid to cry! If you feel like it, it's a great option.

Sex it up. Who doesn't feel more energized after a night of great sex? If sex didn't do a body good, then it wouldn't make us feel so fantastic and crave the next session. That's right: for once, something that feels good is actually good for us. Sex makes us happy, and great sex in a loving, intimate relationship makes us even happier. For starters, sex is one of the world's best stress releasers, and as with almost everything else that we've been talking about, it all comes down to hormones—those chemical messengers that dictate how we feel. Beta-endorphins, prolactin, and oxytocin wash through you during sex. Beta-endorphin is a natural opiate produced in the hypothalamus and in the brainstem, contributing to that delicious high you feel. This is the same hormone that diminishes pain levels. Prolactin, a chemical messenger responsible for more than 300 functions, gives you that relaxed sensation, and oxytocin promotes feelings of affection and triggers that nurturing instinct. Yes, it's the same bonding hormone that got pumped out of your brain alongside prolactin after you gave birth to turn your breasts on for feeding (and dare we say energizing) your newborn.

Exactly how these hormones affect sexual desire, arousal, and pleasure is an active area of research, but what is known so far is that all three hormones are released during orgasm and the net effect is satisfaction and contentment. And it's no surprise that your relaxed state of mind and body allow you to fall asleep rather quickly.

The message, in short: sex makes you look good and feel good. But you hopefully knew that from experience. If you don't feel like you're getting enough (and, like sleep, you know when you're deprived), this is something you'll want to address in your life.

Not in a relationship? Then go for the next best thing and treat yourself to more touching through massage. It may seem like a luxury, but it doesn't have to be. If you were to add up the cost of eating dinner out once a week for a month, you'd have plenty of money to get a massage, body scrub, and/or facial and enjoy all the amenities offered at most spas. The healing power of touch is grossly underestimated in our society, yet it's one of the most effective tools for emotional care.

I learned how valuable touch is to the energy of your spirit. I believe humans need and crave touch so powerfully, much more so than we know. A simple gesture communicates love, adoration, positivity, and a sense of value. My mother, my grandmother, my friends, have all taught me the beauty of a hug, a hand hold, a squeeze on the arm, a touch on the cheek. Physically showing love and concern towards your children is so important to their psyches. My grandmother used to always hug me, hold my hand, touch my hair and I knew she adored me. It made me feel alive in some special way. Sometimes we fear that touch will make us feel awkward and vulnerable so we shy away from it, but we shouldn't. It makes me sad when I see children not getting affection from their parents, or couples coexisting without touch and affection.

—VERONICA BOSGRAAF,
Pure Bar founder and mother

Massage not only benefits the muscles and tissues being kneaded and stretched but also has been found to lower stress levels significantly. It's been shown to increase weight gain in premature infants, alleviate depression, reduce pain in cancer patients, improve sleep patterns, and positively alter the immune system. Research from the renowned Touch Research Institute shows that it's as beneficial to touch as it is to be touched. And, more recently, researchers at the University of North Carolina, alongside scientists in Europe, are unraveling how the body responds to pleasurable touch. They have identified a class of nerve fibers in the skin that specifically send pleasure messages. Called the C-tactile nerve fibers, they send feel-good messages to the brain upon stimulation through pleasurable touch.

Healing touch therapy can take many forms, not just classic massage. Experiment with what your local spa has to offer. Bring this concept to home and into the bedroom with your partner, too. In between the more elaborate spa visits, schedule brief, inexpensive manicures, pedicures, or simply exchange five minutes of chair massage with your best friend at work. Studies have shown that these can dramatically reduce job stress while increasing productivity and alertness.

Be consistent. Make personal playtime a consistent habit. The key is to be sure the practice entails no phones, no talking, no way to be pulled back into the vortex of daily life, and it must be something doable on a regular basis. If you fluctuate ("I'll get a massage this week and go the movies with a girlfriend next week, etc.") then you're more apt to lose the habit. And lose your sanity. Having a consistent habit that's relaxing allows you to go into deeper relaxation every time.

Take action. Today, pick just one single habit you want to change and make a commitment to making that happen. It can be an ambitious goal such as quitting smoking or a small one such as reducing your consumption of fast food or replacing butter with extra-virgin olive oil in your cooking.

The Ten Essential Nutrients . . . they aren't found in food, but have everything to do with what food you choose and how your body uses it.

1. Nutrient L—for LAUGHTER . . .

2. Nutrient M—for MASSAGE . . .

3. Nutrient N—for NURTURE (YOURSELF as well as OTHERS) . . .

4. Nutrient O—for OXYGEN . . .

5. Nutrient P—for PHYSICAL ACTIVITY . . .

6. Nutrient Q—for QUIET . . .

7. Nutrient R—for RELAXATION . . .

8. Nutrient S—for SLEEP . . .

9. Nutrient T—for TIME . . .

10. Nutrient U—for UNDERSTANDING . . .

Take time to see where these nutrients fit into your plan. We promise, they make a huge difference

Source: Exceprted from Ashley's *Recipes for IBS: Great-Tasting Recipes and Tips Customized for Your Symptoms* (Fair Winds Press, 2007)

REFRESHED AND REJUVENATED

We hope that you understand the importance of play in your life. It's not something just for children. When you think about it, do you know anyone who comes back from a playful vacation complaining of exhaustion? Even if the vacation was physically demanding, the time away from the demands of everyday life was invigorating. But finding time to play needn't require two weeks off a year—or even a whole day to yourself. It can entail smaller, little pockets of time that you use to just exhale for a moment and recharge. It can be as simple as a 10-minute massage, or a movie night with friends or a loved one once a week. And it's not so much about finding time as it is about *making* time. All of us are overscheduled. The ones who can move meetings and commitments around to accommodate playtime are the happier survivors of that overscheduled life.

MOM UP! JUMP-START YOUR TRANSFORMATION

Right this moment, take out your calendar—the thing you use to organize and schedule your life. Maybe it's all on your cell phone or perhaps you keep a traditional calendar on your wall at home. However you plan out your days, weeks, and months, now is the time to plan your playtime over the next 30 days. Pick at least one day a week (that's four times over the next month) when you carve out at least one hour for play (this doesn't include playtime with your kids, the bedtime hour, or even sex time; make this playtime totally separate and all about you minus the demands of everyday life). See if you can fill that one hour with something fun, such as lunch with a friend, a manicure or pedicure, or a dinner date with your spouse without the kids. Every month, when you pull out your calendar to plan ahead, see if you can plan your playtime in advance. The added challenge: try to find more than an hour here and there to play. Go away for a long weekend when the opportunity presents itself. Make a deposit on a vacation 6 to 12 months in advance so you don't let the whole year go by without a serious time-out.

The Choice Is Yours

Health is dynamic. Energy is, too. In either case, you don't get to achieve it and cross it off your list. It's like becoming a mom. You give your energy to your child from day one and then you're a mom forever . . . giving your energy away. You're a mom forever. You'll never get to be done with seeking optimal health throughout your life. But that's just life!

For many moms, it seems that your ability to choose is a window that is not as wide open as it used to be before giving birth. But it can be as wide open as you want it if you plan and choose carefully. Just as you chose to be a mom, you can choose to live your life a certain way that optimizes your energy and health. It's ultimately up to you to learn what makes you tick and feel fulfilled with that steady flow of energy. It may mean getting up at 5:30 to hop on a stationary bicycle, but then you're done with your exercise and don't have to think about it the rest of the day. You have a choice whether or not to plan at the top of the week and know what's coming down the pipeline. Are you the carpool person this week? On which nights do you have more time to cook? Can you find a night to go out with your husband or girlfriends? What after-school events require your attendance? When will you fit in your gardening? If you choose to lay back and say, "Can someone pick up the kids . . . and where's the pizza?" you'll pay consequences.

Of course, there will be things that go by the wayside, such as perfect nails and hair. In the long run, though, aren't you okay with that? Yes, because you get the important stuff done that ensures a healthy, happy family. And an energized mom who is ready to take on anything.

FINAL NOTE

By now we hope you've gained not only a lot of information on ways to improve your energy, but also a greater appreciation for your health and happiness. Your energy is not a fiction, just as Mom Energy is not an oxymoron. We applaud you in your decision to take better care of yourself, no matter how small a step you take starting today. Just picking up this book gives you points! And as you no doubt understand through personal experience alone, how energetic you feel says so much about you—your confidence, your courage, your character, and even your faith in yourself and the world at large.

Our knowledge about this astonishing link between our bodies and its myriad energy equations will only continue to expand. What we will discover in the future will reinforce the necessity to honor time-tested techniques for reducing and managing stress and choosing to maintain better lifestyles that can support our longevity. Remember, we want to live healthfully for as long as possible. Feeling as naturally energetic as possible in those later years ain't bad, either.

Your dedication to nurturing your body from an energy standpoint will reward you in so many fantastic ways—not just today, but every day forward for the rest of your life. We wish you the best of luck in your journey and encourage you to come back to this book when you need reminders about healthy, energetic living.

The Whole-Body List of Top Exercises

We realize it would be unwise of us to not at least give some specifics to working the body. Again, this is not meant to be a particular program. We just want to give you some of the tried-and-true methods of working the body that minimize your time commitment and maximize energy-generating results. These are great exercises to have on hand when you can't get to the gym or schedule a more formal workout. You'll find that many of these moves can be done in the comfort of your kitchen (while cooking) or den as you watch television and babysit a toddler playing nearby. All of them will pump your heart, get your blood running, and strengthen those little muscular engines that could! Added challenge: see if you can perform these exercises until you pant. Avoid performing the same routines on consecutive days, but try to incorporate all of them into your week, at least twice. Most of these exercises can be done in gyms using equipment, but they also can be done using props at home.

> **Caution:** Speak with your physician if you have specific health issues or physical limitations to contend with prior to commencing an exercise program, especially if you have not been active in a while. Your doctor can also help you gauge your fitness level and help you tailor an exercise program to your physical body. This will help lower your risk for injury or illness, as many people jump-start their fitness goals too quickly and wind up hurt and burned out. You must achieve a fine balance between pushing your body physically and staying attuned to its needs as you move forward.

LOWER BODY

Squat and Knee Lifts

There's a variety of ways to perform this one, but it's so versatile that you can be cooking in your kitchen and go through a couple of these heart pumpers. In a traditional squat and knee lift, you simply stand with feet hip distance apart and dip into a squat. In this position, your hips are back until your knees are bent to about a 90-degree angle. You can hold your hands in front of you around a small medicine ball or free weights. As you squat, sit back into your heels and keep your chest up. You don't want your knees to go in front of your toes. Then rise back up and lift one knee up until your upper leg is perpendicular to your body. Lower the leg and then repeat the squat. When you rise up again, lift the opposite leg.

Lunge and Squat Combo

Instead of a static lunge (returning your forward foot back to the original position), you can do a walking lunge, with a squat in between each step. So you lunge forward with the right foot and then take the left foot up to meet the right foot, then do a front squat. Repeat the sequence on the left side, lunging with the left foot forward, etc. Try making this a walking exercise, and watch your heart start pumping at a higher notch. Can you reach a point where you're starting to pant?

Toe and Hip Lift Hold *(or, How to Be Nice to Your Back and Work Your Butt Off!)*

Use a mat or cushioned floor. This exercise will relieve tension in your lower back and work your butt at the same time. Lie on your back with your arms at your sides with your knees bent and your feet on the floor. Lift your hips toward the ceiling, lifting your feet up on your toes. Hold for 1 count, and then lower back down. Repeat the lifts for 60 seconds, squeezing your glutes and hamstrings at the top of the range of motion. Be careful not to overarch your spine. For an added challenge, extend one leg at the top of the lift. Keep your thighs parallel and hold the lifted position for about 5 seconds. Keeping your hips up, place your foot back on the floor and then lower your hips. Repeat this exercise for 30 seconds; switch sides and do the move for another 30 seconds on the other leg.

Standing Single Leg Lifts

Ideally, this exercise should be done with a stability ball, a giant inflatable ball that you'll find at a sporting goods store or gym. This exercise will work the hip and thigh area. If you don't have access to a ball, try using the back of a chair. What you want to do is balance your weight on one leg while leaning on the exercise ball (or a chair).

To start, place the stability ball on the floor in front of you. Bend at the waist and place both hands shoulder width apart on the stability ball. Have a comfortable distance between your legs and the ball so you can bend comfortably. Your back should be parallel to the floor. Remember to maintain correct posture with a straight back and aligned shoulders; also make sure to place your head in alignment with your spine. Keeping your right foot on the ground, bend your right knee slightly and extend your left leg behind you until it is parallel with the floor. Your lifting leg should be in alignment with the rest of your body. Keep your foot flexed as you lift and tuck in your abdomen. Hold your lifted leg in position for 1 to 2 seconds and return it to the floor. Perform 10 repetitions for each leg. You can increase to 2 to 3 sets of standing leg lifts as your strength improves.

Double Stair Climb

It's proven that climbing stairs two at a time has tremendous advantages over taking one step at a time. When researchers at Pennsylvania State University in 2010 compared the metabolic cost and muscular activity of these two techniques, they found that, indeed, skipping a step leads to a measurable difference in energy usage. Translation: your body will burn more energy, which then cycles back to infuse you with more energy. Case closed.

Find a good set of stairs in your neighborhood, hopefully one that has more than 10 steps, but anything will do. Get into a rhythm of climbing 2 steps at a time, and then walk back down 1 step at a time. Repeat. See if you can go for at least 15 minutes. Vary the speed—you can start by walking, then ramp up your speed to a semi-run or a full-fledged run. Given your comfort level and the depth/size of the stairs, you can also try to walk down the staircase two at a time, or pick up your downstep pace, too. Moving in both directions will pump your heart and give you a great lower-body workout.

Wall Sit with Leg Crossed

Stand in front of a wall (about 2 feet in front of it) and lean against it. Slide down until your knees are at about 90-degree angles and hold, keeping the abs contracted. Find your stability, and then cross one leg over the other. Relax your arms, keep your chest open, and shoulders back against the wall. Hold for as long as you can, about 15 seconds to a minute. Then switch legs, crossing the other and holding. Do 2 or 3 rounds.

CORE

Plank

Lie facedown on a mat or a carpeted floor, resting on your forearms with palms flat on the floor. Push off the floor, raising up onto toes and resting on the elbows. Keep your back flat, in a straight line from head to heels. Tilt your pelvis and contract your abdominals to prevent your rear end from sticking up in the air or sagging in the middle. Hold for 20 to 60 seconds, lower, and repeat for 3 to 5 reps.

On-Your-Side Hip Lift

Lie on your left side with legs extended, right leg slightly in front of the left, body weight supported on your left elbow and left hip. Your right arm rests on your right side, and your left elbow is bent and in line with your left shoulder, palm on floor.

Contract your abs and hold your torso erect; it should form a straight line between your head and your hips. Using your left upper-hip and buttocks muscles and keeping your abs tight, press the side of your left foot into the floor and lift your hips until your body forms a straight line from head to feet. Hold for a count of 3, and then lower your hips to the starting position. Complete 10 reps and switch sides. Do 3 sets on each side. Bonus: perform the last set on one leg by lifting your top leg off the floor and holding it in line with and just above your bottom leg.

Flat-Arm Crunch

The flat-, or long-arm, crunch is sixth in the list of top 10 most effective abdominal exercises. It's been proven to produce 19 percent more muscle activity than a traditional crunch. As with any abdominal exercise, the flat-arm crunch relies on slow, controlled movements. The abdominal muscles should be tightened or engaged in order to make the upper body move. Properly done, this exercise requires very little movement up and off of the floor. Consistent abdominal pressure is the key to this movement.

Lie flat on your back with your knees bent and the feet flat on the floor. Extend your arms above and slightly behind the head (not bent—they remain extended, or "flat"). Your hands should be held close together. Contract your abdominals and bring your shoulder blades off the floor. Then lower your body back down to the starting point. Repeat for at least 20 counts. See if you can do 3 sets of 20.

During the exercise, the arms should remain next to the ears. They should not fall forward and away from the head. The reason for this is to limit the extent to which other muscle groups, other than the abdominals, are used. Throwing the arms forward can grant extra momentum, undermining the effectiveness of the movement. Similarly, straining with the neck or head to raise the trunk of the body should be avoided.

Jump and Touch

Find an object about 18 inches above your tiptoe reach. It can be a bar, the top of a doorframe, or a 5-pound ring you dangle from a doorframe. Jump straight up into the air, touching the object at the peak of the jump. Avoid going into a full squat before each jump. Make sure you can tap the object each time you jump. Try 3 sets of 20 jumps each.

UPPER BODY

Triceps Dips with Straight Legs

Sit on a chair or step. Grasp the front edge of the seat near the thighs. Walk feet forward until hips are slightly bent, legs straight, arms extended (don't lock the elbows). Keep feet hip-width apart. Bend elbows about 90 degrees and lower hips toward the floor. Inhale as you go down. If you feel pain in the shoulders, your elbows are bent too much. As you exhale, press up until elbows are straight, but not locked. Repeat this action 15 to 20 times. Go 3 rounds.

Triceps Dips with One Leg Crossed

Perform the same action as above, but cross one leg over the other. After a round of 15 to 20 dips, switch legs and repeat. Go 3 rounds on each leg.

Push-up

Assume the traditional push-up position on the floor: palms of hands flat on floor slightly more than shoulder width apart; legs straight, with weight on balls of the feet; feet just a few inches apart. If you find this exercise too difficult, you may modify the basic position by having your knees, rather than the balls of your feet, touch the floor. Inhale as you lower your body to the floor; exhale as you lift it. Repeat 15 to 20 times in succession. If doing 2 sets, rest for no more than 30 seconds between sets.

The following exercises require free weights. Get yourself a pair of dumbbells that are comfortable to hold. You're likely to want to increase the weights as you get stronger, so start with a set of 3-pounders and add more as you go. Work up to using 8- and 10-pounders in each hand.

Shoulder Presses

Sit on the end of a bench or use a bench/chair that supports the back. Hold dumbbells in each hand. Hold weights with palms facing out and elbows at 90 degrees, palms at shoulder level.

As you exhale, push weights overhead until arms are straight and in line with shoulders. Don't lock elbows completely. Then, as you inhale, return to starting position to complete 1 rep. Perform 15 to 20 reps, and go for 3 rounds.

Bicep Curls

Stand with feet slightly apart, knees slightly bent, and abs tight. Grasp a dumbbell in each hand with an underhand grip. Lock elbows into the side of your torso and rest weights in your hands, on the front of your thighs. As you inhale, curl one dumbbell to your shoulder. Then, exhale and lower dumbbell to starting position; then curl the dumbbell in your opposite hand.

One curl on each side equals 1 rep. Perform 15 to 20 reps, and go for 3 rounds. (Note: Keeping abs tight will help protect your lower back. If your body leans backward as you curl up the weight, then the weight is too heavy. Keep elbows pressed into your sides for support and to isolate the biceps. This exercise can also be done in a seated position.)

Bicep Curl with Squat

This will get your upper and lower body working simultaneously. With your feet shoulder-width apart, hold the dumbbells by your side. Squat back as if you're going to sit on a chair, and perform a bicep curl on the way up. Inhale on the way down, and exhale on the way up.

Acknowledgments

As with all books, it takes a small army of talented, bright, and energetic people to weave together a manuscript worthy of publication. This one is no different. We owe everyone we've ever worked with through the years a heartfelt thank you, especially the mothers who've been the inspiration for this book. The unwavering support of our families, friends, colleagues, and clients have also paved the path to this book. Your guidance, insights, and feedback were indispensible; *Mom Energy* is as much yours as it is ours.

Collectively we'd like to express our gratitude to the many extraordinary people who trained their efforts on this project from start to finish. To those who provided tips and offered comments, and to the moms who allowed us to quote their remarks, we thank you.

To our indefatigable agent, Laurie Bernstein, who went beyond the call of duty and orchestrated so much of our creative energy when the initial concepts were just beginning to germinate in the proposal phase. You provided the roadmap for this book, and your unwavering support from day one has been invaluable. Thanks to Laurie, we met our talented writer, Kristin Loberg, who took our voice, thoughts, and ideas to the page. You inspire us with your blind plunge into a "mom" project, and during the process became one yourself.

To the team at Hay House, who endured all of our last-minute requests and changes, and whose insights helped produce the best book possible. Thanks especially to Patty Gift, Laura Koch, Sally Mason, Reid Tracy, Margarete Nielsen, Gail Gonzales, Carina Sammartino, and all the other wonderful, hard-working souls at Hay House.

Thank you to Lisa Fyfe for your creative genius and willingness to go the distance.

And now, to a few more individuals that each of us would like to call out:

From Ashley:

So many people contributed to this book, and I thank them for their energy and their role in enabling mine. I thank the team on this book—"the *Mom Energy* gals"—including my co-author, Kathy, an exceptionally talented individual and friend. All of you have shown me that *Mom Energy* has so many different presentations, each of them beautiful, respectful, funny, and inspiring.

To the women in my life: Mom, Irma, Camille, Juliet, my friends, and their moms, too. They support my energy by giving the gifts of example, suggestions, and never-ending encouragement for which I am grateful beyond words. I also thank the men in my life: Dad, Corey, Jon, and Austin. All of you are *Mom Energy* enablers in different ways, and I admire each of you for your unique blend of humor and compassion.

I thank my energy team: Doron, Dr. DG, Brad, Ben, Jason, my agent Amy Stanton, my publicists Melinda and Ryan, and the AKA team: Matthew H. and Matt T., Amy F. and Rerun. Thank you for being there for me and for nurturing my body, voice, and spirit.

From Kathy:

I would love to say that my energy allows me to do it all, but I've had an extra set of hands for many years, and I would like to thank Kathleen Ingle for helping me keep up the pace that I have grown accustomed to.

Thanks to my longtime publicist, Sharon House, whose support through the years eventually led to this important book.

And of course, a special thanks goes to my comrade and tireless book partner, Ashley. Had it not been for your tenacity, enthusiasm, and collaborative wisdom on nutrition and energy metabolism, this book might never have gotten to where it needed to be.

I have great respect for women who take the journey of motherhood, a journey that is sprinkled with trials and tribulations. I could not have found reason to write this book had it not been for my mom and my children.

Finally, I'd like to personally extend another round of applause to all the moms in the world. We are one in the love of our children.

About the Authors

Ashley Koff, R.D., is a registered dietitian with the proven ability to demystify the science of nutrition and communicate the importance of a healthy lifestyle to clients in a way that instills loyalty and trust.

Named among the Top 10 Registered Dietitians in the U.S. by *Today's Dietitian* magazine and Best of LA's "Nutritionist/Dietitians" by *Citysearch* three years running, Koff appears regularly on national media outlets, including *The Dr. Oz Show, The Doctors,* CBS's *The Early Show, Good Morning America Health,* CNN, AOL, and E!; and was the lead expert for *The Huffington Post Living*'s "Total Energy Makeover with Ashley Koff RD." Koff is frequently featured in national publications such as *The New York Times, InStyle, Reader's Digest, Every Day with Rachael Ray, Redbook, Women's Health, Shape,* and *O, The Oprah Magazine.* She is a contributing editor for *Natural Health* magazine, the dietitian for espnW, and a member of the advisory board of *Fitness* magazine. Koff has been the featured dietitian on the CW's couples health transformation show, *Shedding for the Wedding,* and Lifetime's *Love Handles.* In 2007, she authored *Recipes for IBS*, a cookbook and treatment plan for digestive wellness.

As part of her "Qualitarian" mission, Koff is committed to helping consumers, health-care practitioners, and the media easily identify products that contribute to a healthy lifestyle. At her nutrition counseling and consulting company, she created The Ashley Koff Approved (AKA) Lists, a tool to help people identify products that meet a high standard of nutrition and marketing integrity. Curiosity and a desire to get the whole story on food ingredients, Koff routinely "goes to the source" around the world and throughout the U.S. to explore food production and cultural influences in our food system.

Koff maintains a private practice, regularly lectures, is a spokesperson for several national brands, and works to improve the quality of food choices in numerous outlets including on the sets of popular shows like ABC's *Private Practice,* CBS's *CSI: New York,* HBO's *Big Love,* FX's *It's Always Sunny in Philadelphia,* and FOX's *Bones.*

Educated at both Duke and New York Universities, Koff trained at LA+USC and Columbus Children's hospitals and also worked at Cedars-Sinai Medical Center in Los Angeles.

Website: **www.AshleyKoffRD.com**

Kathy Kaehler has devoted her life to helping people live happy, productive, and healthy lives as an author, celebrity trainer, spokesperson, and mom. She is a National Fitness Hall of Famer and continues to shape the bodies and inspire the lives of millions around the world.

For 13 years, she appeared on the *Today* show's exercise segments with Katie Couric, Matt Lauer, and Ann Curry. She has worked out with numerous A-list celebrities including Julia Roberts, Michelle Pfeiffer, Cindy Crawford, Jennifer Aniston, Drew Barrymore, Jennifer Lopez, Denise Richards, Claudia Schiffer, and Kim Basinger. Her work with Kim Kardashian in 2009 led to a downloadable workout series and added yet another DVD video— *Kim Kardashian's Body Beautiful*—to Kathy's large collection.

As a prolific and best-selling author, Kaehler has written many books, including *Teenage Fitness, Fit and Sexy for Life,* and *Kathy Kaehler's Celebrity Workouts.* She has been a contributing writer to *Elle, Self,* and *Women's Sports and Fitness* and her workouts and training tips have appeared in *InStyle, Us Weekly, Shape, Fitness, Family Circle, Health, More, Allure, Marie Claire,* and *Woman's Day,* among many others. Kathy was a regular contributor to MSNBC.com and wrote biweekly columns for the *Los Angeles Daily News,* which was syndicated to several other major markets. In addition to the *Today* show, Kathy has appeared on such shows as *The View,* *The Megan Mullally Show,* *The Best Damn Sports Show,* and *The Oprah Winfrey Show.*

As an in-demand spokesperson, Kathy has worked with a number of brands and products including Boniva, Healthy Ones, Hanes, Propel, Vaseline, Nasonex, Ragu, the Milk Board, Chilean Fresh Fruit, MIO watches, Walkmill portable treadmill, Serta, Breyers, and Enell bras. Kathy is currently the leading health and fitness spokesperson for USANA and creator of Sunday Set-Up™. She also is a Podfitness Premiere Trainer and one of the stars of Lifetime's *My Workout.*

Kaehler believes that everyone, at any age, should adopt a lifestyle that incorporates fitness, good nutrition, and a positive outlook. As a mother to three boys—15-year-old twins and an 11-year old—she knows about Mom Energy.

Website: **www.kathykaehler.net**

HAY HOUSE TITLES
OF RELATED INTEREST

YOU CAN HEAL YOUR LIFE, the movie,
starring Louise L. Hay & Friends
(available as a 1-DVD program and an expanded 2-DVD set)
Watch the trailer at: **www.LouiseHayMovie.com**

THE SHIFT, the movie,
starring Dr. Wayne W. Dyer
(available as a 1-DVD program and an expanded 2-DVD set)
Watch the trailer at: **www.DyerMovie.com**

A COURSE IN WEIGHT LOSS:
21 Spiritual Lessons for Surrendering Your Weight Forever,
by Marianne Williamson

ARE YOU TIRED AND WIRED?:
*Your Proven 30-Day Program for Overcoming
Adrenal Fatigue and Feeling Fantastic Again,*
by Marcelle Pick, MSN, OB/GYN NP

FRIED:
Why You Burn Out and How to Revive,
by Joan Borysenko, Ph.D.

WISHES FOR A MOTHER'S HEART:
Words of Inspiration, Love, and Support,
by Tricia LaVoice and Barbara Lazaroff

All of the above are available at your local bookstore,
or may be ordered by contacting Hay House (see next page).